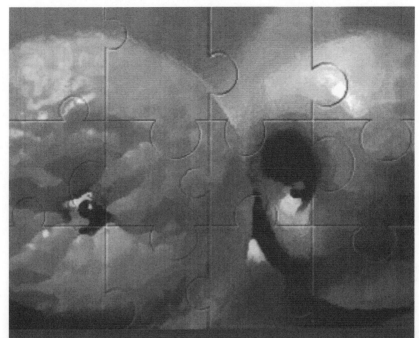

Systematic Reviews in the Social Sciences

A PRACTICAL GUIDE

Mark Petticrew and Helen Roberts

Blackwell
Publishing

BLACKWELL PUBLISHING
350 Main Street, Malden, MA 02148-5020, USA
9600 Garsington Road, Oxford OX4 2DQ, UK
550 Swanston Street, Carlton, Victoria 3053, Australia

First published 2006 by Blackwell Publishing Ltd

12   2012

Library of Congress Cataloging-in-Publication Data

Petticrew, Mark.
  Systematic reviews in the social sciences : a practical guide / Mark Petticrew and
  Helen Roberts.
    p. cm.
  Includes bibliographical references and index.
  ISBN 978-1-4051-2110-1 (hard cover: alk. paper)
  1. Social sciences—Research—Methodology. 2. Social sciences—Statistical methods.
  I. Roberts, Helen, 1949- II. Title.

H62.P457 2005
300'.72'3—dc22

                                              2005011632

A catalogue record for this title is available from the British Library.

Set in 10.5pt/12.5pt Bembo
by SPI Publisher Services, Pondicherry, India

The publisher's policy is to use permanent paper from mills that operate a sustainable
forestry policy, and which has been manufactured from pulp processed using acid-free
and elementary chlorine-free practices. Furthermore, the publisher ensures that the
text paper and cover board used have met acceptable environmental accreditation
standards.

For further information on
Blackwell Publishing, visit our website:
www.blackwellpublishing.com

Systematic Reviews in the Social Sciences

Contents

Foreword – *William R. Shadish*   *vi*
Acknowledgments   *x*
Preface   *xiii*

Chapter 1 Why do we need systematic reviews?   1
Chapter 2 Starting the review: Refining the question
              and defining the boundaries   27
Chapter 3 What sorts of studies do I include in the review?
              Deciding on the review's inclusion/exclusion criteria   57
Chapter 4 How to find the studies: The literature search   79
Chapter 5 How to appraise the studies: An introduction to
              assessing study quality   125
Chapter 6 Synthesizing the evidence   164
Chapter 7 Exploring heterogeneity and publication bias   215
Chapter 8 Disseminating the review   247
Chapter 9 Systematic reviews: Urban myths and fairy tales   265
Glossary   277
Appendix 1 The review process (and some questions to ask
               before starting a review)   284
Appendix 2 MOOSE Guidelines   288
Appendix 3 Example of a flow diagram from a systematic review   291
Appendix 4 Example data extraction form   293
Appendix 5 Variations in the quality of systematic reviews   296

Bibliography   *298*
Index   *324*

Foreword

The idea of evidence-based practice is not new. For example, nearly 60 years ago, the scientist-practitioner model of clinical psychology in the US was based in part on the idea that clinical psychologists would scientifically investigate the effectiveness of their own treatments, and use what proved to be effective. Around 100 years ago, the British Army asked Sir Karl Pearson to review the evidence about the effects of a new typhoid vaccine, to help them decide whether to adopt that vaccine more widely.[1] Such relatively isolated examples are common for hundreds of years. What is new is the widespread acceptance that evidence-based practice is practice whose time has come. Whether it be through the Cochrane Collaboration, the Campbell Collaboration, the What Works Clearinghouse in the US Department of Education, or any of a host of similar efforts, the idea that practices and policies that are supported by scientific evidence can be identified and disseminated has now been institutionalized. That in itself is a remarkable accomplishment.

In this context, this book by Petticrew and Roberts is a timely gem, full of detailed history, pithy quotes, marvelous examples, compelling arguments, practical advice, and transparent demonstrations of how to do one of the most common ways of putting the evidence into evidence-based practice – the systematic review. Practical advice leaps out at the reader from every chapter, with novel information I have not seen in related works.

Let me start with reference to the key justification for systematic reviews, that "single studies taken in isolation are often seriously misleading" (chapter 1, this volume). Or as I tend to put it: Never trust the results of single studies. One need only graph a frequency distribution of effect sizes to see that some studies will show unusually positive effects, and some unusually negative effects, substantially by virtue of chance. Yet the public, the media, and even other scientists routinely place great faith in single studies.

As a result, ineffective or inaccurate policies, practices, or ideas are adopted, accurate or effective ones are dismissed, and all parties get confused. The analogy that Petticrew and Roberts make with a survey is a good one. We would never take seriously the results of a sample survey where the sample was of a single person, and we all understand why – we will often get a different answer by asking a different person. The same is true in systematic reviews. We will often get a different answer when we look at a different study. In sample surveys, only a large sample is capable of giving us a reliable answer. In reviewing literature on a question, only the systematic review process is capable of helping to clarify where the answer really lies.

Yet as Petticrew and Roberts point out in chapter 2 and elaborate in chapter 3, we have had an unnecessarily narrow view of what a systematic review can do – answer questions about cause and effect relationships. Systematic reviews need not only address what works, as important as that question is. Such reviews can address the evidence about nearly any kind of question, for example, about the prevalence of a problem, the correlation of two variables to each other, the implementation of a program, the meaning program stakeholders ascribe to a program or its context, the causal mediating processes that help us understand why it works, and program costs, to name just a few. Similarly, our understanding of the question of what works has often been too narrow. That question involves high quality evidence about cause and effect relationships, to be sure. But we are also informed about what works by, for example, knowledge that some stakeholder groups refuse to participate, that costs are too high to be practical, or that the need for the treatment is questionable.

What is less clear is whether we have well-developed technologies for addressing some of these questions. The technological problem is twofold, how to integrate studies that are all of one kind (e.g., about need) with each other, and how to integrates studies of one kind (e.g., need) with studies of another kind (e.g., treatment effectiveness). The former problem is relatively unproblematic for most kinds of quantitative studies, but is far less clear for qualitative studies. The latter problem is almost completely unaddressed. It is this context that makes me so pleased to see the effort Petticrew and Roberts have put into both these problems. Many people talk about the value of integrating quantitative and qualitative studies, for example, but actual examples of such integration are few and far between. Petticrew and Roberts lay out the logic of such integrations, some of the methods that might be used for doing them, along with examples. And they don't shy away from the difficulties such as a lack of standardized search terms to use in locating qualitative studies on a given topic. For many years, when critics have decried the narrow focus on experiments in systematic reviews of what works, I have responded by saying we are working on that problem. Now I can actually point to the work.

I was also pleased to see the huge number of references in chapter 5 about assessing the quality of different kinds of research designs. Just the compilation itself is a major contribution. Yet we should remember that quality can mean two different things: (a) quality of the implementation of the method (e.g., did the primary study author implement the qualitative method properly); and (b) quality of the inferences from the method (do the methods used support a causal inference). My sense is that the latter kinds of quality scales are pretty common for experiments, though serious question remains about whether those scales are well enough developed to warrant widespread use. But inference quality scales are far less well developed for qualitative methods, where the available scales seem more concerned with whether the methods were implemented well. The problem is that good implementation of a method is orthogonal to whether that method supports a given inference. The best-implemented randomized experiment is rarely going to tell us much about the need for an intervention, just as the best implemented ethnography is rarely going to yield a strong inference about cause-and-effect relationships.

Finally, chapter 8 on dissemination and use of systematic reviews raises a crucial issue. Too often we assume that policymakers and practitioners are likely to adopt interventions that are shown to work. That assumption is at best only partly right. We learned that the hard way in the field of program evaluation in the 1960s and 1970s. The early emphasis in that field was on experimentation to determine effective interventions that could be adopted as policy. We quickly found out that they were frequently not adopted even when they were effective, and began to study the process of use itself.[2] The fate of Fairweather's Lodge for the chronically mentally ill is illustrative.[3] That intervention was far more cost effective than the alternatives, was well-liked by patients and successful on most outcome criteria; but it was relatively little used despite extensive dissemination funding because it had no funding mechanism, conflicted with the extant treatment institutions, and required citizens to accept a house of patients next door. Adopting effective practices involves far more than knowing what works, and Petticrew and Roberts do a commendable job of laying out the issues. The lessons learned are remarkably similar to those we learned in program evaluation years ago, and we would do well to revisit the modern versions of that literature (e.g., Patton)[4] to help us understand more about how to make our work useful.

As you can see, I am a fan of what Petticrew and Roberts have done in this book. They lay out a broad and ambitious agenda for the art and science of systematic reviews, an agenda that cogently presages issues that I think will be at the cutting edge of this field of inquiry in the coming decades. I hope you enjoy it as much as I did.

William R. Shadish
University of California, Merced

REFERENCES

1. Pearson, K. Report on certain enteric fever inoculation statistics. *British Medical Journal* 1904, 3: 1243–6.
2. Shadish, W. R., Cook, T. D., and Leviton, L. C. *Foundations of program evaluation: Theories of practice.* Newbury Park, CA: Sage Publications, 1991.
3. Shadish, W. R. Policy research: Lessons from the implementation of deinstitutionalization. *American Psychologist* 1984, 39: 725–38.
4. Patton, M. Q. *Utilization-focused evaluation* (3rd edn.). Newbury Park, CA: Sage Publications, 1996.

Acknowledgments

Writing books incurs a large number of debts. This one is no different, and we would particularly like to thank Susan Kennedy and Rodney Barker, who have gone well beyond the usual demands of being our partners by reading, commenting, and constructively criticizing.

Professor Will Shadish, one of the foremost meta-analysts in the USA readily and generously agreed to write a foreword. The anonymous peer reviewers of our proposal and, in particular, the reviewer of our final manuscript contributed a great deal to our thinking and the final product. At our request, Blackwell approached them to ask if they would forgo anonymity so that we could acknowledge them by name, and we are happy to say that they agreed to this. Many thanks then, to Trevor Sheldon, at the University of York, who nobly reviewed both the proposal and the book; and to the proposal reviewers Jim Connelly, University of Leeds, Emma Davies, Auckland University of Technology, David DuBois, University of Illinois at Chicago, Loraine Gelsthorpe, University of Cambridge, David Gough, Institute of Education, University of London, Geraldine Macdonald, Commission for Social Care Inspection, Susan Michie, University College London, Deborah Phillips, Georgetown University, and Maggie Savin-Baden, Coventry University. We are also grateful to Kate Pool from the Society of Authors.

Our colleagues in Glasgow and City Universities, our co-researchers and colleagues on the ESRC-funded project on narrative synthesis: Jennie Popay, Amanda Sowden, Nicky Britten, and the late Sally Baldwin, Lisa Arai, Mark Rodgers, and Katrina Roen, and our colleagues in the ESRC Evidence Network, and the Cochrane and Campbell Collaborations (particularly those whose work we have quoted) have all been parties to discussions and conversations that have helped inform our work.

Mark Petticrew would particularly like to thank colleagues in the ESRC Centre for Evidence-Based Public Health Policy, and in his research program (funded by the Chief Scientist Office of the Scottish Executive Department of Health), whose work and thinking the book draws on: among them Pam Attree, Beth Milton, Clare Bambra, Frances Drever, Matt Egan, Hilary Graham, Val Hamilton, Sally Macintyre, Liz McDermott, David Morrison, David Ogilvie, Sian Thomas, Hilary Thomson, and Margaret Whitehead. Colleagues elsewhere who read and commented on parts of the book, or who kindly gave permission to use their work, include Iain Chalmers, Iain Crombie, the EPOC (Effective Practice and Organization of Care) group of the Cochrane Collaboration, Simon Gilbody, David Gough and colleagues at the EPPI Centre, Rebecca Ivers and colleagues, Betsy Kristjansson, Geoffrey Nelson and colleagues, Anthony Petrosino, Steve Platt, Scott Reeves, Roberta Scherer, Fujian Song, Peter Tugwell, and Paul Wilson. Thanks for permission to reproduce various figures or tables go to John Wiley & Sons Ltd (the Forest plots in chapters 6 and 7, which are copyright of the Cochrane Library), The Sainsbury Archive (Figure 6.2 in chapter 6), Hawaii Medical Library, the National Portrait Gallery (for the portrait of Francis Bacon in chapter 4), the *British Medical Journal* (for permission to reproduce material in chapter 9), David Ogilvie (the photograph in chapter 6), and the Centre for Reviews and Dissemination (CRD) at the University of York for permission to reproduce material from their systematic reviews guidance (CRD Report 4). Thanks also to Mary Robins for library support.

Helen Roberts is particularly grateful to colleagues at City University, especially current and past colleagues in the Child Health Research and Policy Unit, and to fellow members of the What Works for Children "node" funded as part of the ESRC evidence network – Trevor Sheldon at the University of York, Kristin Liabo, Madeleine Stevens, Greg Khine, and Alison Moore at City University and Di McNeish, Tony Newman, Sarah Frost, Angela Hutton, and Philippa Roberts at Barnardo's. Shruti Uppal provided valuable assistance with reference and Web checking. Helen has learned a great deal from colleagues at the EPPI Centre at the University of London Institute of Education and others who contributed to the seminar series on research evidence organized by the Evidence Network, funded by the UK Health Development Agency. Other colleagues with whom Helen has worked on systematic reviews including Carol Joughin, Gabrielle Laing, Stuart Logan, Sandra Dowling, Catherine Law, Jos Kleijnen, Patricia Lucas, Janis Baird, and David Fisher have helped her thinking while working on joint systematic reviews. Ruth Gilbert, Ian Roberts, and Dennis Cheek all responded quickly and helpfully to requests for advice. Helen would also like to thank her former colleagues in the R&D team in Barnardo's with whom she worked on some of the material on which we draw in chapter 8, and to ESRC and David Walker for allowing us to draw on their communications toolkit and related work.

Thanks to Getpetsonline for permission to use the photograph in figure 2.2 and to the Thomas A. Edison papers archive at Rutgers University for permission to use the image in Box 4.5.

Sarah Bird, Will Maddox, Joanna Pyke, Rhonda Pearce, Mervyn Thomas, Helen Kemp, and Zeb Korycinska from Blackwell looked after this book as it moved through publication. We thank them for their careful work.

Mark Petticrew
Helen Roberts

Preface

> Research studies use a variety of methods, are of variable quality and may appear to have contradictory findings ... Research information can seem to users like small jigsaw pieces in a box where there may be several pictures, several duplicates and several missing pieces. Under these circumstances it can be difficult for the researcher, research funder or user to make sense of the research or take stock of the knowledge base. (Sheldon, 1998)[1]

Literature reviews have many purposes. They can examine old theories and propose new ones, consider where the balance of evidence lies in relation to a particular topic, and provide a basis for recommendations for interventions, (such as teaching in smaller or larger classes, running an anti-bullying program, or offering parenting education). They can provide guidance to researchers planning future studies, and provide convenient summaries of the literature on a particular issue. They can also be used to examine methodically the reasons why different studies addressing the same question sometimes reach different conclusions – a common and frustrating problem for both researchers and research users.

This book is a guide to planning and conducting a particular type of literature review, one that is increasingly used as a scientific tool: the systematic literature review. The book is aimed at social science researchers, but it provides a more general discussion of systematic reviews for those who want to use and understand them, but don't necessarily want to do one themselves. Most of the recent interest in systematic reviews focuses on reviews of the effectiveness of interventions, reflected in the growth of initiatives like the Campbell and Cochrane Collaborations. This book therefore focuses on reviews of effectiveness, but not exclusively. Systematic reviews are also widely used to synthesize other sorts of evidence, for example in order to answer questions about etiology (causes of problems), or about people's experiences, and we discuss and present examples of such reviews.

The book discusses the following:

- what a systematic review is and why this method of reviewing evidence is increasingly important to social scientists;
- how to decide on an appropriate question for a systematic review;
- how to decide which types of study to include;
- how to design a search to identify those studies;
- how to appraise the quality and relevance of qualitative and quantitative research;
- how to summarize the results of the studies, either narratively, or quantitatively as appropriate;
- how to assess whether the results of the review are robust; and
- how to disseminate the results of the review

In the book we use the term "systematic review" to cover both those reviews that include a statistical summary of the included studies (a meta-analysis), and those that don't. While we also use the phrase systematic "literature" reviews, not all evidence which may be useful for a review will of course appear in the published "literature." Because of this, the term "research synthesis" (or "evidence synthesis") is becoming increasingly common. We have used the term "systematic review" in preference, as it is still so widely used, but we do not assume that only "published" literature can be reviewed.

We also discuss some emerging issues – in particular the part played by different research designs in systematic reviews, including qualitative research; approaches to reviewing complex interventions; the means of dealing with variations between studies in terms of design and study quality; and ways of involving stakeholders in the process of planning, carrying out, and disseminating systematic reviews. Finally we discuss some wider dissemination issues. As our focus is on reviews in social sciences, we draw on examples that examine the effectiveness of social interventions in the fields of crime, education, social welfare, transport, and health. The science of systematic reviewing for social policy purposes is still relatively young, and we do not assume that systematic reviews as presently constituted are perfect, or that they are appropriate for all purposes. Nor do we assume that every review has to be "systematic" to be useful (or even that every "systematic" review is useful). We therefore acknowledge and discuss the limitations of systematic reviews, and the criticisms that have been made of them. However, we believe that they can be used more widely than at present, can often be made more useful, and are an essential scientific tool that *any* scientist (social, or otherwise) should know how to use.

HOW TO USE THIS BOOK

This book can be read either as a "story" about systematic reviews: what they are, why they are important, and what they can tell us, or it can be read as a practical guide. We have therefore organized it so that it can be read from cover to cover, for those starting to explore this area, or used as a practical aid for those carrying out a review themselves. Summaries of key points at the end of each chapter are used to signpost the reader through the systematic review process.

Mark Petticrew
MRC Social and Public Health Sciences Unit
University of Glasgow

Helen Roberts
Child Health Research and Policy Unit
City University, London

June 2005

REFERENCE

1. Sheldon, T. *An evidence-based resource in the social sciences*, Report of a scoping study for the Economic and Social Research Council (ESRC), 1998.

Chapter 1

Why do we need systematic reviews?

Box 1.1 Examples of "social interventions" in UK and international headlines

"City wide initiative to get tramps off the streets"

"Does money buy you happiness? (No, it's the other way round)"

"Prisons too full" says Chief of Parole: "Spending money on imprisonment is a negative spend on crime: spend on communities"

"President sets aside $1.5bn to boost marriage"

1.1 INTRODUCTION

Box 1.1 gives some dramatic newspaper headlines culled from UK and international newspapers, suggesting apparently important but very different initiatives for improving society. The first refers to a program in a UK city, which it was claimed would help homeless people into permanent accommodation. The second refers to a study that found that even large increases in wealth had only limited effects on happiness. The third headline raises the possibility that spending more money on communities would be a better use of taxpayers' money than spending it on prisons.

These headlines have more in common than the fact that they caught the journalist's eye. They are all claims about "what works" – that is, claims about the **effectiveness** of **interventions**. They also involve implicit or explicit claims about how public money could be better spent to improve society. "Marriage programs do work," Wade Horn, the assistant secretary of health and human services for children in the United States is reported to have said.[1] Implicit in each headline is the promise that someone knows how a particular social problem can be fixed. Of course, it takes more than a headline or a bold claim to establish whether any of these initiatives are likely to work or not, and some sort of formal research study frequently lies behind the headline, usually one which suggests that a particular course of action is warranted.

Systematic literature reviews are a method of making sense of large bodies of information, and a means of contributing to the answers to questions about what works and what does not – and many other types of question too. They are a method of mapping out areas of uncertainty, and identifying where little or no relevant research has been done, but where new studies are needed. **Systematic reviews** also flag up areas where spurious certainty abounds. These are areas where we think we know more than we do, but where in reality there is little convincing evidence to support our beliefs. The three commentators in Box 1.2 highlight the importance of knowing about our own ignorance. As Lao-Tze, Confucius, and Donald Rumsfeld all point out, it is important to be able to tell the difference between real and assumed knowledge, and systematic reviews can help us tell which is which. Reviews are important because the results of single studies are generally given much greater credence than they merit. There are few studies that are so methodologically sound, whose results are so generalizeable and that leave us so certain that the results represent a good approximation of the

---

Box 1.2 On the importance of knowing about uncertainty

It is important not only that we know what we know, but that we know what we do not know.

(Lao-Tze, Chinese Philosopher (ca. 604–521 BCE))

When you know a thing, to hold that you know it; and when you do not know a thing, to allow that you do not know it – this is knowledge.
(Confucius, Chinese teacher and philosopher (551–479 BCE))[2]

As we know, there are known knowns. There are things we know we know. We also know there are known unknowns. That is to say we know there are some things we do not know. But there are also unknown unknowns, the ones we don't know we don't know.

(Donald Rumsfeld, 2002)[3]

"truth," that we should accept their findings outright. This is not to deny that single studies with dramatic and important results do exist; but most research can only be understood in context – and a key part of that context consists of the results of other studies that tested the same hypothesis, in similar populations.[4]

One problem with interpreting and using research is that the research behind the headlines is often so far removed from real-life settings that it may be difficult for policymakers or the public (or indeed homeless people, prisoners, young offenders or those considering marriage) to know whether the results are to be taken seriously, or whether they represent no more than the latest unreliable dispatch from the world of science. The more skeptical research-informed policymaker may simply wait patiently, on the grounds that another researcher will soon publish a paper saying the opposite. If one study appears claiming that what delinquents need is a short sharp shock, another is sure to follow suggesting that what they actually need is a teambuilding adventure holiday.

Studies produce such conflicting findings for reasons other than method-ological shortcomings, or authorial **bias**. There may be simple statistical reasons why the results of studies vary; 20 studies of the same intervention will produce a range of estimates of its **impact**, and one of these studies will, by chance alone, produce statistically significant findings even if the inter-vention is ineffective. Moreover the findings may often be statistically significant, but not *socially* significant.

Sometimes, as the headlines at the start of this chapter indicate, claims with strong face validity can be attractive to politicians, and seized on as evidence to support a call to action. Marriage is one example. Mentoring in young people is another (see Box 1.3).

The problem is, we often do not know whether the sorts of important interventions described in the headlines really work or not, without locating and reading the relevant research studies (if any). Even then, if we find studies with contradictory answers we might not know which study to believe, and perhaps the most sensible approach might be to rely on a literature review written by an expert in the field. However, literature reviews may themselves be biased, and by carefully selecting which studies to review, it is possible to produce two similar reviews that come to entirely opposite conclusions.

1.2   BIAS IN TRADITIONAL REVIEWS

Most scientists operate on a double standard; they go to great lengths to define the methods they used to minimise biases and random errors in their reports on the results of new research, but they often do not attempt to apply

Box 1.3 Mentoring to reduce anti-social behavior in childhood

Anti-social behavior in young people is a problem for the police, for communities, and for politicians. This makes finding a solution a political as well as a therapeutic imperative – a potent driver to "do something." One approach to reducing anti-social behavior is through mentoring schemes. The mentor aims to offer support, understanding, experience, and advice. Mentoring is non-invasive and medication-free. It is easy to see why it might work, and why it is attractive to politicians and policymakers.

In February 2003, Lord Filkin, then a minister in the Home Office of the UK Government, announced £850,000 of funding for mentoring schemes: "Mentors can make a real difference to . . . some of the most vulnerable people . . . and help to make our society more inclusive. There are . . . excellent examples of schemes which really work." On the other side of the pond President Bush announced plans in his state of the union address for a $450 million initiative to expand the availability of mentoring programs for young people. This included $300 million for mentoring at-risk pupils and $150 million to provide mentors to children of prisoners: "I ask Congress and the American people to focus the spirit of service and the resources of government on the needs of some of our most vulnerable citizens – boys and girls trying to grow up without guidance and attention and children who must walk through a prison gate to be hugged by their mom or dad."[5]

Unfortunately, mentoring doesn't work for all youngsters all of the time, and it may even harm some vulnerable young people.[6] This does not mean that mentoring never works. Our current state of knowledge on the effectiveness of mentoring is similar to that of a new drug that shows promise, but remains in need of further research and development.

scientific principles in their discussions of how the newly generated evidence accords with previously available information. (Chalmers et al., 1993)[4]

An old scientific joke draws on Newton's Third Law of Motion: "For every expert there is an equal and opposite expert." It is a fair criticism of scientific research that it is often difficult to know which, if any, study to believe. The traditional scientific approach to this problem is to carry out a literature review. This is often conducted by an expert or other well-known figure in the field, but general expertise and high profile may be poor indicators of the ability to produce an unbiased and reliable summary of the evidence. Literature reviews, even those written by experts, can be made to tell any story one wants them to, and failure by literature reviewers to apply scientific principles to the process of reviewing the evidence, just as one would to primary research, can lead to biased conclusions, and to harm and wasted resources.[4] Yet traditional literature reviews frequently summarize highly unrepresentative samples of studies in an unsystematic and uncritical fashion, as highlighted in Box 1.4.[7, 8]

As we shall see in later chapters, researchers can also be influenced, consciously or otherwise, by their own pet theories, by their funders, and

---

Box 1.4   When reviews disagree

Literature reviews are known for often being somewhat haphazard, but this can be difficult to spot. Ann Oakley describes some differences between a series of health education reviews she and colleagues examined. They found six reviews of older people and accident prevention, which included a total of 137 studies. However, only 33 studies were common to at least two reviews, and only one study was treated consistently in all six reviews.[7, 9, 10]

The same was found with two reviews of anti-smoking education in young people: a total of 27 studies were included in one or other of the reviews, but only three studies were common to both. More alarmingly, Oakley et al. knew from their own databases that there were at least 70 studies that, potentially, could have been included.

---

sometimes by the perceived need to produce positive findings in order to get published. All these make it difficult to work out where the balance of truth lies in many areas of science. Systematic reviews, however, provide a redress to the natural tendency of readers and researchers to be swayed by such biases, and they can fulfill an essential role as a sort of scientific gyroscope, with an in-built self-righting mechanism.

Vitamin C and the common cold

Paul Knipschild's description of how he and colleagues set out to find out whether Vitamin C really prevents a cold is illustrative. The received wisdom was that very large doses prevent the common cold, a view which largely derives from the Nobel Laureate Linus Pauling's 1986 book *How to Live Longer and Feel Better*, which reviews the extensive literature in a non-systematic manner. Pauling eventually concluded that: "we should be getting 200 times the amount of vitamin C that the Food and Nutrition Board recommends."[11]

Knipschild and colleagues tested Pauling's claims by carrying out a separate exhaustive search of databases, and hand searches of journals and special collections, eventually identifying 61 trials, of which 15 appeared to be methodologically sound. They concluded on the basis of these trials that even in megadoses Vitamin C cannot prevent a cold, though perhaps it might shorten its duration. Knipschild describes how Pauling's review did not mention five of the "top 15" studies, and two of the others were referred to only in passing. A haphazard review, even one carried out by an expert, can be very misleading.[12, 13]

Of course many traditional literature reviews are excellent. Moreover, not every review needs to be a "systematic" review. However, if a review purports to be an authoritative summary of what "the evidence" says, then the reader is entitled to demand that this is a comprehensive, objective, and reliable overview, and not a partial review of a convenience sample of the author's favorite studies. One way of giving the reader this assurance is by describing the methods used (as for any study). In the absence of this assurance, the review may be still be valid and interesting, but can also be predominantly a vehicle for the author's opinions, rather than a scientific summary of the evidence. We shall see later in the book how reviewer biases may affect the results of literature reviews, just as researcher allegiances can affect the results of primary studies.[14] Shadish, for example, surveyed authors of over 280 articles in psychological journals and found that more often than not studies get cited simply because they support the author's own argument, and not because the study is particularly reliable.[15] Expert reviews are of course a valid use of journal space, for debating findings, developing theory, and much else. But they do not take the place of the reliable, scientifically conducted overview, which is what systematic reviews aim to provide.

1.3 INFORMATION OVERLOAD

The problem is not just one of inconsistency, but one of information overload. The past 20 years have seen an explosion in the amount of research information available to decision makers and social researchers alike. With new journals launched yearly, and thousands of research papers published, it is impossible for even the most energetic policymaker or researcher to keep up-to-date with the most recent research evidence, unless they are interested in a very narrow field indeed. The problem is not a new one. Over 30 years ago, in 1971, Ravetz was writing of the "information crisis" which he put down in part to "pointless publication," and partly to shoddy science: "The majority of journals in many fields are full of papers which are never cited by an author other than their own, and which on examination, are seen to be utterly dull or just bad."[16]

This claim could probably be made at any point in the history of science. Indeed, it seems to have been made regularly over the centuries,[17] though gross information overload is still relatively new simply because most science is "new science;" about 80–90 percent of all research papers ever written have probably been written in our own lifetime. As shown in Box 1.5, over 100 years ago there was concern about the "information mountain."

Box 1.5   The information mountain, 100 years ago

[T]here can be no doubt that our experimental literature is increasing in bulk – not only in the sense that more investigations are being published every year, but also in the sense that the single papers are becoming longer.

(Titchener, 1903)[18]

As well as a huge increase in the publication of science papers, the number of web-based sources of apparently relevant information has increased dramatically. In many ways, this is a welcome democratization of knowledge, or at least a means by which information can be made much more widely available. But it can be difficult to tell whether websites are presenting reliable information or just a partial view of a particular issue. In many cases, the information is simply out of date.

Box 1.6 gives an example of information overload in relation to an important problem: parents, children and teachers often want advice on how to stop bullying. Finding the information itself is not difficult; but finding relevant and reliable information presents more of a challenge.

Box 1.6   Stopping bullying: Information overload

Parents, teachers and pupils interested in finding out how to prevent bullying, or stop it if it does happen will have no shortage of sources of information. There are over a quarter of a million websites that appear to refer to bullying. This includes sites aimed at children (http://www. bullying.org), and sites devoted to racist bullying and bullying by mobile phone (http://www.bullying.co.uk). Among the approaches to this problem described by one government organization (http://www. parentcentre.gov.uk) (The Department for Education and Skills in the UK) are:

- Cooperative group work
- Circle Time
- Circle of Friends
- Befriending
- Schoolwatch
- The support group approach
- Mediation by adults
- Mediation by peers
- Active listening/counseling-based approaches
- Quality circles
- Assertiveness training groups

How can those using the web work out which sites to trust, and which interventions might actually work? Some sites suggest that certain interventions such as using sanctions against bullies can be ineffective, or even harmful – that is, actually increase bullying (e.g., http:// www.education.unisa.edu.au/bullying). Other sites suggest that such approaches may work (http://www.education-world.com/a_issues/ issues103.shtml).

It is no surprise that websites suggest a range of approaches and are not consistent in their conclusions. However the results of research studies that have investigated the effectiveness of anti-bullying interventions often do not agree either.[19] The same intervention may appear to work for some children, but not for others – younger children for example – and some types of bullying, such as physical bullying, may be more readily reduced than others, such as verbal bullying.

For bullying, as for other types of social problem, one can quickly become swamped with well-meaning advice. Navigating one's way through the swamp is tricky, but systematic reviews provide stepping stones – differentiating between the boggy areas (the morass of irrelevant information) and the higher ground (the pockets of reliable research information on what works and for whom, and where and when).

Systematic reviews can provide a means of synthesizing information on bullying, or aspects of bullying, and give a reliable overview of what the research literature can tell us about what works. For example, a systematic review of school-based violence prevention programs identified 44 trials in all, and concluded that while more high **quality** trials are needed, three kinds of programs may reduce aggressive and violent behaviors in children who already exhibit such behavior.[20]

1.4   THE ROLE OF SYSTEMATIC LITERATURE REVIEWS

As noted above, those who use research information, among whom we can number citizens, researchers, and people making decisions about the delivery or organization of services, rely on reviews to help organize and prioritize the most relevant information. Alongside "traditional" or "narrative" reviews, a new type of review has appeared in recent years: the systematic literature review. In this chapter we set out the particular ways in which systematic reviews can be helpful, as well as acknowledging the merits and drawbacks of other kinds of review.

Systematic reviews are literature reviews that adhere closely to a set of scientific methods that explicitly aim to limit systematic error (bias), mainly by attempting to identify, appraise and synthesize all relevant studies (of whatever design) in order to answer a particular question (or set of questions). In carrying out this task they set out their methods in advance, and in detail, as one would for any piece of social research. In this respect, as we shall see, they are quite unlike most "traditional" narrative reviews.

The systematic review is more "fit for the purpose" of answering specific questions and testing hypotheses than the traditional review. It is less of a discussion of the literature, and more of a scientific tool; but it can also do more than this, and can be used to summarize, appraise, and communicate the results and implications of otherwise unmanageable quantities of research. It is widely agreed however that at least one of these elements − communication − needs to be improved greatly if systematic reviews are to be really useful. This issue is discussed in chapters 8 and 9.

Systematic and non-systematic reviews fulfill very different needs. There are many examples of expert reviews that provide valuable summaries over a wide topic area, and which make no pretence to do anything other than present an overview. They may also use a literature review to present an argument. These kinds of review can be an important source of ideas, information, context, and argument, and many historical reviews would fall into this category. The value of expert reviews lies in the fact that they are written by someone with a detailed and well-grounded knowledge of the issues, though they may not be comprehensive or balanced in their selection and use of discussion material.

The systematic review by contrast adopts a particular methodology in an endeavor to limit bias, with the overall aim of producing a scientific summary of the evidence in any area. In this respect, systematic reviews are simply another research method, and in many respects they are very similar to a survey − though in this case they involve a survey of the literature, not of people. Perhaps most importantly systematic literature reviews usually aim to answer a specific question or test a specific hypothesis, rather than simply summarizing "all there is to know" about a particular issue.[8]

We emphasize however that in answering questions about effectiveness or causation, a well-conducted systematic review should be considered the most authoritative source of information. However, broader questions may require the use of other tools from the social scientist's toolbox, and good traditional reviews play an important role. Like so many things, it is a question of "horses for courses."

1.5 WHEN A SYSTEMATIC REVIEW IS OF VALUE

Systematic reviews are particularly valuable as a means of reviewing all the evidence on a particular question if there is some uncertainty about the answer. If it is unclear whether a particular intervention is effective, then a systematic review of the available evidence may help resolve the issue. Examples of questions that can usefully be addressed by a systematic review include whether mentoring is a good way to reduce anti-social behavior or increase school attendance in young people, or whether hearing loss in infancy causes dyslexia in children. A systematic review may be the only way of answering such a question since single studies taken in isolation can be so misleading.

The influence of systematic reviews has grown rapidly as potential users have become aware that they provide a means of dealing with the information mountain, by allowing large amounts of research information to be distilled into a manageable form. A further attraction to users lies in the potential to allow decisions to be made on a transparent and potentially defendable basis, as it draws on *all* relevant scientifically sound research, rather than on single studies. This appeals to the current policy interest in questions about "what works," and in evidence-based policy making more generally.[21]

Systematic reviews to inform policy

Politicians and policymakers are increasingly interested in evidence-based decision making. They are under pressure to look to research for solutions to policy problems, and to justify programs by reference to the knowledge base. For policymakers, systematic reviews may provide robust, reliable summaries of the most reliable evidence: a valuable backdrop of evidence on which decisions about policies can draw.

Politicians and policymakers alike have been criticized for failures to integrate research with decision making,[22] though systematic reviews have in fact been used to guide both US public policy[23] and UK public policy and health care policy (http://www.nice.org.uk; http://www.policyhub.gov.uk).[24] The perceived value of systematic reviews from the social sciences to UK Governmental decision making was spelled out in a speech by a UK minister, entitled "Influence or irrelevance: Can social science improve government?":

> Systematic reviews have not been given sufficient credit compared with new data collection...we're not interested in worthless correlations based on small samples from which it is impossible to draw generalisable conclusions...we welcome studies which combine large-scale, quantitative information on **effect sizes** which will allow us to generalise, with in-depth case studies which provide insights into how processes work. (Blunkett, 2000)[25]

In most policy debates, research evidence is only part (and sometimes a rather small part) of what gets considered. Values and resources are also part of the equation, but well-produced and well-explained and disseminated systematic reviews are likely to increase the part played by research evidence. The incorporation of economics into systematic reviews can also increase their value to policymakers, though for this we need to refer the reader to a more detailed guide to using systematic reviews for economic evaluation.[26]

A good example of the use of a systematic review to inform a contentious policy debate is given in Box 1.7. This review assembled the scientific evidence on the positive and negative effects of water fluoridation as a means of preventing tooth decay. This is also an example of how a good systematic review can actually increase certainty, and, in many cases, shows us that we know less about an issue than we thought we did.

Systematic reviews to support practice

Research has long played a part in informing the practice of those involved in the delivery of social policies, although a part which is sometimes more extensive than practitioners, and less than researchers would like. "Research-informed" practice has always been controversial. In the nineteenth century in the UK, the Charity Organization Society (COS), sometimes known as the "Scientific Charity," aspired, among other aims, to apply a scientific method in order to forecast what would happen to both an individual and his or her social group as a result of a charitable intervention. COS members included the social reformer and subsequent Fabian Socialist Beatrice Webb, and the housing reformer Octavia Hill. While its methods were dissimilar to systematic reviews, relying much more heavily on casework, and some of their philosophies spectacularly divisive between those seen as deserving and undeserving, they were early proponents of the view that there could be a gap between the intention to do good, and actually having a beneficial effect.

While the turf wars between research and practice are now less well defined, the growth of interest in evidence-based practice has increased pressure on practitioners to demonstrate that their existing work and their new practices are based on the best available research evidence. The increasing amount of research information, which varies in quality and relevance, can make it difficult to respond to these pressures, and can make the integration of evidence into practice difficult.[29] Systematic reviews there-

Box 1.7   Systematic review of water fluoridation[27, 28]

In 1999, the UK Department of Health commissioned the Centre for Reviews and Dissemination (CRD) at the University of York (England) to conduct a systematic review into the **efficacy** and safety of the fluoridation of drinking water. As this is a highly controversial topic, a review advisory panel was carefully selected to provide balanced representation from both sides of the debate, as well as those who were neutral. The panel included medical doctors, dentists, scientists, consumers, epidemiologists, and representatives of the water industry. Its role included overseeing the review, refining the review questions, and helping to identify relevant literature.

It was felt that the review had to be transparent and seen to be free from bias towards either side of the fluoridation debate. To keep members of the public updated on the review's progress and to provide information on how it was conducted, a website was created (http://www.york.ac.uk/inst/crd/fluorid.htm). This website explained how and why systematic reviews are undertaken and gave details of all involved in the review process, the review methods and **protocol**, all included and excluded studies, a list of frequently asked questions and a feedback and enquiry facility.

The review conclusions can be read in full on the website. Briefly, the evidence suggested that water fluoridation was likely to have a beneficial effect, but that the range could be anywhere from a substantial benefit to a slight disbenefit to children's teeth.[27, 28] This beneficial effect appears to come at the expense of an increase in the prevalence of fluorosis (mottled teeth) – though the quality of this evidence is poor. An association with water fluoride and other adverse effects such as cancer, bone fracture and Down's syndrome was not found, though it was concluded that not enough was known about this issue because the quality of the evidence was again poor.

fore provide a key source of evidence-based information to support and develop practice as well as to support professional development – for example, by helping to identify new and emerging developments and gaps in knowledge. For practitioners in social work and social care, an interest in evidence-based practice is also driven by issues of accountability, and decisions about policy and practice based on research evidence as well as on values, professional knowledge, and experience.[30, 31]

The following hypothetical situation highlights some of the key issues. Suppose someone planning services wants to evaluate the impact of discussion groups aimed at improving the parenting of a group of mothers and fathers living in poverty. Suppose also that a particular program runs for eight weekly sessions, and is considered by the workers and parents to have been a success for those who did not drop out. Their judgment is based on the self-reports of the parents, the workers' observations of parents' increasing self-esteem, and improvements in the apparent well-being of the children (who have been cared for in a playgroup during the parents' discussions). The work is carefully carried out and gets good local publicity. The researchers and the family present the work well, and it is picked up for a national early morning news program. Before asserting that "discussion groups work" we need to be as certain as possible that in this particular case:

- improvements *have* taken place; and
- they have been brought about as a result of the discussion group.

It is difficult to do this if we do not have mechanisms for ruling out competing explanations, such as:

- The parents might have improved simply with the passage of time, and increased confidence in their own parenting ability. There is evidence from other fields that many psychological problems, for instance, improve spontaneously over time in two-thirds of cases.[32] This provides a reason for having a "no treatment control," so that the effects of the intervention can be identified separately from any effects due to the passage of time.
- The children might have become more manageable through spending time with skilled playgroup workers.
- Other external factors might be responsible for changes, such as improved income support or additional help from social services.
- The perceived improvement in the parents might be due to their having learned the "right" things to say in the course of the intervention, having been asked the same kind of questions at the beginning and end of the program, and become familiar with the expectations of the workers.
- The parents who stayed might have been highly motivated and would have improved anyway. Alternatively, those parents who dropped out might have done just as well as those in the program. We simply don't know.

What is more, we also need to know what other studies have found, and how robust those studies are. Maybe this study showed it worked because of the play of chance, and not because the intervention really was generally effective. Maybe other studies show that it doesn't work, or that it only works in some types of setting, or for certain types of parent. After all, we are well used to seeing research studies reported in the media and elsewhere that show that something works one year, only to be contradicted by a different study (or a different researcher) the next. What happens if the results of all these studies are examined together? Would we still conclude that discussion groups "work"? Or, having seen all the relevant evidence, would we conclude the opposite? Or remain uncertain? These problems demonstrate the difficulties that arise whenever we plan to do something that we claim produces clear **outcomes**, whether good or bad (adapted from Macdonald and Roberts, 1995).[33]

Systematic reviews provide a good way to help us resolve this kind of issue. They are a method of critically appraising, summarizing, and attempting to reconcile the evidence in order to inform policy and practice.[34, 35] The value of systematic reviews is that they provide a synthesis of robust studies in a particular field of work which no policymaker or practitioner, however diligent, could possibly hope to read themselves. Systematic reviews are thus unlike "reviews of the studies I could find," "reviews of the authors I admire," "reviews that leave out inconveniently inconclusive findings or findings I don't like," and "reviews that support the policy or intervention I intend to introduce." Not only do they tell us about the current state of knowledge in an area, and any inconsistencies within it, but they also clarify what remains to be known.

1.6   WHY DO A SYSTEMATIC REVIEW? A RATIONALE

Single studies can usefully be seen as similar to single respondents in a survey. The results from one respondent may say something, and sometimes something very important, but one might well get the opposite answer from the next respondent. It is more likely that one will learn more by examining data from other respondents, by looking at the range of answers and examining why those answers vary, and by attempting to summarize them. Literature reviews are also, in essence surveys, and it is worth remembering that they share very similar biases with other forms of social surveys. One would not base any conclusion on the data from one survey interviewee, and the same goes for a review of the literature.

1.7   AN UNSYSTEMATIC HISTORY OF SYSTEMATIC REVIEWS

The idea of systematically reviewing research has been around for many decades. According to Iain Chalmers et al., many research fields first recognized the need to organize and evaluate the growing mountain of new research just after World War II, with US social scientists leading the way.[17] However, the history of this general approach to research synthesis goes back even further and a Victorian proto-systematic review can be found in the *American Journal of Psychology* in a paper written by Herbert Nichols in 1891.[36] This review accumulated evidence from 22 **experimental** studies to test the validity of Weber's Law. This is a psychological "law" which describes the smallest noticeable difference that can be perceived between two stimuli – such as two dim lights, or two similar sounds. The review tabulates quantitative information and systematic descriptions of 20 such **experiments**, with a summary statement that "the majority of the evidence" is against Weber's Law. This was not a systematic review in name, but the general aims and methods would be familiar to modern reviewers.

From the 1930s onwards, and possibly even before, the specific term "systematic review" was being used to refer to literature reviews. Many other early examples of literature reviews explicitly describe themselves as "systematic literature surveys."[37-39] In one case we see the use of the literature review explicitly used to test a hypothesis,[40] and in a 1954 review describing itself as systematic, we see included a summary table displaying the mean effect sizes which have been extracted from each included study.[41] In later examples we can see clear attempts to appraise and synthesize a body of experimental or other literature in order to answer specific questions. (Selected examples are shown in Table 1.1). Pawlicki (1970) carries out an appraisal of the quality of the included studies using a set of *a priori* methodological criteria.[42] In a 1972 paper we see a "review of reviews," in which Meltzer and colleagues systematically identify and appraise the quality of existing literature reviews in industrial psychology – an approach to literature reviewing which is becoming more common today.[43, 44] In a paper presented to a 1973 meeting William Kuvlesky suggests a need for the systematic codification and synthesis of past research on family disability – an early echo of calls by Archie Cochrane and Iain Chalmers for systematic reviews of healthcare interventions.[45]

Lavin and Sanders (1973)[46] also used language familiar to modern systematic reviewers:

> This is a systematic effort to review the knowledge and practice in management programs. In synthesizing the knowledge base, the study establishes and

Table 1.1 Selected early examples of systematic reviews (systematic in intent, if not always in name)

Title of review	What the authors said they did
The psychology of time (Nichols, 1891)[36]	"Reviews the theoretical and experimental work on the psychology of time . . . Conclusions based on 22 experimental works are as follows: (1) most studies found a particular length of interval more accurately judged than others, (2) the indifference point of judgments was variable for different individuals, times and conditions, (3) the sign of Constant Error was usually constant in both directions from the indifference point, and (4) the evidence points against the validity of Weber's law."
Review of research on effects of psychological stress upon performance (Lazarus et al., 1952)[49]	"The present report represents a systematic review of the literature dealing with the effects of stress on performance. First . . . experimental procedures which have been used to produce stress are analyzed and evaluated. . . . This is followed by a review of experimental studies of performance under stress. Based upon this review the authors undertake an evaluation of the problem . . . including a consideration of theoretical constructs."
Behavior-therapy research with children: A critical review (Pawlicki, 1970)[42]	"Evaluated behavior-therapy research with children published from 1965–1969 as to experimental design and execution. Studies were examined for use of control groups, base line, systematic variation of treatment, unbiased observation, and follow up. Results indicate most studies to be inadequate."
Educational production functions for teacher-technology mixes: Problems and possibilities (Anderson and Greenberg, 1972)[50]	"A systematic review of past and current experiments with educational applications of computers and television is coupled with a study of the social milieu in which public schools can be expected to operate in the near future. The paper is divided into four sections: a general overview of the social conditions which characterize schools today, an overview of the many studies which have been done in the use of television and computers in education, and economic analysis of some of the best studies."

(Continued)

Table 1.1 (Cont'd)

Title of review	What the authors said they did
Review of reviews in industrial psychology, 1950–1969 (Meltzer, 1972)[43]	"Analyzes the contributions dealing with industrial psychology that were published in the *Annual Review of Psychology* in the 1960s, with references to and comparisons with a similar analysis for the 1950s previously published.... Individual review articles in each year were appraised by 4 raters in terms of their orientation, systematic rationale, and interpretation and evaluation. Differences of opinion among the raters were relatively small.... The trend of thinking on 10 major issues in industrial psychology, as shown by the articles of the 1960s compared with those of the 1950s, is discussed."
Disability and family stress: Conceptual specification and research possibilities (Kuvlesky, 1973)[45]	"The objective of this paper was to develop a broad, systematic conceptual framework for studying psychological and biological based disabilities of individual family members.... A research review demonstrated an eclectic array of studies that were conceptually deficient and difficult to integrate because of varying frameworks." Suggestions for future research were presented, one of which was the systematic codification and synthesis of past research in the area.

emphasizes the great need to link the knowledge banks of the producers' world with the users' stations.

Many other examples from the late 1900s onwards could be given. In short, contrary to what is commonly supposed, neither the term "systematic review" nor the general approach of systematic literature reviewing are particularly new, nor particularly biomedical.

Many systematic reviews involve a statistical pooling of the findings of the primary studies. This approach, **meta-analysis**, probably derives in its current form from Glass and Smith's work, which began in the late 1970s (e.g., Glass et al., 1981).[47, 48] Glass and Smith's seminal meta-analysis involved pooling the results of 375 studies of the effectiveness of psychotherapy, though statistical approaches to the statistical synthesis of data (including data from individual studies) are probably much older than this (see chapter 6, section 6.11). Box 1.8 defines three types of reviews.

Box 1.8 Systematic review and meta-analysis

- *Systematic (literature) review*: A review that strives to comprehensively identify, appraise, and synthesize all the relevant studies on a given topic. Systematic reviews are often used to test just a single hypothesis, or a series of related hypotheses.
- *Meta-analysis*: A review that uses a specific statistical technique for synthesizing the results of several studies into a single quantitative estimate (i.e., a summary effect size).
- *Narrative review*: The process of synthesizing primary studies and exploring **heterogeneity** descriptively, rather than statistically.

1.8 THE **COCHRANE** AND **CAMPBELL** COLLABORATIONS: INTERNATIONAL COLLABORATIONS OF SYSTEMATIC REVIEWERS

With the boost provided by the new tool of meta-analysis, systematic reviews began to proliferate and, in the US in particular, they were seen as a valuable means of synthesizing relevant data for policymakers' use.[17, 22] By the 1980s systematic reviews in health care in particular began to be published in greater numbers, and in the UK in the early 1990s two centers were established to prepare and maintain systematic reviews of the effects of health care interventions – the UK Cochrane Centre in 1993, and the NHS Centre for Reviews and Dissemination in 1994.[17] The goals of the Cochrane Collaboration have been adopted more recently by the Campbell Collaboration, which aims to prepare, maintain, and disseminate the results of systematic reviews of social, educational, and criminological interventions.[51] Many other international centers also currently carry out systematic reviews of public policies (for example, in the case of education, the EPPI Centre).[52] These are discussed in other chapters (for instance, see chapter 4 for links to relevant organizations).

Systematic literature reviews, even when done scientifically, have in the past been seen as being lower status than primary research, perhaps because their role and potential was not often appreciated. This is no longer the case: "Preparing reviews takes time, effort, intelligence and commitment, and it is a branch of scientific endeavour as important as primary research".[53]

1.9 SYSTEMATIC REVIEWS AS PARADIGM SHIFTERS

> Every learner hath a deference more or less to authority, especially the young learners, few of that kind caring to dwell long upon principles, but inclining to take them upon trust: And things early admitted by repetition become familiar: And this familiarity at length passeth for evidence.
>
> *(Bishop Berkeley (1685–1783): from* **The principles of human knowledge***)*

Systematic reviews offer a challenge to the role of the expert, and to much received wisdom. Much current theory and practice are based on assumptions about what works, about what is appropriate, and on past practices. Over time these become crystallized and resistant to challenge. New researchers in a field may doubt the theory, or the strength of evidence offered by certain studies, but often no direct challenge is possible. Moreover, much social research – and other research – is conducted within "schools" – schools of thought, which direct the type of science that is conducted, and to some extent can control the outcomes – by controlling how and when (and if) studies with particular approaches or reporting particular findings are published. "Invisible colleges" prefer orthodoxy; researchers work within a paradigm (or, more likely, several paradigms) in which there is unwritten consensus about what is to be researched. Systematic reviews allow challenge to the paradigm to occur – a challenge permitted by close examination of the underpinning evidence.

The science of systematic reviewing is still evolving, and there are particular opportunities for wider use in relation to theory building and theory testing. Shadish[54] has pointed out that meta-analysis for example has focused too much on descriptive causation (simply describing the size of an effect) and too little on the development of explanatory theories, yet systematic reviews – whether of qualitative or quantitative research – are likely to be much more **powerful** than single studies for these purposes.[55, 56] This is one area where systematic reviews have significant untapped potential.

1.10   WHEN TO DO A SYSTEMATIC REVIEW

In summary then, we can begin by outlining some pointers to when to do a systematic review:

1.   When there is uncertainty, for example about the effectiveness of a policy or a service, and where there has been some previous research on the issue.
2.   In the early stages of development of a policy, when evidence of the likely effects of an intervention is required.
3.   When it is known that there is a wide range of research on a subject but where key questions remain unanswered – such as questions about treatment, prevention, diagnosis, or **etiology**, or questions about people's experiences.
4.   When a general overall picture of the evidence in a topic area is needed to direct future research efforts.
5.   When an accurate picture of past research, and past methodological research is required to promote the development of new methodologies.

It is also worth seriously considering whether a systematic review is needed before embarking on *any* new piece of primary research. This is done too infrequently at present, though increasingly funders require this as a condition of funding for major primary research studies (see Box 1.9 from the website "Netting the Evidence," which suggests how systematic reviews may be attractive to funders in relation to the cumulation of knowledge). Even if it is not a condition of funding, it is simply good scientific practice to know how a new study builds on existing evidence. As Newton knew, cumulation is the heart of good science: "If I see further than others, it is because I stand on the shoulders of giants."

Box 1.9 Systematic reviews in support of funding applications

- To show whether (and, if so, how well) your research topic has been tackled previously: Pilot studies, although necessary, are time-consuming and costly. Access to the published experiences of previous researchers in your topic may well inform your pilot and possibly limit the range of questions that it seeks to address.
- To put your research in the context of other work in this field: This is stipulated by a majority of funding agencies.
- To establish relevance: A proposal for original research is strengthened by supporting literature that can demonstrate that your question is worth answering and, indeed, that it has not already been satisfactorily resolved.
- To support bids for funding and sponsorship: In the competitive arena that is research funding a research proposal is strengthened if it can demonstrate that it is not "reinventing the wheel," that the research question has been identified as an important gap still to be addressed, and that it builds on previous research.

(From SCHARR: School of Health and Related Research (University of Sheffield), online at: http://www.shef.ac.uk/scharr/ir/netting/)

It has long been a criticism of most scientific disciplines that activity is characterized by independent working, lack of dissemination of research findings, and no attempt at synthesis. This applies to the hard and pure sciences just as much as to social sciences. Mathematics for example has been criticized for fragmentation and for lacking institutions for synthesizing or sharing its work.[57] Physicist John Ziman echoes this: "Basic scientific knowledge is typically fragmented into little islands of near conformity surrounded by interdisciplinary oceans of ignorance."[58, 59]

Key learning points from this chapter

- Information overload is a problem for decision makers and researchers alike; single studies are rarely definitive, and the amount of conflicting information often makes deciding where the "balance of evidence" on any question lies difficult.

- Syntheses of evidence are one approach to this problem, but traditional literature reviews are often biased, and often disagree.
- By comparison, systematic reviews aim to provide an objective, comprehensive summary of the best evidence (whether it appears in the published literature, or not – and much of it does not).
- Systematic reviews have been in use in one form or other in the social sciences for many decades, and are increasingly being used to support practice and policy, and to direct new research efforts.

REFERENCES

1. Younge, G. President sets aside £1.5bn to boost marriage. *The Guardian*, January 15, 2004, online at: http://www.guardian.co.uk/international/story/0,,1123417,00.html [accessed February 2, 2005].
2. Legge, J. T. *The Analects of Confucius*: Project Gutenberg, 1930.
3. Rumsfeld, D. Department of Defense news briefing, Feb. 12, 2002, online at: http://slate.msn.com/id/2081042/ [accessed February 2, 2005].
4. Chalmers, I., Enkin, M., and Keirse, M. Preparing and updating systematic reviews of randomized controlled trials of health care. *Millbank Quarterly* 1993, 71: 411–37.
5. Bush, G. *State of the Union Address, 2003*, online at:http://www.whitehouse.gov/news/releases/2003/01/20030128-19.html [accessed February 2, 2005].
6. Roberts, H., Liabo, K., Lucas, P., DuBois, D., and Sheldon, T. Mentoring to reduce antisocial behaviour in childhood. *British Medical Journal* 2004, 328: 512-14, online at: http://bmj.bmjjournals.com/cgi/content/full/328/7438/512 [accessed February 2, 2005].
7. Oakley, A. Social science and evidence-based everything: The case of education. *Educational Review* 2002, 54: 277–86.
8. Mulrow, C. D. Systematic reviews: Rationale for systematic reviews. *British Medical Journal* 1994, 309: 597–9.
9. Oliver, S., Peersman, G., Harden, A., and Oakley, A. Discrepancies in findings from effectiveness reviews: The case of health promotion for older people in accident and injury prevention. *Health Education Journal* 1999, 58: 66–77.
10. Oakley, A. and Fullerton, D. *A systematic review of smoking prevention programmes for young people*. London: EPPI Centre, Institute of Education, 1995.
11. Chowka, P. Linus Pauling: The last interview. 1996, online at: http://members.aol.com/erealmedia/pauling.html [accessed February 2, 2005].
12. Knipschild, P. Some examples of systematic reviews. In I. Chalmers and D. Altman (eds.), *Systematic reviews*. London: BMJ Publishing Group, 1995.
13. Knipschild, P. Some examples of systematic reviews. *British Medical Journal* 1994, 309: 719–21.

14. Gaffan, E., Tsaousis, I., and Kemp-Wheeler, S. Researcher allegiance and meta-analysis: The case of cognitive therapy for depression. *Journal of Consulting and Clinical Psychology* 1995, 63: 966–80.
15. Shadish, W. Author judgements about works they cite: Three studies from psychological journals. *Social Studies of Science* 1995, 25: 477–98.
16. Ravetz, J. *Scientific knowledge and its social problems.* Middlesex: Penguin University Books, 1973.
17. Chalmers, I., Hedges, L., and Cooper, H. A brief history of research synthesis. *Evaluation and the Health Professions* 2002, 25: 12–37.
18. Titchener, E. A plea for summaries and indexes. *American Journal of Psychology* 1903, 14: 84–7.
19. Rigby, K. *A meta-evaluation of methods and approaches to reducing bullying in pre-schools and in early primary school in Australia.* Canberra: Commonwealth Attorney-General's Department. 2002. (See: http://www.education.unisa.edu.au/bullying/countering.htm [accessed February 2, 2005] for details of how to obtain this report.)
20. Mytton, J., DiGuiseppi, C., Gough, D., Taylor, R., and Logan, S. School based violence prevention programs: Systematic review of secondary prevention trials. *Archives of Paediatrics and Adolescent Medicine* 2002, 156: 748–9.
21. Solesbury, W. Evidence based policy: Whence it came and where it's going. ESRC UK Centre for Evidence Based Policy and Practice: Working Paper 1, 2001, online at:http://www.evidencenetwork.org/Documents/wp1.pdf [accessed February 2, 2005].
22. Chelimsky, E. On the social science contribution to governmental decision-making. *Science* 1991, 254: 226–30.
23. Hunt, M. *How science takes stock.* New York: Russell Sage Foundation, 1997.
24. Boaz, A., Ashby, D., and Young, K. Systematic reviews: What have they got to offer evidence based policy and practice? ESRC UK Centre for Evidence Based Policy and Practice, Working Paper 2, 2002, online at: http://www.evidence-network.org/cgi-win/enet.exe/biblioview?538 [accessed February 2, 2005].
25. Blunkett, D. Influence or irrelevance: Can social science improve government? Swindon: Economic and Social Research Council, 2000, online at: http://www.bera.ac.uk/ri/no71/ri71blunkett.html [accessed February 2, 2005].
26. Donaldson, C., Mugford, M., and Vale, L. (eds.) *Evidence-based health economics: From effectiveness to efficiency in systematic review.* London: BMJ Books, 2002.
27. Wilson, P. Muddy waters: The use and abuse of findings from the "York Review" on fluoridation, ESRC Research Methods Festival, July 2, 2004.
28. McDonagh, M., Whiting, P., Wilson, P., Sutton, A., Chestnutt, I., Cooper, J., et al. Systematic review of water fluoridation. *British Medical Journal* 2000, 321: 855–9.
29. Taylor, B., Dempster, M., and Donnelly, M. Hidden gems: Systematically searching electronic databases for research publications for social work and social care. *British Journal of Social Work* 2003, 33: 423–39.

30. Macdonald, G. Evidence-based social care: Wheels off the runway? *Public Money Management* 1999, 19: 25–32.
31. Sheldon, B. and Macdonald, G. Mind the gap: Research and practice in social care. Centre for Evidence Based Social Services, 1999, online at: http://www.ex.ac.uk/cebss/files/MindtheGap.pdf [accessed February 2, 2005].
32. Rachman, S. and Wilson, G. *The effects of psychological therapy.* New York: Pergamon Press, 1980.
33. Macdonald, G. and Roberts, H. *What works in the early years.* London: Barnardo's, 1995, Report summary is online at: http://www.barnardos.org.uk/resources/researchpublications/documents/WW-E-YRS.PDF [accessed February 2, 2005].
34. Petticrew, M. Systematic reviews from astronomy to zoology: Myths and misconceptions. *British Medical Journal* 2001, 322: 98–101.
35. Gough, D. and Elbourne, D. Systematic research synthesis to inform policy, practice, and democratic debate. *Social Policy and Society* 2002, 1: 225–36.
36. Nichols, H. The psychology of time. *American Journal of Psychology* 1891, 3: 453–529.
37. Uttl, K. Vegetative centres in the diencephalon. *Review of Neuroogical Psychiatry (Praha)* 1935, 32: 104–14.
38. Mibai, S. An experimental study of apparent movement. *Psychological Monographs* 1931, 42: 91.
39. Harris, D. The socialization of the delinquent. *Child Development* 1948, 19: 143–54.
40. Winsor, A. The relative variability of boys and girls. *Journal of Educational Psychology* 1927, 18: 327–36.
41. Klebanoff, S., Singer, J., and Wilensky, H. Psychological consequences of brain lesions and ablations. *Psychological Bulletin* 1954, 51: 1–41.
42. Pawlicki, R. Behavior-therapy research with children: A critical review. *Canadian Journal of Behavioural Science* 1970, 2: 163–73.
43. Meltzer, H. Review of reviews in industrial psychology, 1950–1969. *Personnel Psychology* 1972, 25: 201–22.
44. Morrison, D., Petticrew, M., and Thomson, H. Effectiveness of transport interventions in improving health: Evidence from systematic reviews. *Journal of Epidemiology and Community Health* 2003, 57: 327–33.
45. Kuvlesky, W. Disability and family stress: Conceptual specification and research possibilities. Report: TAES-216-15-69; USDA-CSRS-RP-NC-90, paper presented at the Association of Southern Agricultural Workers Meeting, Atlanta, Georgia, February 1973, Washington, DC: Cooperative State Research Service (DOA).
46. Lavin, R. and Sanders, J. *Synthesis of knowledge and practice in educational management and leadership.* Volumes 1 and 2. Project No. ED 73-241: Dayton, OH: Charles F. Kettering Foundation, 1973.

47. Glass, G. and Smith, M. *Meta-analysis of research on the relationship of class size and achievement*. San Francisco: Far West Laboratory for Educational Research and Development, 1978.

48. Glass, G., McGaw, B., and Smith, M. *Meta-analysis in social research*. Beverly Hills: Sage, 1981.

49. Lazarus, R. S., Deese, J., and Osler, S. The effects of psychological stress upon performance. *Psychological Bulletin* 1952, 49(4): 293–317.

50. Anderson, B. and Greenberg, E. Educational production functions for teacher-technology mixes: Problems and possibilities: Report: M-72-2. Washington, DC: National Aeronautics and Space Administration, March 1972.

51. Davies, P. and Boruch, R. The Campbell Collaboration. *British Medical Journal* 2001, 323: 294–5.

52. Elbourne, D., Oakley, A., and Gough, D. EPPI Centre reviews will aim to disseminate systematic reviews in education. *British Medical Journal* 2001, 323: 1252.

53. Muir Gray, J. A. *Evidence-based healthcare*. London: Churchill Livingstone, 1997.

54. Shadish, W. Meta-analysis and the exploration of causal mediating processes: A primer of examples, methods, and issues. *Psychological Methods* 1996, 1: 47–65.

55. Riemsma, R., Pattenden, J., Bridle, C., Sowden, A., Mather, L., Watt, I., et al. A systematic review of the effectiveness of interventions based on a stages-of-change approach to promote individual behaviour change. *Health Technology Assessment* 2002, 6, online at: http://www.hta.nhsweb.nhs.uk/fullmono/mon624.pdf [accessed February 2, 2005].

56. Miller, N. and Pollock, V. Meta-analytic synthesis for theory development. In H. Cooper and L. Hedges (eds.), *The handbook of research synthesis*. New York: Russell Sage Foundation, 1994.

57. Spohn, W. Can mathematics be saved? *Notices of the American Mathematical Society* 1969, 16: 890–4.

58. Gilland, T, Mayer, S., Durodie, B., Gibson, I., and Parr, D. *Science: Can we trust the experts?* London: Hodder & Stoughton, 2002.

59. Ziman, J. Is science losing its objectivity? *Nature* 382 (1996): 751–4.

Chapter 2

Starting the review: Refining the question and defining the boundaries

---

Box 2.1   The seven stages in carrying out a systematic review

1. Clearly define the question that the review is setting out to answer, or the hypothesis that the review will test, in consultation with anticipated users (this chapter)
2. Determine the types of studies that need to be located in order to answer your question (see chapter 3)
3. Carry out a comprehensive literature search to locate those studies (see chapter 4)
4. Screen the results of that search (that is, sift through the retrieved studies, deciding which ones look as if they fully meet the **inclusion criteria**, and thus need more detailed examination, and which do not) (see chapter 4)
5. Critically appraise the included studies (see chapter 5), and
6. Synthesize the studies (see chapter 6), and assess heterogeneity among the study findings (see chapter 7)
7. Disseminate the findings of the review (see chapter 8)

See Appendix 1 for a more detailed overview of the systematic review process.

2.1   IS A SYSTEMATIC REVIEW THE RIGHT TOOL
FOR THE JOB?

Before starting the review, it is worth asking a question that is often over-looked. Is a systematic review *really* needed? There is no doubt that systematic reviews are currently in favor with research-informed policymakers, practitioners, and many researchers. As a result it is often assumed that a systematic review must be done, but in some cases it is not clear that a new systematic review would be the best use of the researcher's time and the funder's money. Most importantly, a systematic review may not be the right type of study for answering the question in hand. One needs to be sure that a new systematic review will be more useful than a new **primary study**, though, as discussed in chapter 1, a systematic review can be a useful precursor to new research. A systematic review will be of particular value when there is uncertainty about what the evidence on a particular topic shows: for example when there is uncertainty about the effectiveness of a particular intervention (such as the effectiveness of government welfare-to-work policies in getting people back into employment),[1] or debate about the relationship between two variables (for example, the relationship between health in childhood and educational and employment outcomes in adulthood).[2] In these circumstances a system-atic review may help clarify the question, provide an authoritative overview of the current evidence, and suggest directions for future research.

Even if a systematic review really is the right tool for the job, a new systematic review might still not be appropriate. This could be because the review has already been done and the question has already been answered satisfactorily. Chapter 8 discusses the importance of dissemination and implementation, and it may be that a gap in the dissemination process means that the right people do not know about that review.

Finally, a review may simply not be the best research method for answering that particular question, or testing that particular hypothesis (see Box 2.2).

2.2   FRAMING THE REVIEW QUESTION

The review question itself may be "wrong" if it is focused on the wrong intervention (in the case of reviews of effectiveness), or more generally, if it asks the wrong question. For example, the reviewer may be most interested in the effectiveness of an intervention, whose effectiveness is already estab-lished (reducing road traffic accidents in children by preventing them from going outside, for instance). However, decision-makers (practitioners or

Box 2.2 Situations when a new systematic review may not be appropriate

- If a systematic review is not the right research tool to answer the question.
- If there are already one or more good systematic reviews in the same area, which could more usefully be summarized, or updated.
- If someone is already carrying out a review in the same area, which is not yet published.
- If the review question is too vague, or too broad.
- If the question is too limited in scope, or narrowly (or wrongly) focused – so that the results of the review are unlikely to be useful to researchers, funders, or other decision makers.
- If you, or your institution have insufficient resources to support a reliable systematic review.

policymakers) may need to know about more child-friendly interventions whose effectiveness is less clear, such as how to employ different kinds of traffic management, while balancing the needs of child pedestrians with the needs of other road users. In general, the review is likely to move further up the shopping list for non-academic users if the reviewer works with them in developing the question, rather than contacting them when the review is finished (see Box 2.3).

Box 2.3 Setting review questions jointly with users

Review questions are best defined together with potential users of the review. Users or stakeholders are the people who are intended to read and/or use the review's findings. They include funders, practitioners, policy and other decision makers, and end-users of interventions. They should be consulted at an early stage to find out their exact information needs. For example, there is no point in doing a systematic review of the literature on parents' *needs* for child care, if what is really required is a systematic review of what *kinds* of childcare are associated with the best outcomes for children, or a review of the *effects* of childcare on parents' and children's lives. Having consulted users, involved them, or been

(Continued)

Box 2.3   *(Cont'd)*

involved by them, review questions can be refined further by reading existing reviews, and consulting other experts in the area.

Two examples:

- *INVOLVE* <http://www.invo.org.uk/index.htm> is a UK organization that promotes public health involvement in the NHS, public health and social care research. It aims to improve the way that decisions are made about what should be research priorities, and the ways in which research is commissioned, carried out, and communicated.
- The *Centre for Reviews and Dissemination* at the University of York (CRD), spends time working with stakeholders including clinicians and user groups. One example is a systematic review funded by the Enuresis Society. They wanted a review, the reviewers were able to identify funding, and once it was produced, there was a ready organization who wanted to use the findings. (See: <http://www.york.ac.uk/inst/crd/ehc82.pdf>.)

There are a number of other ways in which users can be (and are) involved in systematic reviews. These include:

- *The formulation of questions*: Many of the most meaningful research questions come from people who use or provide front line services. Users (and front line providers) are well placed to know what the most important questions are. Reviewers often seek out questions from interested parties, including users. This includes the Cochrane Child Health Field <http://www.cochranechild-health.org/> which asks "Are consumers pushing you for answers in areas for which no answers are available?" and suggests how a question can be asked.
- *Commenting on protocols*: Once the question has been formulated and a protocol drawn up, users may have a view on the process proposed to address the question, and can often comment on every stage, including the protocol (see also Box 1.7).
- *Helping to carry out reviews*: Carrying out good systematic reviews can be very time-consuming. Searching for relevant literature, and in particular **hand searching**, are among the tasks with which people who are enthusiasts for answering particular questions can help.

Users can also be given the opportunity to comment on the completed review – an opportunity offered by Cochrane and EPPI-Centre reviewers <http://eppi.ioe.ac.uk/EPPIWeb/home.aspx>.

It is particularly important to take account of stakeholders' views when interventions are widely used, or where there are powerful stakeholders who might have a commercial interest (such as the developers of a particular intervention), or a professional interest (such as parent educators), or some other kind of interest (such as motorists). "Taking account of their views" does not of course mean that they should dictate the review's findings, but it ensures that their concerns and their priorities are known about. This can help give a review a clearer focus.

It should be remembered that all interventions have the capacity to do harm as well as good, and "involving users" is itself an intervention. It can be a time-consuming exercise for all concerned, and involving users for PR purposes, or as a gimmick, can reduce their willingness to become engaged in future exercises. There is no point consulting on issues where there is no real room for change. There is still a lot to learn about how different "voices" can best be heard in the research agenda and efforts to involve users can easily slip into tokenism unless fully thought through. Users are not a homogenous group. Different approaches are needed to take account of age, gender, ethnicity, and culture and to ensure the participation of "hard to reach" people – those who are even less likely to have a voice but who may have specific expertise on the important questions to be asked on topics such as homelessness, learning disability, or the prison system. Consulting people in the preparation of reviews is only the first stage, and reviewers need not only to listen but also to respond. People quickly become disillusioned unless they see that their views are listened to. This means that review teams need to be clear and honest about what is, and what is not negotiable. They also need to face up to situations where the views of users may be contrary to those of more powerful stakeholders.

Box 2.4 outlines some questions reviewers may want to ask themselves at the beginning of the review process, before spending six months or more doing a systematic review.

It is sometimes the case that a new systematic review is proposed, when what is really needed is new primary research. It is also common to see calls for systematic reviews addressing such general issues that it is difficult to see how a useful question could be answered. The main warning sign is when a review does not appear to have a specific question, but instead aims to be a review of a very wide topic area. Hypothetical examples might include: "A systematic review of stress at work," or "A systematic review of home-work." Unless the underlying topic and question are much more clearly defined, the review will run the real risk of being unmanageably large and non-systematic. To take the first example, one would want to know what specific aspects of stress are of interest: Methods of reducing it?

Box 2.4   What makes you think your review is asking a meaningful question?

Below are three questions that a reviewer might wish to consider:

1.   Do I know anything about the topic? – It is sometimes assumed that anyone can do a review with little prior background knowledge. This can be true, but if the reviewer knows nothing of the area, then they are unlikely to know which questions most need to be answered, what research has already been carried out in the area, where to find it, and how to make the review useful to users. This is why review teams bringing together people from different backgrounds, such as information science, topic experts, and so on is so important.
2.   Who do I envisage will use the results of my review? How will they use this information? – If you don't have a clear idea what contribution the review will make, and who might use its results, then why do it?
3.   How do I know that anyone wants this question answered? – Assuming that you have a clear question in mind, you will want to ensure that the question is the right one – by discussing it with potential users. There is a mountain of social science literature (including systematic reviews) that precisely and authoritatively answers questions that no one asked. You'd better have a good reason for adding to it!

Determinants of stress at work? Theories and concepts of stress in work settings? All of these?

For these broad topics, **scoping studies**, and/or traditional, narrative reviews, presenting an argument may be more helpful, and may themselves lead to clearer questions being asked. These in turn may become the subject of a systematic review (or new primary research).[3]

Framing policy issues as answerable questions

Policy questions in particular may need careful work to frame and clarify them so that a useful systematic review can be carried out. While systematic reviews often aim to answer single questions, or test a single hypothesis (see

Section 2.3), policy questions may often be much broader than this and work may be needed to identify what the question or more likely questions are that need answering. For example, at the time of writing childhood and adult obesity is in the news in many countries, and is a major policy issue. It is also a major issue for the public and the media, with "junk" food, and food producers and retailers currently seen as major contributors to the problem. How can systematic reviews contribute to the debate? The first step is to identify which questions need answering, and the most obvious ones may relate to the likely impact of interventions to promote healthy eating. At a policy level, a systematic review of the impact of legislative interventions (for example, those governing food labeling or nutritional content of foods) may help suggest which interventions may be effective, and what some of the adverse effects may be. Systematic reviews of the relationships between diet, physical activity, the physical environment, and obesity may elucidate the relative contributions made by each of these, and may suggest further areas where policies may be adopted to influence the obesity epidemic. Systematic reviews of qualitative research may shed light on the extent to which interventions are likely to be adopted or resisted. All these reviews are addressing different questions and the answers will come from different sources. Not all of the relevant information may come from systematic reviews, of course; information on the ethics of government intervention in diet may come from other sources, and information on the costs and benefits may come from new economic studies and decision modeling (though these new studies may themselves involve systematic reviews).

Wallace et al. provide a useful reflection on the process of carrying out a systematic review of a UK policy intervention: mortgage "safety nets," which provide support to home owners experiencing financial difficulties. These "safety nets" (which include different types of insurance, and flexible mortgages), aim to affect outcomes such as rates of home repossession, and levels of mortgage arrears.[4] As might be expected, experimental approaches to assessing the impact of safety nets are uncommon, so the review did not take randomized controlled trials (**RCTs**) as the only source of evidence, and did not restrict itself to identifying "ideal" studies (though all studies were assessed as to their robustness). The authors point out that in the case of social policy reviews the changing context within which the evidence is collected makes its interpretation and application to other settings difficult. In the case of mortgage safety nets, the reviewers describe how the outcomes may be mediated by shifting economic cycles, changes in the interventions, and other policy changes. This issue of shifting context was illustrated by these reviewers using a timeline that outlined the key milestones, against which the included studies were plotted. A contextual map was also included which displayed schematically the macro-, meso- and micro-level factors affecting outcomes. Both these approaches may prove particularly useful for illustrating and interpreting the findings of other systematic reviews of policy interventions (see Figure 2.1).[4]

Greenhalgh et al. have developed a new approach ("**meta-narrative mapping**") based on systematic review methods, which may be particularly useful for very complex review questions (such as policy questions) where no one theoretical framework can be applied. They systematically reviewed the literature on the diffusion, dissemination, and sustainability of innovations in health service delivery and organization.[5] This involved mapping the different research traditions, methods of ranking evidence, preferred research methodologies and theoretical models within each of the research traditions that appeared relevant to the review question. The synthesis phase involved assessing the contributions of these traditions (and the evidence they produced) to answering the review question. Such an approach may be of particular value for answering highly complex policy questions where simple questions of effectiveness alone are insufficient.

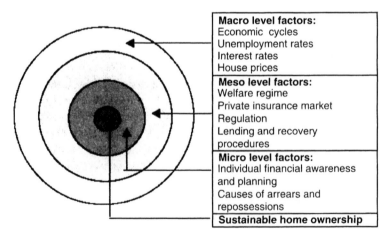

Figure 2.1 Contextual map of sustainable home ownership
Source: Wallace et al. (2004)[4]

2.3 SYSTEMATIC REVIEWS AS HYPOTHESIS TESTS

Cynthia Mulrow has described systematic reviews as hypothesis-testing mechanisms.[6] This is helpful as it reminds the reviewer to frame the questions in a way that they can be clearly answered – and framing a review question as a hypothesis, or a series of related hypotheses allows it to be clearly framed, then accepted or rejected. This may not always be possible (for methodological reviews it might be more difficult, for example), but it will make defining the inclusion and **exclusion criteria** easier, and will help keep the whole review on track. The basic rule is: *Never start a systematic review until a clear question (or clear questions) can be framed.*

2.4 WHEN SHOULD ONE DO A REVIEW – EARLY IN THE DEVELOPMENT OF THE FIELD? OR LATER, WHEN THERE ARE MANY PRIMARY STUDIES TO REVIEW?

It has been suggested that a literature review may be less valuable when a field is immature – that is when there are too few studies to yield data.[7] In this situation however, a systematic review can highlight the absence of data, and point up the fact that any understanding is based on limited empirical underpinnings – in itself an important contribution. Further, even when a field is immature, it is important to cumulate prospectively rather than wait for some later date when "enough" evidence has accumulated, and consolidation can occur. Systematic reviews can identify gaps and direct future research efforts. Cumulating data can also help the early identification of effective interventions. For example Antman et al. showed how a systematic review of existing trials could have identified that "clot-busting" drugs for heart attacks were effective in 1979, 20 years before they were finally licensed for use in the US.[8]

As discussed in chapter 1, some researchers and funders take the view that all new primary research should be preceded by a systematic review. The UK's Medical Research Council for example gives the following guidance: "Potential applicants are encouraged to conduct a systematic review of the available evidence (where a recent such review does not already exist)." In general, carrying out a review is an important first step in designing new interventions, and new evaluations. It can point to where improvements in evaluation methods are required, and can indicate where changes in the intervention may be needed to improve effectiveness.

2.5   START BY FINDING EXISTING SYSTEMATIC REVIEWS

It makes sense not to do a systematic review that has been done before, unless it is clear that previous systematic reviews were significantly biased, or are significantly out of date – for example, if new studies have been published since the older review was completed. For this reason it is important to start any new review by searching for existing systematic reviews, to avoid duplication. This task could be incorporated into the **scoping review** if one is being carried out.

The two keys to effective systematic reviewing are collaboration and avoidance of duplication. These principles have been emphasized by the Cochrane and Campbell Collaborations and are good practice for systematic reviewers more generally. It is wasteful to duplicate existing work, and the obvious place to start the search for prior systematic reviews would be to search specialized databases (Box 2.5). Other sources (apart from mainstream databases such as Medline, ASSIA, Psychlit and so on) include the NICE website in the UK, which includes details of systematic reviews in public health <http://www.publichealth.nice.org.uk>, and the Effective Public Health Practice website in Canada <http://www.city.hamilton.on.ca/ PHCS/EPHPP/EPHPPResearch.asp>. The latter includes full versions of reviews of interventions targeting food safety, child mental health, parenting, domestic abuse, suicide prevention, and summaries of dozens of other reviews. In the UK, CRD at the University of York maintains a database of ongoing systematic reviews which can be consulted freely <http:// www.york.ac.uk/inst/crd/>.

In the US, the What Works Clearinghouse (WWC) <http://w-w-c. org> was established by the US Department of Education's Institute of Education Sciences in 2002 to meet the growing need for systematic reviews. The WWC aims to develop standards for reviewing and synthe-sizing educational research and disseminates reviews of potentially replicable interventions (programs, products, and practices) that are intended to en-hance student outcomes. MDRC <http://www.mdrc.org>, which carries out Social Policy Research, has also published many meta-analyses of US government programs, for example, a meta-analysis of the effect of welfare programs on marriage and co-habitation.[9]

Box 2.5   Databases that contain reports of systematic reviews (See also chapter 4)

- The *DARE* database <http://www.york.ac.uk/inst/crd/crddatabases.htm> contains abstracts of systematic reviews of the effects of healthcare and some social interventions. Each abstract is accompanied by a detailed commentary on the soundness of the methods, and whether the review's conclusions appear to be justified. Potential implications of the review for policy and practice are outlined.

- The *Cochrane Database of Systematic Reviews* contains full versions of systematic reviews, covering a wide range of health care, and some social and public health interventions. For example there are systematic reviews examining the effects of traffic calming measures, day care provision, smoke alarm ownership, reviews of health promotion, and some educational interventions. The database is freely available in the UK <http://www.nelh.nhs.uk/cochrane.asp> and some other countries (including Australia, Ireland, Finland, Denmark, and Norway). The titles and abstracts of Cochrane reviews can be freely accessed online at http://www.cochrane.org.

- *The Campbell Collaboration* "Does for public policy what Cochrane does for health."[10] Now in its fifth year, the Campbell Collaboration (C2's) objectives are to prepare, maintain and disseminate systematic reviews of studies of interventions. C2 builds summaries and electronic brochures of reviews and reports of trials for policymakers, practitioners, researchers, and the public.[11] The *Campbell Library* is compiled by the Campbell Collaboration <http://www.campbellcollaboration.org>. Their website has links to ongoing and completed systematic reviews in crime, education, social welfare, and criminal justice. At the time of writing about 80 systematic review titles are registered including reviews on the means of preventing high school dropout, treatments for sex offenders, and on the impact of marriage and relationship programs. These appear in a register (called C2-RIPE), which is freely accessible online.

- The *Research Evidence in Education Library* (REEL) <http://eppi.ioe.ac.uk/reel/>, at the Institute of Education in London is

(Continued)

Box 2.5   *(Cont'd)*

a database of reviews of educational interventions, located at the Centre for Evidence-Informed Policy and Practice in Education, funded by the Department for Education and Skills, England. Examples of completed reviews include a systematic review of effective literacy teaching in 4 to 14 year olds, and a systematic review of the impact of school head teachers and principals on student outcomes.

Published systematic reviews can also be located in relevant bibliographic databases, such as Medline. If an existing good quality review is identified, but it is slightly out of date (for example, new studies have been published since the search was carried out) then it may make more sense to update it than carry out a new one. This will involve carrying out additional searches and including new studies. If only a few studies post-date the review, and they are small and/or significantly methodologically unsound, the review conclusions may not change significantly.

If you feel the earlier review was inaccurate in some way, because it missed a significant proportion of the relevant literature, or because it did not carry out any **critical appraisal** of the included studies, it may be appropriate to carry out a new, more comprehensive systematic review. Good collegial practice would also involve correspondence with the authors of the earlier review.

2.6   ALTERNATIVES TO SYSTEMATIC REVIEWS

Alternatives to the full systematic review are available. These may be useful for example as a prelude to refining the question for a systematic review, or to map out a general topic area. Some approaches to synthesizing research are outlined in Table 2.1.

2.7   DEFINING THE QUESTION: BREAK THE QUESTION DOWN

It is helpful to start by breaking the review question down into sub-questions. If the review aims to answer a question about effectiveness, the question can be framed using a model called PICO (population, intervention, comparison, outcomes),[23] which encourages the researcher to consider the components of the question, as follows:

Table 2.1 Some common approaches to research synthesis

Type of review	Definition	Example
Systematic review	A review that aims to comprehensively identify all relevant studies to answer a particular question, and assesses the validity (or "soundness") of each study taking this into account when reaching conclusions	Effects of school-based social problem-solving interventions on aggressive behavior[12] A systematic review of the effects of private and public investment on health[13]
Narrative review	Sometimes used to refer to a systematic review that synthesizes the individual studies narratively (rather than by means of a meta-analysis). This involves systematically extracting, checking, and narratively summarizing information on their methods and results	Social consequences of poor health in childhood: A systematic review[2]
Conceptual review/conceptual synthesis	A review that aims to synthesize areas of conceptual knowledge that can contribute to a better understanding of these issues. The objectives of these syntheses are "To provide an overview of the literature in a given field, including the main ideas, models and debates."[14]	Conceptual synthesis 1: Learning from the diffusion of innovations[15]

(Continued)

Table 2.1 (Cont'd)

Type of review	Definition	Example
Rapid review	A literature review carried out (often systematically) but within a limited time (sometimes weeks or a couple of months) and with restrictions on the scope of the search (for example, restricted by year, or country)	The state of children in the UK ("The project aims to provide a comprehensive picture of how children are doing, how their well-being varies within the countries of the UK and by gender, age, ethnicity, family type, and level of income")[16]
Realistic review (or **realist synthesis**)	Approach to reviewing studies which involves synthesizing individual studies with a view to producing generalizable theories (rather than synthesizing outcomes across studies (as systematic reviews do)	Realist synthesis review of "Megan's law" (a US law that mandated the registration and community notification of sexual offenders)[17]
Scoping review	A review sometimes carried out in advance of a full systematic review to scope the existing literature – that is to assess the types of studies carried out to date, and where they are located. This can help with refining the question for the full review, and with estimating the resources that will be needed.	Housing for people with dementia – a scoping review: "This work encompasses issues of design, location, technology and finance... The substantive interest... is in generating evidence on the various elements that constitute more, and less, effective forms of housing for people at different stages of dementia in different settings..." <http://www.york.ac.uk/inst/chp/srpsc/projects.htm>

"Traditional" review	Term sometimes used to refer to a literature review that does not use systematic review methods. Such reviews can still represent excellent overviews of wider literature and concepts – not just reviews of outcomes.	Day services for people with learning disabilities in the 1990s[18]
Critical review	Term sometimes used to describe a literature review that assesses a theory or hypothesis by critically examining the methods and results of the primary studies, often with a wealth of background and contextual material, though not using the formalized approach of a systematic review	Organizational story and storytelling: A critical review[19] *Pathological gambling: A critical review*[20]
Expert review	Literature review, common in medicine and in basic sciences, written by an acknowledged expert (or group of experts) in the field.	Expert review of an approach to functional capacity evaluation (method of assessing capacity to work, as part of work rehabilitation).[21]
"State of the art" review	This term is sometimes used to refer to reviews designed to bring readers up to date on the most recent research on a specific subject. What constitutes "recent" can vary, as can the reviews' methods. State of the art reviews tend to focus on technical subjects such as engineering or transport.	A state of the art review of income security reform in Canada.[22]

- *Population*: What population am I interested in (Children? If so, what age groups? People using a particular service? People with a particular social or health need? All of the above?)
- *Intervention*: What intervention exactly am I interested in reviewing? Is it one intervention, or a cluster of interventions (as in a social program). There may be several related interventions used to address the same problem. Take, for example, road traffic injuries in children. The relevant interventions might include education of children and motorists, law enforcement on the road, traffic calming, and so on. At other times, it may be appropriate to select the most relevant intervention in a particular context, or the most widely used. To take another example, consider a hypothetical review of the effectiveness of interventions to reduce antisocial behavior in young people. With enough resources, the reviewer's net could be cast very widely, and any intervention aimed at preventing or reducing this problem could be addressed. This might include a wide range of interventions aimed at parents and at children (such as parenting interventions, mentoring, schools-based interventions to prevent truanting, and interventions aimed at communities, such as community wardens), and the interventions themselves might address a range of behaviors from crime and aggressive behavior, to health behaviors such as alcohol and drug misuse. However, it is often the case that a narrower range of interventions is reviewed, in a particular setting, and this is often justified by the view that what works in one setting or one population may not work in another.
- *Comparison*: With what is the intervention being compared? For example in research into the effectiveness of a particular form of sex education, with what is it being compared? A different form of sex education?[24] No sex education? Programs advocating abstinence?
- *Outcomes*: For many social interventions there is a wide range of outcomes, and the assessment of effectiveness involves collecting information on both positive and negative impacts, and assessing the balance between them. In specifying the review question it is important to determine which outcomes are the most relevant for answering the question. In the example of sex education, a range of outcomes is possible, from very immediate (proximal) outcomes such as increased knowledge, and changed attitudes to sexual behavior, to later (distal) ones such as rates of early sexual activity, rates of teenage pregnancy and terminations of pregnancy among those receiving the intervention, compared to a control group.
- *Context*: For reviews of social interventions there is a further component, which needs to be considered – the *context* within which the intervention is delivered. It is possible to review the

scientific evidence, but still learn little about how the intervention was delivered, what aided and/or hindered its impact, how the process of implementing it was carried out, and what factors may have contributed to its success or failure. Users of "social" systematic reviews are increasingly seeking this information. It is not enough to say that a particular social policy or intervention "worked" or "did not work," without taking into account the wider context.

For **complex interventions** with a strong social component to how they are delivered (and received), we often need to know more than just "what works" – we need robust data on how and why it works; and if it "works," we need enough information to know whether this was a reflection of the environment within which it was developed and delivered. This information is often not included in systematic reviews at present, but increasingly it is seen as important to broaden the scope of systematic reviews of effectiveness, such that they include a range of study designs to answer different review questions. This issue is discussed further in chapter 6.

2.8   NO MAGIC BULLET

One reason why information on processes and meanings underlying interventions is excluded from most reviews is that many interventions are reviewed as if they were "magic bullets." If some intervention can be shown to "work" in one setting then it is sometimes assumed that it can also "work" elsewhere, particularly if the mechanisms by which it works are similar in different populations. This is sometimes the case, and healthcare treatments such as aspirin for headache are generalizable to other cultures because the physiological pathways by which they act do not vary greatly. However this is not always the case; there are ethnic differences in the efficacy of treatments for hypertension, for example. For many social interventions, the recipient's capacity to benefit and ability to access the intervention vary widely with educational and socioeconomic status, gender, and ethnicity, as well as location. Blanket judgments about effectiveness are, therefore, frequently meaningless because they involve extrapolating from the average study (which may not exist) to the average citizen (who certainly does not exist). Saying something meaningful about effectiveness in social systematic reviews involves generalizing from studies about effectiveness. This generalization requires capturing contextual and process-related information from the primary studies.

Specifying some review questions may often therefore involve asking multiple, related questions. Perhaps there will be a primary question about effectiveness, and a set of secondary questions about the process of implementation of the intervention. These questions will of course require reviewing different types of study (that is, studies of different designs) within the same review. Defining the question for social systematic reviews therefore involves not four components, but five: *Population*, *Intervention*, *Comparison*, *Outcomes*, *Context* (*PICOC*, see Figure 2.2).[23]

2.9   REVIEW PROTOCOLS

Like any research study, a systematic review needs a detailed protocol that describes in advance the process and methods that will be applied. This protocol includes a description of and rationale for the review question, and the proposed methods, and includes details of how different types of study will be located, appraised, and synthesized. Information on the review's dissemination strategy is also included. Detailed review protocols can be found on the Campbell and Cochrane websites (see Box 2.5).

Protocols of systematic reviews frequently change after the review begins. Silagy et al. found that the greatest variability was in the methods section, and that 68 percent of the protocols they examined had undergone major

Population
Intervention
Comparison
Outcomes
Context

Figure 2.2   PICOC: Five components of a clear systematic review question (By permission of Getpetsonline)

change. There may be good reasons for modifying a protocol,[25] but it is essential to document any changes and even more essential that the decision to make revisions is not made simply on the grounds that the primary studies do not give the "right" answers.

2.10   WHAT SORTS OF QUESTIONS CAN SYSTEMATIC REVIEWS ANSWER?

Many systematic reviews address questions about effectiveness. However, systematic reviews can also answer questions about risk factors, and about associations between characteristics of populations, and can explore associations between risk factors or predictors and outcomes. For example, they can examine observational associations between social phenomena and social outcomes – such as "Does gentrification help or harm urban neighborhoods?,"[26] or "Is poverty and income inequality associated with violent crime?".[27] Reviews that explore direct relationships between risk and protective factors and psychological or health or well-being outcomes are also common, for example, one meta-analysis (that is, a systematic review that includes a statistical summary of the included studies) has examined the association between the sexual orientation of the parents and their children's wellbeing.[28] Another recent meta-analysis examined the health consequences of care-giving, by reviewing 23 observational studies that had compared care-givers to non-care-givers on a range of health-related outcome measures.[29] Reviews that explore etiological issues like this are commonly used where the evidence does not consist of evaluations, such as trials, in situations where they are impossible and/or unethical, or have just not been carried out.

Systematic reviews can also be used to contribute answers to a range of other questions about the screening and diagnosis of health and non-health conditions, about prognosis, and about economic issues (Table 2.2). It should also be noted however that systematic reviews on their own often only provide *partial* answers to questions. For example, questions about the appropriateness of providing a particular service will only be partly answered by a systematic review of effectiveness; the decision to provide the service will require other sources of evidence – including evidence on the cost, acceptability, and sustainability of the service (among many other things). Systematic reviews may contribute to evidence-based decision-making, but are not themselves decisions.

After clarifying the type of question the review is aimed at, the next step – which is closely related to defining the inclusion and exclusion criteria – is

Table 2.2 What sort of questions can systematic reviews answer?

This type of review question . . .	. . . is likely to include these study designs (though not necessarily exclusively)	Some examples of questions answered by systematic reviews
Effectiveness	Experimental and non-experimental studies (e.g., RCTs, **controlled studies**). Observational studies (e.g., longitudinal, before-and-after studies, quasi-experimental studies).	Does using daytime running lights on cars reduce the risk of accidents?[30] Do "welfare to work" programs work?[1]
Screening and diagnosis	Trials of screening tests to assess impact on outcomes; observational studies can be used to assess whether tests can accurately detect the problem or issue of interest (Detailed guidance on systematic review of screening and diagnostic tests is available elsewhere.)[31, 32, 33, 34, 35]	Is screening women and elderly adults for family and intimate partner violence effective?[36]
Exploring risk or protective factors	Longitudinal studies (such as cohort studies); retrospective studies examining risk factors (including cross-sectional studies such as surveys)	Can criminal and violent recidivism be predicted among mentally disordered offenders?[37] Does the sexual orientation of the parent matter to the emotional wellbeing and sexual orientation of child?[28]
Observational associations between interventions and outcomes	Cross-sectional surveys, longitudinal studies following populations over time	Does money matter? A meta-analysis of studies of the effects of differential school inputs on student outcomes[38]

Questions about prevalence	Surveys, or other observational studies that have recruited a random sample	Effects of US television programs on foreign audiences: A meta-analysis[39] How prevalent are mental health problems in Pakistan? (a systematic review of surveys).[40]
Questions about meanings or processes of social interventions, or about how interventions are implemented, or about the detail of influences and events in peoples' lives	Qualitative studies,[41] or quantitative studies such as surveys which collect information from study participants on perceptions, use, or impact of an intervention	What are the needs and experiences of young mothers?[42]
Methodological questions to examine the performance of particular research tools, or to synthesize information on best practice in research methods	Any study design is potentially relevant here, depending on the review question	A systematic review of questionnaires measuring the health of resettling refugee women.[43] Systematic review investigating the effects and measurement of biases in non-randomized studies[44]
Economic questions including questions of cost-effectiveness and cost-benefit analyses	Depending on the approach taken, potentially any study design presenting relevant data could be included (including trials and observational studies)[45]	What impact do payment systems have on primary care physician behavior?[46]

to decide what types of study are most appropriate to answer the review question (or questions). This issue is discussed further in chapter 3.

2.11   SCOPING REVIEWS

It is good practice to carry out a "scoping" review if time and resources are available. This can help cost a review for the purpose of drawing up a funding proposal, and can help with estimating how long it is likely to take, and what mix of skills might be needed to carry it out. A scoping review involves a search of the literature to determine what sorts of studies addressing the systematic review question have been carried out, where they are published, in which databases they have been indexed, what sorts of outcomes they have assessed, and in which populations. It may include restricted searches across a limited number of key databases, limited to a certain time period (say, the last 10 years), and perhaps restricted by language (for example, English language only). As well as helping define the review question, this will allow an estimate to be made of the nature and the scale of any new review. It is methodologically acceptable, indeed, good practice, to refine the systematic review question in the light of what is learnt from the scoping review.

Box 2.6   Lumping and splitting in systematic reviews

"Lumpers" and "splitters" are terms used by taxonomists. "Lumpers" tend to lump concepts into broad categories, while "splitters" are more interested in exploring differences; they usually try to avoid grouping together categories into "lumps" unless they are obviously conceptually very similar. In systematic reviews, these "lumps" might include variations in types of intervention and/or types of outcome, as well as different study designs, or different populations.

It is impossible to say in general whether systematic reviewers should aim to be lumpers or splitters; the size and the nature of the lumps, and the size and position of the splits depends on your underlying theoretical model of the intervention, and how it works in different groups, and the extent to which the data from different studies in different populations are generalizable.

The scoping review can also be helpful in deciding how much lumping or splitting is needed with respect to the review question (Box 2.6). This lumper/splitter differentiation has important implications for the utility of systematic reviews and sorts of questions they try to answer. Policymakers may prefer to obtain answers to big, lumpy questions about the most efficient way of organizing particular types of services; they sometimes suspect that researchers are splitters, only happy when producing finely detailed answers to very narrow sub-questions – answers which may only apply to very particular circumstances.

2.12   COSTING A SYSTEMATIC REVIEW

A scoping review will allow an estimate of the cost of the review to be made, though this is an inexact science. Costing a review depends on the volume of literature, how dispersed it is, how much of it is in English (for those who speak English only of course), how much of it is easily locatable in journals and how much in the **"gray" literature**, how easily defined the intervention is, how far back the search needs to go, how quickly the review needs to be done, how much input from experienced reviewers is needed, and how experienced the reviewer is. As an example, the median cost of the healthcare systematic reviews funded by the UK Health Technology Assessment Agency <http://www.hta.nhsweb.nhs.uk/main.htm> between 1993 and 2002 was about £57K per review, rising to about £80K per review in recent years (based on funding information which appears on their website). However the range is large, from £25K up to £140K, though the larger reviews may include several sub-reviews and other methodological or economic analyses (as well as salary costs).

2.13   HOW LONG WILL IT TAKE?

Allen and Olkin[47] have provided a useful estimate of the amount of time that one can expect to spend doing a systematic review, based on an examination of 37 reviews that had included meta-analyses. They found that the average amount of time needed was 1,139 hours (with a median of 1,110 hours), however this figure ranged widely from 216 to 2,518 hours. They broke this figure down further to show the time spent on the different review tasks (see Table 2.3).

Table 2.3   Mean time spent on systematic review tasks (based on 37 meta-analyses)

Task	Time (hours)
Protocol development, searching and retrieval of references, paper screening, data extraction and quality assessment, data entry, and tabulation	588
Statistical analysis	144
Report writing	206
Administrative tasks (including proposal development, project meetings, training, and project management)	201

Source: Allen and Olkin (1999)[47]

Allen and Olkin further analyzed these 37 reviews to produce a formula for estimating the number of hours work, based on the number of potential papers the search would retrieve:

Number of hours $= 721 + 0.243x - 0.0000123x^2$
(where $x =$ the number of retrieved references before applying the inclusion and exclusion criteria).

This median figure of 1,110 hours represents about 29 weeks, full time – that is, about 7 months (excluding holidays). However this is strongly dependent on the type of topic being reviewed. For some topic areas references are easily retrievable: that is, they are relatively easily located through searches of electronic databases, with relatively few studies (such as unpublished reports) in the "gray" literature. This tends not to be the case with more social policy-oriented reviews, which may be likely to rely much more heavily on non-journal sources, for example, non-English language reports, reports from government and research institutes, and websites. This requires a much more extensive, and slower search. Moreover, for these sorts of studies the abstracts of social science literature are often uninformative, or missing. This means that many more papers have to be retrieved for checking for relevance than in other topic areas such as reviews of health care interventions. The effect of this is that the literature search often needs to cast its net much more widely (that is, it tends to be more sensitive, and less specific – see chapter 4) to avoid missing relevant studies. Both the complexity of the search, and the need to obtain many more copies of articles will significantly increase the length and cost of the review.

This chapter ends with Box 2.7, from a paper by Reeves et al.,[48] giving some excellent advice to any group starting their first systematic review.

Box 2.7   Twelve tips for undertaking a systematic review

1. Pay attention to group-forming processes. Be careful not to underestimate the effort required to form your review group. These processes are crucial in providing firm foundations for your review.

2. A number of initial tasks need to be undertaken in the early stages of your review. Take time to complete this early work as decisions you make at this stage will influence the subsequent direction of your review.

3. Expert input is advantageous in progressing your systematic review. This input is especially invaluable for inexperienced review groups.

4. Hold regular meetings. Coming together in the same space enables in-depth discussion and debate to occur. This not only maximizes opportunities for making good progress with your review; it also helps produce high-quality work.

5. Developing a protocol for your review is vital. It provides an explicit plan of your proposed work. Such transparency ensures you produce a rigorous review.

6. The development of an effective database **search strategy** is crucial. Spend time testing your strategy and be sure to amend it when using different databases. Also, think carefully about the range of sources you will search.

7. Be flexible. Where you encounter problems, consider refocusing the review to make it more manageable within the restrictions of time, cost, and the available literature.

8. An ongoing process of quality assurance is vital within any systematic review. It ensures that potential biases introduced by your group are minimized.

9. Dedicate time to developing a data extraction form sheet that can reliably record the key information you need for included studies. Be prepared to produce and test a number of drafts before your group is satisfied.

10. Ensure that your group develops a reliable data-handling system to manage the vast amounts of material generated from your review. Nominating one member to take charge of this work can be effective. Also, consider the use of specialized computer software.

(Continued)

Box 2.7 *(Cont'd)*

11. The analysis stage of your review can be a slow and complex process. Ensure you dedicate sufficient time to develop, discuss, and explore all emerging analyses.
12. If possible, incorporate "workshop time" during your review. This can nurture a deeper level of thinking and collaboration within your group.

(Reeves et al., 2002)[48]

Key learning points from this chapter

- The review needs to start with a meaningful and useful question, and this question should be refined in discussion with users, and other experts (if they have not suggested the question in the first place).
- The reviewer needs to determine whether there are already any completed or ongoing systematic reviews addressing the same question.
- To refine the question, it is necessary to consider the population, intervention, context, outcomes, and users of the review.
- It is important to draw up a detailed protocol, and have it reviewed. This should include details of the proposed methods, and an estimate of the likely timescale and resources that will be required.

REFERENCES

1. Bambra, C., Whitehead, M., and Hamilton, V. Does "welfare to work" work? A systematic review of the effectiveness of the UK's "welfare to work" programmes for people with a disability or chronic illness. *Social Science and Medicine* 2005, 60(9): 1905–18.
2. Milton, B. and Whitehead, M. Social consequences of poor health in childhood. *Child* (in press).
3. Arksey, H. and O'Malley, L. Scoping studies: Towards a methodological framework. *International Journal of Research Methodology, Theory and Practice* (in press).

4. Wallace, A., Croucher, K., Quilgars, D., and Baldwin, S. Meeting the challenge: Developing systematic reviewing in social policy. *Policy and Politics* 2004, 32: 455–70.

5. Greenhalgh, T., Robert, G., Bate, P., Kyriakidou, O., MacFarlane, F., and Peacock. R. How to spread good ideas: A systematic review of the literature on diffusion, dissemination and sustainability of innovations in health service delivery and organisation. Report for the National Co-ordinating Centre for NHS Service Delivery and Organisation R & D (NCCSDO) 2004. Full report available online at: http://www.sdo.lshtm.ac.uk/pdf/changemanagement_greenhalgh_report.pdf [accessed February 24, 2005].

6. Mulrow, C. D. Systematic reviews: Rationale for systematic reviews. *British Medical Journal* 1994, 309: 597–9.

7. Ravetz, J. *Scientific knowledge and its social problems*. Middlesex: Penguin University Books, 1973.

8. Antman, E., Lau, J., Kupelnick, B., Mosteller, F., and Chalmers, T. A comparison of results of meta-analyses of randomized control trials and recommendations of clinical experts. *Journal of the American Medical Association* 1992, 268: 240–8.

9. Gennetian, L. and Knox, V. Staying single: The effects of welfare reform policies on marriage and cohabitation. New York and Oakland CA: MDRC Working Paper 13, 2002, online at: http://www.mdrc.org/publications/373/full.pdf [accessed February 24, 2005].

10. Davies, P. and Boruch, R. The Campbell Collaboration. *British Medical Journal* 2001, 323: 294–5.

11. Turner, H., Boruch, R., Petrosino, A., Lavenberg, J., De Moya, D., and Rothstein, H. Populating an international web-based randomized trials register in the social, behavioral, criminological, and education sciences. *Annals of the American Academy of Political and Social Science* 2003, 589: 203–23.

12. Wilson, S. and Lipsey, M. Effects of school-based social information processing interventions on aggressive behavior, *Campbell Collaboration Systematic Review*, 2004, online at: http://www.campbellcollaboration.org/doc-pdf/agbhprt.pdf, [accessed February 24, 2005].

13. Egan, M., Petticrew, M., Ogilvie, D., and Hamilton, V. Privatisation, deregulation and state subsidies: A systematic review of health impacts of interventions affectingdirect public investment in business (in press), online at: http://www. msoc-mrc. gla.ac.uk/Evidence/Research/Review%2004/Review4_MAIN. html.

14. Nutley, S., Davies, H., and Walter, I. What is a conceptual synthesis? University of St. Andrews, Research Unit for Research Utilisation Briefing Note 1, 2002, online at: http://www.st-andrews.ac.uk/~ruru/Conceptual%20synthesis.pdf [accessed February 24, 2005].

15. Nutley, S., Davies, H., and Walter, I. Conceptual synthesis 1: Learning from the Diffusion of Innovations. University of St. Andrews, Research Unit for Research Utilisation, 2002, online at: http://www.st-andrews.ac.uk/~ruru/Learning%20from%20the%20Diffusion%20of%20Innovations.pdf [accessed February 24, 2005].

16. Bradshaw, J. (ed.) *The well-being of children in the UK*. London: Save the Children, 2002.

17. Pawson, R. Does Megan's Law work? A theory-driven systematic review: ESRC UK Centre for Evidence Based Policy and Practice, Working Paper, 2002, online at: http://www.evidencenetwork.org/Documents/wp8.pdf [accessed February 24, 2005].

18. Simons, K. and Watson, D. Day services for people with learning disabilities in the 1990s. Exeter: Centre for Evidence-Based Social Services, University of Exeter, 1999, online at: http://www.cebss.org/files/LDReview.pdf [accessed February 24, 2005].

19. Boyce, M. Organizational story and storytelling: a critical review. *Journal of Organizational Change Management* 1996, 9: 5–26.

20. Committee on the Social and Economic Impact of Pathological Gambling [and] Committee on Law and Justice, Commission on Behavioral and Social Sciences and Education, National Research Council *Pathological gambling: A critical review*. Washington: National Academy Press, 1999.

21. Gibson, L. and Strong, J. Expert review of an approach to functional capacity evaluation. *Work* 2002, 19: 231–42.

22. Pulkingham, J. and Ternowetsky, G. A state of the art review of income security reform in Canada. Ottawa, Canada: International Development Research Centre, 1998.

23. Booth, A., and Fry-Smith, A. Developing the research question. *Etext on Health Technology Assessment (HTA) Information Resources*, 2004, online at: http://www.nlm.nih.gov/nichsr/ehta/chapter2.html [accessed February 24, 2005].

24. DiCenso, A., Guyatt, G., Willan, A., and Griffith, L. Interventions to reduce unintended pregnancies among adolescents: Systematic review of randomised controlled trials. *British Medical Journal* 2002, 324: 1426–34.

25. Silagy, C., Middleton, P., and Hopewell, S. Publishing protocols of systematic reviews: Comparing what was done to what was planned. *Journal of the American Medical Association* 2002, 287: 2831–4.

26. Atkinson, R. Does gentrification help or harm urban neighbourhoods? An assessment of the evidence-base in the context of the new urban agenda. Glasgow: ESRC Centre for Neighbourhood Research, Paper 5, 2002, online at: http://www.bristol.ac.uk/sps/cnrpaperspdf/cnr5pap.pdf [accessed February 24, 2005].

27. Hsieh, C. C. and Pugh, M. D. Poverty, income inequality, and violent crime: A meta-analysis of recent aggregate data studies. *Criminal Justice Review* 1993, 18: 182.

28. Allen, M. and Burrell, N. Comparing the impact of homosexual and heterosexual parents on children: A meta-analysis of existing research. *Journal of Homosexuality* 1996, 32: 19–35.

29. Vitaliano, P., Zhang, J., and Scanlan, J. Is caregiving hazardous to one's physical health? A meta-analysis. *Psychological Bulletin* 2003, 129, online at: http://www.apa.org/releases/caregiving_article.pdf [accessed February 24, 2005].

30. Elvik, R. A meta-analysis of studies concerning the safety of daytime running lights on cars. *Accident, Analysis and Prevention* 1996, 28: 685–94.
31. Devillé, W., Buntinx, F., Bouter, L., Montori, V., de Vet, H., van der Windt, D., et al. Conducting systematic reviews of diagnostic studies: Didactic guidelines. *BMC Medical Research Methodology* 2002, 2, online at: www.biomedcentral.com/1471-2288/2/9 [accessed February 24, 2005].
32. NHS Centre for Reviews and Dissemination. Undertaking systematic reviews of research on effectiveness: CRD's guidance for those carrying out or commissioning reviews. CRD Report Number 4 (2nd edn), York: University of York, 2001, online at: http://www1.york.ac.uk/inst/crd/report4.htm
33. Deeks, J. Systematic reviews of evaluations of diagnostic and screening tests. In M. Egger, G. Davey Smith, and D. Altman (eds.) *Systematic reviews in health care. Meta-analysis in context.* London: BMJ, 2001.
34. Hasselblad, V. and Hedges, L. Meta-analysis of screening and diagnostic tests. *Psychological Bulletin* 1995, 117: 167–78.
35. Greenhalgh, T. How to read a paper: Papers that report diagnostic or screening tests. *British Medical Journal* 1997, 315: 540–3.
36. Nelson, H., Nygren, P., McInerney, Y., and Klein, J. Screening women and elderly adults for family and intimate partner violence: A review of the evidence for the US Preventive Services Task Force. *Annals of Internal Medicine* 2004, 140: 387–96.
37. Bonta, J., Law, M., and Hanson, K. The prediction of criminal and violent recidivism among mentally disordered offenders: A meta-analysis. *Psychological Bulletin* 1998, 123: 123–42.
38. Hedges, L. V., Laine, R. D., and Greenwald, R. Does money matter? A meta-analysis of studies of the effects of differential school inputs on student outcomes. *Educational Researcher* 1994, 23: 5–14.
39. Ware, W. and Dupagne, M. Effects of US television programs on foreign audiences: A meta-analysis. *Journalism Quarterly* 1994, 71: 947–59.
40. Mirza, I. and Jenkins, R. Risk factors, prevalence, and treatment of anxiety and depressive disorders in Pakistan: Systematic review. *British Medical Journal* 2004, 328: 794.
41. Popay, J., Rogers, A., and Williams, G. Rationale and standards for the systematic review of qualitative literature in health services research. *Qualitative Health Research* 1998, 8: 341–51.
42. McDermott, E. and Graham, H. Resilient young mothering: Social inequalities, late modernity and the "problem" of "teenage" motherhood. *Journal of Youth Studies* 2005, 8(1): 59–79.
43. Gagnon, A., Tuck, J., and Barkun, L. A systematic review of questionnaires measuring the health of resettling refugee women. *Health Care for Women International* 2004, 25: 111–49.
44. Deeks, J., Dinnes, J., D'Amico, R., Sowden, A., Sakarovitch, C., Song, F., et al. Evaluating non-randomised intervention studies. *Health Technology Assessment*

2003, 7, online at: http://www.hta.nhsweb.nhs.uk/fullmono/mon727.pdf [accessed February 24. 2005].

45. Donaldson, C., Mugford, M., and Vale, L. Using systematic reviews in economic evaluation: The basic principles. In C. Donaldson, M. Mugford, and L. Vale (eds.) *Evidence-based health economics: From effectiveness to efficiency in systematic review.* London: BMJ Books, 2002.

46. Sønbø Kristiansen, I. and Gosden, T. Evaluating economic interventions: A role for non-randomised designs? In C. Donaldson, M. Mugford, and L. Vale (eds.) *Evidence-based health economics: From effectiveness to efficiency in systematic review.* London: BMJ Books, 2002.

47. Allen, I. and Olkin, I. Estimating time to conduct a meta-analysis from number of citations retrieved. *Journal of the American Medical Association* 1999, 282: 634–5.

48. Reeves, S., Koppel, I., Barr, H., Freeth, D., and Hammick, M. Twelve tips for undertaking a systematic review. *Medical Teacher* 2002, 24: 358–63.

Chapter 3

What sorts of studies do I include in the review? Deciding on the review's inclusion/exclusion criteria

The previous chapter emphasized the need to clarify the review question, as this will influence what kinds of study are included in the review. Different research designs are obviously appropriate to answering different questions. If one wants to know "what works," the review may include randomized controlled trials (RCTs), if there are any. If one wants to investigate "what matters," qualitative data are going to be important. Many reviews do not have to address either one or other of these types of questions alone. Systematic reviewing is, or has the potential to be, a broad church and can deal with a variety of questions, study designs, and methods within the same review.

This chapter begins by considering which types of research are appropriate to answering different review questions, as it throws light on a number of misunderstandings about the nature of systematic reviews, and their methods. The "hierarchy of evidence" is relevant in this context.

3.1 HIERARCHIES OF EVIDENCE

Many social scientists have found the concept of a "hierarchy of evidence" difficult to accept. They might be reassured to know that the word "hierarchy" is one of those singled out for criticism in the 1977 edition of *Thorne's Better Medical Writing* – a guide to writing a medical article for publication. "Hierarchy" appears in an appendix labeled "Pseud's Corner" – "an appendix of words that are so awful that you use them at your peril."

Others in the list include "overview," "methodology," "evaluative," and "multidisciplinary." (All of these words appear in this book, incidentally.)

In some systematic reviews, particularly those carried out by healthcare researchers, the "hierarchy of evidence" (see Box 3.1) is used to describe the process underlying the selection of studies for inclusion in the review, and is sometimes used as a proxy for indicating the methodological quality of the included studies.

Box 3.1   The "Hierarchy of evidence"[1, 2]

- Systematic reviews and meta-analyses
- Randomized controlled trials with definitive results
- Randomized controlled trials with non-definitive results
- Cohort studies
- **Case-control** studies
- Cross sectional surveys
- Case reports

This hierarchy is simply a list of study designs used to assess the effectiveness of interventions, ranked in order of decreasing **internal validity** (that is, increasing susceptibility to bias). Some lists include qualitative studies (towards the bottom), and a non-scientific method, the anecdote, at the bottom. (The latter is defined in the "Scharr guide to the hierarchy of evidence" as "something told to you by a bloke in the bar" <http://www.shef.ac.uk/scharr/ir/units/systrev/hierarchy.htm>.)

This list was developed initially to help decision-makers select what sorts of studies they should prioritize when seeking research evidence to help answer clinical questions, but it was soon adopted more widely. The original purpose of the hierarchy is often forgotten. The intention was not to produce a definitive hierarchy of methodological purity for all purposes, but a guide to determining the most appropriate study designs for answering questions *about effectiveness*. Answering questions about processes, or about the meanings of interventions, would imply the use of a very different type of hierarchy, perhaps with qualitative and other methods at the top, while for some etiological questions, observational studies would be ranked first – for example in cases where randomized controlled trials (RCTs) are impractical or unethical (such as studies of the relationship between lung cancer and smoking).

Hierarchies versus typologies

When carrying out a systematic review it is often more useful to think in terms of "typologies" of evidence, rather than hierarchies – that is, to consider which type of study is most appropriate for answering your review question.[3] For example, controlled trials are suitable for assessing whether an intervention "works" – whether its benefits outweigh its costs. The interventions in question could be in education, welfare, health promotion, or other measures including policies delivered to whole populations, or areas. Where controlled trials are impossible (perhaps for ethical or practical reasons), before-and-after studies, which follow one group over time, may be appropriate. Surveys or other types of cross-sectional study do not however provide robust information about effectiveness, though they are valuable methods of collecting other sorts of information – about the prevalence of particular human behaviors for example (such as smoking, or drinking).

Qualitative studies by comparison provide much more detailed in-depth information about meanings – of interventions, and of behaviors. They can also provide valuable information about processes – for example, *why* an intervention worked as it did (or did not work). They do not, however, provide robust information about *whether* an intervention worked. In fact there are a number of studies where people who have received an intervention report positive effects, perhaps out of loyalty to the people providing a service, to whom they may feel gratitude, or with whom they have formed a relationship, but where other data on outcomes (such as school attendance, truancy, or exam results) present a less rosy picture.

As is clear from Box 3.4 later in the chapter, the choice between qualitative and quantitative studies does not have to be "either/or." Experimental studies can include qualitative data, and increasingly do so.

Table 3.1 describes the appropriateness of different kinds of research design in responding to particular review questions. The example considered in the table refers to the different questions which could be asked about an intervention aimed at children. (The larger the number of crosses, the greater the contribution which that particular study design is likely to make to answering that particular question.)

It is not only social scientists who have queried the usefulness of a hierarchy of research designs. A recent paper in the *British Medical Journal* warned that the "Inflexible use of evidence hierarchies confuses practitioners and irritates researchers."[5] The authors also point out that even within hierarchies decisions need to be made about whether or not a

Table 3.1 Appropriateness of different study designs for answering different types of research question[3, 4]

Research question	Qualitative research	Survey	Case control studies	Cohort studies	RCTs	Systematic reviews
Effectiveness: Does this work? Does doing this work better than doing that?				+	++	+++
Process of service delivery: How does it work?	++	+				+++
Salience: Does it matter?	++	++				+++
Safety: Will it do more good than harm?	+		+	+	++	+++
Acceptability: Will children/parents be willing to take up the service offered?	++	+			+	+++
Cost effectiveness: Is it worth buying this service?					++	+++
Appropriateness: Is this the right service for these children?	++	++				++
Satisfaction with the service: Are users, providers, and other stakeholders satisfied with the service?	++	++	+	+		+

particular study has what it takes to answer the research question. A small, or poorly designed RCT, or one where those who drop out are not followed up, should not appear further up the hierarchy than other well-conducted studies with apparently less robust designs. Nonetheless, not all research evidence (qualitative or quantitative) is of equal validity or relevance, so a means of determining what type of research is relevant for what purpose is needed. As emphasized above, the hierarchy of evidence was originally developed to help with this task, but its purpose seems subsequently to have been widely misunderstood.

3.2 SETTING INCLUSION/EXCLUSION CRITERIA: DECIDING WHAT TYPES OF STUDIES TO INCLUDE AND EXCLUDE

The inclusion and exclusion criteria describe the types of study, intervention, population, and outcomes that are eligible for in-depth review, and those that are excluded. These criteria need to be specified in the report or article describing the review.

Studies of effectiveness: Randomized controlled trials

For answering questions about effectiveness, such as: "Do psychological interventions for preventing smoking really work?," or "Are interventions directed at drink-drivers effective in preventing injury?," trials examining the effects of the intervention compared to a control group should be prioritized for inclusion. Among these, randomized controlled trials (RCTs), will represent the most internally valid (i.e., does this intervention work for this population at this time) though not necessarily the most externally valid (are these findings generalizable to all populations) studies for answering questions about effectiveness. If one wants to know, for instance whether:

- sex education reduces the rate of teenage pregnancies;
- providing an income supplement for pregnant women at risk of a low birth weight baby leads to bigger babies;
- exercise programs for young people can reduce the number of cigarettes they smoke;

then a randomized controlled trial will provide us with the best evidence of a causal relationship between an intervention and an outcome. True randomization can only occur where all clients have an equal chance of being allocated to either group.

RCTs, however, do not remove all our problems; for example they may not identify which component, or components of the "intervention" actually worked, whether the results are generalizable to other populations, and whether the outcome measures used are meaningful, and unbiased (for example, are not subject to observer bias). These are problems that have to be considered in any **outcome evaluation**, whether or not it employs randomization.

Researchers and others worry about the ethics of randomization, particularly randomization to "no treatment," and people will go to considerable lengths to subvert the randomization process, because of concerns about client welfare.[6] The starting point for randomization, however, is that we frequently do not know what works, or what works best. Box 3.2 gives an example of a randomized controlled trial in social care.

Box 3.2   The effectiveness of out-of-home day care for disadvantaged families: A randomized controlled trial

The trial was conducted at an Early Years center in the London Borough of Hackney. The demand for day-care places at the center greatly exceeded the number of places available, and, in response to a request from the trial team, the borough's education department agreed to use random **allocation** as the method of rationing places. Families living within the catchment area who had applied for a place at the center for a child aged between 6 months and 3.5 years were invited to take part. All available places were randomly allocated, whether or not a family agreed to take part in the trial, and those who had consented to participate were followed up for 18 months.

The intervention was high quality flexible day care for children under 5 years old. Unlike standard nursery care in Hackney, the Early Years center employed qualified teachers, and education was integrated into the care of the children. The integration of health and social services was also encouraged. The center was unusual in offering parents full time or part time places, with the option to change depending on circumstances. It also offered extended care outside the normal nursery times for working parents.

Control group families were expected to use a range of childcare provision that they secured for themselves, including other day care facilities. However, demand for day care places in Hackney was greatly in excess of supply, with about eight children for every available place. The main outcome measures were maternal paid employment, household income, child health and development. The results suggested that day care may have increased maternal employment in the intervention group, but did not seem to increase household income.

As a postscript, the effectiveness of day care for pre-school children had been the subject of a Cochrane review by Zoritch et al. in 2000.[7] With the publication of the new trial above, the Cochrane review was quickly updated, to incorporate this new evidence. This illustrates one of the strengths of systematic reviews: that they are regularly updated to take on board new research.

(For results and a full description, see Toroyan et al., 2003).[8]

It is sometimes the case that systematic reviews seek to include only RCTs and in their absence the reviewers conclude that there is no evidence, or insufficient evidence. While this may be methodologically satisfying to the reviewer, it is often seen by users as unhelpful and yet another example of researchers' "high concept" notions of evidence – and a preference for lamenting the lack of "gold standard" evidence, rather than a willingness to work with "best available" evidence.[9]

For some social interventions (in particular public policies) RCTs are often not available, sometimes for misplaced ethical or political reasons, despite the long history of casting or drawing of lots to help deal with uncertainty and ensure fairness.[10, 11] Non-randomized controlled trials or quasi-experimental designs, (such as non-randomized **prospective studies** with a control group) are likely to represent the best available evidence and should be included in reviews of effectiveness where there are no RCTs. Reviewing non-RCT evidence can give an estimate of the nature, direction, and size of effects, on which future RCTs could be based, but more importantly may represent the best evidence in some fields.

Studies with quasi-experimental designs

These studies benefit from the use of one or more control groups, but without random allocation of participants (see Box 3.3 for an example). A wide range of such studies is described by Shadish et al. in their book on experimental and quasi-experimental designs.[12] One example of this type of study might be where some clients receive a service, while others do not,

Box 3.3   An example of a quasi-experimental design: Breathing space: Evaluating a community-based anti-smoking intervention in a low income area (Research Unit in Health and Behavioural Change, University of Edinburgh)[13, 14]

This study aimed to contribute to an assessment of community-based interventions for reducing social class variations in the prevalence of cigarette smoking. Using a quasi-experimental design, the effectiveness of an experimental health promotion initiative was assessed in terms of its capacity to alter the culturally normative status of smoking in a low-income area of Edinburgh. It was contended that the "normative shift" towards less community tolerance of smoking would contribute towards behavior change in the medium to long term.

The effectiveness of "Breathing Space" as the intervention was known was assessed by comparing differences in relevant outcomes between the experimental area and three control areas over 2.5 years (from baseline survey in 1999 to follow up survey in 2001). Two main types of analysis were carried out: impact analyses aimed to assess awareness and reach of the intervention, and comparing the "dose" of relevant health promotion activity across the four survey areas; and outcome analyses aimed to assess the net "effect" of the program and test the null hypothesis that there was no difference between the intervention and control areas in the amount of change in pre-defined measures of effect. A qualitative **process evaluation** was undertaken in the intervention area in order to elucidate issues relating to the design, development, scope, intended purpose and implementation of the program. Monitoring in all areas of smoking cessation activities, which were not part of the formal Breathing Space program, was carried out so that the validity of the assumption of similar external (non-experimental) influences in both intervention and control areas could be tested. (For the findings of the "Breathing Space" study, see <http://www.chs.med.ed.ac.uk/ruhbc/research/projects/rl4.php>.)

or receive a different service. Instead of randomly allocating clients to one or other service, researchers use control and intervention groups that occur "naturally." For example, they might establish a suitable control group matched on characteristics thought to be important, such as socio-economic status, or the severity and duration of the problem. One problem with matching is that it is impossible to match in a way that takes account of all relevant factors, known and unknown. Quasi-experimental studies with control groups are, however, particularly relevant for inclusion in many systematic reviews of social interventions, as RCTs may not be available.

Uncontrolled studies

In many cases, no controlled studies will have been carried out, but there will have been some other type of evaluation employed. For example, investigations of the effects of policies, or evaluations that assess the effects of innovations such as new ways of organizing services, or new technologies, may involve recording and comparing outcomes (such as changes in health status, or traffic volumes, or crime levels) before and after the new technology is introduced. Data may be collected from a group of individuals before and after they receive some treatment or intervention, with an assessment of how some outcome (such as a health condition, or risk behavior) has changed. In some cases comparisons with historical controls or national trends may be included. A review of non-randomized comparison studies has been carried out by Deeks et al. for the UK Health Technology Agency.[15] The example given in the opening chapter of this book, which described an attempt to evaluate parenting classes, is a study of this type.

Uncontrolled studies are more susceptible to bias than studies with control groups, so their results should be treated with caution. The main problem is that in the absence of a control group the counterfactual is unknown; that is, it is difficult to know what would have happened in the absence of the intervention, and it is correspondingly difficult to be sure that any change in the outcome of interest is really due to the intervention, and not to some other factor.

Systematically reviewing a number of similar uncontrolled studies will not necessarily allow a definitive attribution of **causality**, but will allow consistency in findings among the studies to be explored, and this may provide indicative evidence that the intervention is having an effect.

However, there is no systematic review "alchemy" by which systematically reviewing many biased studies magically produces a single unbiased summary. A multiplicity of biased studies will remain biased after passing though the review process; base metal remains base metal. Some of the problems with interpreting data from uncontrolled studies include susceptibility to problems with **confounding**, seasonality, and regression to the mean. Study biases and their impact on study findings are discussed in more detail in chapter 5.

The Cochrane EPOC (Effective Practice and Organization of Care) group <http://www.epoc.uottawa.ca/>, has been active in producing guidance in the synthesis of this type of evidence, including the appraisal of time series studies.[16] Some systematic reviews of mass media and community interventions have also included uncontrolled studies, and time series studies, for example, some of the systematic reviews carried out by the Cochrane Tobacco Addiction Group.[17, 18]

The decision is sometimes taken to exclude uncontrolled studies of effectiveness from reviews. Sometimes this decision is justified, such as when there are already many controlled (randomized and non-randomized) studies available. However, if no controlled studies are available, there seems little convincing rationale for excluding uncontrolled studies *a priori*.[19, 20] This is particularly true given recent calls for more frequent evaluations, and reviews of evaluations of "natural experiments," such as government policies.[21–24]

Studies assessing etiological relationships: Prospective cohort studies and case control studies

Many systematic reviews are not concerned with issues of effectiveness at all, but with investigating the causal association between some variable (such as a risk factor) and a health, behavioral, or psychological outcome, for example, "Does poverty in childhood affect health and social outcomes in adult life?" To answer such etiological questions, prospective studies are needed. These involve recruiting a cohort of individuals before the outcome has occurred, and following them over a period of years. This could be a large birth cohort, or a cohort recruited for a particular study. It can also be done retrospectively – by the analysis of retrospective cohort and case control studies, and using survey data. In such cases, the data are analyzed after the outcomes have already emerged – for example, individuals with a particular health problem may be compared to healthy individuals on a range of demographic and other variables, for example, risk behaviors. Any difference between the two groups may be causally related to the health problem. This approach (the case control study) helped to determine the causal link between smoking and lung cancer. In the landmark case control studies of the 1950s researchers showed that lung cancer patients were more likely to smoke than healthy controls, and concluded (after controlling statistically for other explanations) that smoking was a definite cause of lung cancer.[25, 26]

Cohort studies

The impacts of poverty in early life on adult health were discussed in an earlier example. Probably the best source of data on the association between early childhood events and later outcomes are cohort studies, which collect both health and social data about children at intervals, often from shortly after birth into adulthood. From these studies, it is known that risks of death and serious illness are greatest for those brought up in the most disadvantaged circumstances, and so are the chances of relatively high blood pressure, poor respiratory health, obesity, and short stature.[27, 28]

Cohort studies enable the identification of factors that seem to have a protective effect. In other words they can help us understand why some children, given a poor start in life, do well. Identifying those factors that seem to have made a difference to the children who have overcome a poor start in life, is the first step towards identifying interventions that may be further evaluated in trials. It would be misleading to suggest that cohort studies can give confident answers to questions about what works in family and social policies, but they can give helpful pointers, and will be relevant to systematic reviews exploring issues of causation, as such studies offer the best opportunity of testing etiological hypotheses.

For some review questions, both cohort and case–control studies testing the same or a very similar hypothesis are often available. However, it is generally taken to be the case that prospective studies are the more reliable source of information. Depending on the number of studies available for review, it may be instructive to include both study designs and separately review both types of study. It has been found previously that the **effect sizes** from case control studies may be inflated compared to prospective studies, and including both designs in the review allows this assumption to be explored.

It does not necessarily follow, however, that the prospective observational studies themselves offer unbiased effect size estimates. Egger et al.[29] illustrate the problem clearly with respect to studies of smoking as a risk factor for suicide, where most of the prospective cohort studies that have been carried out have shown a positive association. A systematic review of these studies shows that the risk of suicide increases with the daily number of cigarettes smoked and indeed a meta-analysis of four of these studies with a total of over 390,000 men showed this clearly. The risk was increased by about 40 percent for light smokers (1–14 cigarettes daily), and by about 90 percent for heavier smokers (15–24 cigarettes daily), and more than doubled for those smoking 25 or more cigarettes a day. However, smoking is unlikely to increase the risk of suicide. It is more likely that both smoking and suicide are themselves related to some other confounding factor such as some social or psychological variable (for example, financial worries, or depression), which are associated with both rates of smoking and risk of suicide. This example has two useful lessons for systematic reviewers; that reviewers should be aware of the risk of confounding in observational studies, and that systematically reviewing biased studies does not remove that bias. Indeed it is likely to produce misleadingly precise inflated estimates of an association, when the studies are statistically synthesized using meta-analysis. As Egger et al. have warned: "The thorough consideration of possible sources of heterogeneity between **observational study** results will provide more insights than the mechanistic calculation of an overall measure of effect, which will often be biased."[29] This advice can also be applied to systematic reviews of other study designs. Meta-analyses of observational studies are very common – about as common as meta-analyses of randomized controlled trials.

3.3   USE OF QUALITATIVE RESEARCH IN SYSTEMATIC REVIEWS

Some of the most important research questions are those that are addressed (if not always answered) by qualitative research. These are the questions that enable us to know whether a particular intervention is salient for the people to whom it is offered, and what they consider the important outcomes to be. Those to whom health, educational, or welfare services are offered have a reservoir of expertise on their own lives, and they may also have views on questions they feel are important to have answered. Without qualitative studies, we would be hard pressed to understand the social worlds of those with whom we work, and without this understanding, cannot begin to conceive of interventions that will be acceptable, let alone effective. Chapters 5 and 6 describe a number of the ways in which qualitative data, and user views, might be included in systematic reviews. We have already suggested that the strongest research design in attributing a particular result to a particular intervention is the RCT. Qualitative research done prior to, and incorporated within, RCTs can help to identify which interventions and outcomes are most likely to be important, and how particular interventions should be delivered. They can also help researchers understand the process of implementing an intervention, what can go wrong, and what the unexpected adverse effects might be when an intervention is rolled out to a larger population. These are all key questions that a systematic review of effectiveness would be expected to address. Box 3.4 provides an example of qualitative work as part of a smoke alarm trial funded by the Medical Research Council in the UK.

Box 3.4   Qualitative work in an RCT of smoke alarms

One of the ways in which primary studies that go to make up systematic reviews of effect may be improved is through the use of mixed methods. An example is given below.[30]

A randomized controlled trial of smoke alarms does not appear at first sight to be one of science's most interesting studies. But fire deaths are an important problem and one with a steep social class gradient contributing to inequalities in health. Signs outside London fire stations used to say: "Smoke alarms save lives." This is only the case, of course, if they are working.

Eighty-one percent of British households reported having an alarm in 1999.[31] However, in two deprived inner London boroughs only 16 percent of homes were found to have working alarms.[32] Several different types of smoke alarm are available but there has been a lack of evidence on which type is most likely to remain working after initial installation. In order to investigate this, a randomized controlled trial was conducted.[33] A key finding was that when alarms were tested 15 months later, only 51 percent, and an even smaller proportion in smokers' households, were working.

Public health interventions, like clinical ones, can have both beneficial and adverse effects, and those on the receiving end can provide important insights into why some interventions may be less effective than anticipated.[34, 35] Using data collected from participants at trial enrolment, households were identified across a range of ethnicities, ages, disability, household and housing types, housing tenure, and incorporating all alarm types used in the trial, as well as households that had been randomized but ultimately refused or otherwise did not

(Continued)

Box 3.4   *(Cont'd)*

receive the intervention (6.6 percent of trial sample). Recruitment ensured that people with infants under 4 years and people aged over 65 were sampled. Discussions were also held with trial recruiters and alarm installers to gather information on reasons for refusing participation in the trial.

Data were collected using a range of qualitative methods. These included individual and group interviews with adults, and questionnaires and 'draw and write' techniques and group interviews with children. Questions were based around a topic guide, with follow up prompts. Critical incidents were explored in more depth with interviewees, including two cases where alarms would not stop.

Factors that encouraged continued alarm use included early warning in the event of fire and an increased sense of security. Those who refused alarm installation said they already had one, or were concerned at receiving an intervention that involved giving a stranger access to their homes. Those who received alarms but discontinued their use cited a range of adverse effects, including problems with maintenance and alarm sensitivity, leading to nuisance alarms and stress.

This provides a context for the low level of functioning smoke alarms 15 months after installation. Although trial participants, including children, considered themselves at high risk for fires and would recommend smoke alarms to others, respondents' reports on the distress caused by false alarms, and problems with maintenance, suggest that by disabling alarms people are making rational decisions about their immediate health and wellbeing. In a population already managing a range of health risks, a public health intervention that makes mealtimes more, rather than less, stressful, and where noise can threaten leisure or relationships with fellow occupants, could pose a threat to immediate wellbeing.

In a successful implementation program, effective maintenance support, as well as installation of the type of alarm most likely to be working after 15 months may be associated with higher rates of smoke alarm functioning. Manufacturers may need to explore other ways of ensuring that smoke alarm users can feel in better control of the alarms in their home.

Is qualitative work relevant to systematic reviews: Are systematic reviews harmful to qualitative work?

Some view the inclusion of qualitative research in systematic reviews of both quantitative and qualitative data with caution. On the one hand, there are hard-line quantitative meta-analysts who find it difficult to see the point of including 'soft' qualitative data, and who question whether it can ever be more than anecdotal. On the other hand, there are equally hard-line qualitative researchers who are wary of what they see as inappropriate use of their methods. This book adheres to neither of these views, but focuses mainly on systematic reviews of mixed methods, although systematic reviews of qualitative research alone are important (one is described in chapter 6). There is clearly enormous scope for improving the means of accumulating the knowledge gained through qualitative studies. These studies play important roles in systematic reviews in relation to processes, implementation, and ensuring the inclusion of user and provider views – as well as contributing to the formulation of meaningful review questions in the first place.

As Dixon-Woods and Fitzpatrick point out, a place for qualitative research in systematic reviews has been established, but the inclusion of qualitative work in a systematic manner is an ongoing challenge.[36] Some of the methodological problems this raises are being addressed by the Cochrane and Campbell Collaborations, which have set up a joint methodological group to develop methods for systematic review of qualitative research (Box 3.5).

3.4 INCLUSION CRITERIA FOR OUTCOMES

Earlier sections have described how to define inclusion criteria, focusing mainly on study design. However, there are other aspects of studies that need to be considered when drawing up inclusion and exclusion criteria. It is important, for example, to specify the outcomes on which the review is seeking information. For reviews of effectiveness, the intervention may have a range of impacts on those receiving it. Some of these impacts will be "primary outcomes" – the effects in which we are most interested. Others will be "surrogate outcomes" – short-term outcomes that are often easier to measure. Sometimes it is necessary for the review to synthesize data on these outcomes, because there may be little evidence on longer term

Box 3.5 The Cochrane and Campbell qualitative methods group

There is a joint website for the Cochrane Qualitative Research Methods Group and the Campbell Implementation Process Methods Group: <http://mysite.freeserve.com/Cochrane_Qual_Method/index. htm>. It is suggested by this group that qualitative studies can: (a) contribute to the development of a more robust intervention by helping to define an intervention more precisely; (b) assist in the choice of outcome measures and assist in the development of valid research questions; and (c) help to understand heterogeneous results from studies of effect.

The Cochrane and Campbell qualitative methods groups share similar aims, which are to:

- Demonstrate the value of including evidence from qualitative research and process evaluations into systematic reviews.
- Develop and disseminate methods for including qualitative research and studies of implementation processes into Cochrane and Campbell reviews.
- Establish and maintain a database of relevant methodological papers.
- Provide a forum for discussion and debate about the role of qualitative research and studies evaluating implementation in systematic reviews.
- Provide links for Cochrane and Campbell Review Groups to people with expertise and experience of qualitative research and process evaluations.
- Provide training for members of Cochrane and Campbell Review Groups.

outcomes available (these are sometimes not measurable within the life-span of the typical research project). One should however be aware of the difference between primary and secondary outcomes, and if one wishes to extract information on all outcomes, be clear which of the outcome data being extracted are specifically relevant to the review question.

For example, an issue of interest to health researchers and psychologists alike is the question of whether particular psychological variables (such as personality types) are risk factors for illness. The best known one is the hypothesized association between the Type A behavior pattern (TABP) (which is characterized by time urgency − an obsession with time and deadlines − hostility and competitiveness), and coronary heart disease (CHD). There have been many dozens of studies over the past four decades that have examined the association between Type A behavior and a range of psychological and physiological outcomes − including heart rate, blood pressure, psychological measures, and a range of hormonal and other measures.[37] However, if the question we are primarily interested in is whether TABP causes CHD, then we would be most interested in reviewing studies which include a direct measure of CHD in the study. There are many fewer of these studies. As it happens, these studies have in fact been systematically reviewed, and the existing evidence for a relationship between TABP and CHD seems equivocal.[37]

More on surrogate (intermediate) outcomes

The problem of which outcomes matter, and which to focus on when conducting a review, is discussed by Peter Gøetsche in a paper entitled "Beware of surrogate outcome measures."[38] Gøetsche points out that to reduce the time one needs to spend on conducting a primary study, and to reduce expense, surrogate outcome measures are often helpful as substitutes for the real outcomes of interest. Sometimes those outcomes of interest (for example, delinquency in later years, changes in health status) are not easily measurable, and short-term outcomes are assumed to be good predictors of long-term outcomes. However, there is a risk that these **intermediate outcomes** are related to the primary outcome, but not *causally* related − and particularly in social science few relationships are simple and unifactorial. Gøetsche concluded that we should "beware of surrogate outcomes," and warns that they can lead reviewers to the wrong conclusions.

Take the example of the effects of the program known as "Scared Straight" on reoffending.[39] This showed how the intervention was popular with a range of stakeholders: participants in the program, police officers, and victims. However, popularity of the program proved a poor predictor of the main outcome of interest, that is, reoffending rates.

3.5 "NARROW" VERSUS "BROAD" REVIEWS

This chapter concludes with a few further words on the issue of "narrow" versus "broad" reviews (see also Table 2.2). Systematic reviews are often seen by critics as being too narrowly focused, and overly-concerned with assessing a meager selection of outcomes from restricted study designs, within closely defined populations; this leads to a concern among some users that systematic reviews are only able to take a reductionist approach, which involves answering simplistic questions which are mainly of interest to other reviewers. This narrow focus is, however, often necessary when reviews aim to test a very specific hypothesis, or to answer a specific, tightly defined question – for example, a question about the effectiveness of a specific intervention within particular contexts or populations. In these cases tightly defined inclusion criteria are necessary, and this approach is no different from any other type of hypothesis–testing research.

In other cases, however, it will be necessary to include a much broader range of evidence (see Box 3.6), though if the review question is *too* broad a systematic review may not be the most appropriate tool. For example, in a review of day services for people with learning disabilities, the authors considered and rejected the possibility of conducting a systematic review, because they wished to include material on the wider debates and discussions within the learning disability field, and on the availability and types of different services. Within such a broad review however, a systematic review of effectiveness (or a systematic review to answer other questions) can still be valuable.

Box 3.6   Promoting walking and cycling as an alternative to using cars: What works? A systematic review with a broad focus[40]

David Ogilvie, lead reviewer on this review, describes some of his reasons for using an inclusive approach in a review that synthesized data on a range of interventions, populations, and study designs:

"Our rationale for specifying a broad research question was that no previous attempt had been made to review systematically ANY of the evidence in this area. The only way to begin to address the question 'what works in achieving X?' is to conduct a broad review that takes account of a multiplicity of possible interventions. Richard Smith (until 2004, editor of the *British Medical Journal*) has written about the need for systematic reviews investigating both 'specific' and 'broad' questions. The Cochrane reviewers' handbook also acknowledges a role for this type of review, and offers three relevant justifications for such an approach:

1. Narrowly focused reviews may not be generalizable to multiple settings, populations and formulations of an intervention.
2. A narrow focus is at high risk of resulting in biased conclusions when the reviewer is familiar with the literature in an area and narrows the inclusion criteria in such a way that one or more studies with results that are in conflict with the reviewer's beliefs are excluded.
3. The known results of a series of studies of a class of interventions might influence the choice of a specific intervention from this class for a narrow review.

A particular strength of our review [on modal shifts[40]] is that we searched widely for evidence applicable to whole populations, rather than the more clinically or individually focused interventions which have been the subject of previous systematic reviews in the field of physical activity promotion. A further strength of our review is that we made no assumptions about the nature and type of intervention that might have resulted in the outcomes of interest."

Key learning points from this chapter

- It is essential to describe and record the inclusion criteria at the start of the review, and to record any changes subsequently made.
- The inclusion/exclusion criteria should describe clearly which study designs, populations, interventions, and outcomes are included and excluded in the review.
- These criteria should be described in the final report or journal article.

(Continued)

Key learning points from this chapter

(Cont'd)

- The choice of studies to include and exclude is not an inherent feature of the systematic review method, but a decision made by the reviewers, guided by the review question, by theoretical considerations, and by the needs of users.
- Systematic reviews can include a range of study designs, as required to answer the review question.

REFERENCES

1. Guyatt, G., Sackett, D., Sinclair, J., Hayward, R., Cook, D., and Cook, R. Users' guides to the medical literature. IX. A method for grading health care recommendations. *Journal of the American Medical Association* 1995, 274: 1800–4.
2. Guyatt, G., Haynes, R., Jaeschke, R., Cook, D., Green, L., Naylor, C., et al. Users' Guides to the Medical Literature: XXV. Evidence-based medicine: Principles for applying the Users' Guides to patient care. Evidence-Based Medicine Working Group. *Journal of the American Medical Association* 2000, 284: 1290–6.
3. Petticrew, M. and Roberts, H. Evidence, hierarchies and typologies: Horses for Courses. *Journal of Epidemiology and Community Health* 2003, 57: 527–9.
4. Muir Gray, J. A. *Evidence-based healthcare.* London: Churchill Livingstone, 1997.
5. Glasziou, P., Vandenbroucke, J., and Chalmers, I. Assessing the quality of research. *British Medical Journal* 2004, 328: 39–41.
6. Silverman, W. *Retrolental fibroplasia: A modern parable.* New York: Grune and Stratton, 1980.
7. Zoritch, B., Roberts, I., and Oakley, A. Day care for pre-school children (Cochrane Review). *The Cochrane Library,* Chichester, UK: John Wiley & Sons, Ltd, 2004, issue 2.
8. Toroyan, T., Roberts, I., Oakley, A., Laing, G., Mugford, M., and Frost, C. Effectiveness of out-of-home day care for disadvantaged families: Randomised controlled trial. *British Medical Journal* 2003, 327: 906.
9. Petticrew, M., Whitehead, M., Bambra, C., Egan, M., Graham, H., Macintyre, S., et al. *Systematic reviews in public health: The work of the ESRC Centre for Evidence Based Public Health Policy. An evidence-based approach to public health and tackling health inequalities.* Milton Keynes: Open University Press (in press).
10. Oakley, A. *Experiments in knowing: Gender and method in the social sciences.* Cambridge: Polity Press, 2000.

11. Silverman, W. and Chalmers, I. Casting and drawing lots: A time honoured way of dealing with uncertainty and ensuring fairness. *British Medical Journal* 2001, 323: 1467–8.

12. Shadish, W., Cook, T., and Campbell, D. *Experimental and quasi-experimental designs for generalized causal inference.* Boston: Houghton-Mifflin, 2002.

13. Ritchie, D. "Breathing Space" – reflecting upon the realities of community partnerships and workers' beliefs about promoting health. *Health Education Journal* 2001, 60: 73–92.

14. Parry, O., Bancroft, A., Gnich, W., and Amos, A. Nobody home? Issues of respondent recruitment in areas of deprivation. *Critical Public Health* 2001, 11: 305–17.

15. Deeks, J., Dinnes, J., D'Amico, R., Sowden, A., Sakarovitch, C., Song, F., et al. Evaluating non-randomised intervention studies. *Health Technology Assessment* 2003, 7, online at: http://www.hta.nhsweb.nhs.uk/fullmono/mon727.pdf [accessed February 24, 2005]

16. Effective Practice and Organization of Care Group. In P. Alderson, L. Bero, R. Grilli, J. Grimshaw, L. McAuley, A. Oxman, et al. (eds.) *The Cochrane Library.* Chichester, UK: John Wiley & Sons, 2004, issue 2.

17. Stead, L. and Lancaster, T. Interventions for preventing tobacco sales to minors (Cochrane Review). *The Cochrane Library.* Chichester, UK: John Wiley & Sons, 2004, issue 2.

18. Sowden, A. and Arblaster, L. Mass media interventions for preventing smoking in young people (Cochrane Review). *The Cochrane Library.* Chichester, UK: John Wiley & Sons, 2004, issue 2.

19. Thomson, H., Hoskins, R., Petticrew, M., Ogilvie, D., Craig, N., Quinn, T., et al. Evaluating the health effects of social interventions. *British Medical Journal* 2004, 328: 282–5.

20. Rychetnik, L., Frommer, M., Hawe, P., and Shiell, A. Criteria for evaluating evidence on public health interventions. *Journal of Epidemiology and Community Health* 2002, 56: 119–27.

21. Mackenbach, J. Tackling inequalities in health: The need for building a systematic evidence base. *Journal of Epidemiology and Community Health* 2003, 57: 162.

22. Macintyre, S. Evidence based policy making. *British Medical Journal* 2003, 326: 5–6.

23. Acheson, D. *Independent inquiry into inequalities in health.* London: Department of Health, 1998.

24. Wanless, D. *Securing good health for the whole population: Final report.* London: HM Treasury, 2004.

25. Doll, R. and Hill, A. A study of the aetiology of carcinoma of the lung. *British Medical Journal* 1952, ii: 1271–86.

26. Doll, R., Peto, R., Boreham, J., and Sutherland, I. Mortality in relation to smoking: 50 years' observations on male British doctors. *British Medical Journal* 2004, 328: 1519–33.

27. Power, C. and Hertzman, C. Social and biological pathways linking early life and adult disease. *British Medical Bulletin* 1997, 53: 210–21.

28. Wadsworth, M. *The imprint of time: Childhood, history and adult life.* Oxford: Oxford University Press, 1991.

29. Egger, M., Schneider, M., and Davey Smith, G. Spurious precision? Meta-analysis of observational studies. *British Medical Journal* 1998, 316: 140–4.

30. Roberts, H., Curtis, C., Liabo, K., Rowland, D., DiGuiseppi, C., and Roberts, I. Putting public health evidence into practice: Increasing the prevalence of working smoke alarms in disadvantaged inner city housing. *Journal of Epidemiology and Community Health* 2004, 58: 280–5.

31. National Statistics. *Britain update: November 2000.* London: National Statistics, 2000.

32. DiGuiseppi, C., Roberts, I., and Speirs, N. Smoke alarm installation and function in inner London council housing. *Archives of Disease in Childhood* 1999, 81: 400–3.

33. Rowland, D., DiGiuseppi, C., Roberts, I., Curtis, K., Roberts, H., Ginelli, L., et al. Increasing the prevalence of working smoke alarms in disadvantaged inner city housing: A randomised controlled trial. *British Medical Journal* 2002, 325: 998–1001.

34. Freeman, R. The idea of prevention: A critical review. In S. Scott, et al. (eds.) *Private Risks and Public Danger.* Ashgate: Avery, 1992.

35. Roberts, H., Smith, S., and Bryce, C. Prevention is better … *Sociology of Health and Illness* 1993, 15: 447–63.

36. Dixon-Woods, M. and Fitzpatrick, R. Qualitative research in systematic reviews has established a place for itself. *British Medical Journal* 2001, 323: 765–6.

37. Hemingway, H. and Marmot, M. Evidence based cardiology: Psychosocial factors in the aetiology and prognosis of coronary heart disease: Systematic review of prospective cohort studies. *British Medical Journal* 1999, 318: 1460–7.

38. Gøetsche, P., Liberati, A., Torri, V., and Rosetti, L. Beware of surrogate outcome measures. *International Journal of Health Technology Assessment* 1996, 12: 238–46.

39. Petrosino, A., Turpin-Petrosino, C., and Buehler, J. Scared Straight and other juvenile awareness programs for preventing juvenile delinquency: A systematic review of the randomized experimental evidence. *Annals of the American Academy of Political and Social Science* 2003, 589.

40. Ogilvie, D., Egan, M., Hamilton, V., and Petticrew, M. Promoting walking and cycling as an alternative to using cars: What works? A systematic review. *British Medical Journal* 2004, 329: 763.

Chapter 4

How to find the studies: The literature search

Poor current information policy resembles the worst aspects of our old agricultural policy which left grain rotting in thousands of storage files while people were starving. We have warehouses of unused information "rotting" while critical questions are left unanswered and critical problems are left unresolved. (*Al Gore, cited in Smith*[1])

4.1 INTRODUCTION

How difficult can it be to find studies for a literature review? After all there is no shortage of literature "out there," and for most researchers it is not too difficult to obtain copies of research papers or journal articles. Quite a lot of the relevant material is now available electronically. Someone doing a systematic review on physical activity, ironically enough, can probably do much of it without leaving her desk, and she probably feels that she knows the main studies in her own area anyway. Why all the fuss about searching for more of them?

This chapter explains why. It discusses the main sources of studies for systematic reviews (including electronic databases) and the main methods used to locate them. It also gives some pointers on when to stop searching (on the assumption that reviewers have neither the resources nor patience to continue searching indefinitely) and because, fun though it may be to spend months trawling through back issues of defunct journals, any review eventually reaches the stage where the yield no longer justifies the effort. The identification of relevant studies has been called "the most fundamental challenge" for systematic reviewers,[2,3] requiring information skills not usually taught to researchers. While there are now many tools (and experts) to help reviewers carry out healthcare systematic reviews, such as search strategies for use with electronic databases, these sorts of aids are in short supply in social science topic areas, where some databases can prove frustrating when using anything more sophisticated than the simplest search strategy. It is important not to cut corners with the literature search, and this means seeking expert (that is, information scientist) help.

4.2   WHERE TO START?

There are many sources of information to consider, but a search of electronic databases is often the main starting point. However such databases are not the only source of literature, and sometimes they are not even the most useful. In many research areas, particularly in the social sciences, the bulk of the relevant evidence may not appear in journals, but will be located in reports in the "gray literature," much of which may not be indexed in electronic databases. There is thus a real risk that electronic searches alone will fail to locate a good deal of relevant information. For example, in a systematic review of housing studies only about one-third of the relevant studies were retrieved through database searches;[4] the rest were identified through contacting other researchers, hand-searching bibliographies, and contacting experts.

The type of information being sought will depend on both the review question and the inclusion criteria. Published journal papers, and other published and unpublished reports of studies will probably be included. The latter may be located through searches of conference proceedings, abstracts of dissertations and other "gray" literature. Searches need to include book chapters because (particularly in the social sciences) these may report the results of studies never published in journals.[5] Bibliographies of other literature reviews (systematic or not) and of primary studies should also be searched by hand (see section 4.20). Again, book chapters may be a useful source of this information. Methods of conducting electronic and other searches of journal articles, books, and unpublished literature are described in more detail below, and lists of databases and other sources of evidence are referred to throughout the chapter.

4.3   USING ELECTRONIC DATABASES: SEARCH STRATEGIES

It should be clear from the review question and from the inclusion/exclusion criteria what types of studies need to be identified. In many cases specific search strategies have been developed by information scientists to help identify particular study designs (such as trials) in electronic databases. These have usually been designed to be used with specific databases, most notably Medline, but they may also provide pointers to how to identify other types of study, while excluding a great deal of irrelevant literature. These search strategies all work in broadly the same way. For an intervention, this involves listing the different ways in which it can be defined, perhaps by drawing up a list of synonyms. Then the population is specified, and the outcome of interest – again, including relevant synonyms. These are combined (usually using the terms AND and OR and NOT) to allow only the most relevant studies to be retrieved.

A search strategy for systematic reviews was described in chapter 2. Detailed strategies for finding reviews, developed by information scientists at the Centre for Reviews and Dissemination (CRD) at the University of York, are also available online <http://www.york.ac.uk/inst/crd/search. htm>.[6] CRD makes available filters for identifying primary studies for systematic reviews (see <http://www.york.ac.uk/inst/crd/revs4.htm>). However, it should be noted that many filters are mainly intended for use in identifying clinical trials, and the search terms used reflect this (using words and phrases like double-blind, randomized, clinical trial, and so on). For social systematic reviews of effectiveness the range of eligible study designs may be wide. Searching for controlled trials alone may either uncover few studies or may not identify other relevant evaluative research, and is likely to exclude studies reporting on process and implementation issues. Similarly, evaluations of the effects of social policies may involve randomized and non-randomized controlled studies, but a range of other study designs and search terms will be relevant depending on the study question. Such evaluations often use quasi-experimental designs, which may be defined in different ways. Some possible search terms to consider are listed in Box 4.1, which describes search terms for *non-experimental* evaluations. Variations of these terms should also be used (for example, experiments, experimental).

4.4 THE RIGHT STUFF: SENSITIVITY AND SPECIFICITY

Perhaps contrary to expectations, the aim of the literature search is not to retrieve everything. It is to retrieve everything *of relevance*, while leaving behind the irrelevant. The terms **sensitivity** and **specificity** refer to these aims. A highly sensitive search is one that retrieves a high proportion of the relevant studies that are waiting to be retrieved; a highly specific search is

Box 4.1 Additional search terms for non-clinical studies of effectiveness (such as policy evaluations)

Quasi-experiment or quasi-experimental
Comparison group or comparative study
Policy experiment
Natural experiment
Policy evaluation
Social experiment
Interrupted time series, time series studies, time series analysis (ITS)
Before and after study, controlled before and after study (CBA)
Longitudinal study, cohort study
Impact evaluation, impact assessment, outcome evaluation

Other methodological terms include **ARIMA** (Auto Regressive Integrated Moving Average) methods, propensity scoring, reflexive comparison, pretest-post-test non-equivalent groups design, regression-discontinuity design, post-test only, non-equivalent control group design.

If the review is also to include information on process or implementation then a range of other search terms will be required (for example, qualitative research, surveys, case studies).

one that retrieves a low proportion of irrelevant studies (see Box 4.2). The sensitivity and specificity of particular searches are often not known, because the true number of studies theoretically available for retrieval cannot usually be determined. However the sensitivity and specificity of different search strategies can sometimes be estimated when the review is completed.

High levels of sensitivity can often be straightforward, if laborious to achieve: they require extensive search terms, and exhaustive searches of a wide range of databases and other sources. However, there is generally a trade-off between sensitivity and specificity, so that highly sensitive searches tend to have low specificity, as the relevant studies are hidden among many thousands (or perhaps tens of thousands) of irrelevant citations, which can be slow and costly to sort through. Often, however, when searching for studies of "difficult to define" interventions there is little alternative. When

---

Box 4.2   Sensitivity and specificity (or how to get the right stuff and avoid getting the wrong stuff)

Sensitivity = proportion of all studies that were retrieved by the search (sometimes called recall)

Specificity = proportion of studies that were retrieved, that were relevant (sometimes called precision)

An example: A hypothetical search retrieves 200 "hits" (abstracts and/ or titles) in total – some relevant, and some irrelevant, as always. However there are known to be 100 studies which need to be retrieved, and the aforementioned search retrieved 97 of these. It is therefore very sensitive (sensitivity = 97/100, or 0.97, or 97 percent), but its specificity is lower: the proportion of studies that were retrieved *and* were relevant is 97/200 studies (specificity = 0.485, or 49 percent).

Say, however, a different search strategy retrieves 1,000 titles and abstracts, and again locates 97 of the 100 studies that we need to find. The sensitivity is still 0.97 (97 of the 100 were found), but the specificity is much lower, because 903 studies were not relevant ("false positives"). The specificity of the new search was therefore 0.097 (or about 10 percent).

Sensitivity and specificity have been more simply, and just as accurately described as "how to get the right stuff and avoid getting the wrong stuff".[7]

---

searching for a clinical intervention – say a drug – it may be possible to list all synonyms for the intervention. The quality of abstracting and description of study designs (such as RCTs) is also increasing in some databases such as MEDLINE (though it is by no means perfect), and this can make the task slightly easier. This is not the case, however, for many social interventions. Structured abstracts and keywords are less common in social science journals, methodological information is often less clearly reported by authors, and a wider range of study designs is often eligible for inclusion in the reviews. The searches therefore often tend towards lower specificity, in the pursuit of high sensitivity. For example, in a recent review of the effects of new road building on communities over 23,000 titles and abstracts were retrieved by electronic searches and hand searching in order to identify the final set of 32 studies.[8] Search terms for social science reviews may often be less specific, and the searches may need to be more exhaustive to identify all the relevant studies, than is the case for other types of review.

As an illustration, Wentz et al. have described the challenges they faced in identifying controlled trials of road safety interventions for a systematic review.[9] They aimed to develop a sensitive and specific search strategy, using search terms identified by word frequency analysis.[10] This proved difficult, because while search terms like "traffic" had high sensitivity, a high proportion of the studies identified which used this term did not prove to be relevant (that is, the term had "low positive predictive value"). The authors make several useful recommendations to authors, editors, and database producers which should help improve the retrieval of studies in this field. These include ensuring consistent indexing of study methods, ensuring that the study design is clearly described in the title, abstract, and methods of the paper, and (for editors) ensuring that structured abstracts with details of study methods are used (see Box 4.3).

Box 4.3   Who writes the abstracts?

The creation of abstracts and indexes for bibliographic databases is usually carried out on a freelance, piece-work basis. The work is not well paid but is a flexible and interesting source of income for home-based workers and provides an opportunity to keep up with professional developments. All abstracters and indexers will have a background in the subject area.

The impression that standards, guidelines, and editorial input vary greatly between databases is confirmed in a survey by Armstrong and Wheatley.[11] Some publishers, such as Medline where the added-value emphasis is on indexing, do not employ abstracters, but use author abstracts only. However, Medline indexers are instructed not to read these abstracts but to work from the full-text of the article, and they have detailed rules and guidelines.

Creating a succinct summary of a lengthy report and identifying salient keywords are satisfying, but researchers who call for universal use of structured abstracts should note that they are hard to create from unstructured articles.

(Val Hamilton, Information Scientist, University of Glasgow)

4.5 THE INFORMATION SCIENTIST

It will be clear from the above description that there are particular skills involved in carrying out sensitive and specific searches, and these tend not to be part of the core training of social researchers. This is why systematic reviewers usually seek expert help from an information scientist, as these specialists are trained in searching electronic and other sources. They will know which databases are available and how to access them through the various interfaces and providers, as well as differences between them with respect to search terms and indexing. They are also skilled in locating gray literature. It is useful for researchers to know about the general principles of truncation, Boolean operators, and so on, but the mechanics of a comprehensive literature search requires expert help.[12]

The rise of information scientists and systematic reviewers was (like many other modern scientific developments) foreseen in some detail by seventeenth-century scientist Francis Bacon (see Box 4.4). Inventor Thomas Edison also knew the value of a comprehensive literature search (Box 4.5).

Strategies for identifying a range of study designs have been made available on the Web and elsewhere by information scientists. Some of these strategies were developed by researchers working with the Cochrane Collaboration, and many are specifically designed for use in Medline, but nonetheless provide a valuable guide to designing a search strategy for use with other databases.[13, 14] Strategies for trials and other study designs are discussed briefly below, and links to electronic versions of the strategies are given on the website accompanying this book <http://www.msoc-mrc.gla.ac.uk/Evidence/Evidence.html>.

Identifying controlled trials and reviews

Examples of search strategies are listed on the CRD Information Services website at <http://www.york.ac.uk/inst/crd/revs.htm>. The SCHARR website at the University of Sheffield is an excellent resource for systematic reviewers and provides a list of sources of MEDLINE filters <http://www.shef.ac.uk/scharr/ir/filter.html>. The CRD site also gives an example of a search strategy for identifying published systematic reviews and meta-analyses.

Identifying qualitative research

There is considerable interest in incorporating qualitative research into systematic reviews, particularly reviews of social interventions. For most

Box 4.4   Depredators, compilers, and merchants of light: Seventeenth-century systematic reviewers at work

"For the several employments and offices of our fellows; we have twelve that sail into foreign countries, under the names of other nations (for our own we conceal); who bring us the books, and abstracts, and patterns of experiments of all other parts. These we call Merchants of Light ...

"We have three that collect the experiments which are in all books. These we call Depredators ...

"We have three that draw the experiments of the former four into titles and tables, to give the better light for the drawing of observations and axioms out of them. These we call Compilers."

Source: **The New Atlantis** *(Francis Bacon, 1627)*
By permission of The National Portrait Gallery

of its history the systematic review has been used to synthesize quantitative information, but the answers to many key questions about interventions can come only from qualitative data. However, identifying qualitative studies for inclusion in reviews is certainly more difficult than identifying trials. There seems to be no ongoing initiative to identify and index qualitative research in a dedicated database, as is the case for clinical trials, for example, the Cochrane Central register of Controlled Trials (CENTRAL). In fact the indexing of qualitative research on existing electronic databases is generally inconsistent, and there is often no methodological information in the study's title or abstract to allow it to be clearly identified as a qualitative study. This makes it difficult to define specific search terms. However, Evans[15] suggests that the following terms may be useful:

Box 4.5   The Wizard of Menlo Park

The first step in any new scientific project has always been the search for previous studies, partly to establish precedence but also to build on previous work. A good example of this is the work of inventor Thomas Edison, who moved to Menlo Park in 1876 to establish his laboratory and within two years had invented a general electric lighting system. With the general principle of underground distribution of electricity clear in his mind, he engaged his assistant Francis Upton to carry out an extensive literature search. Upton did this by searching through indexes (by hand, of course), systematically extracting

data on the design and function of previous lamps, and presenting them in his notebooks with a commentary on their feasibility (The notebooks have been digitized by Rutgers University and can be viewed online at: http://edison.rutgers.edu/.)

The picture shows a cartoon from the *Daily Graphic* of July 9, 1879 showing Edison as "The Wizard of Menlo Park," with the caption "The Wizard Searches …" Bacon, Edison, and Upton thus demonstrated a common application of systematic review methods: using previous research as a way of improving existing methods and developing new ones.

(Courtesy of the Thomas A. Edison papers, Rutgers University.)

Ethnography; Qualitative; Grounded theory; Thematic analysis; Content analysis; Observational methods; **Meta-ethnography**; Constant comparative method; Field notes; Participant observation; Narratives; Field studies; Audio recording; Focus group/groups.

A full search strategy developed by the Hawaii Medical Library for the CINAHL database also provides a good basis for developing a tailored search strategy (Box 4.6). Shaw et al.[16] add "glaser adj2 strauss$" (referring to the qualitative methodologists Glaser and Strauss) to the list of

Box 4.6 Hawaii Medical Library evidence-based filters for CINAHL (Ovid)

Filter for qualitative research (long version):

1.   Qualitative Studies/
2.   Ethnographic Research/
3.   Phenomenological Research/
4.   Ethnonursing Research/
5.   Grounded Theory/
6.   exp Qualitative Validity/
7.   Purposive Sample/
8.   exp Observational Methods/
9.   Content Analysis/ or Thematic Analysis/
10. Constant Comparative Method/
11. Field Studies/
12. Theoretical Sample/
13. Discourse Analysis/
14. Focus Groups/
15. Phenomenology/ or Ethnography/ or Ethnological Research/
16. or/1–15
17. (qualitative or ethnog$ or phenomenol$).tw.
18. (grounded adj (theor$ or study or studies or research)).tw.
19. (constant adj (comparative or comparison)).tw.
20. (purpos$ adj sampl$4).tw.
21. (focus adj group$).tw.
22. (emic or etic or hermeneutic$ or heuristic or semiotics).tw.
23. (data adj1 saturat$).tw.
24. (participant adj observ$).tw.
25. (heidegger$ or colaizzi$ or spiegelberg$).tw.
26. (van adj manen$).tw.
27. (van adj kaam$).tw.
28. (merleau adj ponty$).tw.
29. (husserl$ or giorgi$).tw.
30. (field adj (study or studies or research)).tw.
31. lived experience$.tw.
32. narrative analysis.tw.
33. (discourse$3 adj analysis).tw.
34. human science.tw.

35.   Life Experiences/
36.   exp Cluster Sample/
37.   or/1–36

(See: http://hml.org/WWW/filtrcin.html#qr-long)

search terms, and additional terms like "multi-method," "multi-modal," **"triangulation," "formative evaluation,"** and "process evaluation" may pick up instances where qualitative methods have been used alongside quantitative methods (for example in evaluation studies). Terms referring to qualitative analysis software could also be added, as these may be specific to qualitative studies (e.g., NUDIST, N6, NVivo, Ethnograph). Used alone such terms will of course have low sensitivity.

Shaw et al. have developed a search strategy that involves using indexing terms where available (for example on MEDLINE), plus free text terms plus broad terms.[16] Their findings suggest that a combination of the three strategies is required for a sensitive search, as any one strategy alone risks missing relevant studies.

Hawker et al.[17] have described the lengths they went to in order to identify qualitative studies for a review of strategies for, and the effectiveness of, the transfer of information about elderly patients between the hospital and the community. They describe an iterative process in which the studies identified from their early searches were used to refine the search strategy, for example by examining how they were keyworded. (This strategy can usefully be applied to searching any type of study, qualitative or otherwise.) Their search strategy also included using "related" searches, in which "similar" studies can be located on PubMed, as well as hand searching journals and searching bibliographies.

Qualitative filters should be used with caution until the indexing and reporting of qualitative studies is improved. Methodological work in this area is being undertaken by methods groups of the Cochrane and Campbell Collaborations – in the latter case the Campbell Implementation Process Methods Group <http://www.duke.edu/web/c2method/>.

Searching for qualitative literature can be a challenge for all of the reasons described above. Booth suggests that searching within a qualitative paradigm is different to searching for quantitative studies, and asks whether it is necessary for a qualitative review to be as comprehensive in its coverage.[18] It is more appropriate, he suggests, to identify groups of papers relevant to the phenomena studied. Within these, themes can be identified, and preferably, important "key informants," in much the same way as they might in primary qualitative research. The concept of data saturation, he suggests, is also important. For Booth, literature searching for qualitative systematic reviews should demonstrate:

- The identification of major schools of thought in an area while being alert to variants, minority views, and dissent;
- Searching a broad range of disciplines to introduce different disciplinary (e.g., health economics, statistics) and stakeholder (e.g., user, clinician, manager) perspectives; and
- The use of both electronic and manual search techniques to ensure that materials are not missed through indexing or coverage inadequacies.

4.6   IDENTIFYING "GRAY" LITERATURE

The term "gray" (or "fugitive") literature is often used to refer to literature that is not obtainable through normal publishing channels. It includes reports published independently by academic and non-academic organizations – such as working papers, occasional papers, reports on websites, and informal publications in short print runs, which are not necessarily widely distributed[19] (see Box 4.7). Conference proceedings and theses are sometimes included in this category, and are discussed separately below.

Box 4.7   Sources of gray literature, including (in some cases) conference proceedings, dissertations, and theses

COPAC: provides free access to the merged online catalogs of 24 major university research libraries in the UK and Ireland, plus the British Library and the National Library of Scotland <http://www.copac.ac.uk/copac/>

Dissertation Abstracts: This contains details of dissertations from the UK (1988–present) and US (1861–present) along with selected MSc dissertations.

Index of conference proceedings: The British Library (BL) receives all published conference proceedings; these are listed in the Index, now compiled annually. It can be searched freely through the BL Public Catalogue (BLPC) by selecting the "Advanced search" option, then "Select Individual Catalogues". See <http://blpc.bl.uk/>

Index to Scientific and Technical Proceedings <http://www.isi-net.com/products/litres/istp/> is available through Web of Knowledge, and includes proceedings from many health-related conferences

Index to Social Sciences and Humanities Proceedings: Includes multidisciplinary coverage of conference proceedings, as well as reports, preprints, and monographs <http://www.isinet.com/products/litres/isshp/>

Ovid HealthSTAR Database comprises literature from MEDLINE, from the Hospital Literature Index, from selected journals, and from the National Library of Medicine's now-defunct HealthSTAR database <http://www.ovid.com/site/products/ovidguide/hstrdb.htm>

Planex: The Planning Exchange database covers regeneration and development, including community, economic, environmental, and physical impacts. It is now part of the **IDOX** information service <http://www.i-documentsystems.com/iii/infoservices/index.htm>

PolicyFile: Indexes mainly US public policy research and practice reports <www.policyfile.com>

SIGLE: SIGLE (System for Information on Gray Literature) is a bibliographic database covering European non-conventional literature in the fields of pure and applied natural sciences and technology, economics, social sciences, and humanities. (1974–present). Produced by EAGLE (European Association for Gray Literature In Europe) <http://www.kb.nl/infolev/eagle/frames.htm>

TRANSPORT, TRIS, ITRD, Transdoc: The **TRIS** Database contains almost half a million records relating to books, technical reports, conference proceedings, journal articles, and ongoing transport research, and is produced by the US Department of Transportation <http://trisonline.bts.gov/sundev/search.cfm/>. **ITRD** (International Transport Research Documentation) includes international transport literature provided by research organizations from 23 countries <http://www.itrd.org/>. Both are available on the Transport database, along with the **ECMT TRANSDOC** database, which includes literature on transport economics, making **TRANSPORT** the most comprehensive source of transportation literature. Available from various database providers including Ovid and SilverPlatter.

(Continued)

Box 4.7   *(Cont'd)*

Urbadisc: Compilation of databases from British, French, Italian, and Spanish sources focusing on urban and regional planning and policy issues with citations from journals, books, government documents, and other sources. Includes the databases **Acompline** and **Urbaline** from the UK <http://www.urbandata.org/en/urbadisc/>
Urban Studies Abstracts (published by Sage) may also be of interest to those reviewing urban literature, as will **Housing Information Digest, Housing Abstracts (HABS),** and the **New Towns Record (from Planex),** which is a CD-ROM containing literature relating to the experiences of Britain's New towns (1946–96) <http://www.planex.co.uk/ntr/>

There are a number of databases specifically dedicated to abstracting gray literature. Among the better-known are SIGLE, and, in the US, PolicyFile, which includes gray literature on social and public policy deriving from, for example, the World Bank, the Rand Corporation, the Cato Institute, as well as other material from universities and research organizations. Specialist libraries are another valuable source for gray literature.

4.7   IDENTIFYING ONGOING RESEARCH

Many funders publish details of the research they support, and it is worth checking their websites or databases (if available) for details of completed or ongoing primary studies. Such searches may identify ongoing studies which the reviewer should be aware of, either because they may be included in the review if they are completed in time, or because they are significant to the review in other ways. For example, if an ongoing study is the first, or largest trial of the intervention of interest, it would make sense to refer to it. Knowing about ongoing research may even allow a "best-before" date to be included in the review – that is, an estimate of how long the review is likely to remain current. The "Effective Health Care Bulletins" – systematic reviews of healthcare interventions produced by CRD at the University of York – include such a statement. This is good practice, but rarely done at present.

UK and non-UK funders

In the UK much ongoing social science research is funded by the Economic and Social Research Council (ESRC) and is listed in the Regard database <http://www.regard.ac.uk>. Health-related research appears in the National Research Register (NRR) a database of ongoing and recently completed research projects funded by, or of interest to, the UK's National Health Service (NHS). It includes the MRC's clinical trials directory, freely available online <http://www.update-software.com/national/> and in the Cochrane Database of Systematic Reviews. In the UK, the National Electronic Library for Health <http://www.nelh.nhs.uk/> contains links to various research registers such as the Research Findings Register. Some of the main UK, US, and other research funders are listed below:

CORDIS: The European Community's Research and Development Information Service (EU funded research <http://www.cordis.lu/en/home.html>) offers a means of searching for EU-funded research and development projects.

The Home Office (UK Government) <http://www.homeoffice.gov.uk/> The Research Development and Statistics Directorate of the Home Office funds and carries out research. Reports on research undertaken by, or on behalf of, the Home Office from 1995 to the present including research studies of relevance to crime and justice are accessible on its website.

The Joseph Rowntree Foundation <http://www.jrf.org.uk/> JRF is one of the largest charitable social policy research and development funders in the UK, and supports projects in housing, social care, and social policy. Their website includes details of currently funded research projects, details of research reports, including systematic reviews, awaiting publication, and archives of past press releases.

MIRIAD, the Midwifery Research Database, is no longer online, but a book is available, which provides an overview of midwifery research from 1988–96.[20] The MIDIRS (Midwifery Information and Resource Service) database <http://www.midirs.org/> includes details of over 100,000 journal articles and other information relevant to midwives.

The Office of the Deputy Prime Minister (ODPM; UK Government) <http://www.odpm.gov.uk/> is responsible for policies affecting (among other things) housing and homelessness, urban renewal, social exclusion, and commissions and carries out research in these areas, including some systematic reviews. Details are available on the website, some located within the online Research Management Database.

The Policy Hub <http://www.policyhub.gov.uk/> includes a section focusing on evaluating policy. The report *A framework for assessing qualitative research*, developed by the Cabinet Office and National Centre for Social Research is also online <http://www.policyhub.gov.uk/evalpolicy/index.asp>. There is an excellent set of links to national and international government and non-government academic and other bodies which produce social and economic research (labeled "evidence hotlinks").

Social Policy and Practice <http://www.ovid.com/spp/>. This new database from Ovid Technologies covers published and unpublished literature, as well as government and other reports from public health, social care, homelessness and housing, crime and law and order, families, children and older people, and public and social policy. (See the Evidence Network Resources pages for more details on this, and other social science databases, at <http://www.evidencenetwork.org/cgi-win/enet.exe/resourcesmain>)

SOSIG <http://www.sosig.ac.uk> and other gateways. SOSIG, the Social Science Information Gateway, is an extensive source of selected, high quality Internet information for researchers and practitioners in the social sciences, business, and law. Subject areas include anthropology, economics, education, geography, government policy, homelessness, psychology, research methods, social inclusion, social welfare, sociology, transport, and women's studies. The resources include links to bibliographies, websites, databases of English and non-English language literature, data, educational materials, online papers and reports, and links to learned societies and research centers. Other gateways include **OMNI**, for health and medicine <http://www.Omni.ac.uk>, **Bubl**, which covers health and social sciences <http://bubl.ac.uk/link/>, and **EEVL** <http://eevl.ac. uk/> which covers engineering (including occupational safety). Gateways also exist for other fields (such as **NMAP** for nursing, and numerous education gateways).

UK Research Councils <http://www.rcuk.ac.uk/>. This links to the websites of the seven UK research councils, which fund academic research in the UK, with details of the research they fund.

CRD maintains a register of ongoing systematic reviews in the UK. Researchers can submit details of their systematic review for entry on this database <http://www.york.ac.uk/inst/crd/ongoing.htm>, which is freely available through the National Research Register <http://www.update-software.com/national/>.

The **Evidence Network** <http://www.evidencenetwork.org/> was
funded by the ESRC to contribute to evidence-informed policy in the
UK. The website provides access to full copies of reports and a bibliography of articles related to systematic reviews and evidence-based policy.
The network itself consists of a coordinating center <http://www.
evidencenetwork.org/nodes.asp>, and a series of "nodes" which carry
out research including systematic reviews and other secondary research in
a diverse range of areas, including research utilization, ethnicity and
health, public health, neighborhoods, economic evaluation, child and
social welfare, and social and economic policy. These are:

- **What works for children**: <http://www.whatworksforchildren.
  org.uk/>
- **Centre for Evidence-based Public Health Policy**: <http://
  www.msoc-mrc.gla.ac.uk/evidence/evidence.html>
- **Centre for Neighbourhood Research**: <http://www.
  neighbourhoodcentre.org.uk/>
- **Centre for Economic Evaluation**: <http://www2.warwick.ac.
  uk/fac/soc/economics/>
- **Research Unit for Research Utilisation (RURU)**: <http://
  www.st-andrews.ac.uk/~ruru/>
- **Centre for Evidence in Health, Ethnicity and Diversity**:
  <http://users.wbs.warwick.ac.uk/group/ceehd>
- **Social Policy and Social Care**: <http://www.york.ac.uk/inst/
  chp/srspsc/index.htm>
- **Centre for Economic Policy Research**: <http://www.cepr.org/
  ccepe/>

A guide to searching in the social sciences also appears on the Evidence
Network website <http://www.evidencenetwork.org/searching.asp>,
along with a related discussion paper: <http://www.evidencenetwork.
org/Documents/wp19.pdf>. The Centre has also recently launched a
wide-ranging new interdisciplinary journal, called *Evidence and Policy*:
<http://www.evidencenetwork.org/JournalOfResearch.html>.

Selected US sources

American Institutes for Research (AIR) <http://www.air.org/> is
an important source of social research, including evaluations of social

interventions in education, health, and employment among others (for example studies of the effectiveness of adult literacy training).

The **Centers for Disease Control and Prevention (CDC)** in Atlanta, Georgia, conducts and commissions research. It includes a number of National Centers focusing on (among other issues), environmental health, health promotion and education, injury prevention, epidemiology, public health practice, HIV, STD, and TB prevention. Publications are accessible through its website <http://www.cdc.gov/>. Some of the CDC systematic reviews are also available online – for example the Task Force on Community Preventive Services' systematic review of evidence on the effectiveness of firearms laws in preventing violence.[21]

The **General Accounting Office (GAO)** is the audit, evaluation, and investigative arm of the US Congress, and as such is an important source of information for reviewers. It evaluates federal programs, and provides analyses, program reviews and evaluations, and other services. The GAO database archives are available online <http://www.gao.gov/> and include full versions of published reports –"Blue books"– of evaluations of US Federal programs, from about 1993 to the present.

MDRC is an independent, non-profit, non-partisan, social policy research organization, which was set up to assemble evidence of the effectiveness and cost-effectiveness of US social programs targeting low-income individuals and families, such as education, employment, and welfare programs. It has carried out major experimental and quasi-experimental studies, along with rigorous qualitative evaluations of the impacts of those programs, and makes available the data files on which those evaluations were based. Full reports are online <http://www.mdrc.org/index.html> along with papers from its research methodology series, which covers quantitative and qualitative research methods and data analysis, and experimental and quasi-experimental methods.

National Institutes of Health (NIH): The **CRISP** (Computer Retrieval of Information on Scientific Projects) database <http://crisp.cit.nih.gov/> covers federally funded biomedical research projects conducted at US universities, hospitals, and other research institutions. It includes projects funded by NIH, the Substance Abuse and Mental Health Services (SAMHSA), the Health Resources and Services Administration (HRSA), the Food and Drug Administration (FDA), the Centers for Disease Control and Prevention (CDCP), the Agency for Health Care Research and Quality (AHRQ), and the Office of Assistant Secretary of Health (OASH).

The **Office of Policy** in the US carries out research for the US Government's Social Security Administration, exploring for example the effects

of social security, insurance, disability, retirement, and income maintenance programs. The website <http://www.ssa.gov/policy/index.html>
includes details of research from 1995 onwards, with full versions of more
recent publications, organized by subject area.

The **Urban Institute** is a not-for-profit independent research and educational organization, which carries out social and economic policy
research among other tasks. It has carried out research projects in the
areas of education, immigration, homelessness, housing, welfare, teenage
pregnancy, delinquency, and crime, among many others, including
evaluations of the national welfare-to-work programs. Full versions and
summaries of many reports are available on its website <http://www.
urban.org/>.

The **What Works Clearinghouse (WWC)** <http://www.w-w-c.
org/> acts as a central point for quality-assessed evidence on the effectiveness of educational interventions, established by the US Department of
Education's Institute of Education Sciences in 2002. It systematically
appraises studies of effectiveness, and produces evidence reports – which
involve systematic reviews – in a range of topic areas. Interventions
currently being reviewed include interventions for beginning reading,
programs for preventing high school dropout, and programs for increasing
adult literacy.

There are many other US and international organizations producing primary
studies evaluating the effectiveness of social interventions including policies,
and conducting social research of other types which may be of relevance to
social systematic reviewers. Some are listed in Boxes 4.8 to 4.13.

Theses

In the UK and Ireland the titles and abstracts of theses can be consulted at
<www.theses.com>. This includes details of all theses accepted for higher
degrees by universities in Great Britain and Ireland since 1716, which
should cover most systematic reviewers' needs (subscription required).
The thesis itself may be obtained from the University, or from the British
Library (in microfiche form). For US, Canadian, and other European theses,
the database **Dissertation Abstracts International** (http://library.dialog.
com/bluesheets/html/bl0035.html) lists titles and abstracts of theses from
1861 onwards, and full versions of more recent theses can be downloaded.
Canadian theses also appear at <http://www.collectionscanada.ca/theses

canada/index-e.html> (provided by Library and Archives Canada), and full-text is available from 1998 onwards.

The Australian Digital Theses (ADT) project: Australian theses are generally deposited at the university where the dissertation was completed and can be located via the respective university library <http://www. nla.gov.au/libraries/>, though searching for a particular topic on a library-by-library basis would be a laborious task. Be grateful, therefore, for the Australian Digital Theses (ADT) project, which aims to create a national collaborative distributed database of digitized theses produced at Australian Universities. In a similar vein, about 180 universities and institutes around the world have collaborated to produce the Networked Digital Library of Theses and Dissertations <http://www.ndltd.org/>, which covers all topic areas.

Conference proceedings

Unpublished studies may be located through indexes of conference proceedings. (Why this is important is discussed in chapter 7.) Some databases include conference proceedings if they are relevant to their topic area; for example CancerLit (produced by the National Cancer Institute of the US <http://www.nci.nih.gov/>) includes proceedings of cancer conferences. The Index of Conference Proceedings, for the truly committed scientific completist, goes back to 1787.

4.8   CITATION SEARCHING

Searching for articles which themselves cite a key reference (sometimes referred to as "pearl growing") can be a useful means of widening a search.[22] It is unlikely that, say, a major trial of interventions to reduce school bullying would not be cited by subsequently published trials, so forward searching can be a helpful adjunct to the usual searches of databases and bibliographies. This may be less useful if the cited study (the "pearl") is relatively recent, as it may take up to two years for papers citing it to get into print, and then onto electronic databases. Citation searching can be carried out in Web of Science (a "cited reference" search). Another form of citation searching involves using the index terms of retrieved articles, and searching for other papers which use the same terms. This is useful when the indexing of studies in the topic area under investigation appears to be inconsistent, and citation searching may increase the percentage of references retrieved by about a quarter.[23]

Medline and Web of Science also offer the facility to search for articles related to a selected reference. Medline does this by comparing words from the title, abstract, and subject heading (MeSH) terms from the selected reference. Web of Science uses a different approach, involving searching for references which cite at least one of the sources cited by the original article. The articles are ranked by the number of references they cite in common with the "parent" article.

4.9   CURRENT AWARENESS

While the reviewer is slaving away at a systematic review, other thoughtless researchers are not idly waiting for the conclusions, but instead are relentlessly hewing away at the coalface of science by carrying out new primary research. This means that the literature search can get out of date quite quickly in topic areas where studies are being published rapidly, given that the literature searches will often have been completed some months before the "writing-up" stage. In reality, if the search has included research registers and conference proceedings and contacts with experts, the reviewer should be aware of any important forthcoming studies, and will be keeping track of these. These should be referred to in the review and their findings included if they are completed in time, or, if not, then details of their methods, interventions, populations being studied, and outcomes can be included. Even the most public-spirited researchers are unlikely to allow a reviewer to report their findings before they have had the chance to do so themselves. It is sensible to subscribe to current awareness services such as Current Contents and Web of Science, so that details of studies of interest can be obtained automatically. Tables of contents of core journals can be obtained via journal websites and many of these offer alerting services. Other alerting services such as ZETOC, the British Library's Electronic Table of Contents service, should also be considered. Many social research organizations (such as MDRC <http://www.mdrc.org/>) also have email alerting services.

4.10   THE WEB

Searches of the web – as opposed to purposive searching of specific websites – can be a hit or miss affair. In some topic areas the gain may be marginal when compared with a thorough search of more traditional sources, but this approach may be particularly important in social science systematic reviews, as some of the most important social science research is never published in academic journals. Web-searching using search engines such as Google may uncover papers as yet unwritten, (conference presentations and the like), and unpublished literature from government-funded and other research organizations. Meta-search engines (such as <http://vivisimo.org>, and <http://www.metacrawler.com>) may also be helpful in locating this information. It is becoming common to see web searches included in the methods sections of systematic reviews.

4.11   HOW DO YOU KNOW WHEN TO STOP SEARCHING? SOME STOPPING RULES

The short answer to this question is funds, time, and logic. Quite often at the beginning of a review it is unclear just how much literature is out there, and how extensive the search should be. In reality, one can never know whether every study really has been found, because of the difficulty of proving a negative. Logic, however, would suggest that there must be a cut-off point for each search, otherwise the review would never end. "Stopping rules" are often used in trials to identify when clear evidence of benefit or harm has emerged and the trial should be stopped. However there are no hard and fast "stopping rules" for systematic reviews, though there probably should be. Chilcott et al. do in fact describe their decision about when to stop searching in just those terms.[23] They discontinued their search of a database if the yield of relevant articles fell below 1 percent, or if it failed to yield articles that were not already identified. They note, however, that such an approach would not be appropriate in a systematic review of effectiveness, where the aim is comprehensiveness, as opposed to achieving saturation. See chapter 7 for discussion of a review by Egger et al.[24] on the value of comprehensive literature searches.

In practice the stopping point may be approaching when the search has covered all the most relevant databases and bibliographies, and when further searches of databases, and scanning of bibliographies of review papers do not add to the tally of included studies. The cut-off point may therefore become clear if the yield from the searches is monitored.

The approach may vary with different types of review. For example, if a review is aiming to systematically identify and review a range of theoretical perspectives on an issue, then the concept of "saturation" may be more useful than "comprehensiveness." "Saturation" here is analogous to the concept of "theoretical saturation" employed in the analysis of qualitative data. To return to the example given by Chilcott et al., based on their methodological systematic review: "Optimally a methodological search will reach a point of data saturation, where no further perspectives or schools of thought are added by further acquisition of articles." The same principle of saturation may usefully be applied to systematic reviews of qualitative literature, and reviews of theories, methods, and models.[25]

Theoretically it is possible to identify all relevant studies for some reviews. For example, one may often be reasonably sure that all relevant large randomized controlled trials have been identified. If the search includes databases, book chapters, and large reviews, contacts with experts, conference proceedings, and funders' websites, all such studies should be identifiable. It is unlikely that further extensive searches will uncover large, hitherto unknown RCTs (though the possibility can never be ruled out). Smaller studies may be overlooked much more easily - and this is particularly true of small, **non-experimental studies**, such as surveys. In reality, one's efforts should be directed towards ensuring that all reasonable measures are taken to identify all the relevant literature, and then to estimate the likely effect of missing any relevant studies (see chapter 7).

One can run a simple check on the effectiveness of a new search strategy by listing the key studies that one would expect to identify. These studies can be identified from existing literature reviews. If the new search strategy has not identified these, then it may need revision. Perhaps studies are being overlooked because the databases have not included study abstracts, only study titles, and the search terms being used do not appear in the title of the journal article. Titles that do not describe the study purpose, design, or question certainly seem to be more common in social science areas than in clinical areas. How many reviewers searching for studies of women's experiences of visits to the gynecologist would immediately locate the paper "A funny thing happened on the way to the orifice," for instance?[26, 27] These kinds of titles make the papers (or their titles, at least) more memorable, but may also make them more difficult to locate, and more difficult to identify for inclusion in systematic reviews. This is one reason why accurate keywords are important.

4.12   HOW MANY DATABASES SHOULD ONE SEARCH?

The number of databases or other sources that one needs to search varies from topic to topic, and depends on the time and resources available. It also clearly depends on one's tolerance to the risk of missing a relevant study or studies, and one's assessment of the cost of missing it. For some clinical topics it has been shown that for comprehensive searching one needs to search a minimum of two or more databases plus hand searching selected journals.[28] Certainly no search is complete if it does not also include searching the bibliographies of a selection of key traditional reviews and major discussion papers. This may uncover studies that have not been listed in electronic databases.

4.13 KEEPING RECORDS

It is essential to keep a detailed record of how and where the studies in the review were found. This adds transparency to the review process and will help subsequent researchers identify the most efficient search strategies for finding similar studies. Also record the search terms and filters used, when the sources were searched, and (for databases) which years were included. For some journals it is also a requirement of publication that a flowchart is included to indicate how the final selection of studies was made – that is, how many titles and abstracts were identified, from what sources, and how the numbers were whittled down by applying the inclusion criteria. (See Appendices 1 to 3 for an example flowchart, and details of the QUORUM and MOOSE guidelines.) In practice, however, the search and selection of studies can often be much less linear than the flowchart implies.

4.14 1966 AND ALL THAT: HOW FAR BACK SHOULD ONE SEARCH?

The answer to this question depends on the review topic, and is best arrived at logically rather than by following hard and fast rules. If the review has the objective of assessing the effects of an intervention, and that intervention has only recently been developed, then the researcher can argue that the search should date from the publication of the first trial (or other study) assessing effectiveness, or perhaps its first use in humans. It may be worth remembering however that the intervention may have been in use (or in development) for long before the first trial was published in an academic journal, so it is best to allow a wide margin of error around the start date.

Many systematic reviews in health and related topic areas use 1966 as a start date for their searches. This is not just coincidence, or because 1966 represents any particular scientific milestone, but because until recently Medline only included articles from that date onwards. A search strategy which starts at 1966 may miss trials published after 1948, (the date the *British Medical Journal* published the first randomized clinical trial of streptomycin), and will miss any relevant studies of other designs carried out before that period. This may not always be crucial. Most interventions evolve and change, sometimes rapidly, and so do the populations and contexts in which they are evaluated. In some cases, older studies may simply not be relevant – but equally it can be important to identify earlier studies to document this change and in some cases to demonstrate consistency (or inconsistency) of effects over time. In general, there is little to be lost by searching as far back as possible and documenting any studies that were identified, and then noting whether they are to be excluded on grounds of age. Their details should be included in the review in a list of excluded studies (perhaps as an appendix). Journal referees may ask for this information. As an example, Badger et al.[27] chose 1983 as the start date for their review of the epidemiology of mentally disordered offenders, as this is the year that the UK Mental Health Act (1983) was passed. (By comparison, a systematic review on the health effects of housing renewal used 1887 – the date of the earliest study indexed on PsycLit – as a start date, because it was known that there were likely to be very early studies, which would not have been previously reviewed.)[29]

In any case, the cut-off points (that is, the start and end dates) for the search need to be decided and stated clearly in the protocol and methods section of the review, and an explanation given as to why those dates were chosen. If updating an existing good-quality systematic review, then the search obviously needs to start from the end date of that review's searches. This information should be available from the methods section of that review. It is sensible to allow some overlap. For example, if the methods section of the old review states that the literature was searched up until December 1997, then it would be sensible to begin the search from at least several months, and probably a year before that date. The added effort of sifting through an additional year of abstracts is more than offset by the added confidence that relevant studies were not overlooked.

4.15   DECIDING WHICH ARTICLES TO OBTAIN IN HARD COPY

Box 4.8 lists of some of the main databases that may be worth searching for reviews in health and related topic areas. Many may only be accessible on a subscription basis, and it should be noted that this is a selected sample out of the hundreds of databases available. It should also be noted that there are sometimes considerable overlaps between databases in terms of content. Some abstracts will appear on all of Medline, Embase, PsycINFO, and ASSIA for example. Moreover in some cases a database will include only titles, rather than titles and abstracts, making the decision about whether to order a particular paper to check for inclusion in the review more difficult. It may be tempting to order every paper that looks remotely relevant to reduce the risk of missing a relevant study, but this clearly has costs in terms of both time and money. A more (cost) efficient method is to start by ordering a selected sample of those which cannot be excluded or included on the basis of the title alone, but which look promising, to get a clearer idea of what sort of information these documents contain. This will inform subsequent decisions about ordering full copies of papers.

4.16   MANAGING THE REFERENCES

It is important to manage the results of the searches in a good bibliographic database such as Endnote, Reference Manager, or similar software. This can help with identifying duplicate entries, but more importantly it ensures that the progress and eventual fate of every paper through the review process can be tracked. Bibliographic databases also permit abstracts from online databases to be imported directly, and allow the citations to be directly inserted in the appropriate journal style into the finished report or journal article.

4.17   CONTACTS WITH EXPERTS

It can be worthwhile, and is standard systematic review practice, to contact experts working in the field in order to identify other studies they may be aware of which may have been missed by database searches. It is important to do this in a way that will maximize response and interest in the review, and minimize pressure on fellow scholars' and practitioners' email inboxes. It would be unwise (as well as unsystematic) to write to people before doing the initial searching. However, later, it can be helpful to email corresponding authors to ask whether they have published anything of relevance (or are about to) that you have not traced. Your advisory group can also be helpful in drawing your attention to literature, or even bodies of literature, you may have missed. Sometimes, scholars will be more receptive to responding to younger researchers at the start of their careers, and sometimes to peers and colleagues where a decade or two of trading favors is likely to get a result. Even if no additional studies are turned up by the experts, you will have greater confidence that you have identified all the relevant studies, and it also offers an opportunity to let other experts know that the review is under way.

The effectiveness of writing to experts in this way probably varies with the subject area. Hetherington et al.[31] contacted 42,000 obstetricians and paediatricians in 18 countries to obtain details of unpublished clinical trials, and obtained details of 395 unpublished RCTs, though only 18 of these had been completed over 2 years before the survey was carried out. In a later study McGrath et al. obtained further data in 17 percent of cases.[32] Chilcott et al. contacted experts and obtained little relevant material,[23] but noted that the process was useful in raising the review's profile, and McManus et al. found that 24 percent of references would have been missed entirely if they had not contacted experts.[2]

A systematic review has compared the additional yield from hand searching with searches of electronic databases,[33] and found that searching an electronic database using a complex search strategy would identify most trials published as full reports in English language journals, provided, of course, that the relevant journals have been indexed in the database. This finding may not apply to reviews of social interventions. One way of checking to make sure that relevant journals are picked up in the electronic searches is to check where the key journals are indexed and abstracted. Most journals have this information on their websites.[34]

4.18   SOCIAL WORK AND WELFARE DATABASES

Databases of relevance to those carrying out literature reviews in social work and social welfare are shown in Box 4.8, and some of the main databases and other sources of relevance to those carrying out systematic reviews in the area of education are listed in Box 4.9. Databases of interest to reviewers working in criminology and justice appear in Box 4.10, while Box 4.11 provides details of some sources of economic and related information. Your local librarian or information scientist should be able to advise you about access to these.

4.19   TRIALS REGISTERS

"The design of all studies should be publicly available"
(Declaration of Helsinki. Principle 16[35])

Many funders and research organizations maintain registers of trials they fund; however there is no single comprehensive source of information

Box 4.8   Selected electronic databases that cover health, social policy, and social work and related literature

(See also Taylor et al.[30] Please note that databases listed in the other boxes will also be relevant.)

Ageinfo: <http://www.cpa.org.uk/ageinfo/ageinfo2.html> Information service about old age and ageing provided by the Centre for Policy on Ageing in London (UK). It requires a subscription, but may be freely available through university or other libraries.

AIDSInfo: <http://www.aidsinfo.nih.gov/> was formed from a merger of the HIV/AIDS Clinical Trials Information Service (ACTIS) and the HIV/AIDS Treatment Information Service (ATIS).

AIDSLINE: from NLM includes citations derived from MEDLINE, POPLINE, HealthSTAR, BIOETHICSLINE, and conference and meeting abstracts.

AMED: Database of articles on Allied and Complementary Medicine (1985–present). Mainly European articles with most titles in English. Available on the Internet and on CD-ROM but NHS professionals in England and Wales can access it freely via the NHSnet.

ASSIA: Applied Social Sciences Index and Abstracts. Covers social sciences including social services, health, economics, politics, and education from about 650 English language journals (1987–present). Provided through Cambridge Scientific Abstracts' Internet Database Service.

BIOSIS: <http://www.biosis.org/> Provider of life sciences databases. Books, reports, and conference proceedings are included, and journal and non-journal material. Database and data services are also provided in the UK by **BIDs** <http://www.bids.ac.uk/> and **EDINA** http://edina.ac.uk/>.

British Education Index: <http://www.leeds.ac.uk/bei/bei.htm> Subscription database covering over 300 education and training journals published in the British Isles, including report and conference literature.

CareData: <http://www.elsc.org.uk/caredata/caredata.htm> Database of social care articles (see **eLSC**).

Cancerlit: Free on the web at <http://www.cancer.gov/> Database from the US National Cancer Institute containing more than 1.8 million citations and abstracts, including biomedical journals, proceedings, books, reports, and doctoral theses.

ChildData: (National Children's Bureau, London) <http://www.childdata.org.uk/> gives access to the NCB Library's four databases covering policy, legislation, practice, and research on children and young people. It includes details and abstracts of over 57,000 books, reports, and journal articles. By subscription.

CINAHL: <http://www.cinahl.com/prodsvcs/cinahldb.htm> Database for nursing and allied health literature (1982–present). Includes literature from biomedicine, management, behavioral sciences, health sciences, education, and consumer health.

ClinPSYC: <http://www.psycinfo.com/clinpsyc.html> a clinical subset of the PsycINFO database, concentrating on clinical literature of relevance to clinical psychology and medicine.

CommunityWISE: <http://www.oxmill.com/communitywise/> contains community, voluntary, and development studies information (including research) spanning seven databases, with data obtained from Barnardo's, the Joseph Rowntree Foundation, Community Development Foundation and the National Centre for Volunteering. Includes abstracts.

Department of Health and Human Services (US): <http://www.hhs.gov/> reference collections include links to online reports, databases, and other research information in many areas of health and welfare.

ELSC: Electronic library for social care <http://www.elsc.org.uk/>, produced by the UK's Social Care Institute for Excellence (SCIE). It includes the database **CareData** <http://www.elsc.org.uk/caredata/caredata.htm>, with titles and abstracts of social care articles.

EMBASE: <http://www.embase.com/> covers human medical and related biomedical research, including drugs and toxicology, clinical medicine, biotechnology and bioengineering, health affairs, and psychiatry. It includes data from 3,500 biomedical journals dating back to 1980.

ERIC: <http://www.eric.ed.gov/> Educational Research Information Center (funded by the US Department of Education's Institute of Education Sciences) contains more than 1 million abstracts of documents and journal articles on education research and practice (1966–present).

ETOH: <www.etoh.niaaa.nih.gov> Alcohol and Alcohol Science Database, produced by the US National Institute on Alcohol Abuse and Alcoholism, contains over 110,000 records from the 1960s to present across a wide range of subject areas of relevance to alcohol. It includes journal articles, books, dissertation abstracts, conference papers and proceedings, reports and studies, and book chapters.

(*Continued*)

Box 4.8   *(Cont'd)*

HMIC: (Health Management Information Consortium) <http://www.ovid.com/site/index.jsp> A database comprising three different databases: **DH Data** (the UK Department of Health Library and Information Services' Database), **King's Fund Database** (1979–), and **HELMIS** (Health Management Information Service) produced by the Nuffield Institute for Health. Together these cover health policy, health services management, health inequalities, health and social care services, health economics, among others. Mainly UK and European literature. Subscription-based.

HSTAT: <http://www.nlm.nih.gov/pubs/factsheets/hstat.html> Free database from NLM offering access to health-care and health technology assessment documents, including guidelines and health technology evaluations, and links to other databases, including **PubMed**.

International Bibliography of the Social Sciences: <http://www.lse.ac.uk/collections/IBSS/> (1951–present), a huge database indexing social science literature from journals, books, and book chapters, including non-English language literature.

LexisNexis: <http://www.lexisnexis.com/> US Legal and business database, including newspapers, company reports and financial information and public records.

LILACS   <http://www.unifesp.br/suplem/cochrane/lilacs.htm> Index of Latin American and Caribbean healthcare literature, which indexes 670 journals and produces abstracts in English, Spanish, and Portuguese, and has little overlap with Medline.

Medline: This is the main international biomedical database, and is the electronic equivalent of *Index Medicus, Index to Dental Literature*, and the *International Nursing Index* (1966–present). About 40,000 new abstracts are added monthly. **PubMed** <http://www.ncbi.nlm.nih.govquery.fcgi> includes Medline citations as well as citations from other life sciences journals, and includes **OLDMEDLINE** (citations from biomedical journals from 1953–65).

National Clearinghouse on Child Abuse and Neglect Information (US): <http://nccanch.acf.hhs.gov/index.cfm> Online database of publications produced by the Clearinghouse and other organizations and selected records from ERIC. See also the US Department of Health and Human Services Administration for Children and Families webpage <http://www.acf.hhs.gov/index.html>, which has links to online publications, bibliographies, and databases.

National Childcare Information Center Online Library: <http://128.174.128.220/cgi-bin/nccic/searchnccic.cgi>

Nutrition Abstracts and Review Series A: Human and Experimental: <http://www.cabi-publishing.org/AbstractDatabases.asp?Subject Area=&PID=79> Human nutrition research from international journals, books, and conference proceedings.

OSH-ROM: <http://www.rose-net.co.ir/products/PRODUCTS1/SP/oshrom.htm> is a collection of bibliographic databases covering occupational health and environmental medicine: includes **CISDOC** (International Occupational Safety and Health Information Center of the International Labor Organisation (ILO) Geneva), **HSELINE** from the UK Health and Safety Executive, **NIOSHTIC** from the National Institute of Occupational Safety and Health (NIOSH) Technical Information Center (USA), and the **MEDLINE** Occupational and Environmental Medicine subset, among others.

POPLINE: <http://db.jhuccp.org/popinform/basic.html> population information database, from the Johns Hopkins University Center for Communication Programs (JHU/CCP) Population Information Program. Includes citations on population, family planning, reproductive health, and breastfeeding.

PsycINFO: Database produced by the American Psychological Association which includes over 1,300 journals from psychology and related disciplines including medicine, psychiatry, nursing, sociology, education, pharmacology, physiology, linguistics, and other areas (1887–present). It also includes book chapters. **PsycLit** is a sub-set of PsycINFO.

Sociofile: (see also Sociological Abstracts, below) this database contains sociological abstracts from about 2,000 journals (1974–present). It includes abstracts of articles published in Sociological Abstracts, as well as books and book chapters.

Sociological abstracts (formerly Sociofile) <http://www.csa.com/csa/factsheets/socioabs.shtml> a database of abstracts from sociology and behavioral sciences, from Cambridge Scientific Abstracts. Includes books, book chapters, dissertations, and conference papers.

Social Sciences Citation Index: <http://www.isinet.com/products/citation/ssci/> Database of abstracts and cited references from over 1,700 social science journals, including anthropology, criminology, education, social work, health, ethics, nursing, transport, and others. See also **International Bibliography of the Social Sciences**.

(Continued)

Box 4.8   *(Cont'd)*

Social Services Abstracts: <http://www.csa.com/csa/factsheets/socserv.shtml> Covers social work, human services, social welfare, social policy, and community development, abstracted from over 1,406 serials publications. Includes dissertations.

Social Work Abstracts: <http://www.naswpress.org/publications/journals/abstracts/swabintro.html> Produced in the US by the National Association of Social Workers; contains abstracts from over 400 US and international journals. NASW available on CD-ROM and the Internet through SilverPlatter.

SPORTDiscus: <http://www.sportdiscus.com> sport, fitness, and sports medicine bibliographic database of articles, theses, and dissertations (1975–present).

Box 4.9   Databases of relevance to educational researchers

Note that some of the databases listed in previous boxes (such as Medline, CCTR, PsycINFO, ASSIA and others) will also be of relevance, but other sources of information include the following:

Research into Higher Education Abstracts 1980: <http://www.tandf.co.uk/journals/titles/00345326.asp> has a UK and British Commonwealth and European focus but with some US literature. Produced on behalf of the Society for Research into Higher Education <http://www.srhe.ac.uk/>

Higher Education Abstracts: <http://highereducationabstracts.org/> (published by The Claremont Graduate University), has a US focus and is a compilation of abstracts of journal articles, conference papers, research reports, and books relating to higher education. It includes publications from professional organizations, government agencies, and foundations. It also includes Canadian and other English language material.

Educational research abstracts (ERA): <http://www.tandf.co.uk/era/> Large database of abstracts of international research in education.

Current Index to Journals in Education (CIJE) and Resources In Education: index articles from 750 educational and related journals; these are obtainable through ERIC (above).

Multicultural Education Abstracts: <http://www.tandf.co.uk/journals/titles/02609770.asp> (Carfax Publishing). Abstracts are included in the ERA database.

The EPPI Centre: <http://eppi.ioe.ac.uk/EPPIWeb/home. aspx?& page=/reel/databases.htm> website provides access to several databases including REEL, a database of references in education, and a database of research into personal development planning (PDP), as well as systematic reviews carried out by the EPPI Centre reviews and review groups).

Other sources include the National Clearing House for Bilingual Education (NCBE) <http://www.ntlclearing.qpg.com/> database and numerous gateways: a list of links to other research resources including databases is provided at <http://www.library.uiuc.edu/edx/eleced.htm>

Sociology of Education Abstracts: Abstracts are included in ERA database.

Special Educational Needs Abstracts includes abstracts of journal articles, and conference papers, reports, and theses. These abstracts are included in the ERA database.

Box 4.10   Selected databases of relevance to criminology and justice

The US NCJRS Abstracts Database (National Criminal Justice Reference Service) <http://www.ncjrs.org/> contains titles and abstracts of more than 180,000 criminal justice publications and is freely searchable online. (Searches of the NCJRS Virtual Library are also available via this link – this permits searches of the NCJRS website and the websites of the agencies of the US Department of Justice, Office of Justice Programs and the White House Office of National Drug Control Policy <http://fulltextpubs.ncjrs.org/content/FullTextPubs.html>.

(Continued)

Box 4.10 (Cont'd)

Criminal Justice Abstracts indexes published and unpublished literature (including dissertations, government reports, books, and unpublished papers) on crime prevention and control, juvenile delinquency and juvenile justice, policing, courts and the legal system, punishment and sentencing, and victimology. It is available through CSA <http://www.csa.com> and SilverPlatter <http://www.silverplatter.com/catalog/cjab.htm>.

LMS Bibliographic Database: <http://www.unicri.it/bibliographic_database.htm> United Nations database of international research in crime and justice.

The **Australian Domestic and Family Violence Clearinghouse** <http://www.austdvclearinghouse.unsw.edu.au/> provides a central source for Australian research and practice on domestic and family violence. Its website includes two databases, one containing details of Australian research in the area, the other (The Good Practice database) containing details of over 110 past and present programs.

Box 4.11 Additional sources of economic and related information

CHEPA: Centre for Health Economics and Policy Analysis: <http://www.chepa.org/home/default.asp> Based at McMaster University in Canada, mainly focused on healthcare and health services. Includes a database of publications and working papers.

Econlit: <http://www.econlit.org/> Database of international economic literature, with abstracts, produced by the American Economic Association (AEA).

HEED: <http://www.ohe-heed.com/> is produced by the Office of Health Economics and includes details of economic evaluations of medicines and other treatments and medical interventions.

NHS EED: (NHS Economic Evaluation Database) <http://agatha.york.ac.uk/nhsdhp.htm> is a freely searchable online database containing economic evaluations of healthcare interventions, identified from hand searching and electronic searches, each with a commentary on the study.

Labordoc: <http://www.ilo.org/public/english/support/lib/labor doc/> is the International Labor Office (ILO) Library's searchable online database of its international collection of books, reports, journals, and documents relating to work. It also includes references to journal articles, documents, and much unpublished material, many with abstracts.

REPEC: <http://repec.org/> Research papers in economics: Database of working papers, journal articles, links and software.

World Bank: <www.worldbank.org> Grimshaw [19] suggests that the World Bank website is a valuable source of research studies on development. It includes databases of abstracts and full working papers.

Independent research organizations such as the **US National Bureau of Economic Research** based in New York and Stanford <http:// www.nber.org/> and the **Institute for Fiscal Studies** (IFS) in the UK <http://www.ifs.org.uk/index.shtml> publish working papers and other documents pertaining to social policy, welfare and health, and health inequalities, as does the **London School of Economics** <http://www.lse.ac.uk/>.

Other literature can be accessed directly though the websites of individual organizations (such as the **Institute of Health Economics** <http://www.ihe.ab.ca/>, the Health Economics Resource Centre at the University of York, England <http://www.york.ac.uk/res/ herc/>, and the **Office of Health Economics,** <http://www. ohe.org/>).

about ongoing trials in any topic area (including healthcare).[36] The US has its own register <http://www.clinicaltrials.gov> and in the UK the Medical Research Council and the NHS Research and Development Programme contribute to a meta-register of controlled trials <http:// www.controlled-trials.com>.[37] There is increasing pressure on researchers to ensure that all trials are prospectively registered, by obtaining a unique International Standard Randomized Controlled Trial Number (ISRCTN) from the above site. This ensures that once a trial is initiated it cannot subsequently be lost from view. This is known to be an important source of bias in systematic reviews. Prospective registration also makes it easier for subsequent systematic reviewers (and others) to unambiguously identify trials that are reported in multiple publications. Research registers (many of which include non-trial research), and links to organizations that fund social research are listed in Box 4.12.

As noted previously, do not neglect to search databases of existing systematic reviews (such as DARE, REEL, and the databases and websites of the Cochrane and Campbell Collaborations) as appropriate. Box 4.13 lists some other possible information sources.

Box 4.12 Trials registers and research registers

CCTR: Cochrane Controlled Trials Register: This is the world's largest database of controlled trials, and is searchable as part of the Cochrane Library, which is available on CD and should be available at any university or health library.

Clinicaltrials.gov (US Clinical trials register): <http://www.clinical trials.gov/> Database of information on federally and privately supported clinical trials for a wide range of diseases and conditions.

CRiB (Current Research in Britain): Database of research being carried out at British academic and other research institutions. Includes **NOD** (Nederlandse Onderzoek Databank), the Dutch Current Research Database. Covers physical and biological sciences, Social Sciences and Humanities. Available in paper and CD-ROM versions.

HSRProj (Health Services Research Projects in Progress): <http://www.nlm.nih.gov/pubs/factsheets/hsrproj.html> US database of ongoing grants and contracts in health services research, awarded by public and private funding agencies and foundations.

ISRCTN Register: <http://www.controlled-trials.com/> Database of randomized controlled trials with an International Standard Randomized Controlled Trial Number (ISRCTN).

NHMRC: <http://www.ctc.usyd.edu.au/trials/registry/registry. htm> in Australia runs a national cancer trials registry (restricted access), and is collaborating with the Perinatal Society of Australia and New Zealand in the establishment of a perinatal trials registry <http://www.ctc.usyd.edu.au/6registry/impact2.htm>.

PDQ (Physician Data Query): <http://www.cancer.gov/cancer-info/pdq/cancerdatabase> is the National Cancer Institute's database of cancer clinical trials, covering cancer treatment, screening, prevention, genetics, and supportive care, and complementary and alternative medicine; includes a registry of approximately 15,000 US and international trials.

C2-SPECTR: This is an international web-based register of randomized controlled trials (RCTs) and possible RCTs in the social, behavioral, criminological, and education sciences. It is compiled by the Campbell Collaboration <http://www.campbellcollaboration.org>.[38]

Federal Research in Progress (FEDRIP): <http://www.nisc.com/factsheets/qfdr.asp> information about ongoing federally funded projects in the US in the physical sciences, engineering, and life sciences. Records contributed by (among others) the Federal Highway Administration, the Departments of Agriculture and Veterans Affairs, and the National Institutes of Health (from the CRISP database).

HERO: Higher Education and Research Opportunities in the UK <http://www.hero.ac.uk/> includes extensive information on UK research funding with links to UK and other funders.

Meta-register of controlled trials (MRCT): <http://www.controlled-trials.com/> International database combining registers of ongoing randomized controlled trials in all areas of healthcare. (Includes the Association of the British Pharmaceutical Industry voluntary register of clinical trials). Also includes MRC-sponsored clinical trials.

Regard: <http://www.regard.ac.uk> Database of ESRC-funded research, including abstracts of journal articles arising from ESRC projects.

UKCCCR: <http://www.ctu.mrc.ac.uk/ukcccr/register.html> UK National Register of Cancer Trials (held at the MRC Clinical Trials Unit in London, UK).

Unreported trials register: <http://www.ncehr-cnerh.org/english/communique2/Negative.html> Editors of nearly 100 international medical journals have called an unreported trial amnesty: the "Medical Editors Trial Amnesty." Unreported trials can be notified to the BMJ.

(Continued)

Box 4.12   *(Cont'd)*

Other sources of information

The **Canadian Institutes of Health Research (CIHR)** <http:// www.cihr-irsc.gc.ca/e/193.shtml> maintain an online database The websites of the 13 institutes that make up the CIHR are accessible through this gateway. These detail research in the areas of aboriginal people's health, ageing, population and public health, gender and health, and policy research, and human development, child, and youth health (among others).
The **Canadian Health Services Research Foundation (CHSRF)**: <http://www.chsrf.ca/home_e.php> funds management and policy research in health services and nursing, and details of past and current research appear on its home page, including research reports and useful links to other Canadian, Australian, and other international resources <http://www.chsrf.ca/links/databases_e.php>.

4.20   HAND SEARCHING

Hand searching journals is often seen as essential, because electronic searches depend on the studies being indexed correctly in the databases, and errors in

Box 4.13   Other possible information sources

Geographical abstracts: <http://www1.elsevier.com/homepage/ sah/spd/site/locate_geobase.html> Human Geography part of the GEOBASE database, which itself includes published and unpublished international literature from geography, ecology, and related fields.
International Development Abstracts: <http://www1.elsevier. com/homepage/sah/spd/site/locate_geobase.html> cover agriculture and rural development; environment and development; industrial policy; social policies such as health, housing, and education; health, gender and culture; aid, international relations, and politics. Part of GEOBASE.

Leisure, Recreation and Tourism Abstracts: <http://www.leisur
etourism.com/Abstracts/index.asp> which also cover travel, transport, and social inclusion issues.

Studies on Women and Gender Abstracts: <http://www.tandf.
co.uk/journals/titles/1467596x.asp> focuses on education, employment, women in the family and community, medicine and health,
female sex and gender role socialization, social policy, the social
psychology of women, and other issues. Includes empirical research
studies.

African Studies Companion: A guide to information sources can be
found at http://www.africanstudiescompanion.com/intro.shtml.

British Humanities Index: Wide coverage, including education,
economics, the environment, gender studies, religion; list of contributing journals can be found at <http://www.csa.com/csa/fact
sheets/bhi.shtml>.

The list of social science information sources and databases is extensive and being extended continually. An excellent UK guide on how
to find information in the social sciences is available.[19]

Qualitative data

DIPEx: <http://www.dipex.org> the Database of Interviews on
Patient Experience is potentially an important resource for narrative
data (and analysis) of patient experience of health problems and
treatments/services. The website includes video, audio, and written
clips from each interview, while the DIPEx research group at the
Dept of Primary Health Care, University of Oxford, has a growing
collection of full narrative interviews copyrighted for use in research,
teaching, and broadcasting which they will share with other research
groups in return for a small contribution to the charity.

indexing are common. This is because it is sometimes difficult for those
writing and coding the abstracts on electronic databases to determine the
appropriate keywords to assign to the study – particularly as authors themselves are sometimes unclear when describing issues such as study design. If a
study's title, abstract, and index terms or keywords are not informative or
are inaccurate, it may be missed by electronic searches. Hand searching –

checking by hand the contents of key journals in the field – allows reviewers to be sure that they have picked up all relevant studies. If it is not clear which journals need to be hand searched, the database SERLINE, which provides details of health and related journals, may be useful. Badger et al.[27] found in their review in the field of education that some key British journals were not included in electronic databases and had to be searched by hand, and pointed out that some databases of interest existed only in printed form (for example, *Criminology, Penology,* and *Police Science Abstracts*). Although the need for hand searching in healthcare reviews has been well demonstrated, there is less research in other areas. One recent study however has shown that in systematic reviews of education 26 percent of studies were located by hand searching alone, and 57 percent through searches of commercial databases alone (such as ERIC, ASSIA, and PsycInfo).[39] A recent systematic review of trials of hand searching has suggested that this method is likely to find a higher proportion of RCTs than searches of electronic databases.[40]

4.21 AN EXAMPLE OF A COMPREHENSIVE LITERATURE SEARCH: EXPERIMENTS IN CRIME REDUCTION

Anthony Petrosino is a member of the Crime and Justice Group of the Campbell Collaboration, which carries out systematic reviews of the effects of crime reduction interventions. Petrosino's best-known systematic review is an evaluation of "Scared Straight" and similar programs. These interventions aim to scare at-risk or actual delinquent children from a life of crime, by exposing them to aggressive presentations about life in prison, presented by inmates. The review aimed to synthesize all previous randomized controlled trials evaluating the effectiveness of this intervention in reducing offending. Some of the key decisions the authors made in their search, and the impact this had on their review, are described in a 1995 paper "The hunt for experimental reports."[41] The considerable lengths they went to when they updated and extended their Campbell Collaboration review are outlined in Box 4.14.

4.22 WHAT HAPPENS NEXT? SIFTING THROUGH THE EVIDENCE

Having carried out the searches and collated them in a database, the reviewer must screen the titles and abstracts in order to identify those studies

Box 4.14   Scared straight: The hunt for randomized reports of a crime reduction intervention in juveniles[42]

First, randomized experiments were identified from a previous larger review of trials in crime reduction.[43] This identified more than 300 randomized experiments by means of (1) hand searching (i.e., visually inspecting the entire contents) of 29 leading criminology or social science journals; (2) checking the citations reported in the *Registry of Randomized Experiments in Criminal Sanctions*;[44] (3) electronic searches of Criminal Justice Abstracts, Sociological Abstracts and Social Development and Planning Abstracts (Sociofile), Education Resource Information Clearinghouse (ERIC) and Psychological Abstracts (Psyc-INFO); (4) searches of 18 bibliographic databases; (5) letters soliciting information were sent to over 200 researchers and 100 research centers; (6) solicitations were published in association newsletters; and (7) tracking of references in over 50 relevant systematic reviews and literature syntheses; and in relevant bibliographies, books, articles, and other documents. Seven randomized trials were found this way.

Second, the Campbell Collaboration Social, Psychological, Educational & Criminological Trials Register (C2-SPECTR) was searched; there was also a check of citations from more recent systematic or traditional reviews to provide coverage of more recent studies; citation checking of documents relevant to "Scared Straight" and like programs; email correspondence with investigators; and searches of the Cochrane Controlled Trials Register (CCTR).

Third, 12 relevant electronic databases for published and unpublished literature (including dissertations and government reports) were searched. The bibliographic databases and the years searched were:

Criminal Justice Abstracts, 1968–September 2001
Current Contents, 1993–2001
Dissertation Abstracts, 1981–August 2001
Education Full Text, June 1983–October 2001
ERIC (Education Resource Information Clearinghouse) 1966–2001
GPO Monthly (Government Printing Office Monthly), 1976–2001
MEDLINE 1966–2001

(Continued)

Box 4.14   *(Cont'd)*

National Clearinghouse on Child Abuse and Neglect (through 2001)
NCJRS (National Criminal Justice Reference Service) –2001
Political Science Abstracts, 1975–March 2001
PAIS International (Public Affairs Information Service), 1972–October 2001
PsycINFO (Psychological Abstracts) 1987–November 2001
Social Sciences Citation Index, February 1983–October 2001
Sociofile (Sociological Abstracts and Social Planning and Development Abstracts) January 1963–September 2001

that appear to meet the review's inclusion criteria. It is usually seen as best practice for two reviewers to do this. If the review is large, thousands of abstracts may need to be sifted in this fashion. The systematic review of mentally disordered offenders referred to earlier in this chapter by Badger and colleagues identified about 10,000 titles from the searches, which the reviewers reduced to 2,500 by reading the titles.[27] Where resources are restricted, a second reviewer will screen a sample – perhaps 10 percent of the titles and abstracts – to ensure that studies are not missed, or the inclusion/exclusion criteria misapplied. If the search has been very non-specific, and has retrieved a very large number of entirely non-relevant studies (that is studies where there is no uncertainty about their exclusion) – these can be excluded by one reviewer alone. While it can take two reviewers several weeks to double-screen several thousand titles and abstracts, an experienced reviewer can remove the clearly irrelevant studies and duplicates in a day or two, leaving a subset of studies to be screened by two reviewers. A sample of these excluded studies can then be examined by a second reviewer to check that this process is working, and that no babies are being accidentally thrown out with the bathwater.

Whatever method is adopted, it is important to ensure that excluded studies are not permanently deleted – it will probably be necessary to return to the original database more than once to check the number of "hits," or to search it for additional studies – for example if, as sometimes happens, the inclusion/exclusion criteria change in the course of the review (as described in chapter 2), or to reply to referees' or readers' queries about the implications of rejecting certain subsets of studies.

Similarly, each paper that is ordered for possible inclusion in the review will need to be read carefully to identify whether it really meets the inclusion criteria, and again it is best for two people to do this, working independently and keeping note of the number of papers on which they agree and disagree. Some journals also require reviewers to report **Kappa test** statistics to show the level of agreement.

Having decided on the studies that meet the inclusion criteria and that need to be reviewed in detail, the reviewer next needs to tabulate each included study. The table should contain details of the study design, setting, number of participants, length of follow-up, and the main findings of the study. This information is sometimes extracted from each article onto a data extraction form, to ensure that relevant information is not missed and to ensure accuracy; an example is given in Appendix 4. This process is discussed in more detail in the next two chapters.

Key learning points from this chapter

- Searches of electronic databases alone will not identify all relevant studies.
- Both published and unpublished (gray) literature should be sought.
- Bibliographies of review papers are a valuable source of studies.
- For reviews of the impacts of policies, a wide range of methodological terms should be considered to ensure that quasi-experimental and other non-randomized studies are retrieved.
- Searching for qualitative studies requires special methods, and may require "snowballing" – using retrieved studies to identify other qualitative studies in the same area.

REFERENCES

1. Smith, R. Doctors information: Excessive, crummy, and bent. *British Medical Journal* 1997, 315: 13, online at: http://bmj.bmjjournals.com/cgi/content/full/315/7109/0
2. McManus, R., Wilson, S., Delaney, B., Fitzmaurice, D., Hyde, C., Tobias, R., et al. Review of the usefulness of contacting other experts when conducting a literature search for systematic reviews. *British Medical Journal* 1998, 317: 1562–3.

3. Chalmers, I., Dickersin, K., and Chalmers, T. Getting to grips with Archie Cochrane's agenda. *British Medical Journal* 1992, 305: 786–8.

4. Thomson, H,, Petticrew, M., and Morrison, D. Housing interventions and health – a systematic review. *British Medical Journal* 2001, 323: 187–90.

5. Sheldon, T. *An evidence-based resource in the social sciences,* Report of a scoping study for the Economic and Social Research Council (ESRC), 1998.

6. Glanville, J. Identification of research. In K. Khan, G. ter Riet, J. Glanville, A. Sowden, and J. Kleijnen (eds.) *Undertaking systematic reviews of research on effectiveness: CRD's guidance for carrying out or commissioning reviews*: York: CRD, University of York, online at: http://www.york.ac.uk/inst/crd/report4.htm, 2001.

7. *Searching for the best evidence in clinical journals.* Oxford: Centre for Evidence-Based Medicine, online at: http://www.cebm.net/

8. Egan, M., Petticrew, M., Hamilton, V., and Ogilvie, D. Health impacts of new roads: A systematic review. *American Journal of Public Health* 2003, 93(9): 1463–71.

9. Wentz, R., Roberts, I., Bunn, F., Edwards, P., Kwan, I., and Lefebvre, C. Identifying controlled evaluation studies of road safety interventions: Searching for needles in a haystack. *Journal of Safety Research* 2001, 32(3): 267–76.

10. Boynton, J., Glanville, J., McDaid, D., and Lefebvre, C. Identifying systematic reviews in MEDLINE: Developing an objective approach to search strategy design. *Journal of Information Science* 1998, 24: 137–57.

11. Armstrong, C. and Wheatley, A. Writing abstracts for online databases: Results of an investigation of database producers' guidelines. *Program* 1998, 32: 359–71.

12. A useful glossary of information science terms appears at: http://www.fact-index.com/i/in/information_science_glossary_of_terms.html

13 McDonald, S., Lefebvre, C., Antes, G., Galandi, D., Gøetsche, P., Hammar-quist, C., et al. The contribution of handsearching European general health care journals to the Cochrane Controlled Trials Register. *Evaluation & the Health Professions* 2002, 25: 65–75.

14. Lefebvre, C. and Clarke, M. Identifying randomised trials. In M. Egger, G. Davey Smith, and D. Altman (eds.) *Systematic reviews in health care: Meta-analysis in context.* London: BMJ, 2001.

15. Evans, D. Database searches for qualitative research. *Journal of the Medical Library Association* 2002, 90: 290–3.

16. Shaw, R., Booth, A., Sutton, A., Miller, T., Smith, J., Young, B., et al. Finding qualitative research: An evaluation of search strategies. *BMC Medical Research Methodology* 2004, 4, online (free) at: http://www.biomedcentral.com/1471-2288/4/5

17. Hawker, S., Payne, S., Kerr, C., Hardey, M., and Powell, J. Appraising the evidence: Reviewing disparate data systematically. *Qualitative Health Research* 2002, 12: 1284–99.

18. Booth, A. Cochrane or cock-eyed? How should we conduct systematic reviews of qualitative research? Qualitative Evidence-Based Practice Conference, Coventry University, May 14-16, 2001, online at: http://www.leeds.ac.uk/educol/documents/00001724.htm, 2001.

19. Grimshaw, J. *How to find information: Social sciences.* London: British Library, 2000.

20. McCormick, F. and Renfrew, M. E. *MIRIAD, The Midwifery Research Database, A sourcebook of information about research in midwifery,* 2nd edn. Hale: Books for Midwives Press, 1996.

21. Hahn, R., Bilukha, O., Crosby, A., Fullilove, M., Liberman, A., Moscicki, E., et al. First reports evaluating the effectiveness of strategies for preventing violence: Firearms laws. Findings from the Task Force on Community Preventive Services. *Morbidity and Mortality Weekly Report* 2003, 52: 11–20.

22. Hartley, R., Keen, R., Large, J., and Tedd, L. *Online searching: Principles and practice.* London: Bowker-Saur, 1990.

23. Chilcott, J., Brennan, A., Booth, A., Karnon, J., and Tappenden, P. The role of modelling in prioritising and planning clinical trials. *Health Technology Assessment* 2003, 7, online at: http://www.hta.nhsweb.nhs.uk/htapubs.htm

24. Egger, M., Jüni, P., Bartlett, C., Holenstein, F., and Sterne, J. How important are comprehensive literature searches and the assessment of trial quality in systematic reviews? *Health Technology Assessment* 2003, 7, online at: http://www.hta.nhsweb.nhs.uk/htapubs.htm

25. Alderson, P., Green, S., and Higgins, J. (eds.) *Cochrane Reviewers' Handbook 4.2.2 [updated March 2004].* In *The Cochrane Library,* Issue 1, 2004. Chichester, UK: John Wiley & Sons, Ltd.

26. Scully, D. and Bart, P. A funny thing happened on the way to the orifice. *American Journal of Sociology* 1973, 78: 1045–50.

27. Badger, D., Nursten, P., Williams, P., and Woodward, M.. Should all literature reviews be systematic? *Evaluation and Research in Education* 2000, 14: 220–30.

28. Suarez-Almazor, M., Belseck, E., Homik, J., Dorgan, M., and Ramos-Remus, C. Identifying clinical trials in the medical literature with electronic databases: MEDLINE alone is not enough. *Controlled Clinical Trials* 2000, 21: 476–87.

29. Thomson, H., Petticrew, M., and Morrison, D. Health effects of housing improvement: Systematic review of intervention studies. *British Medical Journal* 2001, 323: 187–90.

30. Taylor, B., Dempster, M., and Donnelly, M. Hidden gems: Systematically searching electronic databases for research publications for social work and social care. *British Journal of Social Work* 2003, 33: 423–39.

31. Hetherington, J., Dickersin, K., Chalmers, I., and Meinert, C. Retrospective and prospective identification of unpublished controlled trials: Lessons from a survey of obstetricians and pediatricians. *Pediatrics* 1989, 84: 374–80.

32. McGrath, J., Davies, G., and Soares, K. Writing to authors of systematic reviews elicited further data in 17% of cases. *British Medical Journal* 1998, 316: 631.

33. Hopewell, S., Clarke, M., Lefebvre, C., and Scherer, R. Handsearching versus electronic searching to identify reports of randomized trials (Cochrane Methodology Review). In *The Cochrane Library*, Issue 2, 2004. Chichester, UK: John Wiley & Sons, Ltd.

34. Hamilton, V. Personal communication, May 2005.

35. Declaration of Helsinki, online at: http://www.wma.net/e/policy/b3.htm, 1964.

36. Manheimer, E. and Anderson, D. Survey of public information about ongoing clinical trials funded by industry: Evaluation of completeness and accessibility. *British Medical Journal* 2002, 325: 528–31.

37. Tonks, A. A clinical trials register for Europe. *British Medical Journal* 2002, 325: 1314–15.

38. Turner, H., Boruch, R., Petrosino, A., Lavenberg, J., De Moya, D., and Rothstein, H. Populating an international web-based randomized trials register in the social, behavioral, criminological, and education sciences. *Annals of the American Academy of Political and Social Science* 2003, 589: 203–23.

39. Rees, R., Potter, S., and Penn, H. Searching for studies of the outcomes of education: A bibliometric study. XI Cochrane Colloquium: Evidence, health care, and culture, Barcelona, 2003.

40. Hopewell, S., Clarke, M., Lefebvre, C., and Scherer, R. Handsearching versus electronic searching to identify reports of randomized trials (Cochrane Methodology Review). In *The Cochrane Library*, Issue 2, 2004. Chichester, UK: John Wiley & Sons, Ltd.

41. Petrosino, A. The hunt for experimental reports: Document search and efforts for a "What works?" meta-analysis. *Journal of Crime and Justice* 1995, 18: 63–80.

42. Petrosino, A., Turpin-Petrosino, C., and Buehler, J. "Scared Straight" and other juvenile awareness programs for preventing juvenile delinquency. *The Cochrane Library*, Issue 2, 2004. Oxford: Update Software, 2004.

43. Petrosino, A. What works revisited again: A meta-analysis of randomized experiments in delinquency prevention, rehabilitation, and deterrence. Doctoral dissertation. Rutgers University (New Jersey, USA): University Microfilms Inc., 1997.

44. Weisburd, D., Sherman, L., Petrosino, A. *Registry of randomized experiments in criminal sanctions, 1950–1983*. Los Altos, CA: Sociometics Corporation, Data Holdings of the National Institute of Justice, 1990.

Chapter 5

How to appraise the studies: An introduction to assessing study quality

5.1 INTRODUCTION

If synthesizing evidence is like assembling a jigsaw, then most of the preceding chapters have been about finding the pieces – in this case, the individual studies. In the next stage, each individual piece is examined critically to determine whether it really is part of the picture, and where to place it (if anywhere) – and to find out how it fits with other pieces (if at all). In the context of a systematic review, this involves determining whether any of the individual studies are affected by significant bias, as this may affect the weight to place on them when it comes to putting the whole picture together. This involves assessing whether the study is representative of the wider population, whether the numbers add up (for a quantitative study), and whether the study was affected by problems or other events that might affect your interpretation of its results.

The process of assessing the methods and results of each study is often referred to as critical appraisal, and sometimes as "assessing study quality." In a systematic review, this exercise aims to determine whether the study is adequate for answering the question. Research evidence can be produced by a wide range of methods and approaches, and some of it is produced by studies, which for reasons of cost, practicality, or accident will be subject to some degree of systematic error (bias). For example, in the case of trials, some participants enrolled at the start of a study later refuse to take part, and their outcomes may remain unknown (though research tells us that their outcomes are likely to be worse than among those who stayed in the study). Similarly in surveys, a large percentage of people will not respond. In each of these cases the non-responders will often differ systematically from the responders. Some of the difficulty with interpreting social (and other) research is due to such biases, but it can also be due to non-reporting of essential information by the study authors. This is the case not only in large-scale quantitative research, but also in studies aimed at collecting qualitative data, where too little information on the context, methods, analysis, and background to the study may be presented by authors to allow the data to be interpreted meaningfully.

The effect of bias

It is clear that particular methodological biases may affect the results of the study. They have been shown in some cases to be a common source of inflated estimates of effect size, for instance. This finding is the basis of Rossi's Iron Law of Evaluation,[1] which implies that simply including all studies in a systematic review without taking this into account will lead to a biased review. This is a strong argument against "vote counting" reviews – those which count the number of studies with positive findings, and those with negative findings (see chapter 6).[2] If biased studies do indeed overestimate effects, then this increases the risk that the review will falsely reject the null hypothesis. The review will then conclude that an intervention is effective, when it is not.

The list of potential research biases in quantitative studies is long. Sackett identified over 30 biases to which case-control studies alone were suscep-tible.[3] It has been suggested that there are three important biases to which randomized controlled trials are particularly subject: lack of **blinding, attri-tion bias**, and inadequate randomization.[4] (See: http://www.bmjpg.com/rct/chapter4.html for a readable summary of the issue of bias in RCTs.) Although other criteria should be considered when appraising an RCT (for example, the extent to which the study is representative of the users of the intervention), these are the three criteria that have been explored most extensively (see section 5.12). As described later in the chapter, critical appraisal questions for qualitative studies have also been suggested.[5]

5.2   NON-REPORTING BY AUTHORS: WHEN NO NEWS ISN'T ALWAYS GOOD NEWS

Critically appraising a study is often made difficult because too little informa-tion is presented. In such situations it is common practice for reviewers to contact the original authors for additional information, and occasionally to request access to the original data (for example, in order to perform meta-analysis on the individual-level data).[6, 7] Contacting the author for verification of study details avoids confusing inadequate reporting with a poor-quality study.

Huwiler-Müntener et al. examined this issue in a review of 60 RCTs, in which they analyzed the association between a quantitative measure of reporting quality,[8, 9] and various indicators of methodological quality. They concluded that reporting quality *is* associated with methodological quality, but that similar quality of reporting may hide important differences in methodological quality, and that even well-conducted trials may be reported badly. This led them to suggest that a distinction be made between the quality of reporting and the methodological quality of trials.[10]

5.3   WHAT IS STUDY QUALITY?

Study quality means different things to different people working in different disciplines. For those doing systematic reviews, assessing study quality is often used as a shorthand to mean "internal validity" – that is, the extent to which a study is free from the main methodological biases (such as **selection bias**, response bias, attrition bias, and observer bias). Jadad,[11] for example, suggests that the following items may be relevant to assessing the quality of trials:

- the relevance of the research question;
- the internal validity of the trial (the degree to which the trial design, conduct, analysis, and presentation have minimized or avoided biased comparisons of the interventions under evaluation);
- the **external validity** (the precision and extent to which it is possible to generalize the results of the trial to other settings);
- the appropriateness of data analysis and presentation; and
- the ethical implications of the intervention they evaluate.

By comparison, a recent report on types and quality of knowledge in social care includes a wider set of sources of knowledge, and criteria on which a study may be judged. Here "quality assessment" is used in a wider sense to include issues of transparency (clarity about how the knowledge was generated), accuracy, purposivity (the extent to which the methods used were appropriate or "fit for purpose"), utility ("fit for use"), and propriety (which includes legal and ethical considerations).[12]

Quality assessment is often used in a more restricted fashion than this in systematic reviews of quantitative studies, focusing primarily on identifying methodological problems. This information is used to "weight" each study summarized in the review, and may help with making appropriate methodological recommendations regarding future research. This weighting is usually done narratively, by differentiating clearly between higher and lower quality studies. The impact of study quality can also be investigated by means of a **sensitivity analysis**, which involves testing how sensitive the review findings are to the inclusion and exclusion of studies of different quality.

5.4   CRITICAL APPRAISAL: TOO MUCH CRITICISM, NOT ENOUGH APPRAISAL?

Critical appraisal aims to ensure that the reader directs her attention to all the key aspects of the study – its design, methods, participants, setting, and any key measures or variables. This is rather different from simply reading a study closely to see if it is "good enough," Instead, it often involves using a checklist or scale to formalize the process of appraising the study. This ensures that the main methodological issues are examined systematically, using the same approach for each study, and this makes it less likely that problems or biases will be overlooked. Of course, a reader often implicitly assesses the quality of any paper they read as a matter of course; however this may not be done in an unbiased or transparent manner.

While critical appraisal is essential to sound systematic reviewing, being "critical" is not an end in itself. No study is perfect, and it is easy to find flaws in every piece of research. Steven Woolf, of the US Preventive Services Task Force, which has done much to promote the judicious use of critical appraisal techniques, warns against taking critical appraisal to extremes:

> critical appraisal can do harm if valid evidence is rejected. . . . At one extreme of the spectrum, where data are accepted on face value (no appraisal), the risk of a **type I error** (accepting evidence of efficacy when the intervention does not work or causes harm) is high, and that of a **type II error** (discarding evidence when the intervention actually works) is low. At the other extreme (excessive scrutiny) the risk of a type II error is great.[13]

The skill in critical appraisal lies not in identifying problems, but in identifying errors *that are large enough to affect how the result of the study should be interpreted*. For reviewers assessing social science research studies, care should be taken when using "off-the-shelf" critical appraisal tools, because they may have originally been designed for use with clinical interventions, and may encourage inappropriate criticism of evaluations of social interventions, where, for example, double-blinding will often be impossible. Similarly, what are considered "appropriate" methods or standards varies between disciplines, so intelligent adjustment of checklists for use in other disciplines is sometimes needed – though of course this may affect the validity of the scale.

Assessing the susceptibility to bias of each study is the key to critical appraisal. Study methods do significantly affect study outcomes. For example, Heckman et al. have shown how drop-outs from a trial (people who drop out of the intervention group, and do not participate further in the study), can result in inaccurate findings in a trial of a classroom training program.[14] Contamination (where participants in a trial receive an intervention which they were not intended by the experimenters to receive, perhaps because they sought it out for themselves from another source) can have the same effect.[14] Bias due to drop-outs is not confined to trials of course; participants who drop out of studies are likely to differ significantly from those who remain in the study, and so the study findings may be based on a biased sample. In one US-based longitudinal study of smoking, the drop-outs tended to be of lower academic achievement, have lower knowledge about tobacco and health, and were more likely to be smokers.[15] Educational status and ethnicity have also been shown to be related to attrition in other research studies.[16, 17, 18]

Just because a critical appraisal checklist or tool has been widely used in other systematic reviews, this does not mean that it produces the "right" answer about a study's validity. One should be wary in particular of adding up the individual items in a checklist to get a summary score. Jüni et al. for example warn that very different results may obtained by scoring the same studies with different checklists.[19] They used 25 different scales to score 17 RCTs and examined the relationship between summary scores and pooled treatment effects in a series of meta-analyses of medical RCTs. The results showed that, depending on the scale used, very different (even opposite) results could be obtained. They concluded that it is more important to examine the methodological aspects of studies individually, rather than in summary form.

5.5   THE HIERARCHY OF EVIDENCE AGAIN

Many reviews have used a "hierarchy of evidence" to appraise studies. However, this is not the same as critical appraisal. The hierarchy of evidence ranks studies according to the degree to which they are affected by bias, but it is more useful in reviews as an aid to determining study appropriateness, than for exploring issues of study "quality." Moreover, an assessment of study quality alone is unlikely to be informative; one at least needs also to know whether the study results are likely to be generalizable. For example, one can imagine a situation in which a systematic review includes an RCT and an observational study both evaluating the same intervention. Although the RCT may have higher internal validity (that is, it will be affected less by selection and possibly other biases), it may include a highly selected sample of participants. It is known that women, the elderly, and people from ethnic minority groups are more likely to be excluded from trials.[20] Moreover, those participating in trials of treatment tend to be poorer, less educated, and more severely ill than those who do not, while the opposite appears to be the case for trials of prevention (such as health promotion interventions).[21] The types of intervention evaluated in RCTs and observational studies are likely to differ. RCTs are more common in evaluations of interventions delivered to individuals, while interventions delivered at the population level have more often been evaluated using non-randomized study designs. Appraising a study involves making a series of judgments (and trade-offs) about the population, intervention, and methodological biases together.

5.6   IN SEARCH OF THE METHODOLOGICAL "HOLY GRAIL"

The apparent obsession of systematic reviewers with methodological adequacy and bias can seem obsessive and hypercritical, even to other social scientists. One argument goes that most research is good enough for its purpose, and that scientific nit picking contributes little to the understanding of social phenomena. A second argument suggests that formalizing the process of critical appraisal is unnecessary, as any intelligent reader is likely to critically examine the studies that he or she reviews.

However, a century or more of psychological research on human information processing suggests otherwise. We often cannot tell when the numbers do not add up, we recognize patterns in the data that are not there, we miss those that *are* there, and we use rules of thumb (heuristics) which often work but sometimes don't, to help us manage large amounts of information (such as those in a review). It is well known from the work of Kahneman, Tversky and others that we select, evaluate, and remember information in a way that supports our individual preferences, we fail to look for evidence that disconfirms our pet hypotheses, and we cannot spot errors in our own reasoning: for example, we examine evidence that contradicts our own views more critically than when it supports them.[22, 23, 24]

Critical appraisal is not carried out in pursuit of some "holy grail" of perfection. If reviewers were only interested in perfect studies they would have nothing to review. Moreover, like physical perfection, our views of methodological perfection are subject to change over time. Critical appraisal, therefore, involves assessing the degree to which a study is affected by bias and whether the degree of bias is large enough to render the study unusable. It is not simply a matter of "sorting the wheat from the chaff," but an assessment of whether the research is "fit for purpose." We would probably be both surprised and pleased if we found that a study was methodologically perfect, but we would be more interested in whether it is evidentially adequate.

5.7 CRITICAL APPRAISAL: TOOLS, SCALES AND CHECKLISTS

Wortman describes quality assessment tools as deriving from two main frameworks.[25] The first derives from work in the social sciences by Campbell and colleagues and involves identifying the main threats to validity in mainly non-randomized (quasi-experimental) studies.[25, 26] This approach led to the development of a 33-item checklist which can be used as a guide to the overall quality of the study, by assessing whether the study is affected by any of Cook and Campbell's threats to validity.[27] The second approach, used initially for assessing the quality of RCTs, was developed by Thomas Chalmers and colleagues and focuses on the objective methodological characteristics of the study.[28] The reviewer codes each of these in turn, using this to generate an overall measure of study quality. This widely used tool also allows the coding of many study details in addition to methodological items.[28, 29]

Many of these "tools" take the form of checklists, some of which have been designed along strict psychometric principles, so that their reliability and validity is known. Others have not gone through this process, but are based on lists of the most common or well-documented biases to which certain types of study are susceptible. The simplest checklists highlight the main sources of bias for each type of study, and the reader uses this information to guide their overall assessment of the study's soundness. This information is then used in one of several ways:

- To "weight" the studies qualitatively, when summarizing the results; for example, on the basis of the results of the critical appraisal, studies may be categorized as high, intermediate, or low quality, and this may be taken into account when deriving conclusions from the review.

- To weight the studies quantitatively; a score may be derived for each study, and this may be used to "weight" the study in a meta-analysis – with low-scoring, more biased studies contributing less to the final summary effect size estimate. This is not often done as weights derived in this fashion are not usually empirically based.[30]

Examples of checklists appear below. Some checklists have been extensively validated (for example, Downs and Black),[31] while others have been developed solely for one-off use in a particular review.

Randomized controlled trials

One of the most widely used scales for assessing RCTs with respect to these criteria is the Jadad Scale[4, 11] (see Box 5.1).

Jadad suggests that the total score obtained using the scale can be used to help decide which trials to include in the review, as well as being an overall guide to the methodological soundness of the included studies. The validity of the scale has been demonstrated with the finding that studies that score low on the scale produce treatment effects that are 35 percent larger than those produced by trials with 3 or more points – another demonstration of the Iron Law of Evaluation.[1]

For behavioral or **population-level** interventions, it may be impossible to achieve a maximum score on the Jadad scale – for example, one cannot imagine double-blinding recipients of a juvenile delinquency intervention. Participants and providers alike would be pretty sure to notice that they were in a prison or in a boot camp, rather than on a safari trip (though blinded outcome assessment is possible). However the principles of assessing

---

Box 5.1   Assessing the validity of RCTs using the Jadad Scale[4, 11]

1. Was the study described as randomized?
2. Was the study described as double-blind?
3. Was there a description of withdrawals and drop outs?

and dealing with dropouts (attrition, and **intention to treat** analysis) and quality of randomization remain relevant.

Kristjansson et al. have used the Jadad scale in a Campbell Collaboration review of school feeding programs for reducing inequalities in health.[32] The scale was supplemented with four other items (relating to allocation concealment, baseline measurement, reliable primary outcome measures, and protection against contamination), and as the review included other study designs, a range of other checklists from the EPOC group (see Box 5.5) was used to assess methodological quality.

Using the Jadad scale does not preclude the assessment of other quality issues relating to trials. One could use a further set of questions to assess the extent to which the results are transferable, and other issues could be assessed. A framework for assessing the ethics of trials in systematic reviews has also been proposed.[33]

Assessing the quality of cluster RCTs

Cluster RCTs, in which allocation to intervention or control arms takes place at the cluster level (such as clusters of individuals, or organizations such as schools, workplaces, or prisons, or geographical areas) are subject to particular biases.[34] Puffer et al. have produced a summary of the main sources of biases in cluster RCTs.[35] They point to the need to assess bias at the cluster level, and at the individual level. Allocation to clusters, as with individuals in RCTs, should be done in such a way that it cannot be subverted, and clusters should be retained in the study to avoid attrition bias at a cluster level. Identifying and obtaining consent from participants before randomization should also reduce the risk of selection biases, which are introduced if individuals are recruited differentially into the intervention and control arms of the trial, and inclusion/exclusion biases, in which participants may be included or excluded from the different arms of the trial at differential rates after randomization has taken place (see Box 5.2).

Observational studies (including prospective controlled studies)

The phrase "observational studies" covers a wide range of study designs and purposes. It includes controlled and uncontrolled studies used to evaluate the effects of an intervention, such as studies with a control or comparison

Box 5.2   Assessing sources of bias in cluster RCTs

1.   Did cluster allocation seem secure?
2.   Cluster allocation stratified?
3.   Evidence of cluster imbalance?
4.   How many clusters lost after randomization?
5.   Patients identified before randomization?
6.   Could selection have been biased?
7.   Evidence of risk of bias?

(Based on Puffer et al., 2003)[35]

group, but where no random allocation has taken place. It also includes prospective studies where a population is followed over time to determine the effects of an intervention (sometimes called before-and-after studies; or, if a control group is involved, controlled before-and-after, or CBA studies). Studies used to assess etiology also fall into this category, such as (prospective) cohort studies, and case-control studies (retrospective). There are many other variants of these basic study types (such as retroprospective studies, nested case-control studies, crossover trials, and limited-prospective, or quasi-prospective studies). Interrupted Time Series studies are a special case of observational study and are discussed separately below.

There is no shortage of tools for assessing the validity of non-randomized studies. Deeks et al. found 194 of them in their systematic review, of which six appeared to be of use to systematic reviewers, on the grounds that they allow an overall assessment of quality to be made and compared between studies, and they covered all major threats to validity (see Table 5.1).[29] Deeks and Cooper concur that tools which follow a mixed-criteria approach may be most useful for systematic reviews; this approach involves assessing objective aspects of the study methods, followed by a judgment as to quality.[29, 36] For example, one might record how confounding was dealt with, followed by a judgment as to whether this was adequate. The other important issue to take into consideration when choosing a tool for critical appraisal is useability. Long, complex questionnaires can be slow to use and difficult to interpret, and while this is not a problem in reviews with a small number of primary studies, it is unwieldy in much larger reviews. A general rule of thumb is to try to avoid unvalidated tools, and tools that have not previously been used (and useful) in similar reviews to your own, though this is not always possible. The use of untested tools may be difficult to defend on scientific grounds when it comes to publishing the completed review in a journal. Box 5.3 gives details of the quality criteria for critical appraisal of observational studies, adapted from the CRD handbook.

The *Maryland Scientific Methods Scale* (SMS) has been applied to studies in Campbell systematic reviews of crime reduction strategies.[43, 44] The SMS uses a five-point scale which describes five study designs, ranked in order of internal validity, somewhat similar to a "hierarchy of evidence." It has been employed along with assessments of statistical and other aspects of internal validity such as response rate, and attrition, and validity of outcome assessment, in a major set of systematic reviews of crime prevention interventions. These reviews used the Maryland SMS to help categorize the interventions into one of four categories: "What works," "What does not work," "What is promising," and "What is unknown." For example, in the case of school-based crime prevention, strategies that focus on changing the environment were more effective than those focusing only on changing an individual's attitudes, behaviors, or beliefs (except for effects on truancy and dropout).[45]

Table 5.1 Six tools suitable for use in systematic reviews of quantitative studies

Author(s)	Purpose
Cowley [37]	13 items used for assessing comparative studies
Downs and Black[31]	27 questions for the assessment of randomized and non-randomized studies
Newcastle-Ottawa tool (Wells et al.)[38]	8 items relating to cohort studies examining causation; (further changes needed to apply it to cohort studies assessing effectiveness). See: <http://www.ohri.ca/programs/clinical_epidemiology/nosgen.doc>
Thomas: Quality assessment tool for quantitative studies[39]	Any study design (randomized or non-randomized) 21 items; items on non-randomized allocation methods
Reisch et al.[40]	57 items, applicable to any study design
Zaza et al.[41] Tool used for the US Community Preventive Services Reviews	Any study design; 22 items; may require detailed understanding of validity issues

Source: Deeks et al. (2003)[29]

Box 5.3   Quality criteria for critical appraisal of observational studies

1. Are the study participants adequately described? For example, look for adequate descriptive data on age, sex, baseline health status, and other relevant variables.

2. If there is a comparison or control group, are they similar to the intervention group, in terms of variables that may affect the outcome of the intervention (including demographic and other socio-demographic characteristics). This may be achieved by matching or other means – it may be taken into account in the statistical analysis – for example, by means of ANCOVA or regression techniques.

3. If the study involves an assessment of an intervention, is the intervention clearly described, with details of who exactly received it?

4. If the study is an etiological study (e.g., does maternal stress cause behavior problems in children?) were the independent and dependent variables adequately measured (that is, was the measurement likely to be valid and reliable)? This may include valid reliable measures, such as well-validated questionnaires if appropriate.

5. Are the measures used in the study the most relevant ones for answering the research question?

6. If the study involves following participants up over time, what proportion of people who were enrolled in the study at the beginning, dropped out? Have these "drop-outs" introduced bias?

7. Is the study long enough, and large enough to allow changes in the outcome of interest to be identified?

8. If two groups are being compared, are the two groups similar, and were they treated similarly within the study? If not, was any attempt made to control for these differences, either statistically, or by matching? Was it successful?

9. Was outcome assessment blind to exposure status? (That is, is it possible that those measuring the outcome introduced bias?)

(Adapted from the CRD handbook)[42]

Case control studies

Case control studies compare groups of individuals with, and without a particular disease or condition, and examine their past history to attempt to determine the cause. There are fewer validated tools for assessing case-control studies, but the main sources of bias in these studies are well known. A useful appraisal checklist is shown in Box 5.4. One of the well-known biases is recall bias, in which cases may be more likely to recall potential risk factors for the outcome in question – for example, in case-control studies of stress and breast cancer, women with breast cancer and healthy controls are often asked about stressful life events in the past year, or several years.[46] Breast cancer patients are indeed more likely to recall more such events, but this is less likely to be due to the events "causing" the cancer, than to women seeking harder to recall stressful events which might help to explain a subsequent diagnosis. This is understandable as it is a common but probably mistaken belief that stress causes cancer. In general, recall bias may introduce spurious associations between apparent risk factors and outcomes. One way to avoid this is to ensure that information is sought

---

Box 5.4   Appraising case-control studies

1. Are the study participants adequately described (with descriptive data on age, sex, baseline health status and other variables as appropriate to the research question)?
2. If the study is an assessment of an intervention, is the intervention clearly described, with details of who exactly received it?
3. If it is an etiological study (e.g., do food additives cause behavior problems?) were the independent and dependent variables adequately measured (that is, was the measurement likely to be valid and reliable)? Were they measured in the same way in both cases and controls?
4. Are the outcome measures used in the study the most relevant ones for answering the research question?
5. Are the two groups being compared similar, from the same population, and were they treated similarly within the study? If not, was any attempt made to control for these differences, either statistically, or by matching? Was it successful?

(Adapted from NHS CRD Report 4)[42]

in exactly the same way from cases and controls – in the example given above, information should ideally be elicited by means of a **standardized** questionnaire, which should be administered by an interviewer who is blind to whether the interviewee is a case or a control.

Interrupted time series (ITS) studies

For some social interventions, few RCTs will have been carried out and the main evaluation methods will have been longitudinal studies, such as interrupted time series studies (ITS) (which are usually seen as part of the family of quasi-experimental studies). This is the case, for example, with evaluations of many fiscal interventions. For example the association between taxation levels and tobacco consumption can be examined by collecting data at several time points before and after the policy of interest was introduced. The Cochrane Effective Practice and Organization of Care (EPOC) group, which publishes systematic reviews of educational, behavioral, financial, organizational, and regulatory interventions as part of the Cochrane Collaboration (and which contributes to the work of the Campbell Collaboration), has developed a guide to the quality assessment of ITS studies (Box 5.5). Some of the items in this and other checklists will not apply to all types of social intervention, but nevertheless provide a valuable framework. The EPOC criteria were used as a guide to assessing the quality of ITS studies in a systematic review of new road building (Box 5.6).[47] Longitudinal studies are already commonly included in systematic reviews that aim to assess the impact of policies, where RCTs or controlled studies have not been carried out. Examples include the Cochrane Tobacco Group's systematic reviews, which have examined the impact of interventions delivered to communities to reduce smoking among young people and adults, and interventions that included the use of the mass media (such as advertising and television campaigns).[48]

Cross-sectional surveys

Many of the study designs discussed above have a temporal dimension; that is, they involve following study participants over time, and recording events that happen to those people. However, many research studies have simple cross-sectional designs, where data are collected at just one point in time. Surveys are the most common example,[49, 50] and are commonly used to collect information on the use and acceptability of services. This type of process information is increasingly included in reviews of effectiveness – not

Box 5.5   Seven quality criteria for ITS designs from the EPOC group

A.   Protection against **secular changes**

1.   The intervention is independent of other changes:
     DONE if the intervention occurred independently of other changes over time
     NOT CLEAR if not specified, and will be treated as *NOT DONE* if information cannot be obtained from the authors
     NOT DONE if it is reported that the intervention was not independent of other changes in time
2.   Sufficient data points to enable reliable statistical inference
     DONE if at least 20 points are recorded before the intervention AND the authors have done a traditional time series analysis (ARIMA model)
     OR at least 3 points are recorded pre- and post-interventions AND the authors have done a repeated measures analysis
     OR at least 3 points are recorded pre- and post-intervention AND the authors have used ANOVA or multiple t-tests AND there are at least 30 observations per data point
     NOT CLEAR if not specified in the paper (e.g., the number of discrete data points is not mentioned in the text or tables; treat as *NOT DONE* if the information cannot be obtained from the authors)
     NOT DONE if any of the above conditions are unmet
3.   Formal test for trend (complete this section if the authors have used ANOVA modeling)
     DONE if formal test for change in trend using an appropriate method is reported
     NOT CLEAR if not specified in the paper (treat as *NOT DONE* if information cannot be obtained from the authors)
     NOT DONE if formal test for trend has not been done

B.   Protection against detection bias

4.   Intervention unlikely to affect data collection
     DONE if the authors report that the intervention itself was unlikely to affect data collection (for example, if sources and
     (Continued)

Box 5.5   *(Cont'd)*

methods of data collection were the same before and after the intervention)

NOT CLEAR if not reported (treat as *NOT DONE* if information cannot be obtained from the authors)

NOT DONE if the intervention was likely to affect data collection (for example, any change in source or method of data collection)

5. Blinded assessment of primary outcomes

DONE if the authors state explicitly that the primary outcome variables (that is, the main outcomes relating to the author's main hypothesis or question) were assessed blindly OR the outcome variables are objective (e.g., length of hospital stay, or other objective, independently recorded measure of effect, such as length of prison sentence). If some primary outcomes were assessed blindly, and others not, score each separately.

NOT CLEAR if not specified (treat as *NOT DONE* if information cannot be obtained from the authors)

NOT DONE if the outcomes were not assessed blindly

6. Completeness of data set

DONE if the data set covers 80–100 percent of the total number of participants or episodes of care in the study

NOT CLEAR if not specified (treat as *NOT DONE* if information cannot be obtained from the authors)

NOT DONE if the data set covers less than 80 percent

7. Reliable primary outcome measures

DONE if the study used two or more raters with at least 90 percent agreement, or with Kappa ≥ 0.8 OR the outcome is obtained from some automated system

NOT CLEAR if reliability is not reported for outcome measures that are obtained by extracting information from medical or other charts, or are collected by an individual researcher (treat as *NOT DONE* if information cannot be obtained from the authors)

NOT DONE if agreement is < 90 percent, or Kappa is < 0.8

(If some outcome variables were assessed reliably and others not, score each separately)

(See the EPOC group website http://www.epoc.uottawa.ca/resources.htm)

Box 5.6   Quality assessment criteria used in a systematic review of the health and social impact of new road building

Nine quality criteria were developed, based on previous epidemiological criteria for assessing longitudinal studies, and on additional criteria relevant to new road building:

1. Whether the researchers controlled for general trends;
2. Whether the data appeared to be a reliable/representative sample;
3. Whether sufficient data were presented to validate results;
4. Whether the authors controlled for regression to the mean (an approach commonly used in transport research when control groups are absent);
5. Assessment of whether data are available for at least 3 years before and after the intervention was implemented;
6. Compares more than one new road;
7. Injury severity considered;
8. Number of individual casualties included;
9. Whether accident migration across wider road network was considered.

(Egan et al., 2003)[47]

least because it helps us understand not just whether something "works," but whether it is likely to be used. Some questions that should be borne in mind when reading a report of a survey are outlined in Box 5.7.

As a final word on surveys, it is worth emphasizing, as Roger Jowell has pointed out in relation to the British Social Attitudes Survey, that no finding from a survey is definitive: "Every finding is an approximation, part of a body of evidence which needs to be examined in the context of other evidence."[52]

There are many useful guides to critical appraisal of quantitative studies; Crombie provides one readable overview[51] and the NHS CRD Guide to Systematic Reviews provides detailed guidance on this topic.[42] Examples of critical appraisal in education can also be found in the reviews of the EPPI-Centre <http://eppi.ioe.ac.uk/EPPIWeb/home.aspx>, in the Research Evidence in Education Library; these reviews show how the quality of each study can be used to assess the overall "weight of evidence" in a review.

Box 5.7   Framework for appraising a survey

General orientation questions

- What question(s) is the study aiming to answer?
- Was the survey specifically designed with this question in mind?
- Do the survey measures used allow this question to be answered clearly?
- Is the population surveyed clearly described?
- How was the survey carried out?

Selection of the sample

Those who respond to surveys differ systematically from those who do not. For example, responders to household surveys are more likely to be at home and willing to answer the door; children who spend a lot of time out of the house or who live in residential care or a boarding school are likely to be under-represented in surveys of children of adult respondents to surveys. The size and nature of the biases is likely to vary from topic area to topic area (and from culture to culture).

- What is the response rate? If it is not reported, calculate it yourself, if enough data are presented. Is the response rate high enough to ensure that response bias is not a problem, or has response bias been analyzed and shown not to significantly affect the study?
- Is the denominator reported? (What information is given about the size and type of population from which the survey sample is drawn?)
- Is the sample surveyed representative? (i.e., representative of the population to whom the results will be generalized)

Measurement issues

- Are the measures reported objective and reliable? (e.g., in a study of diet, is a standardized, valid measure of diet used?)

- Are these the most appropriate measures for answering the study question?
- If the study compares different subgroups from the survey, were the data obtained using the same methods from these different groups? (Bias may be introduced if data were collected using different methods in different groups.)

Survey methods

- How was the survey carried out? (e.g., postal survey, interview, web-based survey)
- Is the survey method likely to have introduced significant bias? (e.g., sampling method could include random versus quota sampling; web-based surveys, and so on)

Data and statistical issues

- Is the study large enough? (e.g., sample size justification, or discussion of statistical power)
- Is there an adequate description of the data? (including tables and summary statistics describing the sample, and adequate information on the results of any analyses)
- Is there evidence of multiple statistical testing, or large numbers of post hoc analyses?
- Are the statistical analyses appropriate?
- Is there evidence of any other biases? (e.g., funding bias)

(Adapted from Crombie, 1996)[51]

5.8 INSIDE THE BLACK BOX: ASSESSING THE IMPLEMENTATION OF THE INTERVENTION

Many of the study designs described above could probably be included in a review of effectiveness, though they would be used to answer different questions. Surveys for example might be included to answer questions on the likely take-up and acceptability of an intervention, while some of the other study designs would be more likely to be used to assess its effectiveness. However evaluating interventions requires knowing more about the intervention than whether it works, and systematic reviews increasingly seek to include detailed information on the content and implementation of the intervention. This information is often overlooked in systematic reviews in favor of extracting information on methodological biases. However, without knowing what actually was done, information on whether something "worked" or not is unhelpful. We now discusses some of the process data that may be included in a systematic review. Not all of this information is likely to be reported in the original study, and contact with study authors may be necessary to obtain it.

5.9   TREATMENT INTEGRITY, IMPLEMENTATION, AND CONTEXT

Treatment integrity (sometimes referred to as program adherence) refers to the degree to which an intervention was implemented as prescribed by the study protocol. The rationale for assessing this in systematic reviews is that it is assumed that effectiveness is directly related to the fidelity with which the intervention is implemented.[53,54] One approach to assessing treatment integrity is to code information from each study relating to aspects of the content and delivery of the intervention, and then to examine the association between these indicators and outcomes (such as effect sizes, as was done by Devine and Cook in their meta-analysis of the effects of psychoeducational interventions on lengths of stay in hospital).[25,55] For many reviews, however, and particularly for reviews of complex social interventions, more is required than simply coding methodological aspects of the study. One also needs to assess both the fidelity and the "intensity" of the intervention as it was delivered.

DuBois et al.'s meta-analysis of 55 studies of youth mentoring programs examined these issues, in each case assessing 125 aspects of the program.[56] They rated each study on 11 features relating to the quality of implementation of the intervention. These features had been included in previous recommendations for establishing effective mentoring programs, and the reviewers used these to produce a theory-based "index of best practice" (Box 5.8). This in turn was used to explore the association between best practice and effect size. Larger effect sizes were found in the programs that had engaged in a majority of the 11 "best practices." This gives a demonstration of how implementation can be assessed and used to explore

Box 5.8   Assessing implementation in a meta-analysis of the effectiveness of youth mentoring programs

DuBois et al. began with an extensive coding of the characteristics of each study. This included not just methodological issues, but also the geographical location, program goals, characteristics of the mentors and participating youths, characteristics of the mentor–mentee relationships, among many others. They also created a theory-based index of best practice to provide an assessment of the program and its implementation. Eleven program features were assessed, and a score was calculated based on the number of best practices each program adhered to. The program features included:

- Monitoring of program implementation
- Screening of prospective mentors
- Matching of mentors and young people
- Mentor pre-match training
- Ongoing training of mentors
- Supervision of mentors
- Existence of support group for mentors
- Structured activities for mentors and young people
- Parent support or involvement component
- Expectations for both frequency of contact
- Expectations for length of relationships

(DuBois et al., 2002)[56]

moderator effects in a systematic review (in this case a meta-analysis was carried out).

Lumley et al. describe how their review of smoking cessation interventions aimed at pregnant women sought to include a range of non-trial data.[57] This review included reports on who developed the interventions, how they were developed, their theoretical basis, and how they were delivered. They describe how reviewing these process indicators helped explain some of the heterogeneity in outcomes, as there was heterogeneity in how the interventions were delivered (some poorly, some not), and some were delivered more intensively than others. The reviewers found that those interventions delivered more intensively and those that were theoretically based appeared to have the greatest impact.

The following list of issues to consider when describing interventions in a systematic review may be helpful. This list draws on existing criteria for appraising process evaluations:[58]

- Details of intervention activities (what the intervention consists of, where, how, how often, and by whom it is delivered, and for how long);
- Resources: this includes: time, money, people, information, technology, and other assets needed to conduct the intervention;[58]
- Staffing, and where appropriate to the intervention, the level of skills of staff;
- Context (as described above, this may include the political, community, organizational, and other contexts);
- The stage of development of the intervention[53] (whether it is a mature, well-developed intervention, which perhaps has been implemented elsewhere);
- Sustainability (including any measures taken to ensure retention of people in the study);
- Whether any adverse or negative effects were observed or reported by researchers or participants; and
- The logic model: how the intervention is theorized to bring about change in the desired outcome – that is, by what steps, or by what theorized causal pathway.[53]

This last point may be difficult to identify or may not be reported in the research paper or report, but it will help the user of the review to understand the purpose of the intervention, and why anyone ever thought it could work. As illustration, this information was extracted by Secker-Walker et al.[48] in their review of community level smoking cessation interventions:

> In 23 studies (72%) there was a description of the theoretical background for the interventions. Fourteen (44%) drew explicitly on social cognitive theory, 11 (34%) on communication theory and 10 (31%) on diffusion of innovation theory. All three theories were specified in seven studies (22%). In 18 (56%) studies, other theories were used including community participation in seven (22%), stages of change in five (16%), social marketing in three (9%), and planned behaviour or reasoned action in three (9%). The PRECEDE model of planning and evaluation for health education and policy interventions was used in six (19%) studies.

Anderson et al. provide another example of a logic model, in which they clearly outline the theoretical framework underlying their systematic review of the effectiveness of early childhood development programs.[59] In this, they describe the pathways linking the components of childhood development programs, which run from intermediate social, health, and other outcomes (such as improvement in social skills), through to final outcomes such as educational attainment, and changes in health-related outcomes (such as risk behaviors like drug and alcohol use). Their approach uses the "Guide to community preventive services,"[60] which has been used to produce a wide range of reviews of healthcare and social interventions. For example, another review in this series summarizes evidence on the effectiveness and economic efficiency of interventions to promote healthy social environments, which covers housing, educational, and other programs (see <http://www.thecommunityguide.org/>).

The EPPI Centre has also produced a 12-question checklist to help with assessing process evaluations in health promotion. The full version of this checklist can be found at: <http://eppi.ioe.ac.uk/EPPIWeb/home.-aspx?page=/hp/reports/phase/phase_process.htm>.

Incorporating information on context

The context within which a study is carried out also affects the effectiveness of the intervention; this will vary between studies within a single review. Rychetnik et al. suggest that important contextual characteristics could include factors in the political or organizational environment, as well as socioeconomic or demographic characteristics of the population in the study,[53] though some of these contextual factors may not be reported consistently (Box 5.9).

If enough information is reported (or can be gleaned from the authors) context can be taken into account in interpreting the review's results. For example, "welfare to work" programs have been implemented in many places including the US, Scandinavia, and the UK, but they vary in their content, and their impact is likely to depend on the political and other settings within which they are delivered. A systematic review of such studies would need to interpret the data they collect in the light of this variation. Alternatively the reviewers could reduce variability by confining the review to evaluations carried out in countries with similar welfare systems, or could confine the review to one country. One recent review took the latter approach. It examined the evidence on the impact of the UK's welfare to work programs on the employment rates of people

Box 5.9   Finding evidence on implementation: A case study

In a study funded by the Health Development Agency (now incorporated into NICE), Arai et al. started to map the evidence on the
implementation of interventions aiming to reduce accidental injuries,
to explore ways in which this evidence can be quality appraised and
synthesized in a manner accessible to policymakers and practitioners.
Their review found that:

- many papers contained little information on implementation
  processes;
- a majority of the papers containing material on implementation
  processes were judged to have too little information on study
  design to allow study quality to be assessed; and
- in many cases, it was unclear whether "implementation relevant"
  statements were based on research evidence.

Some journal editors have already sought to improve the quality, not
only of research reporting, but also of research conduct, through
guidelines on presentation and content. There is scope for further
improvements in reporting on implementation issues.

(Arai et al., 2005)[61]

with a disability or chronic illness, and included 17 studies in the final
synthesis. Its conclusion was that "welfare to work" has a positive effect
on employment rates.[62]

5.10   ASSESSING EXTERNAL VALIDITY

Even if a study has high internal validity, it may not be generalizable (high
external validity). There is often a trade-off between internal and external
validity. One starting point in determining **generalizability** is to explore
whether the study population appears to be representative of the population
to which you wish to apply the results. However, even if the populations are

similar, they may differ in other ways; as above, differences in the settings, and in cultural or other contextual factors, should also be considered.

If the study involves an evaluation of an intervention, then its transferability needs consideration; what is acceptable to one population at one point in time, may not be acceptable to another. Ethical appropriateness may also vary between populations; an intervention which aims to prevent harm may be ethical in a high-risk population, but not in the general population. This may be the case with screening programs for example. Conversely, categories of interventions that appear effective in some populations may have the opposite effect in others; Pawson gives the example of "naming and shaming" (public disclosure of misdemeanors). This penalty may work when aimed at car manufacturers who make cars that are easily broken into and stolen – but may have the opposite effect in other situations.[63]

Reviewing the results of a number of studies of course itself provides a test of generalizability; if the results have been replicated in several settings with different populations, then this gives an indication of whether the results are transferable. If the number of studies is large enough, it can suggest the range of effect sizes to be expected in different settings. Generalizability is not often assessed separately in systematic reviews, though consideration of the issue is included in some critical appraisal checklists.[29] Rychetnik et al.[53] suggest that assessing this requires obtaining information on the intervention itself, on the context within which it is delivered and evaluated, and on interactions between the intervention and its context – sometimes referred to as effect modification (see also chapters 6 and 7).

As some of the examples above show, theory has an essential role to play in systematic reviews; a theoretical model of how the intervention works, and for whom, is important when deciding on the review question, and what types of studies to review. It will help in interpreting the review's findings, and will be valuable in assessing how widely applicable those findings may be. In turn systematic reviews can contribute to developing and testing the limits of theories, by examining how contextual or temporal variables moderate outcomes.[64] Theories themselves can also be the subject of systematic reviews.[65, 66, 67]

5.11 QUALITY ASSESSMENT AND QUALITATIVE RESEARCH

Information on process and implementation issues will often, though not exclusively, be derived from qualitative research, and there are systematic reviews that have explicitly set out to review only qualitative studies.

For example, systematic reviews may use qualitative research to explore barriers or facilitators of the implementation of interventions, or to synthesize qualitative evidence on people's experiences. An example of the latter is given in Box 5.10.

Box 5.10 Resilient young mothering: A systematic review of qualitative research on the experiences of teenage mothers

The problem: Teenage pregnancy and motherhood is a central focus of the UK government's policies to tackle social exclusion and health inequalities.

The review: It is widely acknowledged that an understanding of the needs and experiences of young mothers is essential for the development of effective services, an understanding provided by studies that record their experiences of their lives. The authors therefore searched for reviews of qualitative studies of teenage mothers and mothers-to-be. To ensure the review's relevance to the UK policy context, it focused on UK studies of teenage pregnancy and motherhood published from 1990 to 2003, seeking out primary studies that recorded and analyzed the accounts of young women. As far as possible, the review used systematic review methodology developed for quantitative studies, but drew on templates developed by qualitative researchers who have tried to adapt this methodology for the critical appraisal and synthesis stages of the review.

The critical appraisal: The authors found that methods for critically appraising qualitative research and for synthesizing their findings are still under development, with as yet no consensus about, and therefore no accepted guidelines for, these two key stages of a systematic review. If there is any agreement, it is that a single set of methods is unlikely to be appropriate for qualitative reviews: it is the purpose and type of the review that should drive the choice of appraisal criteria and synthesis strategy.

In line with this view, they assessed a range of quality criteria and synthesis strategies, and selected the criteria developed by reviewers working at the EPPI Centre, who had previously applied them to a review of barriers to physical activity among young people (Rees et al).[68] Ten of the 22 studies they had identified through their extensive searches met these criteria, and entered the final stages of the review, where two methods of synthesis were used. First, a detailed cross-study analysis was undertaken to generate a coding frame, which enabled the authors to uncover common concerns running through mothers' accounts. Then, they identified a set of overarching themes across the studies: these themes related to the difficulties of being a young, poor mother and to the resilient mothering practices which women develop. The review suggested that an appreciation of these resilient practices is essential for the development of services that respect and meet the needs of young mothers and their children.

(Liz McDermott and Hilary Graham)[69, 70]

There is ongoing debate about the appropriateness of quality assessment methods to qualitative research, and about what the "goals" of such methods of appraisal should be.[71, 72, 73] However, it is clear that one needs to be able to distinguish "good quality" from "poor quality" qualitative research, just as one does for quantitative studies. In some cases, good quality studies may not necessarily be fit for the purpose of a particular systematic review, since, unlike quantitative studies, they will less frequently directly answer the review question. If you are doing a review on maternal views of infant growth for instance, it will be a bonus to find a study on precisely this subject. However, other studies may well present relevant information, and in all cases, it will be appropriate to ask just how well the study was carried out. Nonetheless, while there is now a large number of critical appraisal tools for qualitative research, there are as yet no widely accepted criteria as to "the best" method for qualitative study appraisal. Work exploring this issue is currently in progress.[74, 75]

Other frameworks and guidance have been developed to aid in appraising qualitative research, and these will be of value in systematic reviews which include qualitative studies.[72, 73] A recent example was produced by Spencer et al. at the National Centre for Survey Research in the UK, working on behalf of the UK Government's Cabinet Office.[5] Their framework was developed with particular reference to evaluations concerned with the development and implementation of social policy, programs, and practice. It drew on a systematic review of existing literature on approaches to judging the quality of qualitative research, and was based around 18 open-ended appraisal questions, which are intended to be applied mainly to four methods used in qualitative research: in-depth interviews, focus groups, observation, and documentary analysis (Box 5.11). The authors emphasize that the framework is explicitly designed to aid informed judgments, rather

---

Box 5.11   Eighteen appraisal questions for qualitative research

1.   How credible are the findings?
2.   How has knowledge or understanding been extended by the research?
3.   How well does the evaluation address its original aims and purpose?
4.   How well is the scope for drawing wider inference explained?
5.   How clear is the basis of evaluative appraisal?
6.   How defensible is the research design?
7.   How well defended are the sample design/target selection of cases/documents?
8.   How well is the eventual sample composition and coverage described?
9.   How well was the data collection carried out?
10.   How well has the approach to, and formulation of, analysis been conveyed?
11.   How well are the contexts of data sources retained and portrayed?
12.   How well has diversity of perspective and content been explored?
13.   How well have detail, depth, and complexity (i.e. richness) of the data been conveyed?
14.   How clear are the links between data, interpretation and con-clusions – i.e., how well can the route to any conclusions be seen?
15.   How clear and coherent is the reporting?
16.   How clear are the assumptions/theoretical perspectives/values that have shaped the form and output of the evaluation?
17.   What evidence is there of attention to ethical issues?
18.   How adequately has the research process been documented?

(Spencer et al., 2003)[5]

than to encourage mechanistic approaches to quality assessment (see: <http://www.strategy.gov.uk/files/pdf/Quality_framework.pdf>).

Generalizability and qualitative research

Qualitative research that puts a metric on findings should ring alarm bells. To be told that "most" children don't like greens, or "few" women enjoy an episiotomy on the basis of a qualitative study are unlikely to be the kind of data that would add much to knowledge. Qualitative work depends not on numerical but conceptual analysis and presentation. As Fitzpatrick and Boulton point out, if qualitative data are reported mainly in terms of frequencies and proportions of respondents with a particular view, that is a quantitative study.[76] This is very far from saying that "anything goes" in qualitative research, but in trying to ram qualitative research into a glass slipper of a different research paradigm, the kinds of understandings that sound qualitative research can bring are likely to be lost.

It is more likely that high quality qualitative research can help generate new hypotheses on why quantitative research shows what it does, what the appropriate and acceptable interventions might be, and whether the "right" kinds of questions are being asked. It should of course be presented in a context that describes the background and characteristics of those who are part of the study, and the strengths and limitations of these data in terms of lessons that might be drawn from them. As Green puts it: "Data extracts taken out of context tell us little about the situated nature of beliefs and behaviour, and inferences that are not rooted in a theoretical understanding are unlikely to be generalisable to other settings."[77]

Quality in qualitative research: Are checklists sensible?

Checklists for qualitative research have been criticized for their potential as "tail wagging the dog" exercises, and the possibility that researchers may contort their work to meet checklist criteria, while paying less attention to some of the more basic requirements of scientific rigor.[78] Checklists are not a shortcut to ensuring quality in qualitative research, but when using a research method such as systematic reviewing, one of whose claims to legitimacy is transparency, checklists provide one means of ensuring that included studies contain sufficient information about the sample, the question, the data analysis, and so on. This enables those reading a review to check that the basics are reported in each study.

5.12 DOES QUALITY ASSESSMENT MATTER?

It is sometimes assumed that biases in primary studies are "self-canceling;" that is, that errors occur randomly across the set of studies in the review and so in aggregate (if there are enough studies in the review) they will cancel each other out.[25] If this was the case, then the assessment of internal validity would not be crucial. However, there is now ample evidence that study biases in general operate systematically, and often result in inflated effect sizes. For example non-random assignment in RCTs has been shown to over-estimate effects by at least one-third – though systematic underestimates of effects have also been observed.[25]

Schulz et al.'s study of 250 trials provides a clear empirical demonstration of the effects of study biases on outcomes.[79] Trials in which concealment was either inadequate or unclear yielded larger effect size estimates than those that had adequately concealed the treatment allocation; **odds ratios** were exaggerated by 41 percent for inadequately concealed trials (adjusted for other aspects of quality). Trials that were not double-blinded also yielded larger estimates of effects, with odds ratios being exaggerated by 17 percent.

The case for critical appraisal is also supported by an RCT carried out among general practitioners, which compared critical appraisal (using a checklist) versus "free" appraisal, in which readers were asked to score papers on the basis of "their importance to me in everyday work." This showed clear differences. Those using the critical appraisal tool gave a consistently lower overall score, and applied a more appropriate appraisal to the methodology of the studies.[80]

5.13 DATA EXTRACTION

Critical appraisal is often carried out as an integral part of the data extraction process. Data extraction is the process of extracting the relevant information from each study, either by copying it onto printed pro-forma templates, or by directly entering it into a database or table. An example of a data extraction sheet for quantitative studies appears in Appendix 4. Other example data extraction sheets are available from the EPOC website <http://www.epoc.uottawa.ca/resources.htm> and from the CRD guide to systematic reviews (available on the CRD website <http://www.york.ac.uk/inst/crd/>).

5.14   CHECKING THE RELIABILITY OF CRITICAL APPRAISAL AND DATA EXTRACTION

Wortman and others refer to "data extraction bias" in which the reviewer introduces bias into the review – perhaps by differentially extracting information from studies that are in accord with their own views, or by applying differential judgments of quality or methodological adequacy to different studies.[25] Data-extraction bias may also (in theory, at least) be introduced by the reviewer's awareness of the study authors or the journal, or their disciplinary background, or by awareness of other aspects of the study being reviewed. Some of these issues can be dealt with by blinding the reviewers (for example, by obscuring study details with tape or a marker), by using multiple reviewers, and by validating the data extraction. In the latter case, this can be done by ensuring that all data extraction is checked by another person, (a common practice), or by double data extraction by two people working independently (much less common, but likely to be more reliable).

5.15   EXTRACTING DATA ON DIFFERENTIAL EFFECTS OF INTERVENTIONS

Research studies often report their results at a population-level; that is, the study findings are reported as if the participants were an undifferentiated group. However, for many interventions there are likely to be interactions that modify their effects – for example, interactions between characteristics of the participants and their outcomes. Interactions with level of education are common in many health promotion interventions, as are interactions with age: for example a systematic review by Shepherd et al. found some suggestion that the effectiveness of healthy eating interventions in school-children varied with age, and found a distinct interaction with gender (knowledge and consumption of healthy foods were more likely to improve in young women than in young men).[81] Where data on impacts in sub-groups are reported this should be extracted by the reviewer. This is discussed further in chapter 7.

5.16   TRANSLATING NON-ENGLISH PAPERS

The cost of translating non-English language papers can be significant and difficult to estimate. Full-text translations in particular can be expensive. One way of reducing cost without compromising the quality of the information extracted is to translate only those selected sections of the paper that are essential – this often excludes the introduction, and discussion – and to translate key sections of the methods and results, and headings for tables and figures. One problem with this approach is that important contextual information may be excluded through this process.

An English language abstract is often available, though this is sometimes hidden at the back of the paper. Instead of employing a translator, it may be more efficient to send them a copy of the paper to read, and then question them to decide whether it meets the inclusion criteria. If you are close to a language school or university language department, this can be a useful source of help. Cheaper still is to do it yourself. Even with limited linguistic skills, a knowledge of the main methodological terms in that language can be enough to allow a paper's key details to be extracted. Web-based translators (such as Alta Vista's Babelfish <http://world.altavista.com/>) can be useful as they are often accurate enough to allow the reviewer to determine whether the study meets the review's inclusion criteria (see Box 5.12).

Box 5.12   How to avoid getting "Lost in translation"

The decision about which studies to translate can be made on grounds of relevance. For example, a recent systematic review of infant growth investigated interventions that might lead to optimal growth for children.[82] One of the researchers, Patricia Lucas, started by scanning relevant world literature, including literature from the countries of origin of the UK's main immigrant groups. For this, she used national data on country of origin. Given that most immigrants gravitate towards the larger cities, and in particular capital cities, she then obtained data on the main languages spoken in London. This information helped her develop inclusion and exclusion criteria to help decide (on the basis of the abstract) which articles needed to be translated.

5.17 CONCLUDING COMMENTS

Despite the difficulties in applying critical appraisal, it is an essential part of a systematic review, though unfortunately it still too often remains undone. Ignoring critical appraisal on grounds that studies are probably good enough, or that the biases cancel each other out, is simply misleading and makes for a potentially misleading review. In some cases it may be harmful to take studies at face value, and so systematic reviews that have made no attempt at critical appraisal should not be considered reliable.

Key learning points from this chapter

- Biases in individual studies can affect their conclusions; ignoring this fact can in turn bias the conclusions of a systematic review.
- Critical appraisal is, therefore, an essential step in any systematic review; without this the review may be unreliable.
- Critical appraisal tools are available for all major study designs, and guides to the appraisal of qualitative research have been produced.
- This is generally done with a view to systematizing the assessment of the reliability and utility of the information presented by the studies, and not as an exercise in criticism for its own sake.
- The appraisal of the primary studies is sometimes carried out in tandem with the data extraction; in extracting data, information on subgroup effects, and on **moderator variables** (that is, variables which appear to moderate the effects of other important independent variables) should also be extracted where available.

REFERENCES

1. Rossi, P. The iron law of evaluation and other metallic rules. *Research in Social Problems and Public Policy* 1987, 4: 3–20.
2. Light, R. and Smith, P. Accumulating evidence: Procedures for resolving contradictions among different research studies. *Harvard Educational Review* 1971, 41: 429–71.
3. Sackett, D. Bias in analytic research. *Journal of Chronic Diseases* 1979, 32: 51–63.
4. Jadad, A., Moore, A., Carrol, D., Gavaghan, D., and McQuay, H. Assessing the quality of reports of randomised clinical trials: Is blinding necessary? *Controlled Clinical Trials* 1996, 17: 1–12.

5. Spencer, L., Ritchie, J., Lewis, J., and Dillon, L. *Quality in qualitative evaluation: A framework for assessing research evidence.* London: Government Chief Social Researcher's Office, 2003.

6. Burdett, S., Stewart, L., and Tierney, J. Publication bias and meta-analyses. *International Journal of Technology Assessment in Health Care* 2003, 19: 129–34.

7. Alderson, P., Green, S., and Higgins, J. (eds.) *Cochrane Reviewers' Handbook 4.2.2 [updated March 2004].* The Cochrane Library, Issue 1, 2004. Chichester, UK: John Wiley & Sons.

8. CONSORT Guidelines, online at: http://www.consort-statement.org/

9. Moher, M., Schulz, K. F, and Altman, D. The CONSORT statement: Revised recommendations for improving the quality of reports of parallel-group randomized trials. *Journal of the American Medical Association* 2001, 285: 1987–91.

10. Huwiler-Müntener, K., Jüni, P., Junker, C., and Egger, M. Quality of reporting of randomized trials as a measure of methodologic quality. *Journal of the American Medical Association* 2002, 287: 2801–4.

11. Jadad, A. *Randomised controlled trials: A users guide.* London: BMJ Books, 1998.

12. Pawson, R., Boaz, A., Grayson, L., Long, A., and Barnes, C. Types and quality of knowledge in social care: Social Care Institute for Excellence. Online at: http://www.evidencenetwork.org/project1.asp, 2003.

13. Woolf, S. Taking critical appraisal to extremes: The need for balance in the evaluation of evidence. *Journal of Family Practice* 2000, 49(12), December: 1081–5.

14. Heckman, J., Hohmann, N., and Smith, J. Substitution and dropout bias in social experiments: A study of an influential social experiment. *Quarterly Journal of Economics* 2000, 115: 651–94.

15. Siddiqui, O., Flay, B. R., and Hu, F. B. Factors affecting attrition in a longitudinal smoking prevention study. *Preventive Medicine* 1996, 25: 554–60.

16. Krishnan, E., Murtagh, K., Bruce, B., Cline, D., Singh, G., and Fries, J. Attrition bias in rheumatoid arthritis databanks: A case study of 6,346 patients in 11 databanks and 65,649 administrations of the Health Assessment Questionnaire. *Journal of Rheumatology* 2004, 31: 1320–6.

17. Matthews, F. E., Chatfield, M., Freeman, C., McCracken, C., Brayne, C., and MRC CFAS. Attrition and bias in the MRC cognitive function and ageing study: An epidemiological investigation. *BMC Public Health* 2004, 4: 12.

18. Williams, G., O'Callaghan, M., Najman, J., Bor, W., Andersen, M., and Richards, D. Maternal cigarette smoking and child psychiatric morbidity: A longitudinal study. *Pediatrics* 1998, 102(1): e11.

19. Jüni, P., Witschi, A., Bloch, R., and Egger, M. The hazards of scoring the quality of clinical trials for meta-analysis. *Journal of the American Medical Association* 1999, 282: 1054–60.

20. Prescott, R., Counsell, C., Gillespie, W., Grant, A., Russell, I., Kiauka, S., et al. Factors influencing the quality, number and progress of randomised controlled trials. *Health Technology Assessment* 1999, 3, online at: http://www.hta.nhsweb.nhs.uk/htapubs.htm

21. Britton, A., McKee, M., Black, N., McPherson, K., Sanderson, C., and Bain, C. Choosing between randomised and non-randomised studies: A systematic review. *Health Technology Assessment* 1998, 2, online at: http://www.hta.nhsweb.nhs.uk/htapubs.htm

22. Hogarth, R. *Judgement and choice. The psychology of decision-making.* Chichester: John Wiley & Sons, 1987.

23. MacCoun, R. Biases in the interpretation and use of research results. *Annual Review of Psychology* 1998, 49: 259–87.

24. Kahneman, D., Slovic, P., and Tversky, A. (eds.) *Judgement under uncertainty: Heuristics and biases.* Cambridge: Cambridge University Press, 1982.

25. Wortman, P. Judging research quality. In H. Cooper and L. Hedges (eds.) *The handbook of research synthesis.* New York: Russell Sage Foundation, 1994.

26. Campbell, D. and Stanley, J. *Experimental and quasi-experimental designs for research.* Chicago: Rand McNally, 1966.

27. Cook, T. and Campbell, D. *Quasi-experimentation: Design and analysis issues for field settings.* Chicago: Rand McNally, 1979.

28. Chalmers, T., Smith, H., Blackburn, C., Silverman, B., Schroeder, B., Reitman, D., et al. A method for assessing the quality of a randomized controlled trial. *Controlled Clinical Trials* 1981, 2: 31–49.

29. Deeks, J., Dinnes, J., D'Amico, R., Sowden, A., Sakarovitch, C., Song, F., et al. Evaluating non-randomised intervention studies. *Health Technology Assessment* 2003, 7, online at: http://www.hta.nhsweb.nhs.uk/fullmono/mon727.pdf [accessed February 24, 2005].

30. Sutton, A., Abrams, K., Jones, K., Sheldon, T., and Song, F. Systematic reviews of trials and other studies. *Health Technology Assessment* 1998, 2, online at: http://www.hta.nhsweb.nhs.uk/ProjectData/3_publication_select.asp. Also available as: Sutton et al. *Methods for meta-analysis in medical research.* Chichester: Wiley & Sons, 2000.

31. Downs, S. and Black, N. The feasibility of creating a checklist for the assessment of the methodological quality of both randomised and non-randomised studies of healthcare interventions. *Journal of Epidemiology and Community Health* 1998, 52: 377–84.

32. Kristjansson, B., Robinson, V., Tugwell, P., Petticrew, M., Greenhalgh, T., Macdonald, B., et al. School feeding programs for improving outcomes of low-income children and for reducing socioeconomic inequalities in health (submitted).

33. Weingarten, M., Paul, M., and Leibovici, L. Assessing ethics of trials in systematic reviews. *British Medical Journal* 2004, 328: 1013–14.

34. Ukoumunne, O., Gulliford, M., Chinn, S., Sterne, J., and Burney, P. Methods for evaluating area-wide and organisation-based interventions in health and health care: A systematic review. *Health Technology Assessment* 1999, 3, online at: http://www.hta.nhsweb.nhs.uk/htapubs.htm

35. Puffer, S., Torgerson, D., and Watson, J. Evidence for risk of bias in cluster randomised trials: Review of recent trials published in three general medical journals. *British Medical Journal* 2003, 327: 785-9.
36. Cooper, H. *The integrative research review: A systematic approach.* Newbury Park, CA: Sage, 1984.
37. Cowley, D. Prostheses for primary total hip replacement: A critical appraisal of the literature. *International Journal of Technology Assessment in Health Care* 1995, 11: 770–8.
38. Wells, G., Shea, B., O'Connell, D., Peterson, J., Welch, V., Tugwell, P. et al. *The Newcastle-Ottawa Scale (NOS) for assessing the quality of nonrandomised studies in meta-analyses.* Ottawa: Clinical Epidemiology Unit, University of Ottawa, 1999.
39. Thomas, H. Quality assessment tool for quantitative studies. Effective Public Health Practice Project. Toronto: McMaster University, 2003, online at: http://www.hamilton.ca/phcs/ephpp/Research/Tools/QualityTool2003.pdf
40. Reisch, J., Tyson, J., and Mize, S. Aid to the evaluation of therapeutic studies. *Pediatrics* 1989, 84: 815–27.
41. Zaza, S., Wright-de Aguero, L., Briss, P., Truman, B., Hopkins, D., Hennessy, H., et al. Data collection instrument and procedure for systematic reviews in the "Guide to Community Preventive Services." *American Journal of Preventive Medicine* 2000, 18: 44–74.
42. NHS Centre for Reviews and Dissemination. Undertaking systematic reviews of research on effectiveness: CRD's guidance for those carrying out or commissioning reviews. CRD Report Number 4 (2nd edn): University of York, 2001, online at: http://www1.york.ac.uk/inst/crd/report4.htm
43. Farrington, D., Gottfredson, D., Sherman, L., and Welsh, B. The Maryland Scientific Methods Scale. In L. Sherman, D. Farrington, B. Welsh, and D. MacKenzie (eds.) *Evidence-based crime prevention.* London: Routledge, 2002.
44. Farrington, D. Methodological quality standards for evaluation research. *Annals of the American Academy of Political and Social Science* 2003, 587: 49–68.
45. Gottfredson, D., Wilson, D., and Najaka, S. School-based crime prevention. In L. Sherman, D. Farrington, B. Welsh, and D. MacKenzie (eds.) *Evidence-based crime prevention.* London: Routledge, 2002.
46. Petticrew, M., Fraser, J., and Regan, M. Adverse life events and breast cancer: A meta-analysis. *British Journal of Health Psychology* 1999, 4: 1–17.
47. Egan, M., Petticrew, M., Hamilton, V., and Ogilvie, D. Health impacts of new roads: A systematic review. *American Journal of Public Health* 2003, 93(9): 1463–71.
48. Secker-Walker, R., Gnich, W., Platt, S., and Lancaster, T. Community interventions for reducing smoking among adults (Cochrane Review). *The Cochrane Library*, Issue 2, 2004. Chichester, UK: John Wiley & Sons.
49. Magnus, P. and Jaakkola, J. Secular trend in the occurrence of asthma among children and young adults: Critical appraisal of repeated cross sectional surveys. *British Medical Journal* 1997, 314: 1795.

50. Mirza, I. and Jenkins, R. Risk factors, prevalence, and treatment of anxiety and depressive disorders in Pakistan: Systematic review. *British Medical Journal* 2004, 328: 794.

51. Crombie, I. *The pocket guide to critical appraisal.* London: BMJ Publishing Group, 1996.

52. Jowell, R. Introducing the survey. In R. Jowell and C. Airey (eds.) *British Social Attitudes: The 1984 report.* Aldershot: Gower, 1984.

53. Rychetnik, L., Frommer, M., Hawe, P., and Shiell, A. Criteria for evaluating evidence on public health interventions. *Journal of Epidemiology and Community Health* 2002, 56: 119–27.

54. Hawe, P., Shiell, A., and Riley, T. Complex interventions: how "out of control" can a randomised controlled trial be? *British Medical Journal* 2004, 328: 1561–3.

55. Devine, E. and Cook, T. A meta-analytic analysis of effects of psychoeducational interventions on length of postsurgical hospital stay. *Nursing Research* 1983, 32: 267–74.

56. DuBois, D., Holloway, B., Valentine, J., and Cooper, H. Effectiveness of mentoring programs for youth: A meta-analytic review. *American Journal of Community Psychology* 2002, 30: 157–97.

57. Lumley, J., Oliver, S., and Waters, E. Interventions for promoting smoking cessation during pregnancy (Cochrane Review). *The Cochrane Library*, Issue 2, 2004. Chichester, UK: John Wiley & Sons.

58. CDC Evaluation Working Group: Steps in Program Evaluation: Centers for Disease Control, Atlanta, US, online at: http://www.cdc.gov/eval/steps.htm, 2004.

59. Anderson, L., Shinn, C., Fullilove, M., Scrimshaw, S., Fielding, J., Normand, J., et al. The effectiveness of early childhood development programs. A systematic review. *American Journal of Preventive Medicine* 2003, 24(3 Suppl): 32–46.

60. Briss, P., Pappaioanou, M., Fielding, J., Wright-de Aguero, L., Truman, B., Hopkins, D., et al. Developing an evidence-based guide to community preventive services – methods. *American Journal of Preventive Medicine* 2000, 18 (1S): 35–43.

61. Arai, L., Roen, K., Roberts, H., and Popay, J., It might work in Oklahoma, but will it work in Oakhampton? What does the effectiveness literature on domestic smoke detectors tell us about context and implementation? *Injury Prevention* 2005, 11: 148–51.

62. Bambra, C., Whitehead, M., and Hamilton, V. Does "welfare to work" work? A systematic review of the effectiveness of the UK's "welfare to work" programmes for people with a disability or chronic illness. *Social Science & Medicine* 2005, 60(9): 1905–18.

63. Pawson, R. Evidence and policy and naming and shaming: ESRC UK Centre for Evidence Based Policy and Practice: Working paper no. 5, 2001, online at: http://www.evidencenetwork.org/home.asp

64. Miller, N. and Pollock, V. Meta-analytic synthesis for theory development. In H. Cooper and L. Hedges (eds.) *The handbook of research synthesis*. New York: Russell Sage Foundation, 1994.

65. Pawson, R. Does Megan's Law work? A theory-driven systematic review: ESRC UK Centre for Evidence Based Policy and Practice: Working paper, 2002, online at: http://www.evidencenetwork.org/Documents/wp8.pdf [accessed February 24, 2005].

66. Powell, S. and Tod, J. A systematic review of how theories explain learning behaviour in school contexts. Research Evidence in Education Library. London: EPPI-Centre, Social Science Research Unit, Institute of Education, online at: http://eppi.ioe.ac.uk/EPPIWeb/home.aspx?&page=/reel/reviews.htm, 2004.

67. Pawson, R., Greenhalgh, T., Harvey, G., and Walshe, K. Realist synthesis: An introduction: ESRC Research Methods Programme, University of Manchester. RMP Methods Paper 2/2004, online at: http://www.ccsr.ac.uk/methods/publications/documents/RMPmethods2.pdf, 2004.

68. Rees, R., Harden, A., Shepherd, J., Brunton, G., Oliver, S., and Oakley, A. Young people and physical activity: A systematic review of research on barriers and facilitators. London: EPPI Centre, Institute of Education, University of London, online at: http://eppi.ioe.ac.uk/EPPIWeb/home.aspx, 2001.

69. McDermott, E. and Graham, H. Resilient young mothering: Social inequalities, late modernity and the "problem" of "teenage" motherhood. *Journal of Youth Studies* 2005, 8(1): 59–79.

70. Petticrew, M., Whitehead, M., Bambra, C., Egan, M., Graham, H., Macintyre, S., et al. *Systematic reviews in public health: The work of the ESRC Centre for Evidence Based Public Health Policy. An evidence-based approach to public health and tackling health inequalities*. Milton Keynes: Open University Press (in press).

71. Yardley, L. Dilemmas in qualitative health research. *Psychology and Health* 2000, 15: 215–28.

72. Mays, N. and Pope, C. Assessing quality in qualitative research. *British Medical Journal* 2000, 320: 50–2.

73. Popay, J., Rogers, A., and Williams, G. Rationale and standards for the systematic review of qualitative literature in health services research. *Qualitative Health Research* 1998, 8: 341–51.

74. Dixon-Woods, M., Shaw, R., Agarwal, S., and Smith, J. The problem of appraising qualitative research. *Quality & Safety in Healthcare* 2004, 13: 223–5.

75. Pearson, A., Wiechula, A., and Long, L. QARI: A systematic approach to the appraisal, extraction and synthesis of the findings of qualitative research. XI Cochrane Colloquium: Evidence, health care and culture, 2003, Barcelona.

76. Fitzpatrick, R. and Boulton, M. Qualitative methods for assessing health care. *Quality in Health Care* 1994, 3: 107–13.

77. Green, J. Generalisability and validity in qualitative research. *British Medical Journal* 1999, 319: 418–21.

78. Barbour, R. Checklists for improving rigour in qualitative research: A case of the tail wagging the dog? *British Medical Journal* 2001, 322: 1115–17.
79. Schulz, K., Chalmers, I., Hayes, R., and Altman, D. Empirical evidence of bias. Dimensions of methodological quality associated with estimates of treatment effects in controlled trials. *Journal of the American Medical Association* 1995, 273: 408–12.
80. MacAuley, D., McCrum, E., and Brown, C. Randomised controlled trial of the READER method of critical appraisal in general practice. *British Medical Journal* 1998, 316: 1134–7.
81. Shepherd, J., Harden, A., Rees, R., Brunton, G., Garcia, J., Oliver, S., et al. Young people and healthy eating: A systematic review of research on barriers and facilitators. London: Evidence for Policy and Practice Information and Co-ordinating Centre, Institute of Education, University of London, online at: http://eppi.ioe.ac.uk/EPPIWeb/home.aspx, 2001.
82. Lucas, P. et al. A systematic review of lay perspectives on infant size and growth (for project descrption please see http://www.city.ac.uk.chrpu/projects/infant growth.html).

Chapter 6

Synthesizing the evidence

6.1 INTRODUCTION

This chapter describes the process of assembling the jigsaw of evidence. For some systematic reviews, this stage can be relatively straightforward. If the pieces are similar enough (for example, if the interventions and study designs are similar, and if the studies include a similar set of dependent variables or outcomes) then it may be possible to carry out a meta-analysis. This allows the review question to be answered by calculating a quantitative summary measure, and permits a detailed statistical exploration of other factors that may affect the review's findings. The statistical principles underlying meta-analysis are easily understood, and meta-analysis is increasingly easy to carry out with the aid of various free and commercial software packages. A simple meta-analysis can even be done by hand or on a spreadsheet. Indeed the first meta-analyses were probably in use well before the computer age – perhaps as long ago as the seventeenth century.[1]

However, in social science systematic reviews, the studies are sometimes too heterogeneous to permit such a statistical summary, and, in the case of qualitative studies in particular, different methods of synthesis are more appropriate. In such situations some form of narrative synthesis of the studies is indicated. Carrying out a meta-analysis does not, of course, preclude carrying out a narrative synthesis in tandem. Doing both together may even make for a better and more thorough review. This chapter discusses narrative synthesis and meta-analysis separately, in sections 6.2 and 6.11 below, respectively. Before any such synthesis is attempted however, it is useful to visually inspect the data, for example, by means of a **Forest plot**. This graphical method of displaying study findings is discussed in section 6.12.

6.2 NARRATIVE SYNTHESIS OF QUANTITATIVE STUDIES

Tabulating the included studies

Tabulating the study findings is one of the most important steps towards a narrative synthesis (or indeed a meta-analysis for that matter). One or more tables should be drawn up, which should include a full description of the studies, their populations, methods, and results. Clear, detailed tables increase the transparency of the review. They show the reader which data have been extracted from which studies, and they clarify the contribution made by each study to the overall synthesis. Tables can also reveal something of the review's wider context; that is, they can be used not just to present details of each study's methods and findings, but to organize and present information on the context, setting, and population within which each study was conducted. In short, clear, well-organized tables show how each study's data contribute to the reviewer's final conclusions, and they allow the reader to assess whether they would have come to similar conclusions, based on the same set of data.

Normally, several tables are needed. One table can be used to present information on the study setting, the intervention, the study methods, the participants, and the study findings. A further table may be used to summarize the results of the critical appraisal for each study. It is also helpful to the reader to provide a description of what the tables show, in the form of a short narrative summary of the study results in the main text of the review. This is discussed in more detail later in this chapter.

The tables themselves, although important, do not constitute a "synthesis" of the studies. Rather, the synthesis draws on the tables, and takes into account the biases and other issues identified by the critical appraisal process, which may affect the interpretation of each study's findings. This means that a narrative summary may give greater "weight" to those studies that are the most methodologically sound – but this narrative "weighting" should not be done independently of other aspects of the studies, such as their generalizability. Box 6.1 gives the first steps toward a narrative synthesis.

Dealing with study quality

As discussed in the previous chapter, the included studies are likely to vary in quality (methodological soundness). One means of dealing with this variation is to focus the review solely on the "best" (most methodologically

Box 6.1   First steps toward a narrative synthesis

The initial key tasks involve summarizing the results of the studies, summarizing the range and size of the associations these studies report, and describing the most important characteristics of the included studies (such as the population within which the study was conducted, the study methods, details of interventions that were evaluated, and their outcomes, if relevant). A detailed commentary on the major methodological problems or biases that affect the studies should also be included, with a description of how this appears to have affected the individual study results, and the review's conclusions (see Box 6.3).

robust) studies. This makes sense if there is a large enough "pool" of homogenous, robust studies to draw upon. For example, some systematic reviews synthesize the results of RCTs of the same intervention, carried out in similar populations, in preference to studies of other designs. Depending on the question addressed, this approach is not always possible and, as explained in chapter 2, a more heterogeneous set of studies, such as studies of different designs or studies which use very different methods, will often be included in a review. If the RCTs appear not to be generalizable because they are carried out in highly selected populations, it may be more helpful to select studies for review on the basis of *both* internal and external validity, rather than on the basis of internal validity alone. The results of the experimental studies (if any) can then be usefully compared with the findings from non-experimental studies. This is an approach with some similarities to cross-design synthesis, and triangulation, both of which are described below (see section 6.6).

If a range of study designs is included, then it will be helpful to the reader to compare their findings – for example, by comparing randomized and non-randomized studies, or controlled and uncontrolled studies – rather than treating them as a homogeneous group. It has been found that randomized and non-randomized evaluations of the same intervention can often produce different conclusions. In particular it has been suggested that non-randomized studies over-estimate effect sizes – that is, they may conclude that treatments are more effective than they really are, because of the systematic bias introduced by the non-random allocation of individuals.

As discussed in chapter 5, this may in some cases inflate effect sizes by up to 40 percent.[2] This finding, and other work by Shadish and Ragsdale[3] and others[4] call into question the practice of combining randomized and non-randomized studies in the same meta-analysis. Similarly, in etiological reviews that investigate risk factors, the results of prospective and retrospective studies should be analyzed separately and compared. The direction of relationships and attributions of causality are more difficult to establish in retrospective studies, while prospective studies are usually taken to provide more robust estimates of effect. This assumption can be examined if the studies are synthesized separately.

Selecting studies for analysis on the basis of study quality or study design alone can introduce bias into a review. This can happen if the higher quality studies differ systematically from the other studies in the review on characteristics other than study quality. For example, the types of intervention that tend to be evaluated by means of RCTs typically differ from those evaluated using non-experimental methods; RCTs are less commonly used to evaluate policies, and are less likely to be applied to interventions delivered to communities, areas, and large populations. RCTs are instead more commonly used at present to evaluate interventions delivered directly to individuals. This means that if the review includes (say) only RCTs there may be an in-built bias towards individual-level interventions, and thus the review may present a skewed view of the available evidence within that particular topic area.

This last point is most easily illustrated with an example from a recent systematic review which sought to identify interventions to promote a "modal shift" in transport choice; that is, interventions to influence people to walk and cycle, rather than using their cars.[5] Here, knowing "what works" is of interest to policymakers for reasons of public health, given the increase in levels of obesity in most developed countries. It is also important to policymakers in other sectors, because it may allow us to identify the most effective means of reducing traffic congestion and perhaps environmental damage. The interventions that have been evaluated to date range from offering tailored self-help materials to households and individuals in order to encourage them to leave their car at home, to city-wide initiatives, such as publicity campaigns, new cycle routes, financial incentives, traffic management and congestion charging schemes. Some of these interventions (such as traffic management measures, and financial incentives to motorists) have been evaluated in non-experimental studies. These are often interventions that could be applied at a population level, for example, to an entire city. There are also experimental studies that have evaluated the impact of interventions that have been specifically tailored to individuals, or households. Synthesizing experimental evidence would, therefore, tend to bias the review towards intensive, focused interventions, which target individuals, while overlooking many interventions which could be implemented on a city-wide level – perhaps more easily and cheaply. Moreover, the populations included in the experimental and non-experimental studies are often different; the participants in some of the trials are highly selected, and it is unclear whether the intervention could be applied to the wider population. In this case, synthesizing only RCT evidence would restrict the review to particular types of intervention, and perhaps to particular types of participant, thus limiting the generalizability of the review's findings.

The review in question (see Box 6.2) took an inclusive approach, by including a range of study designs and populations, and then categorizing

---

Box 6.2 Promoting walking and cycling as an alternative to using cars: What works? A systematic review[5]

The question

What interventions are effective in promoting a population shift from using cars towards walking and cycling?

The search for evidence

The authors sought published and unpublished reports in any language from 18 electronic databases, and from bibliographies, websites, and reference lists.

What sort of studies were included?

The review included experimental or observational evaluation studies, with a controlled or uncontrolled prospective design or a controlled retrospective design, of the effects of any policy, program or project applied to an identifiable urban population or area in an OECD member state by measuring outcomes in a sample of local households, residents, commuters, drivers, or school pupils.

What were the outcomes of interest?

Changes in the distribution of transport mode choice between cars and walking and cycling; effects on any measure of human health, fitness, health-related behavior or well-being; and the distribution of effects between social groups.

Synthesizing the study findings

Twenty two studies met the inclusion criteria: three randomized controlled trials, seven non-randomized controlled prospective studies, eleven uncontrolled prospective studies and one controlled retrospective study. Studies were categorized according to the main focus of the intervention assessed, and within each category, the results of the studies were reported in decreasing order of internal validity.

The review's conclusions

There was some evidence that targeted behavior change programs can indeed change behavior, resulting (in the largest study) in a modal shift of around 5 percent of all trips at a population level. Modest effects were also found for commuter subsidies, and a new railway station. The balance of best available evidence about publicity campaigns, engineering measures, and other interventions did not suggest that they were effective.

(Photo: David Ogilvie)

the interventions before summarizing their results, ordered by study quality. This systematic ordering and description of the results of the studies lies at the core of most systematic reviews. Its purpose is to assess in turn each of the studies, "weighing" its quality and applicability, after categorizing them within conceptually and/or methodologically similar groups. The reader's judgment may differ from those made by the reviewer, but the decisions and the results of those decisions are made explicit, and are described in advance. Moreover the data on which those decisions are made is there in the tables and in the text for all interested parties to see, and challenge, if necessary. It is important to consider and describe in advance how the studies will be ordered and synthesized, otherwise there is a risk that the studies will appear to have been selected and reviewed to support some prior belief or hypothesis. The organization and grouping of the studies will instead often be driven by theoretical considerations. For example, it may be based on conceptual or other similarities between the studies.

It is helpful to highlight the higher quality studies in your review, and to explore how their results may be different from the more methodologically biased studies. It is also helpful to the reader to explore how other study characteristics relate to study conclusions. Was the intervention more effective in children than in adults, for example? Were studies that used more objective outcome assessments more likely to report that the intervention was less effective? (This is often the case.) This exploration of heterogeneity and the impact of moderator variables may involve conducting a sensitivity analysis, as described in chapter 7.

Finally, you should aim to produce a short summary statement presenting the results of your review, based on the most methodologically robust studies (see Box 6.3). It may be helpful before attempting to do this to examine the "results" sections of published systematic reviews, to see how they have tackled the same task.

6.3 NARRATIVE SYNTHESIS IN THREE STEPS

The narrative synthesis can be carried out in several ways. Probably the most commonly used approach in reviews of effectiveness starts with a narrative summary of the findings of the quantitative outcome evaluations. It may be helpful to break this process down into three steps: (i) organizing the description of the studies into logical categories; (ii) analyzing the findings *within* each of the categories; and (iii) synthesizing the findings *across* all included studies.

Box 6.3   Example of the description of methodological quality in a systematic review of quantitative studies

Systematic review of interventions for preventing obesity in children[6]

Five of the seven long-term studies were RCTs. All of these five studies randomized by cluster, three by schools, one by classes within schools, and one by families. However, only three of these RCTs statistically accounted for the potential unit of analysis errors. In addition, power calculations were only discussed in two of these studies. Allocation of groups to intervention or control was concealed in two studies, blinded outcome assessment was reported in one study, and baseline differences between intervention and control groups were discussed in all studies. All studies reported follow-up of more than 80 percent of the baseline sample.

The remaining long-term studies were non-randomized trials with concurrent control group. One study had very poor rates of follow-up over the two-year period of the study, while the other did not adequately describe attrition. None of these studies discussed the potential of contamination between study groups.

References to the specific studies appear in the original review.

1.   Organization of studies

The analysis of the data will be helped by a logical organization of the data from the included studies. This becomes particularly important as the number of studies in the review rises. A simple list of studies, their methods and their conclusions may be relatively easy to interpret, and easy for a reader to follow if there are only four studies in the review. By comparison, a list-like presentation of the results of 40 studies may simply be confusing. It is therefore essential to carefully plan the layout of the studies and their findings, and in particular to consider how they can be organized and presented in meaningful categories. There is no definitive approach, as the organization and choice of meaningful categories will be driven in part by the review question. For example, it is likely that the studies will vary in terms of the intervention, population, design, setting, and in the types of outcomes or processes assessed. Thus, in some cases, it will be useful to group studies by type of population (policy-level interventions may be discussed together, then community-level, then individual-level interventions), and within those categories, to order them by study design. In other cases categorizing studies by type of outcome may be more meaningful.

Organizing studies primarily by study design, or by study quality can illustrate where the strongest evidence (in terms of internal validity) lies. Grouping the studies by the outcomes they included will facilitate answering questions about how those outcomes may best be achieved; and grouping studies by intervention type will help answer questions about the relative effectiveness of those interventions. These are different, but, of course, related questions.

Where qualitative and other data on processes or implementation, and on the views of users are available from the primary studies, this may be reported together with the quantitative findings. Explanations of the reasons for impact, or lack of impact, may come from these studies, rather than from the outcome evaluations.

This advice about careful organization and categorization of the studies also extends to preparing the study tables. Logically organized tables facilitate the subsequent analysis and summary of the study findings, and help the investigation of moderator variables, and sources of heterogeneity. However, alphabetical organization of tables (by first study author) is commonly used, as this can make it easier for readers to compare the narrative descriptions in the text of the review with the tabulated data (see Tables 6.1 and 6.2).

The organization of data from qualitative studies similarly requires careful planning, and the approach to critical appraisal and synthesis of the included studies will be different from that taken with quantitative research. While in reviews of quantitative studies statistical synthesis (meta-analysis) may be possible, this approach is not applicable to purely qualitative information. Even so, presentation and synthesis can be aided by the use of tabular summaries of methods, participants, and data. This systematic organization and presentation of the data can help the reader and reviewer to identify themes across studies, as well as facilitating theory-testing by exploring similarities and differences between study findings. There are at present no standard approaches to the synthesis of qualitative research, though meta-ethnography is increasingly widely used. This approach to synthesis involves exploring the relationships and differences between the study findings, and the extent to which they reflect common, higher order, themes.[7,8,9]

Table 6.1 Example: Descriptive table from a systematic review of modal shifts in transport choice

Study	Year	Intervention	Study population	Study design	Primary outcome
Adelaide[23]	1998	Tailored feedback on travel diaries with suggestions on changing travel patterns, supported with customised information (Travel Blending)	Households living, working or visiting in two neighbourhoods of Adelaide	Uncontrolled prospective panel study	Reported frequency of, and time spent on, all trips in a seven-day travel diary by mode
Boston[34]	1978	Car restriction, subsidised bus services and pedestrianisation in central business district	Employees in city centre office buildings in Boston	Uncontrolled repeated cross-sectional study	Reported mode of journey to work on day before survey
California (cashing out)[35]	1992	State legislation requiring employers with at least 50 staff to "cash-out" the cost of rented parking spaces	Employees at workplaces in urban South California	Controlled repeated cross-sectional study	Reported mode of all journeys to work over five consecutive days
California (telecommuting)[29]	1993	Voluntary use of neighbourhood telecommuting centres as an alternative to commuting to their usual workplace	Registered users of telecommuting centres in California	Retrospective study using participants as their own controls	Reported mode of all trips recorded over two periods of three consecutive days
Camden-Islington[25]	NR	Site-specific advice to participating schools from a school travel coordinator	Pupils in primary schools in two London boroughs	Cluster randomised controlled trial	Reported mode of journeys to school on one day
Delft[29]	1982	Upgrading and increased connectivity (+3.3 km) of cycle route network	Households in suburbs of Delft	Controlled repeated cross-sectional study with nested panel study of a subset of respondents	Reported mode of all trips of residents aged 10 and over on one of a number of specified days covering all the days of the week

(Continued)

Table 6.1 (*Cont'd*)

Study	Year	Intervention	Study population	Study design	Primary outcome
Detmold-Rosenheim[30]	1981	Bicycle-friendly demonstration project in two towns, mainly consisting of planning and building improvements to cycle route network (+31 km, +13 km respectively)	Households in both towns	Controlled repeated cross-sectional study	Reported mode of all trips of residents aged 10 and over on one of a number of specified days covering all the days of the week
England (bypasses)[33]	1992	Construction of bypasses, followed by a variety of traffic calming measures and enhanced walking or cycling facilities in each town centre	Residents of six small towns in England	Uncontrolled repeated cross-sectional study	Reported main mode of residents' journeys to town centres
England (20 mph zones)[32]	1996	Construction of 20 mph (30 km/h) zones, enforced using a range of engineering measures	Residents of neighbourhoods in six towns in northern England	Uncontrolled repeated cross-sectional study	Stated change in travel patterns

Table 6.2 Example of tabulated outcome data from the review in Table 6.1

Validity score	Study, primary reference and secondary reference(s) if relevant	Sample size	Response rate	Follow-up rate	Follow-up (months)	Outcome measure	Findings
7	Delft[29] [W13-19]	1937 households	Before: 68% After: NR	NA	36	Reported mode of all trips of residents aged 10 and over on one of a number of specified days covering all the days of the week	In the main intervention area, cycling share increased from 40% to 43% of all trips, the frequency of bike trips increased by 4% and the frequency of car trips did not change. A comparison of similar trips made by a sub-panel of respondents in the intervention area who participated in both survey waves (a sample described by authors as "biased", sample size not reported) found a positive modal shift of 0.6% of all trips from a baseline of 66.2%; 8.8% of cycling trips after the intervention had been shifted from

(Continued)

Table 6.2 (Cont'd)

Validity score	Study, primary reference and secondary reference(s) if relevant	Sample size	Response rate	Follow-up rate	Follow-up (months)	Outcome measure	Findings
							other modes, of which 4.4% came from walking and 3.3% came from the car. In a secondary intervention area which received only improvements to the bike route to the city centre, cycling mode share increased from 38% to 39%. In the control area, the frequency of car trips increased by 15% and the frequency of bike trips did not change. Insufficient data to judge statistical precision of results.

Qualitative research in systematic reviews may either be combined with quantitative findings in order to help "weight" positive, negative, or anomalous findings, or may be reported in its own right, alongside a quantitative synthesis providing insights into the review questions not illuminated by quantitative evidence alone.[10, 11]

2.   Within study analysis

This involves a narrative description of the findings for each study, often with a description of study quality. In the example in Box 6.4 the description presented by the authors is quite detailed, as it is taken from the full version of a Cochrane review of smoking cessation interventions. They also provide extensive tables describing the quantitative outcomes. The summary of each study is likely to be very much shorter than this when a

---

Box 6.4   Description of some of the results of the Stanford Three-city project

The Stanford Three-city Project (Maccoby 1977) aimed to reduce the cardiovascular risk factors of smoking, high cholesterol, high blood pressure, overweight, and inactivity, through the use of mass media and community programmes. In a quasi-experimental design one town, Watsonville, was exposed to both mass media and community programmes, while another town, Gilroy, was exposed to the mass media component alone, and the third town, Tracy, received no intervention and was the comparison community. The innovative mass media component used television and radio spots to model the appropriate skills for behaviour change as well as television and radio programming, newspaper advertisements and stories, billboards, posters and printed materials mailed to participants. People at higher risk for cardiovascular disease were especially targeted in Watsonville for individual risk reduction counselling, which constituted the community component of this intervention.

After two years, compared with Tracy, the non-intervention town, there was a lower per capita cigarette consumption in Watsonville, which received the mass media campaign and the community intervention, with an even lower level among the intensive intervention group. An intermediate reduction in per capita cigarette consumption was observed in Gilroy, the town exposed to the mass media campaign alone.

(Continued)

Box 6.4 *(Cont'd)*

Mediating Variables: Knowledge of cardiovascular risk factors was assessed by a 25-item questionnaire, which included three items about smoking. There were significant increases in overall knowledge scores in the two intervention cities after 2 years, compared with Tracy. The intensive instruction intervention of the high-risk group in Watsonville improved this.

Process evaluation: The media campaign was monitored and feedback used formatively. Network analysis was also used to trace the path of communications within the community, however limited information is presented in relation to this.

Evidence relating to exposure: Information was collected in relation to the number of mass media messages broadcast.

Dose-response: Evidence was presented to suggest a significant dose-response relationship. Increased levels of intervention exposure were associated with improvements in knowledge of CVD risk. No evidence comparing dose in the intervention and comparison areas was found, but the gains in knowledge of CVD risk were greater in the intervention cities than in Tracy.

Maintenance: The two-year programme was followed by a third "maintenance year" of reduced effort.

(From a Cochrane systematic review of community interventions for reducing smoking among adults)[12]

review is written up as a journal article. In reviews that include many primary studies, a limited description of each study (other than that which appears in the tables) may sometimes be all that is possible, for reasons of space.

This example was chosen because the review shows how to provide short, clear, summary information on a range of process and outcome measures for a complex social intervention. Many of the descriptions of primary studies in this particular review are very much longer, depending on the study being described.

3. Cross-study synthesis

Conventionally, the summary of the results of the review often begins with a simple description of the amount of information that the review has uncovered. For example, this might consist of a statement outlining the number of studies that met the inclusion criteria, and describing their designs and settings. This gives the reader an overview of the scale of the review, and the type of evidence that has met the inclusion criteria. An overall statement of the effects of the intervention may also be presented. For example, in the smoking review described earlier, the overall findings are first presented for all adults, and then separately for women and men, as a range of effect sizes: "For all adults, the net decline in smoking prevalence ranged from -1.0% to $+3.0\%$ per year (10 studies). For women, the decline ranged from -0.2% to $+3.5\%$ per year (11 studies), and for men the decline ranged from -0.4% to $+1.6\%$ per year (n = 12)."

Summary information on the effects of mediating variables (such as knowledge and attitudes) is also presented. For example: "Among the seven studies which assessed attitudes to quitting smoking, only one showed a net intervention effect: a significant progression through the stages of change."

The results of the individual studies are then described, study by study, as in Box 6.4. This review also provided detailed summary-level information on a wide range of study characteristics (Box 6.5). The full version of this review can be found in the Cochrane Library, which is freely available through most university libraries <http://www.cochrane.org/>.

The main aim of the cross-study synthesis is to produce an overall summary of the study findings taking account of variations in study quality, and other variations (such as variations in populations, interventions, and settings) that may affect the generalizability of the results. This process is made much easier by well-organized, detailed tables, but is also made easier by using graphical displays of the results of the studies, for example by means of Forest plots, or **stem-and-leaf** diagrams even if no meta-analysis is carried out (see chapter 7).

Box 6.5   Community interventions for reducing smoking among adults: Describing the studies

This review set out to address the questions:

1. Do community-based interventions reduce smoking in adults (measured by prevalence, cigarette consumption, quit rates, or initiation rates) compared with no intervention in comparison communities?

(Continued)

Box 6.5 *(Cont'd)*

2. Which characteristics of these studies are related to their efficacy?

It included trials which randomized either communities or geographical regions, and non-randomized controlled trials, and found 32 studies in total.

To help summarize the evidence presented by these studies, the reviewers included detailed summary descriptions of the following study characteristics.

Description of the studies

- Characteristics of the communities (including the countries in which they were located and the size of the community);
- Characteristics of the participants (including details of gender and ethnicity);
- Characteristics of the interventions (details of the type of intervention, its content, theoretical basis, and of the outcomes it was intended to influence);
- Delivery of the intervention (the channels through which it was delivered, and whether there was community involvement);
- Evaluation methods, and lengths of follow-up;
- Smoking-related outcomes (how they were measured, and validated);
- Moderator variables, and intermediate outcomes (including attitudes to smoking among participants, and degree of social support);
- Sustainability (the extent to which the intervention was maintained in communities after external funding ceased).

Process evaluation

- Including details of programme penetration, and details of any formative evaluations and pilot studies.
- Dose-response assessment (assessment of whether there was a relationship between the "amount" of the intervention received, and a smoking behavioural outcome).

Methodological quality

- Methods of allocation to intervention or comparison groups;
- How participants were selected for the studies;
- Response rates, and rates of attrition;
- Baseline comparability of intervention and comparison groups;
- Whether the evaluations were done independently by those developing and delivering the intervention, or by external evaluators.

  (From a Cochrane systematic review of community interventions for reducing smoking among adults)[12]

The synthesis across studies should also aim to explore differences between studies, often described as investigating study heterogeneity. This entails an examination of any variations between study findings, and an exploration of the reasons behind those variations (see chapter 7). This can also involve examination of the effects of moderator variables.

Another example of a narrative summary is given in Box 6.6. This example comes from a review of the effectiveness of parenting programs. The full review appears on the Campbell Collaboration website <http://www.campbellcollaboration.org>.

6.4   BEST EVIDENCE SYNTHESIS (BES)

The "modal shift" review in Box 6.2 refers to synthesizing the "best available evidence." This approach is commonly used (often implicitly) by systematic reviewers, and derives from an approach described by educational researcher Robert Slavin. In Best Evidence Synthesis (BES), studies that meet minimal standards of adequacy and relevance to the review are included. BES combines the meta-analytic approach of extracting quantitative information in a common standard format from each study with a systematic approach to the assessment of study quality and study relevance.[14, 15]

Box 6.6 Teenage parents and their children: Narrative summary of individual studies[13]

Examples of narrative descriptions can be seen in the reports of completed reviews that appear on the Campbell and Cochrane Collaboration websites. See, for example the review by Coren and Barlow of the effectiveness of individual and group-based parenting <http://www.campbellcollaboration.org/Fralibrary2.html>. This review included only RCTs of programs that had used at least one standardized instrument (such as a questionnaire) to assess the psychosocial and developmental outcomes of teenage parents and their children.

In their summary of the study results, the authors present details of the intervention, the study methods, and the study quality, followed by a summary of the outcomes in a standard format (effect sizes with 95 percent **confidence intervals**; for example: "The results show a large significant effect favoring the parents in the intervention group −0.61[−1.34,−0.11])." This is followed by a discussion of the generalizability of the review's results.

Finally, there is discussion of the implications of the results for practice and for further research. The results of the review suggest that, overall, parenting programs may be effective in improving a range of psychosocial and developmental outcomes in this group.

An example of a systematic review by Robert Slavin and Alan Cheung that used BES can be found on the website of the research organization CRESPAR (Center for Research on the Education of Students Placed at Risk − a collaboration between Johns Hopkins University and Howard University.[16] This report reviews evidence on the effectiveness of methods of teaching reading to English language learners, concentrating on the relative effectiveness of bilingual instruction methods versus English "immersion" classes. In the authors' own words, the review uses: "consistent, clear standards to identify unbiased, meaningful information from experimental studies and then discusses each qualifying study, computing effect sizes but also describing the context, design, and findings of each study." The review includes both randomized and non-randomized out-come evaluations. Among the findings of this extensive review was that native language instruction can be beneficial for the English reading of English language learners.

BES has been used most often to explore educational issues. A range of Best Evidence Syntheses, for example, are available on the New Zealand Ministry of Education website <http://www.minedu.govt.nz/>. The strength of this approach is that it is not prescriptive about the study designs that need to be included. The inclusion criteria vary from review to review, depending on the review question; and because reviews can include more than one ques-tion (perhaps questions about what works, along with questions about *how* it works) then different subsets of studies can be incorporated into the review as appropriate. The "what works" question may be answered by outcome evaluations (both trials and observational studies), while questions about "how it works" may be best answered by reliable studies describing the intervention itself, and how it was implemented (and this information may come from a wide range of types of study, including, but not limited to, qualitative research). Descriptions of the context and other aspects may come from case studies, which include no robust outcome information, but which may give some insight into context and setting. BES aims to identify and synthesize these diverse sources of evidence, but from the above description one may see that BES is simply an example of good systematic review practice, with some small differences. Suri suggests that one of these differ-ences is that in extracting data from the primary studies BES tends towards calculating the median effect size, rather than calculating a weighted mean effect size, as is standard meta-analytic practice.[17]

6.5   VOTE COUNTING

The easiest method of summarizing the results of the studies is by means of a "vote count"; for example, counting which studies show a particular policy to be effective, and which show it is ineffective, and comparing the two numbers. Although easy to use, this approach is usually inappropriate. The problems with this approach were outlined in some detail by Light and Smith over 30 years ago.[18] These include the fact that it ignores sample size (small studies count just as much as large studies), it takes little account of study methods and study quality (poor methods and biased studies count just as much as robust studies), it overlooks qualitative differences between subsets of studies, and it does not permit analysis of interactions between variables in the studies. It is also low-powered for the range of sample sizes and effects most often encountered in the social sciences.[19]

Allowing "parity of esteem" among small, biased studies and larger, well-conducted studies in this way may seem nicely democratic, but it has no place in systematic reviews, where some studies really are "more equal than others," and vote counting can introduce serious bias into a review. Say, for example, the reviewer identifies five RCTs, three of which suggest that a particular intervention is effective, and two of which suggest that it is ineffective. One might conclude on the basis of a quick vote count that the balance of evidence (three trials) suggests that the intervention "works." However, if the first three trials had serious methodological problems, and the other two were more robust, then one might come to quite the opposite conclusion. In short, the balance of the evidence may suggest one thing, but the balance of the *best* evidence can often suggest something quite different. Vote counting should therefore be used with caution. Synthesis of the results of the primary studies should instead be strongly influenced by the results of the critical appraisal. It should differentiate between studies on grounds of size and quality, and other relevant qualitative criteria (such as how, and to whom the intervention was delivered, in the case of reviews of effectiveness).

Many traditional reviews adopt an implicit vote-counting approach, in which the authors list the studies, and summarize those whose results come

Box 6.7   The science of reviewing research

Oxman and Guyatt[20] convened a panel of researchers to judge the methodological rigor of 36 literature reviews, using a set of objective criteria including whether the reviewer had specified his or her methodology, and whether the review's conclusions were supported by the reported data. They also surveyed the reviews' authors about their levels of expertise, the time they had spent on their reviews, and the strength of their prior opinions, and found an *inverse* relationship between self-assessed expertise, and review quality: "Our data suggest that experts, on average, write reviews of inferior quality; that the greater the expertise the more likely the quality is to be poor; and that the poor quality may be related to the strength of the prior opinions and the amount of time they spend preparing a review article."

out "for" the hypothesis being tested, and those that are "against." Some weighing of the evidence in the author's mental scales then takes place, before the conclusion is reached that "most studies show..." This approach is similar to vote counting (but without the scientific rigor). Like vote-counting, it overlooks variations between the studies and it also depends on the reviewers' mental scales being calibrated correctly. (There is some evidence that they are not: see Box 6.7.)

6.6   CROSS-DESIGN SYNTHESIS

Cross-design synthesis is a method proposed by the General Accounting Office in the US to bring together secondary data from database analysis and the results of RCTs. It has been recognized in medicine, as in other fields, that RCTs, while high in internal validity, in some cases may not include a representative sample of the population and so generalizability of the findings of some trials has been questioned. The RCT may be assessing the impact of the intervention in the best possible circumstances (one where the content, delivery, and uptake of the intervention can be well-controlled). In contrast, observational data such as those available from routine databases may be more typical of those who deliver and receive the intervention outside of research settings.[21]

Cross-design synthesis in theory combines the complementary strengths of experimental and non-experimental research – for example by adjusting the results of RCTs by standardizing RCT results to the distributions obtained from database analyses.[22, 23] Such approaches may only infrequently be applicable to systematic reviews of social interventions because large observational datasets derived from routine practice, coupled with RCTs, may often not be available.

6.7   BEST AVAILABLE EVIDENCE

In our own reviews of the effects of social interventions (such as transport, housing, and employment interventions) we have generally taken an approach similar to Best Evidence Synthesis, in which the reviewer works with whatever evidence is available, taking account of study design and quality. This is based on an assumption that a review which simply seeks RCTs in a topic area where logic suggests none are likely, and reports ruefully that there are none, before suggesting that "more research is needed," is likely to be of limited value to decision makers (Box 6.8). In some of our reviews, it is unlikely that randomized controlled trials will exist (the building of new roads being an obvious example),[24] but there is often a wealth of observational evidence. It seems more important to assess and synthesize the existing evidence base, however flawed, than to lament the absence of better studies (though, one usually does both).

This is not to understate the importance of using systematic reviews to identify research "gaps" – areas where new research really is needed. Indeed, every systematic review should aim to include recommendations for future research, and they are the most reliable means of identifying missing pieces of the jigsaw. However in many cases, particularly in the case of reviews that aim to assess the impact of social policies, those who commission a review are probably less likely to want to know about the dearth of evidence, than to find out what the available evidence says about the impacts of the intervention in question, while acknowledging that the evidence base is still far from perfect. In practice this means that "systematic reviews of best available evidence" are often characterized by:

- An initial, inclusive search which initially does not seek to exclude studies on grounds of study design alone.
- Efforts to include *all* evaluative studies of the intervention in question, of any design (controlled and uncontrolled), and, where relevant, other observational studies (such as cohort studies) that may suggest potential interventions.

Box 6.8 "More evidence is needed"

The Walrus and the Carpenter
Were walking close at hand;
They wept like anything to see
Such quantities of sand:
"If this were only cleared away,"
They said, "it would be grand!"

(The Walrus and the Carpenter
Lewis Carroll, 1872)

- Incorporation of all those studies in the review, which implies the use of a range of different critical appraisal (quality assessment) tools, often specially tailored to the topic area.
- A range of approaches to synthesizing that heterogeneous evidence – including the use of schematic diagrams summarizing the range, quality, and type of research evidence available.

Clearly this approach may not always be appropriate, and of course it has costs. One cost of using wide initial inclusion criteria is that the searches generally produce very large numbers of "hits" – sometimes many thousands of titles and abstracts – because studies cannot easily be excluded automatically by means of the search filters. The reviewer may therefore need to search through very large haystacks to find relatively few needles. In some of our own systematic reviews, we have carried out reviews with wide inclusion criteria, but have still located few evaluative studies of any design – and so the final number of studies to be reviewed in depth in many reviews of social interventions is likely to be in the tens, or fewer, depending on the inclusion criteria, rather than in the hundreds (as is the case with studies evaluating the effects of homework[25] or psychotherapy[26]). The numbers are small because many social interventions have not been subject to outcome evaluation; and even where evaluations have been carried out there have often been few replication studies, as Ann Oakley has pointed out.[27, 28] In many social policy areas, despite adopting an inclusive approach to evidence, the final evidence base, which needs to be critically appraised and summarized, often remains relatively small. This is not unusual; the typical Cochrane systematic review contains about six trials, with a median number of participants per review of 945.[29]

6.8   TRIANGULATION IN SYSTEMATIC REVIEWS

Social systematic reviews often draw together a range of evidence comprising studies of varying design and quality. This has similarities to the process of "triangulation"[25] and works on the principle that where hard evidence of outcomes from trials does not exist, other suggestive evidence may be sought from observational evaluative studies such as controlled before-and–after studies, and perhaps etiological studies such as case-control studies, and prospective cohort studies. Triangulating this information across different sources may fill some of the gaps in the evidence base. For many social interventions there will be little evidence from controlled studies to review – but this does not mean that "no" evidence exists (scientist J. B. S. Haldane illustrated how one should not mistake "absence of evidence" for "evidence of absence," by pointing out that in England in the Middle Ages there was "no evidence" for the existence of Australia). Indicative evidence to suggest which interventions may be effective, and require further evaluation, may be found elsewhere. Indications of the range and type of positive and negative impacts may be identified from observational etiological studies, and from qualitative research. When the evidence jigsaw is suspected to have many pieces missing, it makes sense to try to collect as much as possible of the pieces that do exist. Some creative reconstruction or filling in of the gaps may even be possible.[30]

On the other hand, where there is ample evidence from trials, these are likely to represent the least biased estimates of effect. For example, a review which examined the effectiveness of psychological debriefing after traumatic events (such as road accidents, assaults, fires, violent crimes, and traumatic childbirth), included only RCTs (n = 11).[31] The results did not suggest that single session debriefing was helpful in reducing distress, or reducing post-traumatic stress disorder (PTSD), and one trial found an increase in the risk of PTSD after debriefing.

In other topic areas, where RCTs are less common, the inclusion criteria for systematic reviews are appropriately broader. Our systematic review of the health and social impacts of new road building sought a range of study designs, including before-and-after studies involving controls, uncontrolled before-and-after studies, and retrospective studies involving controls (including historical controls).[24] Thirty-two studies made it into the final review (but, as was expected, no RCTs).

6.9 REVIEWING COMPLEX EVIDENCE

It is still common practice to carry out reviews with deliberately restricted inclusion criteria, which include a narrow range of study designs, and seek to answer tightly-focused questions. Systematic reviews work well in these circumstances, because they are very efficient hypothesis-testing tools.[32] It is often assumed that this is the only sort of systematic review that is possible, and that they are only capable of dealing with simple interventions, which are discrete, easily evaluated in RCTs, easily described, and vary little in terms of implementation. Medical interventions are often (erroneously) seen as falling into this category, on the assumption that the context within which they are delivered matters little. While it is true that the mechanisms by which aspirin works on headache are much the same whether it is taken by a patient in York, or New York, this is not the case with all health care interventions, and even for simple interventions, the implementation of the intervention will vary. Very focused systematic reviews testing single hypotheses about effectiveness or efficacy are seen as acceptable in medicine, but are less well-accepted, and may sometimes be less appropriate, in the social sciences.

Systematic reviews of interventions that have a large social component (including policies) may often need to consider and include detailed information on the context within which that intervention was carried out. Such reviews may also frequently focus on clusters, or programs of interventions, rather than single interventions. Take, for example, welfare-to-work programs, which are designed to enable and enhance the transition from out-of-work benefit receipt to paid employment.[33] While the term "welfare to work" is probably recognizable in many western countries, the component parts of the program vary widely, as do the welfare and political systems within which the program is delivered. A review of the international literature on welfare to work would probably not be very meaningful if it did not include detailed information on the welfare, cultural, and political contexts within which the program was delivered, but instead assumed that the intervention was the same everywhere, as if it were some sort of social version of aspirin. Potential users of the review would clearly need to know much more about the context within which such a complex intervention is delivered – and more about the intervention itself than simply its description. "Aspirin" means the same thing in most cultures. "Welfare," and "work," do not.

This has several implications. The first is that reviews of complex social interventions are themselves often complex, extensive, and expensive, because of the need to locate and review very heterogeneous types of evidence. Some of the issues to consider are listed below, drawing on key points from previous chapters.

- *More work is required to define the question, or questions*: A wide range of questions may need to be considered by reviewers of social interventions: not just "what works," but why it worked; how was it implemented or delivered; if it did not work in some settings, why not; and what is known of the context within which it was delivered. A review, may, for example include a primary question about effectiveness and a range of further questions about process and implementation factors.
- *The inclusion criteria for studies will be complex*: At its simplest, a review of the effectiveness of a clearly defined, and unvarying intervention, which is easily evaluated, may be able to restrict itself to single study

designs; RCTs for example. By comparison the answers to questions about the delivery and context of complex interventions may need to be sought from a range of different types of study. Some, but not all of these answers, will be found in qualitative research, and other answers will come from surveys, or from other study designs. Some answers (for example, information about the context) may be found in policy and administrative documents, which are not "research" in the formal sense.

- *The search for studies will be complex*: Some of this information will not be published at all, because past studies have not prioritized the dissemination of this information, and funders have not funded it. Some of it will be well-hidden, appearing in the gray literature, and finding it may present further challenges. Trials are now well-indexed on some databases; qualitative research and other research designs less so. Complex interventions may be difficult to identify, and may be wrongly excluded from searches. It has been shown for example that studies of complex clinical interventions may be excluded from systematic reviews because they do not include single, easily isolated, components.[34]

- *The need for multiple critical appraisal*: If such reviews seek to answer questions not just about effectiveness, but also about other issues (such as process and implementation), then there will be a need for a range of approaches to quality assessment within a single review. One critical appraisal "tool" will not be sufficient. Integrating this information may be challenging, and it is likely that good quality information will be found to answer some questions, but not others. For example, there may be reliable information from outcome evaluations to show that an intervention does not work, but there may little reliable information on how it was implemented, and to explore whether this might explain its lack of impact.

The synthesis of heterogeneous information presents a challenge to reviewers. In particular, while quantitative evidence may be synthesized meta-analytically, other types of evidence may not be so easily dealt with.

6.10   SYNTHESIZING QUALITATIVE AND MIXED METHODS RESEARCH

Qualitative research is not a single method, but involves a range of research designs including in-depth interviews, focus groups, case studies, and participant and non-participant observation. Moreover, qualitative research is not just a non-quantitative method of organizing data. It operates within a different paradigm of analytic induction.[35] Qualitative work has tended to be allocated a rather small (or no) place in many systematic reviews in the past, but this is changing. All cultures include an element of story telling as a powerful means of communication, and synthesis which builds on a narrative tradition is likely to increase in importance.[36, 37, 38] A recent report on approaches to using evidence from diverse research designs demonstrates the wide range of methods under development in this area.[39]

Reviews may have to become longer, and the structure of systematic reviews may need to change to accommodate this additional information. The production of longer versions of reviews, alongside summary versions may become more common, with the longer versions appearing only on websites (as already happens in some journals). This task may be facilitated with the greater availability of new software packages which can aid the synthesis of quantitative and non-quantitative data, such as the SUMARI package, under development at the Joanna Briggs Institute in Australia, which includes a module to aid the synthesis of qualitative data <http://www.joannabriggs.edu.au/services/sumariinfo.php>.[40] New developments in **Bayesian** approaches to synthesizing qualitative and quantitative evidence also offer promising new directions to reviewers who need to integrate complex sets of data within the same review.[41]

A further new development is the use of "realist synthesis," which is described as a new approach to systematic reviewing. Instead of focusing on synthesizing outcomes, it focuses on gathering evidence on how complex social interventions are theorized to work, and evidence to test and refine this theory (or theories). For a guide to the rationale and methods, and a comparison with "traditional" systematic reviews, see Pawson et al.[42] The EPPI-Centre approach to synthesizing different types of evidence is considered in Box 6.9.

Not everything that counts can be counted

Perhaps the least useful way of dealing with qualitative data in systematic reviews is to turn it into quantitative data. While it would make the job of systematizing qualitative research easy if it were restricted to "x participants in y studies said z," this is unlikely to be helpful and is a waste of the qualitative data. If one wishes to know how many people say "z," then a well-designed survey is likely to be the method of choice.

Box 6.9 Synthesizing different types of evidence: The EPPI-Centre approach

The Evidence for Policy and Practice Information and Co-ordinating Centre (EPPI-Centre) is part of the Social Science Research Unit (SSRU), Institute of Education, University of London <http://eppi.ioe.ac.uk/EPPIWeb/home.aspx>. The EPPI-Centre was established in 1993 to address the need for a systematic approach to the organization and review of evidence-based work on social interventions. The Centre engages health and education policymakers, practitioners, and service users in discussions about how researchers can make their work more relevant and how to use research findings.

Researchers at the Centre have described integrating qualitative research with data from trials in systematic reviews, using as an example the question: "What is known about the barriers to, and facilitators of, healthy eating among children aged 4–10 years?"[43] They searched for two kinds of research: trials that explored interventions to promote healthy eating, and studies that examined children's perspectives and understandings, often through qualitative methods. They used conventional systematic review methods and found 33 trials and eight qualitative studies that met their inclusion criteria. Each study was assessed for quality and reliability using criteria appropriate to the study type. They then synthesized the data in three ways. First, a meta-analysis of the trials was carried out, which showed great variations between the findings of the included studies. Second, they synthesized the qualitative work using NVivo software. In the third synthesis, the qualitative and the quantitative syntheses were combined. This involved going back to the original descriptions of the interventions evaluated in the trials, to identify those that built on barriers and facilitators suggested by the children.

6.11 META-ANALYSIS: THE STATISTICAL SYNTHESIS OF QUANTITATIVE STUDIES

Meta-analysis, the statistical pooling of similar quantitative studies, derives in its current form from Glass and Smith's work which began in the late

1970s.[44, 45] They pooled the results of 375 studies of the effectiveness of psychotherapy, and called their statistical approach to synthesis "meta-analysis." The term is now used to describe a range of statistical methods for combining the results of empirical studies, where each study tests the same hypothesis.

This important meta-analysis was the starting point for the wide-scale use of meta-analytic methods in social sciences, but the general statistical approach is much older. Astronomers in the seventeenth century had previously discussed the problem of pooling the results of individual observations in an attempt to limit bias. Statistical approaches to summarizing the results of several quantitative observations to limit error were given a significant boost by the work of Legendre in the eighteenth century.[1] Statistical methods were also considered by Tippett (1931), Fisher (1932) Pearson, Cochrane, Yates, and others in the 1930s and were developed further by US statisticians in the 1950s.[1] The application of the technique to those 375 studies of psychotherapy by Glass and Smith gave a huge impetus to the science of research synthesis and the tools were enthusiastically taken up by other US researchers. Chalmers et al.'s "A brief history of research synthesis" is a readable summary of the work of some of the early protagonists, and a reminder that the need for research syntheses has been recognized for many decades. It also gives an insight into how research synthesis made such rapid headway in the health and social sciences, from the viewpoint of three researchers in the vanguard.[1]

Meta-analysis: does it "work"?

Evidence of the bias-reducing properties of meta-analysis was quickly assembled. Cooper and Rosenthal compared meta-analysis to "traditional" review methods in an RCT, in which 41 researchers were set the task of reviewing the literature on whether there are sex differences in the psychological trait of "persistence" (for example, persistence in pursuing a task). Seven independent studies were included. Participants were allocated either to carry out a meta-analysis of these studies, or were instructed to employ whatever method of review they would normally use. Those using the meta-analytic method reported increased support for the hypothesis (that females are more persistent), and they also estimated a larger effect size than did the "traditional" reviewers.

This finding may be due to the increase in statistical power that results from pooling quantitative studies. The "traditional" literature reviewer may overlook non-significant results reported in single studies, but statistically pooling these studies increases the review's power to detect small effects. Indeed meta-analysis may be most useful when the number of studies to be reviewed is large, because as the number of studies increases it may be difficult to detect patterns in the data. This may be why narrative reviews are more likely to reach uncertain conclusions.[46, 47] However, this is not a problem for meta-analysis and may be a strength, because the more studies that are statistically pooled, the greater the precision with which the summary effect size can be estimated.[19]

To summarize, then, the particular strengths of meta-analysis include:

- increased statistical power, which is particularly important when the effects are likely to be small and thus likely to be missed by individual studies;
- the ability to investigate reasons for statistical variations between studies, and to determine whether this variation is due to chance;
- the ability to weight information from studies according to the amount of information they contain. As described later in the chapter, meta-analysis involves calculating a weighted average from each individual study, with the weighting reflecting the precision with which the effect is estimated;
- increased precision in estimating the overall effect size; and
- the ability to systematically investigate differences between studies and groups of studies, and to explore their causes.

Meta-analytic methods

In its simplest form, meta-analysis involves two steps: the first is to calculate a standard effect size from each study in the review. In the case of quantitative data this might involve calculating the difference between the means of the treatment and control groups, divided by the pooled standard deviations for the two groups. The second step is to pool the summary data from these studies to produce a single overall summary effect size. This is a commonly-used meta-analytic method – the standardized mean difference (though as Glass pointed out there is much more to meta-analysis than pooling mean differences).[48] The method is used when the same outcome is reported in each study, but where it has been measured in different ways – for example, trials may measure the same outcome by means of different scales or questionnaires. Meta-analysis approaches this problem by standardizing the outcome measures to a common scale, before pooling them.

As noted earlier, it can also be helpful to visually inspect the study results – for example by means of a Forest plot – before proceeding with a meta-analysis (see section 6.12).

An example: pooling differences between means

The example below illustrates the pooling of standardized effect sizes from several RCTs, where the outcome data to be pooled are continuous, and are expressed as differences between two means. In this example, a simple statistic can be calculated for each trial to estimate the effect of the intervention. This is the d-Index or d-statistic (or Standardized Mean Difference, SMD), which is calculated as the difference between the mean of the intervention and the mean of the treatment group (that is, $X1-X2$), divided by their common standard deviation (SD). This d-index is calculated for each trial in turn and the individual d values are then combined, with each d weighted to take account of the fact that the ds derived from larger studies will be more reliable. The weighting factor, W_i, is given by:

$$W_i = \frac{2(n_{i1} + n_{i2})n_{i1}n_{i2}}{2(n_{i1} + n_{i2})^2 + n_{i1}n_{i2}d_1{}^2}$$

where n_{i1} and n_{i2} are the number of observations in each of the groups in the study, and d_i is the d-index for the individual study for which the weight is being computed.[25]

The final step is to multiply each d by its corresponding weight (W_i), add these weighted ds, and then divide by the sum of the weights. This gives the combined, weighted effect size.

The upper and lower 95 percent confidence intervals around the pooled effect size are given by:

$$d \pm 1.96\sqrt{(\text{Inverse of the sum of the weights})}$$

The "sum of the weights" referred to above is the sum of all the W_is which have already been calculated.

One caveat to note when using the d statistic is that increasing scores on one scale may signify improvement in performance, but may signify decline in performance on a different scale used in another study. This can be dealt with by multiplying the mean value in the relevant scale by minus 1, or by subtracting the actual score from the maximum possible score on the scale, thus ensuring that all the scales point in the same direction.[49]

In cases where the data are continuous but measured in the same way (for example, using the same scale), there may be no need to standardize the outcome measures to a common scale. In this case each study is weighted by the inverse of its variance (as a measure of the precision with which the effect size is measured). The summary (weighted) mean effect size is then given by:

$$\frac{\text{Sum of (weight} * \text{the effect size for each study)}}{\text{Sum of the weights}}$$

Fixed and random effects and homogeneity

The procedure described above represents the general, fixed effects model for combining effect sizes, which assumes that there is no heterogeneity among the study results (other than that due to sampling error).[19] This assumption can be explored using tests based on the Chi-squared test (such as Cochran's Q). Most meta-analysis software will report the result of these tests for **homogeneity** automatically. A non-significant result suggests that no statistically significant heterogeneity is present, though such tests have low power, so the test may fail to detect heterogeneity even when present.

When this assumption of homogeneity is violated, such that there is additional variation between effect sizes that is not due to sampling error, a random effects model may be more appropriate; this approach attempts to take account of the extra unexplained variation. Unlike fixed effects meta-analysis, which assumes that the studies are estimating the same effect size, random effects meta-analysis assumes that the effect sizes are not derived from the same distribution. Again, meta-analysis software will commonly report the results of both fixed, and random effects analyses. See Sutton et al.[19] and Cooper and Hedges[50] for a full description of the use of (and problems with) fixed and random effects models, and statistical tests for homogeneity.

There are many other approaches to pooling the results of individual studies (not just studies of effectiveness, as in the example above), and meta-analysis deserves a book in itself. Fortunately, there are several excellent and detailed volumes. Guidance on the meta-analysis of a range of types of effect size appears in parts V and VI of Cooper and Hedges' *Handbook of research synthesis*.[50,51] Approaches discussed include: combining correlation coefficients (r) across studies (where r describes the relationship between two continuous variables in each study), odds ratios (example given below) and risk ratios (i.e., **relative risks**). It also discusses in detail the means of dealing with multiple outcomes from the same study (Box 6.10).

Box 6.10   Combining multiple outcomes

Studies often include more than one outcome, and these variables may be inter-correlated. How can these multiple outcomes be incorporated in a meta-analysis?

Several approaches have been suggested. The first point to be made is that not all outcomes will be relevant for answering the review question(s), and one approach is to extract and analyze only the relevant outcomes, separately combining the different classes of outcome. (This approach can, of course, also be applied to reviews that do not employ meta-analysis).

Other meta-analytic approaches include combining all effect sizes within studies, before carrying out a meta-analysis. Such approaches often require the inter-correlation between dependent variables to be either known or calculated from the primary studies.[19]

Combining data on outcomes may often be appropriate, for example where they represent measures of a conceptually similar variable, such as measures of IQ. In other cases however it will not make sense to combine very different outcome measures, such as when they provide different measures of the effect, and where that information is needed to answer very different, separate, questions in the review. Combining effect sizes describing how satisfied clients were with an intervention, with effect sizes describing its adverse effects, for example, is unlikely to be helpful.

Methods for combining multiple outcomes can be found in Cooper and Hedges;[50] Hedges and Olkin;[52] and Sutton et al.[19] The last of these texts is downloadable as a full report from the website of the UK Health Technology Assessment Agency <http://www.hta.nhsweb.nhs.uk/ProjectData/3_publication_select.asp>.

Converting measures of effect

Different types of effect size often need to be extracted from different studies. Not all studies in a review will for example report means and standard deviations to allow a d statistic to be produced. It is, however, possible to convert effect size statistics into each other – or to transform these into a common metric (such as r) to permit pooling. Formulae for converting between Cohen's d, Hedges' g, F, t, r, Z, χ^2 and other effect size measures can be found in Rosenthal[53] and Cooper and Hedges.[50] The latter also cover the use of significance levels as a metric for combining data, when no effect size data are available. If the study author, when contacted, can shed no further light (for example, if the study is an old one and the data have been lost or destroyed), it is possible to use p values to estimate a Z value for each study, before pooling these.

Hanson and Bussière used this approach in their systematic review and meta-analysis to establish the predictors of sexual offender recidivism.[54] Rather than a review of interventions to reduce reoffending, this review involved identifying factors that would predict offending using a meta-analysis of 61 previous studies. Predictor variables were coded from these studies, and the association between that variable and reoffending was recorded (or calculated). Where appropriate, these effect sizes were transformed into a common effect size measure, r, using guidance from Rosenthal, and Hedges and Olkin.[52, 55] Synthesizing these effect sizes first involved calculating the median value of r across all studies, to give a simple measure of central tendency. The formal meta-analysis then involved calculating an adjusted r for each study (adjusted for between-study differences in the baseline rates of recidivism), weighted by the inverse of the variance. This was then used to produce an averaged, adjusted r in the final meta-analysis, giving a summary measure of the correlation between each variable of interest, and sexual offense recidivism. For example, having a negative relationship with mother ($r = .16$), and a greater number of prior offences ($r = .13$) were significantly related to sexual offence recidivism; a negative relationship with the father ($r = -.02$) and sexual abuse as a child ($r = -.01$), were not.

Box 6.11 considers the case where there are no trials making a direct comparison between the interventions under review.

Box 6.11   What if there are no trials directly comparing the interventions in which I am interested?

Most of the examples discussed in this chapter have assumed that an intervention is being directly compared, to "doing nothing," or to another intervention, within the same study. But quite often the two interventions of interest have never been compared directly within the same study. Imagine, for example, a third intervention C. We may be interested in its effectiveness in comparison to A (A versus C), but we only have two trials to help us: Trial 1 compares A versus B, and Trial 2 compares B versus C. No study has ever compared A versus C directly. Can we carry out an indirect comparison, by taking the "A" data from the first arm of Trial 1, and comparing these to the "C" data from Trial 2? What sort of bias will this introduce? After all, the two interventions were never compared directly in the same study.

Song et al.[56] answered this question by examining 44 comparisons of different healthcare interventions from 28 systematic reviews. These reviews were selected so that data could be obtained from both direct and indirect comparisons of competing interventions within the same review. The indirect comparison between any two interventions of interest was adjusted by the results of their direct comparisons with a common intervention (intervention B, in the example above). When two or more trials compared the same interventions in either direct or indirect comparisons, a meta-analysis was carried out.

Song et al. found that, in most cases, the results of the adjusted indirect comparisons were not significantly different from those of direct comparisons. Overall, they suggested that when there is no direct evidence, the adjusted indirect method may be useful to estimate the relative efficacy of competing interventions.

The main caveat here is that these were healthcare interventions, where the assumption was made that their relative efficacy was consistent across trials. Could the same assumption be made of social or behavioral interventions? In many cases, the answer may well be no. The impact of many social interventions is so context and culture dependent that it may not be possible to carry out reliable indirect comparisons in this manner, though the issue merits further methodological research.

6.12   FOREST PLOTS

Meta-analysis is not just about pooling, but also about exploring patterns in the data. These patterns can be better understood if a graphical illustration such as a Forest plot is used. This presents the effect size (with accompanying confidence intervals) derived from each primary study, along with the summary estimate produced by the meta-analysis. Figure 6.1 shows a Forest plot displaying the results of the trials in the Scared Straight systematic review (described in chapter 4). The results of each study are plotted, with the square indicating the effect size and the confidence intervals showing the degree of uncertainty around that effect for the fixed effects meta-analysis. In this case the effect size is an odds ratio (OR), used here to describe the odds of reoffending in the intervention group relative to the controls. (**Funnel plots** can also be used with continuous data. The authors explain that they used ORs here because summary data such as means and standard deviations were rarely reported in the original studies). The actual results for each trial are also presented. In the Lewis (1983) trial, for example, 43 out of 53 participants (81 percent) in the intervention group who were exposed to the Scared Straight intervention had reoffended at follow-up, compared to 37 out of 55 in the control group (67 percent); not a statistically significant difference (as shown by the fact that the confidence intervals include 1.0), but indicative of a trend towards a harmful effect of the program. Most of the other studies also show such a trend, but with few statistically significant results, apart from the Finckenauer (1982) and Michigan (1967) studies. Pooling the data from the trials however shows that the overall effect is statistically significant (shown by the larger black diamond), and this suggests that Scared Straight appears to significantly increase the risk of reoffending – participants are about 68 percent more likely to reoffend than non-participants. The Chi-square test for heterogeneity (which tests for statistical heterogeneity among the outcomes – see chapter 7) is non-significant, suggesting that a fixed effects meta-analysis was appropriate (a random effects meta-analysis of the same seven studies produced very similar results).

The reviewers (Antony Petrosino and colleagues from the Campbell Collaboration Crime and Justice Coordinating Group) also carried out several sensitivity analyses. This involved two further meta-analyses, excluding in turn the results of two studies with methodological problems. The review's conclusions were substantially unchanged. Overall, therefore, the Scared Straight meta-analysis showed what many of the individual studies could not – strong evidence of a negative effect of the program. This effect is also likely to be *socially* significant; an increase in the risk of reoffending by between 60 and 70 percent is certainly something one would want to know about, and prevent. As Petrosino et al. conclude: "Doing nothing would have been better than exposing juveniles to the program."

The Scared Straight review also drew on resources from the Cochrane Collaboration's Development, Psychosocial and Learning Disorders Group.

Review: "Scared Straight" and other juvenile awareness programs for preventing juvenile delinquency
Comparison: 01 Intervention versus Control, Crime Outcome
Outcome: 01 Post-intervention - group recidivism rates - official measures only (fixed effects)

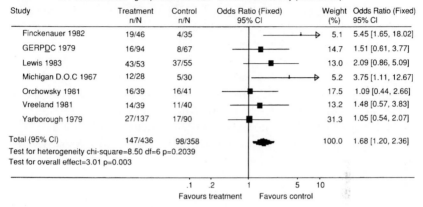

Study	Treatment n/N	Control n/N	Odds Ratio (Fixed) 95% CI	Weight (%)	Odds Ratio (Fixed) 95% CI
Finckenauer 1982	19/46	4/35		5.1	5.45 [1.65, 18.02]
GERPDC 1979	16/94	8/67		14.7	1.51 [0.61, 3.77]
Lewis 1983	43/53	37/55		13.0	2.09 [0.86, 5.09]
Michigan D.O.C 1967	12/28	5/30		5.2	3.75 [1.11, 12.67]
Orchowsky 1981	16/39	16/41		17.5	1.09 [0.44, 2.66]
Vreeland 1981	14/39	11/40		13.2	1.48 [0.57, 3.83]
Yarborough 1979	27/137	17/90		31.3	1.05 [0.54, 2.07]
Total (95% CI)	147/436	98/358		100.0	1.68 [1.20, 2.36]

Test for heterogeneity chi-square=8.50 df=6 p=0.2039
Test for overall effect=3.01 p=0.003

.1   .2   1   5   10
Favours treatment   Favours control

Figure 6.1   Forest plot of "Scared Straight" studies

The full version of the review can be Found in the Cochrane Library (from which Figure 6.1 was reproduced).

6.13   SOFTWARE: STATISTICAL PACKAGES FOR META-ANALYSIS

The actual meta-analysis (and the Forest plot in Figure 6.1) was produced using Cochrane RevMan software, but there are many other free and commercial software packages, and many of the major statistical packages used by social scientists (such as SPSS, STATA, and SAS) can carry out fixed effects and random effects meta-analysis (though not necessarily using integral commands). Sample SPSS syntax for meta-analysis can be found at <http://pages.infinit.net/rlevesqu/SampleSyntax.htm>. The website of the Berkeley Systematic Reviews Group <http://www.medepi.org/meta/> includes guidance on carrying out meta-analysis in STATA and SAS, and includes links to software packages.

There are also a number of freely available programs. An excellent list of free and commercial software and macros for meta-analysis appears on William Shadish's website: <http://faculty.ucmerced.edu/wshadish/index.htm>. Shadish has published many important meta-analyses including a number assessing the effectiveness of psychological therapies. As well as descriptions of, and links to, meta-analysis software, his website includes a comprehensive list of meta-analyses of the outcomes of psychotherapies – over 250 of them so far. Another source is Alex Sutton's home page at Leicester University

<http://www.prw.le.ac.uk/epidemio/personal/ajs22/meta/>, which includes information on available software and useful links to software reviews.

Many of the meta-analysis tasks outlined in this chapter (apart from the graphical ones) can be carried out by Ralf Schwarzer's freeware package <http://userpage.fu-berlin.de/~health/meta_e.htm>.

Among the commercial packages, Comprehensive Meta-Analysis is straightforward to use and can deal with a range of different types of effect size (including group means, standardized mean differences, odds ratios, and correlation coefficients) and permits exploration of moderator variables, as well as producing Forest plots which can be easily exported (a fully working trial version of the package can be downloaded from <http://www.MetaAnalysis.com>). It can also create funnel plots of odds ratios and risk ratios to help explore **publication bias** (see chapter 7).

Is meta-analysis better?

Bushman and Wells carried out an RCT that compared traditional review methods to meta-analysis.[57] Two hundred and eighty participants each reviewed 20 summaries of research studies, after being randomized to use either "narrative review" methods (in this case the term is used to refer to non-systematic review methods, without meta-analysis), or meta-analysis. The 20 studies were reports of investigations into whether interpersonal attraction was related to similarity (that is, whether people who are more similar get on together better). Two further variables were manipulated. The first was whether the order in which the studies were encountered would affect the reviewers' impression of the overall relationship between the similarity and attraction variables. For example, placing all the studies with negative results at the end of the sequence could affect the reviewer's perception of strength of the association. They also manipulated the salience of the titles of the 20 studies, to explore whether the results of the studies with more "memorable" titles would be better remembered, and thus have a greater influence on the reviewers' conclusions about the relationship between similarity and attraction. (For example a salient title would be: "Birds of a feather flock together," compared with "Research examines similarity as a source of liking,") The results were striking: in the "narrative review" group, the title of the article had a significant effect on the reviewers' judgments of the association between similarity and attraction. The relationship was judged by them to be stronger if the studies with positive results had salient titles, than if the studies with negative results had salient titles. Title salience did not affect the reviewer's conclusions in the meta-analysis group. For Bushman and Wells this suggested that superficial properties of the studies (such as title salience) influenced reviewers' impressions of the literature, leading them to overestimate the relationship in the positive studies, and underestimate the relationship in the negative studies. This study shows one of the clear benefits of meta-analysis; that it encourages a focus by the reviewer on the key facts of each study, limiting the influence of reviewer biases.

6.14   CRITICISMS OF META-ANALYSIS

Meta-analysis is not without its critics. One of the main criticisms is that meta-analysis too often seeks to combine dissimilar studies – sometimes called the "apples and oranges" problem, after psychologist Hans Eysenck's and others' accusations that early meta-analyses were combining studies which were too dissimilar.[45] Gene Glass's rejoinder was that combining apples and oranges is fine, if one wants to make generalizations about fruit (Box 6.12).

Eysenck later hardened his stance and extended his metaphor by claiming that meta-analysis combines apples, lice, and killer whales.[60] This is probably a criticism of the inappropriate application of meta-analysis rather than an appropriate criticism of the practice of meta-analysis itself. Meta-analysis is a powerful and easy-to-use tool and this can encourage the pooling of very dissimilar studies – dissimilar in terms of intervention, population, and outcomes, as well as in study methods and study quality. The end result in this situation is indeed likely to be what Eysenck called "an exercise in mega-silliness" [61,62] and what Lipsey and Wilson labeled "a gigantic absurdity."[63] However those who pool data inappropriately do so against the advice of experts on meta-analysis. Harris Cooper's guide, *Integrating research*,[25] provides advice on when and when not to use the technique (Box 6.13).

Statistical assessment of heterogeneity will, in some cases, give an indication of when the outcomes of the studies are too heterogeneous to be combined (see chapter 7) though homogeneous effect sizes may still be obtained from very different sets of studies; statistical homogeneity alone is not a sufficient rationale for a meta-analysis.[64] In Feinstein's example, the weights of small children, small dogs, large cats, and very large fish are homogeneous in terms of weight, but it would be a brave reviewer who

Box 6.12   Meta-analytic fruit cocktail

Meta-analysis is inappropriate for trials which address different hypotheses, or which address the same hypothesis in very different ways... Two apples and three oranges make two apples and three oranges, not five appleoranges, even if the individual fruits are the same size or weight.

(Greenhalgh, 1998)[58]

A common analogy is that systematic reviews bring together apples and oranges, and that combining these can yield a meaningless result. This is true if apples and oranges are of intrinsic interest on their own, but may not be if they are used to contribute to a wider question about fruit.

(Cochrane handbook, 2004)[49]

Some degree of mixing apples and oranges must occur in the tidiest of studies. Even when studies are intended to be direct replications, exact replication probably cannot occur. On the other hand synthesists must be sensitive to the problem of attempting aggregation of too diverse a sampling of operations and studies... of course the final criterion for the extensiveness of the sampling of operations is whether the level of generalization is appropriate to the question being asked.

(Hall et al., 1994)[59]

The question of "sameness" is not an a priori question at all; apart from being a logical impossibility, it is an empirical question. For us, no two "studies" are the same. All studies differ and the only interesting questions to ask about them concern how they vary across the factors we conceive of as important.

(Glass, 2000)[48]

would argue that these should be statistically combined.[64, 65] In short, the "apples and oranges" problem is dealt with by avoiding the mixing of conceptually and methodologically dissimilar studies within the same meta-analysis.

The problem of mixing apples and oranges is of course not specific to meta-analysis, but can also afflict narrative reviews.[66] This acts as a useful reminder that systematic reviews are not immune from methodological and other problems. Systematic reviews should therefore be critically appraised before their findings are acted upon. A brief guide is included in Appendix 5.

Box 6.13   When *not* to meta-analyze

- Meta-analysis should only be applied when a series of studies has been identified for review that addresses an identical conceptual hypothesis, and a reviewer should not quantitatively combine studies at a broader conceptual level than readers or users of the review would find useful.
- It is likely to be inappropriate where interventions received by control groups are clearly different between studies (even if the intervention group is the same). For example, take a review which seeks to assess the effects of a specific violence reduction programme in schools, and the intervention of interest involves extensive school-based education of pupils, involving coursework, seminars, videos, and role-playing ("Intervention A"). In a series of hypothetical trials this could be compared with a range of control groups experiencing a range of interventions: including no intervention, educational plus structural measures (such as searching or screening for weapons), minimal educational measures (such as a leaflet), and more extensive measures (such as educational interventions targetted at pupils and parents together). Even if Intervention A were employed consistently in these trials, it would make little sense to pool this heterogeneous range of control interventions as a comparison group. If all of the control interventions were effective, any pooling of this data might underestimate the effects of Intervention A.

(Cooper, 1989)[25]

6.15   THE META-ANALYTIC SAUSAGE MACHINE

Some of the criticisms of meta-analysis are probably just a modern version of an older argument about the role of quantification in social science: The Sausage Machine argument. For example: "Leaders of influential schools in the social sciences have sincerely believed that real science is done by putting masses of quantitative data through a statistical sausage machine, and then observing the Laws which emerge".[67] This is of course unfair to the fine and ancient craft of the sausage maker (Figure 6.2).

Figure 6.2 Sausage makers, c.1939
(Photo courtesy of the Sainsbury Archive)

The criticism is best reserved for the uncritical meta-analyst – the economy sausage maker of the research world, who indiscriminately includes the unspeakable and the inedible, the raw and the cooked. There is no a priori reason why meta-analysis cannot be used for social interventions and many hundreds have been done, as long as it is remembered that meta-analysis, systematic reviews, and sausage machines share one common rule: garbage in, garbage out.[50] The meta-analysis of observational studies (as opposed to RCTs) has come in for particular criticism (Box 6.14).

Despite these criticisms, meta-analysis has no shortage of supporters. Earlier chapters discussed the potential for bias in traditional reviews, and primary studies. MacCoun points to meta-analysis as one of several "debiasing techniques" which researchers can use (along with thorough

Box 6.14   Meta-analysis of observational studies: Spurious precision?

Most meta-analyses in the social sciences probably include some observational studies; some include *only* observational studies. This approach has been criticized by commentators who have suggested that such meta-analyses are much more prone to bias than meta-analyses of RCTs, because observational studies are themselves much more bias-prone. In particular they may be strongly affected by confounding, which may remain undetected and often unexplored.[68]

Meta-analyses of observational studies are very common; many synthesize the results of quasi-experimental and other observational studies, and others include cross-sectional and prospective cohort studies in order to test hypotheses about etiology.[66] Careful critical appraisal of the primary studies, with particular attention to confounding should be an essential component of meta-analyses of observational studies, and the results of such meta-analyses should be treated as indicative rather than definitive. Egger et al. also suggest that the exploration of possible sources of heterogeneity between study results should be a prominent component of such reviews.[68]

methodological training). The tool is extensively used in this way in other scientific fields, including biology and ecology (see Box 6.15) and economics (see Box 6.16).[69, 70]

Replication of studies alone cannot eliminate bias, but conducting a meta-analysis frequently uncovers errors missed by journal referees.[73] The use of meta-regression may further allow the impact of aspects of study

Box 6.15   Marine meta-analysis

The use of meta-analysis is motivated by the lack of long-term data for any one population. We may never have reliable data on over 100 generations for a natural fish population, yet this is what we need to make reliable statistical inferences. By combining estimates for many populations, we may be able to use much shorter time series to reach reliable conclusions.

(Myers[71] on the use of meta-analysis to analyze marine population data)

Box 6.16   Economic meta-analysis

As well as synthesizing research evidence on effectiveness and etiology, meta-analysis has been used to explore economic questions.
Harmon et al. used meta-analysis to explore the "returns to education," that is, the rate of return to society from investment in education, synthesizing data from 15 European countries and the United
States.[72] This found an average rate of return from this form of
investment of about 6.5 percent, and a range of sub-analyses showed
that this figure was similar across the majority of countries and models
(such as analyses based on men only, and women only). The main
exceptions to the findings were that the returns to schooling for the
UK and Ireland were higher than average, and lower for Nordic
countries, and higher in the 1960s compared to later decades.

design and other factors to be clearly identified and quantified, offering clear
directions to improvements in study methods (see chapter 8).

6.16   IMPROVING RESEARCH SYNTHESIS

As suggested earlier, some of the criticisms of systematic reviews and meta-
analyses outlined in this book are in part a consequence of their perceived
inability to cope with complex sets of evidence. Cooper and Rosenthal
suggested in 1980 that "Some of the confusion and contradiction we often
convey about our research may not be a function of the results we have
found but of how we have chosen to synthesize them."[74] The same may
be said of systematic reviews. Improvements to the methods of synthesis,
and in particular the methods of integrating different types of complex
evidence – perhaps drawing further on methods already in use in qualitative
research – may produce more meaningful reviews for users. Some of this
methodological work is currently being carried out in the Campbell and
Cochrane Collaborations, and in an ESRC-funded project <http://
www.ccsr.ac.uk/methods/projects/posters/popay.shtml>.

The synthesis of qualitative research is in rapid development and the
methods have potential contributions to make to the synthesis of other types
of data.[8, 9, 39, 75] One example is Bayesian reviews, in which prior estimates

of the likely effect are identified through systematic review of qualitative (or other) research combined with the quantitative synthesized data, to produce an estimate that is informed by subjective prior beliefs and other scientific information.[41] The incorporation of systematic reviews into **decision analyses** also holds promise for developing the use of systematic reviews as aids to decision making.[76]

In one of the reviews with which we have been associated on infant growth, <http://www.city.ac.uk/barts/chrpu/projects/infantsizeand growth> systematic reviews of both quantitative and qualitative literature were followed by interviews on experiences of infant growth with parents and grandparents, enabling us to explore with them the concepts that had appeared most important in the literature. As Dingwall et al. remind us, qualitative research can close the gap between our knowledge of what is effective in general terms and our ability to deliver it.[77] Combining methods can be a step towards the development and implementation of effective interventions.

Key learning points from this chapter

- Synthesis of the included studies should start with the detailed tabulation of the studies, with details of the study methods, participants, and findings.
- Assessment of study quality is an essential part of the synthesis, but it is important also to consider the relationship between internal and external validity.
- Graphical presentation of quantitative data should be used where possible to aid interpretation, and permit exploration of heterogeneity.
- In meta-analysis, as in systematic reviews more generally, the aim is to pool conceptually similar studies.
- Assessment of study quality and exploration of heterogeneity between study findings are essential parts of any synthesis.

REFERENCES

1. Chalmers, I., Hedges, L., and Cooper, C. A brief history of research synthesis. *Evaluation and the Health Professions* 2002, 25: 12–37.

2. Schulz, K., Chalmers, I., Hayes, R., and Altman, D. Empirical evidence of bias. Dimensions of methodological quality associated with estimates of treatment effects in controlled trials. *Journal of the American Medical Association* 1995, 273: 408–12.

3. Shadish, W. and Ragsdale, K. Random versus nonrandom assignment in controlled experiments: Do you get the same answer? *Journal of Consulting and Clinical Psychology* 1996, 64: 1290–1305.

4. Deeks, J., Dinnes, J., D'Amico, R., Sowden, A., Sakarovitch, C., Song, F., et al. Evaluating non-randomized intervention studies. *Health Technology Assessment* 2003, 7, online at: http://www.hta.nhsweb.nhs.uk/htapubs.htm

5. Egan, M., Petticrew, M., Ogilvie, D., and Hamilton, V. Privatisation, deregulation and state subsidies: A systematic review of health impacts of interventions affecting direct public investment in business. (in press), online at: http://www. msoc-mrc. gla.ac.uk/Evidence/Research/Review%2004/Review4_MAIN.html

6. Campbell, K., Waters, E., O'Meara, S., and Summerbell, C. Interventions for preventing obesity in children. *The Cochrane Library*, Issue 2, 2004. Chichester, UK: John Wiley & Sons, 2004.

7. Noblit, G. and Hare, R. *Meta-ethnography: Synthesizing qualitative studies.* London: Sage, 1988.

8. Britten, N., Campbell, R., Pope, C., Donovan, J., Morgan, M., and Pill, R. Using meta ethnography to synthesise qualitative research: A worked example. *Journal of Health Services Research and Policy* 2002, 7: 209–15.

9. Campbell, R., Pound, P., Pope, C., Britten, N., Pill, R., Morgan, M., et al. Evaluating meta-ethnography: a synthesis of qualitative research on lay experiences of diabetes and diabetes care. *Social Science and Medicine* 2003, 56: 671–84.

10. Popay, J., Rogers, A., and Williams, G. Rationale and standards for the systematic review of qualitative literature in health services research. *Qualitative Health Research* 1998, 8: 341–51.

11. Dixon-Woods, M. and Fitzpatrick, R. Qualitative research in systematic reviews has established a place for itself. *British Medical Journal* 2001, 323: 765–6.

12. Secker-Walker, R., Gnich, W., Platt, S., and Lancaster, T. Community interventions for reducing smoking among adults (Cochrane Review). *The Cochrane Library*, Issue 2, 2004. Chichester, UK: John Wiley & Sons, Ltd.

13. Coren, E. and Barlow, J. Individual and group based parenting for improving psychosocial outcomes for teenage parents and their children (Campbell Collaboration review), online at: http://www.campbellcollaboration.org/doc-pdf/teenpar.pdf, 2004.

14. Slavin, R. Best evidence synthesis: An intelligent alternative to meta-analysis. *Journal of Clinical Epidemiology* 1995, 48: 9–18.

15. Slavin, R. Best-evidence synthesis: An alternative to meta-analytic and traditional reviews. *Educational Researcher* 1986, 15: 5–11.

16. Slavin, R. and Cheung, A. *Effective reading programs for English language learners: A best evidence synthesis.* Baltimore: CRESPAR/Johns Hopkins University, www.csos.jhu.edu., 2003.

17. Suri, H. A critique of contemporary methods of research synthesis. Paper presented at the Annual Meeting of the Australian Association of Research in Education (AARE), Melbourne, November 29–December 2, 1999, online at: http://www.aare.edu.au/99pap/sur99673.htm

18. Light, R. and Smith, P. Accumulating evidence: Procedures for resolving contradictions among different research studies. *Harvard Educational Review* 1971, 41: 429–71.

19. Sutton, A., Abrams, K., Jones, K., Sheldon, T., and Song, F. Systematic reviews of trials and other studies. *Health Technology Assessment* 1998, 2, online at: http://www.hta.nhsweb.nhs.uk/ProjectData/3_publication_select.asp. Also available as: Sutton et al. *Methods for meta-analysis in medical research*. Chichester: Wiley & Sons, 2000.

20. Oxman, A. and Guyatt, G. The science of reviewing research. *Annals of the New York Academy of Sciences* 1993, 703: 125–33.

21. Black, N. Why we need observational studies to evaluate the effectiveness of health care. *British Medical Journal* 1996, 312: 1215–18.

22. Windle, C. The shift to research synthesis. *Administration and Policy in Mental Health* 1994, 21: 263–7.

23. US General Accounting Office. Cross-design synthesis: A new strategy for medical effectiveness research (GAO/PEMD-92-18), 1992.

24. Egan, M., Petticrew, M., Hamilton, V., and Ogilvie, D. Health impacts of new roads: A systematic review. *American Journal of Public Health* 2003, 93(9): 1463–71.

25. Cooper, H. *Integrating research: A guide for literature reviews*. London: Sage, 1989.

26. Smith, M. and Glass G. Meta-analysis of psychotherapy outcome studies. *American Psychologist* 1977, 32: 752–60.

27. Oakley, A. *Experiments in knowing: Gender and method in the social sciences*. Cambridge: Polity Press, 2000.

28. Oakley, A. Social science and evidence-based everything: The case of education. *Educational Review* 2002, 54: 277–86.

29. Mallett, S. and Clarke, M. The typical Cochrane review: How many trials? How many participants? *International Journal of Technology Assessment in Health Care* 2002, 18: 820–31.

30. Sheldon, T. *An evidence-based resource in the social sciences*, Report of a scoping study for the Economic and Social Research Council (ESRC), 1998.

31. Rose, S., Bisson, J., and Wessely, S. Psychological debriefing for preventing post traumatic stress disorder (PTSD) (Cochrane Review). *The Cochrane Library*, Issue 2, 2004. Chichester, UK: John Wiley & Sons.

32. Mulrow, C. Systematic reviews: Rationale for systematic reviews. *British Medical Journal* 1994, 309: 597–9.

33. Bambra, C., Whitehead, M., and Hamilton, V. Does "welfare to work" work? A systematic review of the effectiveness of the UK's "welfare to work" programmes for people with a disability or chronic illness. *Social Science & Medicine* 2005, 60(9): 1905–18.

34. Muhlhauser, I. Systematic reviews do not allow appraisal of complex interventions. XI Cochrane Colloquium: Evidence, health care and culture, 2003, Barcelona.
35. Boulton, M. and Fitzpatrick, R. Quality in qualitative research. *Critical Public Health* 1994, 5: 19–26.
36. Dixon-Woods, M., Shaw, R., Agarwal, S., and Smith, J. The problem of appraising qualitative research. *Quality & Safety in Healthcare* 2004, 13: 223–5.
37. Stevenson, F. A., Cox, K., Britten, N., and Dundar, Y. A systematic review of the research on communication between patients and health care professionals about medicines: The consequences for concordance. *Health Expectations* 2004, 7(3): 235–45.
38. Hurwitz, B., Greenhalgh, T., and Skultans, V. (eds.) *Narrative Research in Health and Illness*. BMJ Books, 2004.
39. Popay, J. and Roen, K. Synthesis of evidence from research using diverse study designs: A preliminary review of methodological work: Social Care Institute of Excellence, 2003.
40. Pearson, A., Wiechula, A., and Long, L. QARI: A systematic approach to the appraisal, extraction and synthesis of the findings of qualitative research. XI Cochrane Colloquium: Evidence, health care and culture, 2003, Barcelona.
41. Roberts, K. A., Dixon-Woods, M., Fitzpatrick, R., Abrams, K. R., and Jones, D. R. Factors affecting uptake of childhood immunisation: A Bayesian synthesis of qualitative and quantitative evidence. *The Lancet* 2002, 360: 1596–9.
42. Pawson, R., Greenhalgh, T., Harvey, G., and Walshe, K. Realist synthesis: An introduction: ESRC Research Methods Programme. University of Manchester. RMP Methods Paper 2/2004, online at: http://www.ccsr.ac.uk/methods/publications/documents/RMPmethods2.pdf, 2004.
43. Thomas, J., Harden, A., Oakley, A., Sutcliffe, K., Rees, R., Brunton, G., et al. Integrating qualitative research with trials in systematic reviews. *British Medical Journal* 2004, 328: 1010–12.
44. Glass, G., McGaw, B., and Smith, M. *Meta-analysis in social research*. Beverly Hills: Sage, 1981.
45. Hunt, M. *How science takes stock*. New York: Russell Sage Foundation, 1997.
46. Petticrew, M. Why certain systematic reviews reach uncertain conclusions. *British Medical Journal* 2003, 326: 756–8.
47. Petticrew, M., Song, F., Wilson, P., and Wright, K. The DARE database of abstracts of systematic reviews: A summary and analysis. *International Journal of Technology Assessment in Health Care* 2000, 15: 671–8.
48. Glass, G. Meta-analysis at 25. College of Education, Arizona State University, 2000, online at: http://glass.ed.asu.edu/gene/papers/meta25.html
49. Alderson, P., Green, S., and Higgins, J. (eds.) Cochrane Reviewers' Handbook 4.2.2 [updated March 2004]. *The Cochrane Library*, Issue 1, 2004. Chichester, UK: John Wiley & Sons.

50. Cooper, H. and Hedges, L. (eds.) *The handbook of research synthesis*. New York: Russell Sage Foundation, 1994.

51. Shadish, W. and Haddock, C. Combining estimates of effect size. In H. Cooper and L. Hedges (eds.) *The handbook of research synthesis*. New York: Russell Sage Foundation, 1994.

52. Hedges, L. and Olkin, I. *Statistical methods for meta-analysis*. New York: Academic Press, 1985.

53. Rosenthal, R. Parametric measures of effect size. In H. Cooper and L. Hedges (eds.) *The handbook of research synthesis*. New York: Russell Sage Foundation, 1994.

54. Hanson, R. and Bussière, M. Predictors of sexual offender recidivism: A meta-analysis: Public Works and Government Services Canada, online at: http://home.wanadoo.nl/ipce/library_two/han/hanson_96_txt.htm, 1996.

55. Rosenthal, R. *Meta-analytic procedures for social research*. Newbury Park: Sage, 1991.

56. Song, F., Altman, D., Glenny, A., and Deeks, J. Validity of indirect comparison for estimating efficacy of competing interventions: Empirical evidence from published meta-analyses. *British Medical Journal* 2003, 326: 472.

57. Bushman, B. and Wells, G. Narrative impressions of literature: The availability bias and the corrective properties of meta-analytic approaches. *Personality and Social Psychology Bulletin* 2001, 27: 1123–30, online at: http://www-personal.umich.edu/~bbushman/bw01.pdf

58. Greenhalgh, T. Commentary: Meta-analysis is a blunt and potentially misleading instrument for analysing models of service delivery. *British Medical Journal* 1998, 317: 390–6.

59. Hall, J., Tickle-Degnen, L., Rosenthal, R., and Mosteller, F. Hypotheses and problems in research synthesis. In H. Cooper and L. Hedges (eds.) *The handbook of research synthesis*. New York: Russell Sage Foundation, 1994.

60. Eysenck, H. Meta-analysis squared. Does it make sense? *American Psychologist* 1995, 50: 110–11.

61. Eysenck, H. Systematic Reviews: Meta-analysis and its problems. *British Medical Journal* 1994, 309: 789–92, online at: http://bmj.bmjjournals.com/cgi/content/full/309/6957/789

62. Eysenck, H. An exercise in mega-silliness. *American Psychologist* 1978, 33: 517.

63. Lipsey, M. and Wilson, D. Reply to comments. *American Psychologist* 1995, 50: 113–15.

64. Sharpe, D. Of apples and oranges, file drawers and garbage: Why validity issues in meta-analysis will not go away. *Clinical Psychology Review* 1997, 17: 881–901.

65. Feinstein, A. Meta-analysis: Statistical alchemy for the 21st century. *Journal of Clinical Epidemiology* 1995, 48: 71–9.

66. Jones, D. Meta-analysis of observational studies: A review. *Journal of the Royal Society of Medicine* 1992, 85: 165–6.

67. Ravetz, J. *Scientific knowledge and its social problems*. Middlesex: Penguin University Books, 1973.

68. Egger, M., Schneider, M., and Davey Smith, G. Spurious precision? Meta-analysis of observational studies. *British Medical Journal* 1998, 316: 140–4.

69. Petticrew, M. Systematic reviews from astronomy to zoology: Myths and misconceptions. *British Medical Journal* 2001, 322: 98–101.

70. Myers, R., MacKenzie, B., Bowen, K., and Barrowman, N. What is the carrying capacity for fish in the ocean? A meta-analysis of population dynamics of North Atlantic Cod. *Canadian Journal of Fisheries and Aquatic Sciences* 2001, 58.

71. Myers, R. The synthesis of dynamic and historical data on marine populations and communities. *Oceanography* 2000, 13: 56–9.

72. Harmon, C., Oosterbeek, H., and Walker, I. The returns to education: A review of evidence, issues and deficiencies in the Literature. London: Center for the Economics of Education (CEE) Discussion Papers no. 5, London School of Economics, 2000.

73. MacCoun, R. Biases in the interpretation and use of research results. *Annual Review of Psychology* 1998, 49: 259–87.

74. Cooper, H. and Rosenthal, R. Statistical versus traditional procedures for summarizing research findings. *Psychological Bulletin* 1980, 87: 442–9.

75. Dixon-Woods, M., Agarwal, S., Young, B., Jones, D., and Sutton, A. Integrative approaches to qualitative and quantitative evidence: Health Development Agency, London, online at: http://www.publichealth.nice.org.uk/page.aspx?o=508055 2004.

76. Cooper, N., Sutton, A., and Abrams, K. Decision analytic economic modelling within a Bayesian framework: Application to prophylactic antibiotics use for caesarian section. *Statistical Methods in Medical Research* 2002, 11: 491–512, online at: http://www.hs.le.ac.uk/~Keitha/SMMR%202002%20NJC.pdf

77. Dingwall, R., Murphy, E., Greatbatch, D., Watson, P., and Parker, S. Catching goldfish: Quality in qualitative research. *Journal of Health Services Research and Policy* 1998, 3: 167–72.

Chapter 7

Exploring heterogeneity and publication bias

7.1 INTRODUCTION: ARE THE REVIEWS' CONCLUSIONS ROBUST? DIAGNOSING PROBLEMS AND EXPLORING DIFFERENCES

In many social science reviews there will be sizeable differences in the populations, interventions, contexts, and many other variables, which may contribute to wide variations in those studies' findings. This chapter presents some approaches to investigating the different types of heterogeneity that may be encountered, and describes several of the more commonly used methods to summarize quantitative studies and to identify differences between them.

There are of course many challenges to the reliability of systematic reviews' findings, and one of the best-known (and longest discussed) is publication bias. This chapter introduces publication bias and some of the main approaches to detecting and preventing it.

7.2 STUDY HETEROGENEITY AND STATISTICAL HETEROGENEITY

Thomson describes two important forms of heterogeneity.[1] In the case of reviews of effectiveness, one form refers to differences between the studies in terms of methods, participants, and other unknown sources of heterogeneity. While some systematic reviews make efforts to limit this form of heterogeneity by using very precise inclusion criteria, others adopt broader criteria and so some study heterogeneity is to be expected. The other form of heterogeneity, statistical heterogeneity, refers to differences between studies in terms of their quantitative findings. This too may be due to known differences between the studies, including methodological differences, and differences in the baseline characteristics of populations being studied.

Many social interventions are complex because of the characteristics of the interventions, study population(s), outcomes, or other methodological issues relating to the conduct of the **primary studies**.[2] Further complexity is introduced because the effectiveness of the interventions may be modified by the context, and the intervention itself may vary when it is being implemented.[3, 4, 5] Because of these variations, reviewers of social interventions may expect considerable heterogeneity across studies and need to consider this when synthesizing results.

"Social" heterogeneity may incorporate not only socio-demographic and individual differences, but also historical, cultural, spatial, and other differences, which may affect both the delivery and impact of the interventions being reviewed. Some of the main sources of variability are outlined below (adapted from guidance produced by the Cochrane Health Promotion and Public Health Field <http://www.vichealth.vic.gov.au/cochrane/>):

- *Variability in study populations, interventions, and settings*: The content of complex social interventions may vary between specific settings or populations. Some of the variability may be intentional as interventions are tailored to local needs (including characteristics that may influence the outcomes of interest such as race, gender, and socio-economic position).
- *Variability in outcomes*: In clinical interventions variation in outcomes is termed clinical heterogeneity. Variation also exists in social research, however, given the longer causal chains for many social interventions (including public health interventions), proximal/immediate, intermediate, and distal/long-term outcomes may be reported and synthesized.
- *Variability in study designs*: Methodological diversity is common in social systematic reviews. Where the main potential sources of variation are known, heterogeneity between effects can be explored by means of subgroup analysis, based on theories about how the intervention works, and for which groups. For many social and public health interventions, theories about mechanisms and interactions may be under-developed and the exploration and interpretation of heterogeneity complex. It may be difficult to anticipate the main sources of heterogeneity a priori.

7.3   STATISTICAL HETEROGENEITY IN META-ANALYSIS

The meta-analyst is interested in whether statistical heterogeneity is greater than would be expected by chance, suggesting that the studies may not be similar enough to permit statistical combination. This can be tested using the Q statistic, which has a Chi-squared distribution with $N-1$ degrees of freedom (where N is the number of studies). However the test generally has low power to detect heterogeneity. Even if there is no evidence of statistical heterogeneity a meta-analysis may still not be appropriate, because similar effect sizes may be obtained from studies that are conceptually very different.

Because of the problems with statistical methods for detecting heterogeneity, a new quantity has been developed called I^2, which describes the impact of heterogeneity on a meta-analysis, by measuring the degree of inconsistency between studies.[6] I^2 is given by:

$$I^2 = (\chi^2 - df)/\chi^2 \times 100\%$$

Higgins suggests that while I^2 may never reach 100 percent, values in excess of 70 percent should invite caution.[7] However the statisticians who developed this tool also remind us that the quantification of heterogeneity is only one component of a wider investigation of variability across studies.[6]

Heterogeneity in *narrative* reviews may of course simply be due to chance, and in reviews with a small number of studies this may be difficult to investigate and explain. Even with larger reviews, this can be difficult to investigate if the individual studies have not reported data in a common format. Investigation of heterogeneity among quantitative studies (like narrative synthesis) is therefore easier if quantitative outcomes are extracted in a common metric.

Similarly, Forest plots (even in the absence of formal meta-analysis) are a useful diagnostic tool. Like tables they may be ordered by study quality, year of publication and other key variables. Cumulative meta-analysis is one example; this involves the stepwise addition of (or deletion) of studies from a meta-analysis in a pre-specified order.[8] The method has been used to investigate how the summary effect size changes over time – which can indicate (in retrospect) when an intervention could first have been shown to be effective, had a systematic review been carried out at that time.[9]

7.4   SENSITIVITY ANALYSIS

The association between study differences and study outcomes can be investigated using sensitivity analysis. This involves synthesizing different sub-groups of studies, while systematically excluding some studies to determine how this affects the review's conclusions. Subgroups for exclusion could be selected on the basis of any study criterion of interest, to answer "what if?" questions.[10] For example, the following questions could be addressed in a sensitivity analysis: "What if all the unpublished studies were excluded? What if only RCTs were included, and non-experimental studies were excluded? What if only studies carried out in one country, or one type of study participant, were included?" Sensitivity analysis can be used to address issues of study quality (for example, by systematically excluding studies below a certain "quality threshold"), and can help explore implementation issues: for example, the impact of intervention integrity on outcomes could be assessed using this approach by stratifying the studies by the fidelity of implementation of the intervention.

7.5   SUBGROUP ANALYSIS AND MODERATOR VARIABLES

The current received wisdom is that in evaluating social interventions one is less interested in "what works," than in "what works, for whom, and in what circumstances." One would certainly expect that systematic reviews could contribute meaningful answers to this question, and one approach is by means of analyzing moderator variables – that is, variables that moderate the effects of major variables being investigated in the review. This can be done at the study level, by examining characteristics that vary between studies (such as study quality, study design, or study setting) or by analyzing characteristics of the sample (such as groups of outcomes, or patients), based on some underlying theory as to the effects of those variables on outcomes. One approach is to examine the effects of interventions across different social groups, as described in the previous chapter. Tools are currently being developed to assist in this task, among these the World Bank's Equity Gauge, which has been recommended for use in assessing and synthesizing evidence on interventions to address inequalities. This task requires, among other things, consideration of the research evidence across eight key di-mensions: the PROGRESS dimensions (standing for *P*lace of residence, *R*ace and ethnicity, *O*ccupation, *G*ender, *R*eligion, *E*ducation, *S*ocioeconomic status, and *S*ocial capital).[11] For example, Kristjansson's Campbell Collaboration systematic review of school feeding programs for improving outcomes of low-income children has examined socioeconomic status as a moderator variable, in a review driven by the question of whether these programs are differentially effective in children of less well-off compared to better-off families (see Box 7.1).[12] This approach is likely to become more common as reviewers in public health and related areas increasingly turn their attention to the relative effectiveness of interventions (such as social policies) in different socioeconomic groups, in an attempt to identify interventions with the potential to reduce income-related inequalities in health.[13] Some data suggest that the best evidence may be skewed towards non-disadvantaged settings,[14] and that current systematic reviews tend not to provide evidence on differential effectiveness.[15, 16] Equity-focused reviews are currently being carried out under the aegis of the Campbell and Cochrane Collaborations, and systematic reviewers have argued for some years for the importance of exploring moderator effects in systematic reviews.[17–20] Methodological groups working within the Cochrane Collaboration have also contributed extensive empirical and other work on these issues; for example the Cochrane Methods group in Subgroup Analysis has demonstrated some of the methodological and epistemological pitfalls.

Further evidence on this issue is provided by a recent survey of US and European RCTs, which found that American studies were five times more likely than European trials to report information on the ethnicity of participants. The authors suggest that this reflects deliberate recruitment policies to ensure that trials are representative, and the fact that all large federally supported programs are required to report statistics according to race or ethnicity.[21] Nonetheless, only two-fifths of recently published trials from the US report on the ethnicity of participants.

As an example of how information on subgroups can be synthesized and presented clearly see Figure 7.1, from a review by Nelson et al.[22] This involved a meta-analysis, which examined the effectiveness of 34 pre-school prevention programs for disadvantaged children. Outcomes investigated included children's cognitive development, their socio-emotional behavior, and parent–family functioning (for example, parent–child relationships). The reviewers found that for three of four outcomes, the effects were larger

Box 7.1 School feeding programs for improving outcomes of low-income children and for reducing socioeconomic inequalities in health[12]

The problem: Socio-economic inequalities in health are of concern in many developed countries, but there is relatively little evidence of the effectiveness of interventions to reduce them. The objectives of this review were to study the effectiveness of school feeding programs for improving growth, cognition, school attendance, and school performance among economically disadvantaged elementary school children in developing and developed countries.

The review methods: Interventions reviewed included breakfast, lunch, and snacks (food and/or milk) provided at school. Studies were included only if the participants were all poor or on a low income, or if the results could be broken down by income or socioeconomic status. All eligible randomized controlled trials, interrupted time-series, and controlled before-and-after studies of meals in elementary school were included. MEDLINE, Embase, CINAHL, Sociofile, PsycInfo, LILACS (Index of Latin and Carribean health literature), were searched, and reference lists and nutrition journals were hand searched. Methodological quality was assessed, and nutritionists assessed the quality of the intervention in terms of intensity of calories and protein provided. Where possible, results were analyzed by baseline nutritional status (as a proxy for SES).

Results: Eleven studies were included: 5 RCTs and 6 controlled before-and-after studies (CBAs), carried out in children aged from 5 to 13 years. Three studies reported some results by baseline nutritional status. In developing countries (2 RCTs), school meals consistently showed a statistically significant benefit on weight gain over 1 year. Among the CBAs, effects on weight and height were both significant. Benefits were also shown for school attendance, IQ (in one RCT), and verbal fluency (in one RCT). Analysis by initial nutritional status showed mixed results; in some cases the feeding was more effective for undernourished children but in others it was not.

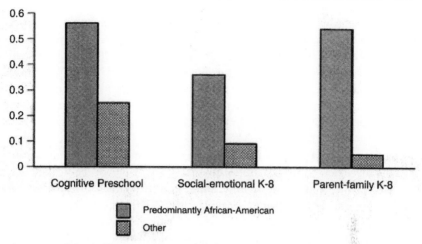

Average weighted effect sizes (*d*) corrected for sample size for different outcomes by ethnoracial background of the study samples.

Figure 7.1   Differential effectiveness of pre-school education programs[22]

for children and families from African–American backgrounds compared to children from other ethnic backgrounds (European–American, Mexican–American, and "Other" ethnic groups).

Subgroup analysis may form a component of a statistical meta-analysis. There are risks involved in this approach however. When examining subgroups, the power to detect differences is lower, and the variance around the summary estimate is greater. When many subgroups are examined, the risk of Type I error is also higher, and this risk increases with the number of subgroups examined. With 20 subgroups in a meta-analysis, one false positive result would be expected (at p <0.05).[23]

Sleight et al. nicely illustrated this problem in their astrological analysis of the ISIS-2 trial of the use of aspirin, compared to another clot-busting drug or placebo, for heart attack. Although aspirin was found to be highly effective overall, when the patients in the trial were analyzed separately by astrological star sign (date of birth had been used as a patient identifier in the study), two subgroups were found in which aspirin was not effective: Gemini and Libra.[24] This does not (unless you are an astrologer) illustrate the need for heart attack victims to be asked their star sign before they are treated; rather, it highlights the need to interpret retrospective subgroup analyses carefully. The same caution applies to systematic reviews, where subgroup analyses may produce spuriously positive findings by chance, and conversely may miss real effects through lack of statistical power. Nonetheless, while subgroup analysis should not be considered as providing definitive answers to questions about impacts in subgroups, they provide a valuable indication of the potential effects in those groups, and an indication of where future primary research may be targeted.[25] Some meta-analysis software allows the user to define a moderator variable to identify the separate groups such as RevMan <http://www.cc-ims.net/RevMan>, and Comprehensive Meta-Analysis <http://www.metaanalysis.com/>.[26]

In many cases, selecting and synthesizing subgroups of studies on the basis of quality alone may be misleading, and it may lessen the usability of the review. For example, in meta-analyses the results observed in subgroups may differ by chance from the overall effect identified by the meta-analysis, and the subgroup findings may not be confirmed by subsequent large trials.[27] In this case, the best estimate of the outcome of the intervention in that subgroup will come paradoxically, by discounting the results from that subgroup, and using the results of the overall meta-analysis (a counter-intuitive state of affairs known as Stein's paradox).[27, 28]

Brookes et al. carried out an extensive analysis that compared the two main approaches to subgroup analysis: separate analysis of effectiveness within subgroups, versus formal statistical analysis of interactions. Using simulated data, they compared the ability of both approaches to correctly identify actual subgroup effects. In the simplest case, where no actual subgroup effects existed, the formal statistical tests identified such effects in 5 percent of cases (as one would expect), whereas for the subgroup-specific analyses the "false positive" rate ranged from 7 to 66 percent (most often appearing in one subgroup only), depending on whether or not there was an overall treatment effect. In general, the formal tests for interaction were superior, and more often identified the correct type of subgroup effect, and, unlike subgroup-specific analyses, were robust to changes in the number and size of intervention groups and subgroups.[29] Box 7.2 gives guidance on interpreting subgroup analyses.

Explorations of effects in subgroups can play an important role in testing and developing theory in systematic reviews. They can be an important tool for assessing the strength of relationships, and for testing the limits of theoretical concepts and explanations, and can contribute to the development of new theories.[30] Box 7.3 quotes Thomas Chalmers on subgroup analysis.

Box 7.2   Guidance on interpreting subgroup analyses in systematic reviews

- Subgroup analyses should as far as possible, be restricted to those proposed before data collection, and any chosen after this should be clearly identified.
- Trials should ideally be powered with subgroups in mind, though for modestly sized interactions this may not be feasible.
- Subgroup-specific analyses are particularly unreliable and are affected by many factors. Subgroup analyses should always be based on formal tests of interaction, although even these should be interpreted with caution.
- The results of subgroup analyses should not be over-interpreted. Unless there is strong supporting evidence, they are best viewed as a hypothesis-generating exercise. In particular, one should be wary of evidence suggesting that the intervention is effective in one subgroup only.
- Any apparent lack of differential effect should be regarded with caution unless the study was specifically powered with inter-actions in mind

(from Brookes et al., 2001)[29]

Box 7.3   Thomas Chalmers on subgroup analysis

"Answering these questions [about subgroup effects] is always difficult both because of the numbers problem and because of the danger of false information resulting from the process of **data-dredging** in each primary study. The numbers problem can be solved by combining groups from individual papers, and the effects of data-dredging biases can be reduced in meta-analyses by proposing prior hypotheses and making cut-off decisions from blinded papers and in duplicate. However, none of this will be successful if the authors of the original papers do not present their data in subgroups that might be combined with subgroup data from other studies."[31]

7.6 META-REGRESSION

The analysis of study-level effects on outcomes as described above can be achieved by meta-regression, in which characteristics of the studies are treated as independent variables in a regression analysis, in an attempt to explain study heterogeneity. A good example of meta-regression comes from a systematic review of the effectiveness of interventions for the prevention of falls in older adults, in which meta-regression was used to assess the independent effects of individual components of the interventions (controlling for other components).[32] The components assessed were exercise programs (such as physical training), education (which could include a range of interventions such as pamphlets or counseling), environmental modifications (such as lighting improvement), and multifactorial programs that incorporated risk assessment and risk management. This latter component appeared effective in reducing the risk of falls, as did exercise. A further meta-regression did not find differences between different types of exercise (such as those which aimed to improve endurance, strength, balance, or flexibility). Another example is given in Box 7.4.

Box 7.4 Meta-regression in transport research

Button and Kerr carried out a meta-regression of 20 international studies to explore the implications of various urban traffic reduction schemes to restrict congestion. The interventions included congestion charging, road pricing, car restrictions, traffic zoning, and improvements in public transport. The meta-regression included variables examining five broad categories of effect; the macro-geographical area within which the study was conducted (such as Scandinavian countries, or the USA); whether the analysis was at the regional or urban level; the type of traffic restraint policy deployed; the level of any public transport improvement which occurred at the same time; and the type of vehicle affected by the policy.

The meta-regression was carried out to demonstrate the use of the technique, and so is not considered by the authors to be definitive but it provides useful insights into the social impacts of transport restraint policies. For example, the meta-regression identified traffic pricing and congestion charging as likely to have a significant impact on traffic reduction.

(Button and Kerr, 1996)[33]

The use of meta-regression is still relatively uncommon, and Higgins and Thomson warn that the risk of false-positive results with meta-regression rises rapidly as the number of characteristics under analysis increases.[34] Sterne et al. also issue several other notes of caution, including the possibility of confounding with other unknown or unmeasured factors.[35]

7.7   GRAPHICAL EXPLORATION OF DIFFERENCES BETWEEN STUDIES: FOREST, FUNNEL, AND L'ABBÉ PLOTS

In 1994 Light et al. found in a survey of systematic reviews in social sciences and psychology that graphical displays were used infrequently.[36] There have been recent improvements, and an increasing use of graphical methods such as Forest plots to display study findings, at least in health care. Nonetheless it is still common for meta-analyses in the social sciences to be published with no graphical displays, and in some cases, no tables describing the studies to help the reader understand the data.

The Forest plot

The Forest plot displays an estimate of the results of each quantitative study in the review, along with its confidence intervals, and the summary estimate (if available). (Lewis and Clarke describe the origins of this method in a 2001 paper.)[37] An example of a Forest plot is described in detail in chapter 6 (see Figure 6.1), and a Forest plot from a recent meta-analysis which synthesized studies examining the effects of helmets on motorcyclists is shown in Figure 7.2. This Cochrane review by Liu et al. carried out a range of meta-analyses for different outcomes. Only the meta-analysis relating to the effectiveness of helmets in preventing death after motorcycle crashes is shown; use of a helmet resulted in a reduction of about 26 percent in the odds of death.[38] This review is also of interest because its inclusion criteria were wide; the authors point out that for obvious ethical reasons RCTs of motorcycle helmet use have not been conducted. Non-randomized prospective and retrospective study designs were therefore eligible for inclusion (another nail in the coffin of the myth that systematic reviews are "really only for RCTs"). The Forest plots shown here and in Chapter 6 used odds ratios, but plots of other types of effect size are of course possible.

Light points out that systematically changing the order in which the effect sizes are plotted can be very informative; there is no reason why the studies need to be plotted alphabetically. Sorting and reordering the display (as with

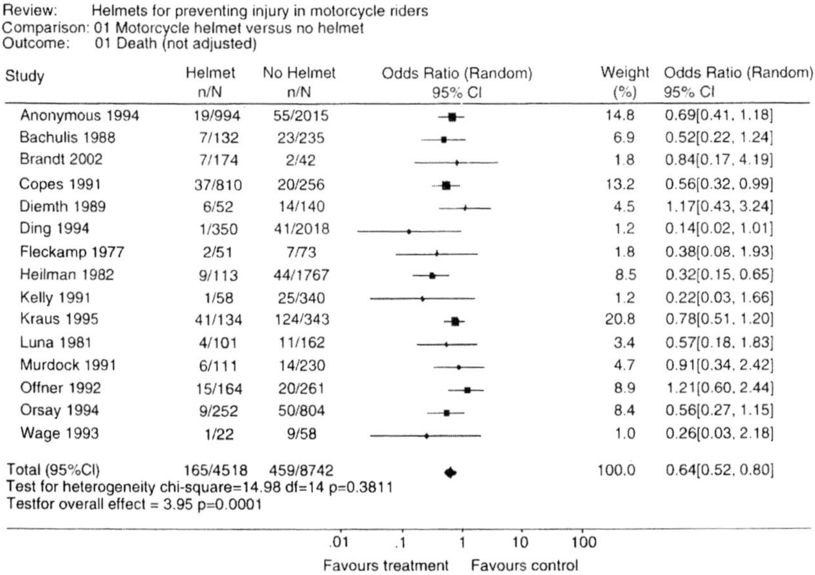

Review: Helmets for preventing injury in motorcycle riders
Comparison: 01 Motorcycle helmet versus no helmet
Outcome: 01 Death (not adjusted)

Study	Helmet n/N	No Helmet n/N	Odds Ratio (Random) 95% CI	Weight (%)	Odds Ratio (Random) 95% CI
Anonymous 1994	19/994	55/2015		14.8	0.69[0.41, 1.18]
Bachulis 1988	7/132	23/235		6.9	0.52[0.22, 1.24]
Brandt 2002	7/174	2/42		1.8	0.84[0.17, 4.19]
Copes 1991	37/810	20/256		13.2	0.56[0.32, 0.99]
Diemth 1989	6/52	14/140		4.5	1.17[0.43, 3.24]
Ding 1994	1/350	41/2018		1.2	0.14[0.02, 1.01]
Fleckamp 1977	2/51	7/73		1.8	0.38[0.08, 1.93]
Heilman 1982	9/113	44/1767		8.5	0.32[0.15, 0.65]
Kelly 1991	1/58	25/340		1.2	0.22[0.03, 1.66]
Kraus 1995	41/134	124/343		20.8	0.78[0.51, 1.20]
Luna 1981	4/101	11/162		3.4	0.57[0.18, 1.83]
Murdock 1991	6/111	14/230		4.7	0.91[0.34, 2.42]
Offner 1992	15/164	20/261		8.9	1.21[0.60, 2.44]
Orsay 1994	9/252	50/804		8.4	0.56[0.27, 1.15]
Wage 1993	1/22	9/58		1.0	0.26[0.03, 2.18]
Total (95%CI)	165/4518	459/8742		100.0	0.64[0.52, 0.80]

Test for heterogeneity chi-square=14.98 df=14 p=0.3811
Testfor overall effect = 3.95 p=0.0001

```
        .01      .1       1       10      100
        Favours treatment   Favours control
```

Figure 7.2   Forest plot of studies of motorcycle helmets and odds of death[38]

tables) can reveal patterns in the data; grouping by other descriptive variables may reveal variations in effectiveness of interventions by country or region, or population; ordering or grouping by study methods or ordering by some measure of study quality may illustrate how study bias may affect study conclusions.[36] Ordering the studies chronologically may also be informative, particularly if a cumulative meta-analysis is carried out. This involves carrying out a new meta-analysis, systematically adding every new study in chronological order. Done retrospectively, this can show how research evidence has accumulated over time.[39]

Further information is provided if the plot symbol is proportionate to the study size, or some measure of its precision, as is done in Liu's Forest plot shown in Figure 7.2.

Forest plots can be carried out even where there has been no meta-analysis. Meta-analysis software (such as RevMan, the Review software used by the Cochrane Collaboration, online at: <http://www.cochrane.org/software/revman.htm>, and Comprehensive MetaAnalysis <http://www.meta-analysis.com/>) can be used to produce Forest plots, but Clark and Djulbegovic[40] have also provided a useful spreadsheet that can be used to produce a Forest plot in Excel (online at: <http://www.evidencias.com/forest01.xls>).

The funnel plot

Another commonly used method of displaying review data is the funnel plot, which has been extensively used to investigate publication and small study bias. This is simply a scatter plot of study precision against effect size, based on the assumption that as the sample size of the studies increases, the range of effect sizes estimated by each study will decrease and those estimates will become more precise. In this case the scatter plot should show an inverted "funnel" shape, as in Figure 7.3 (using hypothetical data). This method is used to detect biases operating in small studies, such as publication bias (described later in this chapter), because asymmetry in the funnel plot – where a part of the funnel appears to be missing – may suggest that some form of small study bias may be operating. See, for example, the shaded area in Figure 7.4; this scatterplot presents the effect sizes from 20 trials of a hypothetical intervention. The more precise, largest studies (at the top of the funnel) suggest that the intervention may be ineffective, clustered close to the vertical line marking no effect (log odds = zero). However, the smaller studies are not symmetrically scattered around this estimate; there appear to be few small studies with large (log) odds ratios, as is shown by the absence of studies in the shaded area of the figure. This asymmetry is sometimes taken as evidence of publication bias (see below). However, it is known that small studies are also prone to a range of other biases; for

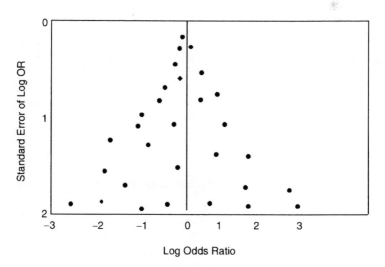

Figure 7.3   Funnel plot (no evidence of bias)

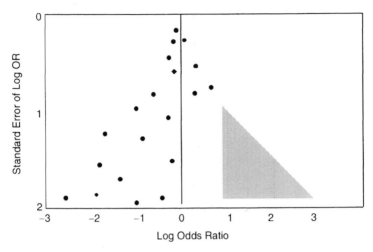

Figure 7.4 Funnel plot (possible bias due to "missing" studies in the shaded area)

example, they are often carried out and analyzed with less rigor than larger studies, so publication bias may not be the only explanation for funnel asymmetry.[41] Other measures of precision can be used by plotting the effect size against the standard error. This emphasizes the differences between the smaller studies, which are the ones of most interest because of their proneness to study bias.[41]

Detecting funnel asymmetry by eye can be difficult, and asymmetry may be difficult to spot particularly when there are few studies. The funnel plot of the data from the review by Liu on motor cycle helmets and mortality is shown in Figure 7.5. Here, there may be some funnel asymmetry, but with 15 studies the pattern is much less clear than in Figure 7.4. (The figure is produced using Comprehensive Meta-analysis software, which adds the diagonal lines signifying 95% confidence intervals to aid detection of funnel plot asymmetry.)[26]

L'Abbé and other plots

The L'Abbé plot is often used to explore the association between the risk of an event and the benefit of the intervention by plotting the proportion of events in the control group against the proportion of events in the intervention group.[42] This can be used to explore whether there are particular

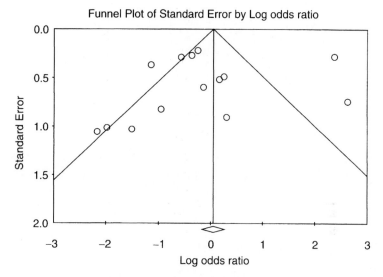

Figure 7.5 Funnel plot, review of motorcycle helmet use and odds of death[38]

subgroups of patients for whom the intervention is more (or less) effective, and to explore heterogeneity (see Figure 7.6). If there is little heterogeneity, the plotted points should lie close to a line showing the pooled treatment effect, based on linear regression analysis (the upper line); and this line should be parallel to the line showing no effect of the intervention (the lower line, which runs through the point (0, 0).[43] The plot in question (based on data from the Scared Straight meta-analysis discussed in Chapter 6) suggests that the intervention effect is similar at all levels of underlying risk (percentage of events in the control group); though the number of points for analysis is small. Sharpe et al. suggest that a L'Abbé plot is a useful adjunct to a Forest plot, but is not appropriate for identifying effective interventions (for example, by using the point at which the two lines cross to identify levels of risk below which intervention is ineffective).

Other simple scatterplots can be used to illustrate study findings and explore statistical or other forms of heterogeneity. Another example is provided from the review by Nelson et al.,[22] discussed earlier, which illustrates differential effects of preschool education in different subgroups of children. Here (Figure 7.7) they explore the relationship between the intensity of the intervention (the length of time the child was enrolled in the program) and one outcome (cognitive development), with an apparent

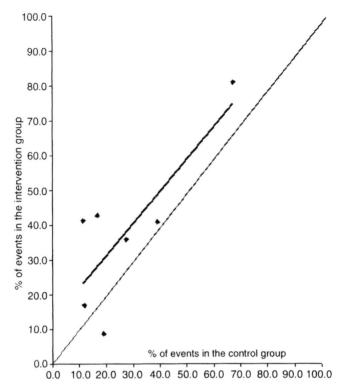

Figure 7.6   Example of a simple L'Abbé plot

increase in impact with increasing length of enrollment in the program. A similar graph was used in this review to examine the relationship between the intensity of the intervention and program outcomes.

One further potential source of bias in systematic reviews is publication bias, which can be explored using some of the methods outlined above.

7.8   PUBLICATION BIAS

A brief history of publication bias

It has been known for a long time – at least since the 1950s, if not before – that about one-half of papers presented at conference are never subsequently fully published in journals or elsewhere. Felix Liebesny referred to this as "Lost Information," and illustrated the problem by following the fate of 383

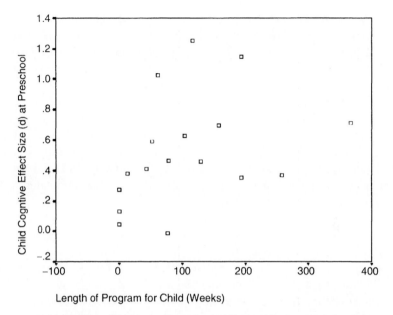

Child cognitive effect sizes (d) at preschool by length of program for child.

Figure 7.7   Scattergram of intensity of delivery of preschool educational intervention by effect size[22]

papers that had been presented at a number of engineering and physics conferences in the late 1940s. Just under 50 percent remained unpublished about 3 years after the event.[44] Liebesny suggested that either the authors had died an untimely death, or, more uncharitably, had suffered a severe attack of amnesia or laziness which prevented them from putting their knowledge into print.

There is, however, another possibility which he did not discuss; that the unpublished papers differ systematically from those that are published, and specifically that they remain unpublished because they contain negative (statistically non-significant) findings which journal editors do not wish to publish, or which authors do not submit to journals in the first place, on the assumption that they are uninteresting and will be rejected. Sterling and others subsequently pointed out that studies reporting negative findings appeared to be under-represented in psychological journals, and subsequent extensive work in the health and social sciences has confirmed that publication bias is a problem, and can be a serious source of bias in literature reviews.[45] Take for example, a hypothetical review of the effectiveness of an intervention which includes only studies which were published in peer-reviewed journals. Those published studies are more likely to have concluded that the intervention was effective, while any unpublished studies with "negative" findings would be overlooked. Such a review may, therefore, over-estimate the effectiveness of the intervention.

Researchers have often blamed journal editors for rejecting negative studies, but this is not the only possibility. Hedges, for instance, suggests that sophisticated authors who do not obtain statistical significance would spare themselves the embarrassment of a rejection.[46] This seems to be the case. Authors do indeed appear to exercise self-censorship, and tend not to submit their negative results for publication; however, among manuscripts submitted to journals, those with negative results are no less likely to be published than those reporting positive findings.[47] Moreover positive studies are published no more quickly.[48] Meta-analyses do not appear to be subject to this bias; Stroup et al. have found that the only predictor of publication of meta-analyses is whether the authors included sufficient detail to allow the meta-analysis to be replicated.[49]

Scherer et al. carried out a systematic review that synthesized the results of all studies of non-publication carried out in the biomedical sciences. This involved synthesizing reports that examined the rate of subsequent full publication of studies initially presented as abstracts (for example, conference abstracts), or in summary form. Scherer's review included 79 reports, which included a total of 29,729 abstracts or summaries. The weighted mean rate of subsequent full publication was found to be 44.5 percent, with a median rate of 47 percent – very similar to Liebesny's 1956 estimate of 48.5 percent.[50] "Positive" studies appeared to be more likely to be published (RR = 1.28). Oral, as opposed to poster presentation, was also significantly associated with full publication, and RCTs, as opposed to other types of study, were more likely to achieve full publication (see Figure 7.8).

The risk posed to systematic reviews by publication bias has been shown by Egger et al.,[51] who have demonstrated how the results of several large meta-analyses have been contradicted by large RCTs of the same intervention.[51,52] In one analysis, discordance was in all cases a consequence of the meta-analyses showing more beneficial effects than the large trials. Egger suggests that the funnel plot could be of value in detecting bias (such as publication or other biases) as described earlier in this chapter.[51]

Publication bias can be at least partially addressed by attempting to locate and include all relevant published and unpublished studies irrespective of their results. However, there are other less obvious biases operating which

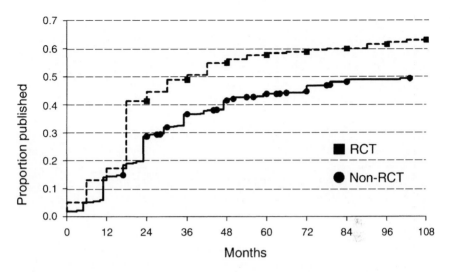

N = 17,344 abstracts for non-RCTs and 2,917 abstracts for RCTs
Circles and squares show points where data censored because reports stopped follow-up.

Figure 7.8   Cumulative rate of publication of abstracts of RCTs and non-RCTs
Source: From Scherer et al.[50]

reviewers should be aware of, as they may affect reviewers' interpretation of the results of any review of quantitative studies. Some of the main location biases are listed in Box 7.5.

Box 7.5   Some location biases in systematic reviews

Publication bias: Studies with statistically significant results are more likely to get published than those with non-significant results. There may be a further related problem with respect to sub-group analyses; Clarke and Stewart[53] have suggested that constraints on journal space and other influences may make it likely that only subgroup analyses with the most interesting, striking, and significant results may be published. Meta-analyses of systematic reviews which synthesize reports of such analyses, for example, to identify differential effects in populations, may therefore be prone to this bias.

(Continued)

Box 7.5 *(Cont'd)*

Funding bias: It has been suggested that the source of funding can affect publication; in particular that the pharmaceutical industry discourages the publication of drug studies that it has funded which have negative findings.[54]

Language and country biases: It has been suggested that authors may be more likely to report positive findings in international, English language journals, and negative findings in a journal in their own countries;[55] a search for only English-language literature may, therefore, over-represent studies with positive findings (though in the case of "social" systematic reviews there may of course be good reasons for only including English language studies, or studies from only one country). Vickers, Egger and others have also found that clinical trials originating in certain countries have a strong tendency to produce only positive results.[56]

Database bias: Many studies are published in journals that are not indexed in any of the major electronic databases. If studies published in an indexed journal differ systematically from those published in non-indexed journals (for example, if positive findings are more likely to appear in indexed journals), then bias may be introduced into the review by only searching the major electronic databases.[54]

Citation bias: Studies that are supportive of a beneficial effect may be cited more frequently than unsupportive trials, regardless of the size and quality of the studies involved.[54] Reviews which rely on only well-known or often-cited studies, or which search only reference lists may thus be biased. One study however has found that journal impact factor is the only significant predictor of study citation rates.[57]

Multiple publication: Studies with significant results are more likely to lead to multiple publications and presentations, and it may be difficult to tell whether several papers represent the same study, or different studies, increasing the risk that both will be inadvertently included in the same systematic review.[54, 58] If in doubt, contacting the authors should be made a priority. Tramer et al. differentiate between overt duplication – the legitimate reanalysis of data with appropriate cross-referencing and covert duplication, which involves re-publication without cross-referencing.[59]

(from Egger (1998)[55] and Song et al. (2000)[53])

See also: <www.jameslindlibrary.org/essays/interpretation/relevant_evidence/reporting_bias.html> for a summary of issues relating to the selective publication and reporting of evidence (Dickersin).[60] Box 7.6 points out the importance of disappointing findings.

Box 7.6   The importance of disappointing findings

Lost hopes aside, methodologically kosher but disappointing findings are very precious. They tell us – particularly in combination – what not to do and potentially at least provide arguments for the release of resources for more promising ventures.

(Sheldon and Chilvers, 2000)[61]

7.9   DEALING WITH PUBLICATION AND OTHER LOCATION BIASES

The main method of dealing with publication bias is to ensure that the risk is minimized. Ideally this should be done by preventing publication bias occurring in the first place, but some measures can also be taken by reviewers.[54] As described in Chapter 2, literature searches should not be confined to electronic databases of peer-reviewed literature, but should consider the inclusion of non-peer-reviewed and other gray and unpublished literature, and, where relevant to the intervention and the context, the inclusion of non-English language studies. Even where these measures are taken, it will be useful to explore the possibility of publication and other biases using relevant graphical plots. Egger et al.,[62] however, warn that in some cases an exhaustive literature search may actually introduce bias. They examined 60 healthcare meta-analyses that had included published and unpublished studies, and others that included studies in other languages than English (n = 50), and non-indexed versus MEDLINE-indexed studies (66 meta-analyses). They examined the effect of systematically excluding trials that were difficult to locate, and those that were of lower quality. Their conclusion provides a useful lesson for systematic reviewers on the tradeoff between the need for comprehensive searches, and the reality of limited resources:

The finding that trials that are difficult to locate are often of poorer quality raises the worrying possibility that, rather than preventing biases thorough comprehensive literature searches, [it may increase them] by including trials of low methodological quality. We believe that in situations where resources are limited, thorough quality assessments should take precedence over extensive literature searches and translations of articles. (Egger et al., 2000)[62]

7.10   FAIL-SAFE N

Other methods have been proposed to detect, and in some cases adjust for, publication bias. One commonly-used method is the Fail-safe N, which calculates the number of unpublished "negative" studies which remain hidden in researchers' hypothetical file-drawers and which would be required to exist in order to overturn the results of a meta-analysis. This could in theory be done if there were enough studies to reduce the level of significance of the meta-analysis to >0.05. Rosenthal referred to this measure as an assessment of the tolerance of a meta-analysis for null results.[63] However the use of the measure has been much criticized in recent years and it is unlikely to be robust. For one thing, it is sensitive to the effects of publication and other biases; it will produce an effect in the same direction as the meta-analysis, yet as described earlier, the meta-analysis may be in error because (for example) it has failed to include small unpublished, negative studies.[64] The fail-safe N would be meaningful if effect sizes were only affected by sampling error and not by systematic bias, but meta-analyses of biased studies may have a tendency to produce a very large fail-safe N. Fail-safe N may therefore often be an unintended measure of study bias, rather than "tolerance for null results," and can lead to unwarranted confidence in the robustness of a review. The stuff that is hidden in the file drawers is different, and often of poorer quality than the stuff that sees the light of day, and because of this fail-safe N values should be treated with caution.

7.11   TRIM AND FILL, AND OTHER APPROACHES

Statistical methods for detecting and investigating publication bias have been developed by Egger et al.[51] The "Trim and fill" method has also been proposed, which involves estimating the number of missing studies from an asymmetrical funnel plot, and then adjusting the overall summary effect from the meta-analysis to take account of the "missing" effect sizes.[65]

Sutton et al. tested this method on a sample of 48 Cochrane reviews and estimated that 54 percent of these had at least one missing study. In about 20% of cases there was a "strong indication" of missing trials. Imputing the "missing" trials changed the estimates of the overall effect for all meta-analyses with one or more "missing" trials, and in four reviews imputing the missing data would have led to significant changes in their conclusions.[66] Overall, these analyses suggest that whereas there was a strong indication of publication bias in about one-fifth of meta-analyses, this affected the results in less than 10 percent; however they recommend that reviewers always check for publication bias.

Other non-technical solutions for preventing publication bias include the development of journals devoted to the publication of negative findings (see Box 7.7), "amnesties" for unpublished trials,[67] and the establishment of trial registers to ensure that studies do not get lost from view or hidden in the filing cabinet.[67, 68] Some of these registers were listed in Chapter 4.

Box 7.7　Even negative findings can find a home: Three journals of negative results

Scientists' perceptions of the importance of negative findings have clearly changed considerably since the days of Beveridge's *Advice on the art of scientific investigation*, which advised that negative results should be quietly put in the bin.[69] Now there are even whole journals devoted to negative findings:

The Journal of Negative Results in BioMedicine: <http://www.jnrbm.com/home/>: From the 'Instructions to authors':

The Journal of Negative Results in BioMedicine is ready to receive papers on all aspects of unexpected, controversial, provocative and/or negative results/conclusions in the context of current tenets, providing scientists and physicians with responsible and balanced information to support informed experimental and clinical decisions.

Journal of Negative Results in Speech and Audio Sciences: <http://journal.speech.cs.cmu.edu/>

(Continued)

238 EXPLORING HETEROGENEITY AND PUBLICATION BIAS

Box 7.7 *(Cont'd)*

The value of meticulous archiving of negative results cannot be overstated. Today, more so than in earlier years, theories that are extremely plausible but do not bear out in practice, are repeatedly re-invented, re-implemented and re-argued by new investigators who have no way of knowing their outcome a priori except through the scientific grapevine. We hope to transform that grapevine into literature that can be seriously referenced.

Journal of Negative Results: Ecology and Evolutionary Biology: <http://www.jnr-eeb.org/>

The primary intention of *Journal of Negative Results* is to provide an online medium for the publication of peer-reviewed, sound scientific work in ecology and evolutionary biology that may otherwise remain unknown. In recent years, the trend has been to publish only studies with "significant" results and to ignore studies that seem uneventful. This may lead to a biased, perhaps untrue, representation of what exists in nature.

The *Marine Ecology Journal* "Marine Ecology Progress Series" also produced an excellent special issue in 1999 devoted to papers discussing the need to publish negative results in ecology, and outlining the statistical and philosophical issues.[70]

Sterne et al. emphasize that when it comes to publication bias "prevention is better than cure."[41] In practice this is why reviews attempt to locate all relevant studies, and why there is increasing emphasis on the registration of trials and other studies.

7.12 THE CAPTURE–RECAPTURE TECHNIQUE AND SYSTEMATIC REVIEWS

> In one moment I've seen what has hitherto been
> Enveloped in absolute mystery.
> And without extra charge I will give you at large
> A lesson in Natural History-
> > The Hunting of the Snark *(Lewis Carroll, 1876)*

The general problem for systematic reviewers who are worried about publication bias is one of estimating the size of an unknown population; in this case, the population of unpublished studies. This problem is well known to those who carry out surveys of any "difficult-to-locate" population. One approach, the "capture–recapture" method, has been used for many years by ecologists, who need to estimate the size of a given animal population. It involves capturing a sample of the animal then tagging and releasing them, allowing them to mix freely with the original population, then recapturing a proportion of them by means of a second sample. The total population can be estimated by examining the ratio of tagged to untagged animals in this second group. This is sometimes referred to as Petersen's method, after the nineteenth-century Danish biologist who used it to estimate fish populations, but it has been extended to human censuses, and to surveys attempting to estimate the size of difficult to locate populations, such as drug users and sex workers.[71, 72, 73]

The method can be extended to help estimate the size of any unknown population by assessing the degree of overlap between independent samples. Spoor et al. have described its application to systematic reviews, by showing how it can be used to estimate the total population of trials by comparing the results of two searches, one using hand searching, and the other using a search of the MEDLINE database.[74] The total number of trials is given by $N = M(n/m)$, where M is the number of publications identified by MEDLINE, n the number identified by hand searching, and m is the number identified by both types of search. The estimated number unidentified by either method – that is, the trials that have been "missed" by the searches – can then be calculated by subtraction. They also note that Chapman's method is more appropriate for small samples. This method estimates the total population size as $N = (M + 1)(n + 1)/(m + 1)-1$. The 95 percent confidence intervals around the estimate can also be calculated from the variance of N, estimated as $Var(N) = (M + 1)(n + 1)$ $(M - m)(n - m)/((m + 1)2(m + 2))$. Bennett et al. have found that the results of the capture–recapture method are broadly consistent with other methods described earlier in this chapter (Trim and Fill, and statistical techniques).[75]

7.13   PUBLICATION BIAS AND QUALITATIVE RESEARCH

It is interesting to speculate on the ways in which publication bias may operate in relation to qualitative research, what effect it may have on systematic reviews of qualitative studies, and how it might be detected.

There appears not to have been any previous empirical research into this issue, though one ongoing study, which is currently investigating this, involves a retrospective analysis of the fate of qualitative papers originally presented at conferences. One might hypothesize that the rates of non-publication for qualitative studies would be similar to those for other sorts of research, as these seem to be similar across time and across discipline; so about 50 percent of qualitative studies presented at conferences might be expected to remain unpublished at two years (this is no more than an hypothesis at present). It would be more interesting to know whether, and how the unpublished studies differ systematically from the published ones (see also Box 7.8).

Box 7.8   Publication bias: Qualitative research

Qualitative research like other kinds of research, is likely to be subject to publication bias, although it may be more difficult to trace completed but unpublished studies, and to speculate on why they might not have been published. Unlike studies of trials, a lack of "positive" findings is unlikely to be the problem.

One aspect of reporting bias in qualitative research relates to article length. In abridging articles to fit the restrictive word length limit of some key journals, data may be so compressed as to make the methodological and analytical components of an article almost meaningless, and the content reduced to illustrative quotations. The selection of data that this requires may introduce bias into qualitative studies.

In the absence of primary data, it is unclear at present just what publication bias in qualitative work means for systematic reviews. Given that qualitative work is not designed to be generalizable, the consequences of publication bias are likely to be different from those resulting from, for instance, the under-publication of trials which do not show a statistically significant effect. Whether this makes publication bias in qualitative work more or less important for systematic reviews and evidence syntheses than a similar bias in quantitative studies itself remains a research question.

> # Key learning points from this chapter
>
> - There may be significant variation between the studies in a systematic review, and this may affect any interpretation of the review's findings.
> - Among the sources of variation are study heterogeneity and statistical heterogeneity. Some of the main sources of heterogeneity in quantitative studies may be detected statistically and graphically, though some methods have low power.
> - The possibility of publication bias should also be considered routinely. A number of statistical methods of detecting and analyzing publication bias have been proposed; however many of these are low-powered and even more so when the number of studies in the review is small.
> - In the case of publication bias, prevention is better than cure.

REFERENCES

1. Thompson, S. Systematic review: Why sources of heterogeneity in meta-analysis should be investigated. *British Medical Journal* 1994, 309: 1351–5.
2. Grimshaw, J., Freemantle, N., Wallace, S., Russell, I., Hurwitz, B., Watt, I., et al. Developing and implementing clinical practice guidelines. *Quality in Health Care* 1995, 4: 55–64.
3. Rychetnik, L., Frommer, M., Hawe, P., and Shiell, A. Criteria for evaluating evidence on public health interventions. *Journal of Epidemiology and Community Health* 2002, 56: 119–27.
4. Hawe, P., Shiell, A., and Riley, T. Complex interventions: How "out of control" can a randomised controlled trial be? *British Medical Journal* 2004, 328: 1561–3.
5. Campbell, M., Fitzpatrick, R., Haines, A., Kinmonth, A., Sandercock, P., Spiegelhalter, D., et al. Framework for design and evaluation of complex interventions to improve health. *British Medical Journal* 2000, 321: 694–6.
6. Higgins, J., Thompson, S., Deeks, J., and Altman, D. Measuring inconsistency in meta-analyses. *British Medical Journal* 2003, 327: 557–60.
7. Higgins, J. Assessing statistical heterogeneity: Chi-squared or I-squared? *Newsletter of the Cochrane Wounds Group* 2004, 3–4.

8. Lau, J., Ioannidis, J., and Schmid, C. Quantitative synthesis in systematic reviews. In C. Mulrow and D Cook (eds.) *Systematic reviews: Synthesis of best evidence for health care decisions.* Philadelphia: ACP, 1998.

9. Lau, J., Antman, E., Jimenez-Silva, J., Kupelnick, B., Mosteller, F., and Chalmers, T. Cumulative meta-analysis of therapeutic trials for myocardial infarction. *New England Journal of Medicine* 1992, 327: 248–54.

10. Greenhouse, J. and Iyengar, S. Sensitivity analysis and diagnostics. In H. Cooper and L. Hedges (eds.). *The handbook of research synthesis.* New York: Russell Sage Foundation, 1994.

11. Tugwell, P. and Kristjansson, B. Moving from description to action: Challenges in researching socio-economic inequalities in health. *Canadian Medical Association Journal* 2004, 95: 85–7.

12. Kristjansson, B., Robinson, V., Tugwell, P., Petticrew, M., Greenhalgh, T., Macdonald, B., et al. School feeding programs for improving outcomes of low-income children and for reducing socioeconomic inequalities in health (submitted).

13. Mackenbach, J. Tackling inequalities in health: The need for building a systematic evidence base. *Journal of Epidemiology and Community Health* 2003, 57: 162.

14. Gruen, R., Bailie, R., McDonald, E., Weeramanthri, T., and Knight, S. The potential of systematic reviews to identify diversity and inequity in health care interventions. XI Cochrane Colloquium: Evidence, health care and culture, Barcelona, 2003.

15. Ogilvie, D. and Petticrew, M. Smoking policies and health inequalities. *Tobacco Control* 2004, 13: 129–31.

16. Tsikata, S., Robinson, V., Petticrew, M., Kristjansson, B., Moher, D., McGowan, J., et al. Do Cochrane systematic reviews contain useful information about health equity? XI Cochrane Colloquium: Evidence, health care, and culture, Barcelona, 2003.

17. Cooper, H. *The integrative research review: A systematic approach.* Newbury Park, CA: Sage, 1984.

18. Cooper, H. *Integrating research: A guide for literature reviews.* London: Sage, 1989.

19. Cooper, H. and Hedges, L. (eds.) *The handbook of research synthesis.* New York: Russell Sage Foundation, 1994.

20. Shadish, W. Meta-analysis and the exploration of causal mediating processes: A primer of examples, methods, and issues. *Psychological Methods* 1996, 1: 47–65.

21. Sheikh, A., Gopalakrishnan Netuveli, G., Kai, J., and Singh Panesar, S. Comparison of reporting of ethnicity in US and European randomised controlled trials. *British Medical Journal* 2004, 329: 87–8.

22. Nelson, G., Westhues, A., and MacLeod, J. A meta-analysis of longitudinal research on preschool prevention programs for children. *Prevention & Treatment* 2003, Article 31, online at: http://journals.apa.org/prevention/volume6/pre0060031a.html

23. Sleight. P. Debate: Subgroup analyses in clinical trials: Fun to look at – but don't believe them! *Current Controlled Trials in Cardiovascular Medicine* 2000, 1: 25–7.

24. ISIS-2 (Second International Study of Infarct Survival) Collaborative Group: Randomised trial of intravenous streptokinase, oral aspirin, both or neither among 17,187 cases of suspected acute myocardial infarction. *Lancet* 1988 ii: 349–60.

25. Eagly, A. and Wood, W. Using research synthesis to plan future research. In H. Cooper and L. Hedges (eds.) *The handbook of research synthesis*. New York: Russell Sage Foundation, 1994.

26. Borenstein. M. and Borenstein H. *Comprehensive meta-analysis: A computer program for research synthesis*. New Jersey: Biostat <http://www.metaanalysis.com>, 1999.

27. Davey Smith, G., Egger, M., and Phillips, A. Beyond the grand mean? *British Medical Journal* 1997, 315: 1610–14.

28. Effron, B. and Morris, C. Stein's paradox in statistics. *Scientific American* 1977, 236: 119–27.

29. Brookes, S., Whitley, E., Peters, T., Mulheran, P., Egger, M., and Davey Smith, G. Subgroup analyses in randomised controlled trials: Quantifying the risks of false positives and false negatives. *Health Technology Assessment* 2001, 5, online at: http://www.hta.nhsweb.nhs.uk/htapubs.htm

30. Miller, N. and Pollock, V. Meta-analytic synthesis for theory development. In H. Cooper and L. Hedges (eds.) *The handbook of research synthesis*. New York: Russell Sage Foundation, 1994.

31. Chalmers, T. Meta-analytic stimulus for changes in clinical trials. *Statistical Methods in Medicine* 1993, 2: 161–72.

32. Chang, J., Morton, S., Rubenstein, L., Mojica, W., Maglione, M., Suttorp, M., et al. Interventions for the prevention of falls in older adults: Systematic review and meta-analysis of randomised clinical trials. *British Medical Journal* 2004, 328: 653–4.

33. Button, K. and Kerr, J. The effectiveness of traffic restraint policies: A simple meta-regression analysis. *International Journal of Transport Economics* 1996, XXIII.

34. Higgins, J. and Thompson, S. The risk of false-positive findings from meta-regression. 4th Symposium on Systematic Reviews: Pushing the Boundaries; 2002; Oxford, online at: http://www.ihs.ox.ac.uk/csm/pushingtheboundaries/symp2002.html

35. Sterne, J., Egger, M., and Davey Smith, G. Investigating and dealing with publication and other biases. In M. Egger, G. Davey Smith, and D. Altman (eds.) *Systematic reviews in health care*. London: BMJ Publishing Group, 2001.

36. Light, R., Singer, J., and Willett, J. The visual presentation and interpretation of meta-analyses. In H. Cooper and L. Hedges (eds.) *The handbook of research synthesis*. New York: Russell Sage Foundation, 1994.

37. Lewis, S. and Clarke, M. Forest plots: Trying to see the wood and the trees. *British Medical Journal* 2001, 322: 1479–80.

38. Liu, B., Ivers, R., Norton, R., Blows, S., and Lo, S. Helmets for preventing injury in motorcycle riders (Cochrane Review). *The Cochrane Library*, Issue 2, 2004. Chichester, UK: John Wiley & Sons, Ltd., 2004.

39. Egger, M., Davey Smith, G., and Altman, D. *Systematic reviews in health care. Meta-analysis in context*. London: BMJ, 2001.

40. Clark, O. and Djulbegovic, B. Forest plots in Excel software (data sheet), online at: http://www.evidencias.com/forest01.xls, 2001.

41. Sterne, J., Egger, M., and Davey Smith, G.. Systematic reviews in health care: Investigating and dealing with publication and other biases in meta-analysis. *British Medical Journal* 2001, 323: 101–5.

42. Song, F., Abrams, K., and Jones, D. Methods for exploring heterogeneity in meta-analysis. *Evaluation and the Health Professions* 2001, 24: 126–51.

43. Sharpe, S., Thompson, S., and Altman, D. The relation between treatment benefit and underlying risk in meta-analysis. *British Medical Journal* 1996, 313: 735–8.

44. Liebesny, F. Lost information: Unpublished conference papers. *Proceedings of the International Conference on Scientific Information* 1959, 1: 475–9.

45. Sterling, T. Publication decisions and their possible effects on inferences drawn from tests of significance – or vice versa. *American Statistical Association Journal* 1959, 54: 30–4.

46. Hedges, L. Comment on: Selection models and the File Drawer problem (Iyengar and Greenhouse, 1988). *Statistical Science* 1988, 3: 118–20.

47. Olson, C., Rennie, D., Cook, D., Dickersin, K., Flanagin, A., Hogan, J., et al. Publication bias in editorial decision making. *Journal of the American Medical Association* 2002, 287(21): 2825–8.

48. Dickersin, K., Olson, C., Rennie, D., Cook, D., Flanagin, A., Zhu, Q., et al. Association between time interval to publication and statistical significance. *Journal of the American Medical Association* 2002, 287(21): 2829–31.

49. Stroup, D., Thacker, S., Olson, C., Glass, R., and Hutwagner, L. Characteristics of meta-analyses related to acceptance for publication in a medical journal. *Journal of Clinical Epidemiology* 2001, 54: 655–60.

50. Scherer, R., von Elm, E., and Langenberg, P. Full publication of results initially presented in abstracts (Cochrane Methodology Review). *The Cochrane Library*, Issue 2, 2005. Chichester, UK: John Wiley & Sons, Ltd.

51. Egger, M., Davey Smith, G., Schneider, M., and Minder, C. Bias in meta-analysis detected by a simple graphical test. *British Medical Journal* 1997, 315: 629–34.

52. Egger, M. and Davey Smith, G. Misleading meta-analysis. Lessons from "an effective, safe, simple" intervention that wasn't. *British Medical Journal* 1995, 310: 752–4.

53. Clarke, M. and Stewart, L. Obtaining data from randomised controlled trials: How much do we need for reliable and informative meta-analyses? *British Medical Journal* 1994, 309: 1007–10.

54. Song, F., Eastwood, A., Gilbody, S., Duley, L., and Sutton, A. Publication and related biases. *Health Technology Assessment* 2000, 4, online at: http://www.hta.nhsweb.nhs.uk/htapubs.htm

55. Egger, M. Meta-analysis: Bias in location and selection of studies. *British Medical Journal* 1998, 316: 61–6.

56. Vickers, A., Goyal, N., Harland, R., and Rees, R. Do certain countries produce only positive results? A systematic review of controlled trials. *Controlled Clinical Trials* 1998, 19: 159–66.

57. Callaham, M., Wears, R., and Weber, E. Journal prestige, publication bias, and other characteristics associated with citation of published studies in peer-reviewed journals. *Journal of the American Medical Association* 2002, 287: 2847–50.

58. Easterbrook, P., Berlin, J., Gopalan, R., and Matthews, D. Publication bias in clinical research. *Lancet* 1991, 337: 867–72.

59. Tramer, M., Reynolds, D., Moore, R., and McQuay, H. Impact of covert duplication on meta-analysis: A case study. *British Medical Journal* 1997, 315: 635–40.

60. Dickersin, K. Reducing reporting biases. In I. Chalmers, I. Milne, and U. Tröhler, (eds.) *The James Lind Library* <www.jameslindlibrary.org>, 2004.

61. Sheldon, B. and Chilvers, R. *Evidence-based social care: A study of prospects and problems.* Lyme Regis, Dorset: Russell House Publishing, 2000.

62. Egger, M., Jüni, P., Bartlett, C., Holenstein, F., and Sterne, J. How important are comprehensive literature searches and the assessment of trial quality in systematic reviews? *Health Technology Assessment* 2003, 7, online at: http://www.hta.nhsweb.nhs.uk/htapubs.htm

63. Rosenthal, R. The "File Drawer Problem" and tolerance for null results. *Psychological Bulletin* 1979, 86: 638–41.

64. Evans, S. Misleading meta-analysis: Statistician's comment. *Lancet* 1996, 312: 125.

65. Duval, S. and Tweedie, R. Trim and fill: A simple funnel-plot-based method of testing and adjusting for publication bias in meta-analysis. *Biometrics* 2000, 56: 455–63.

66. Sutton, A., Duval, S., Tweedie, R., Abrams, K., and Jones, D. Empirical assessment of effect of publication bias on meta-analyses. *British Medical Journal* 2000, 320: 1574–7.

67. Smith, R. and Roberts, I. An amnesty for unpublished trials. *British Medical Journal* 1997, 315: 622.

68. Chalmers, I. Underreporting research is scientific misconduct. *Journal of the American Medical Association* 1990, 263: 1405–8.

69. Beveridge, W. *The art of scientific investigation.* New York: Vintage Books, 1950.

70. Browman, H. Negative results: Theme section. *Marine Ecology Progress Series* 1999, 191: 301–9.

71. Khan, S., Bhuiya, A., and Uddin, A. Application of the capture-recapture method for estimating number of mobile male sex workers in a port city of Bangladesh. *Journal of Health, Population and Nutrition* 2004, 22: 19–26.

72. Hall, W., Ross, J., Lynskey, M., Law, M., and Degenhardt, L. How many dependent heroin users are there in Australia? *Medical Journal of Australia* 2000, 173: 528–31.

73. Laska, E. The use of capture-recapture methods in public health. *Bulletin of the World Health Organization* 2002, 80: 845.

74. Spoor, P., Airey, M., Bennett, C., Greensill, J., and Williams, R. Use of the capture-recapture technique to evaluate the completeness of systematic literature searches. *British Medical Journal* 1996, 313: 342–3.

75. Bennett, D., Latham, N., Stretton, C., and Anderson, C. Capture-recapture is a potentially useful method for assessing publication bias. *Journal of Clinical Epidemiology* 2004, 57: 349–57.

Chapter 8

Disseminating the review

We need to be able to rely on social science and social scientists to tell us what works and why, and what types of policy initiatives are likely to be most effective. And we need better ways of ensuring that those who want this information can get it easily and quickly. (Blunkett, 2000)[1]

You sometimes feel as if you're serenading outside a window, trying to get them to open it, singing "let me in." Sometimes you want to throw a brick in with a message tied to it. But there's no point in chanting from the outside. You really need to get inside the house, and how do you do that? . . . You always think there are simple solutions. But in fact, it's very hard work. (Barnardo's, 2000)[2]

8.1   INTRODUCTION

For research to fulfill its function as an information base for social policy and practice, we need to know the most effective means of:

- making research findings available to those who commission and provide services;
- ensuring research addresses issues of importance to the people who use those services; and
- translating the practical and theoretical implications of research into the policies, procedures, and activities of organizations.

This chapter deals with an important step in the systematic review process: the communication of the review's findings. Although this is sometimes seen as a final step (and it comes towards the end of this book), communication is core to the use of systematic review findings, and needs to be thought about at the start of the review, when the question the review considers is refined, and when the involvement of an advisory group is being planned. Guidance on how and why to do this is given in chapter 2.

A small study, even a poor quality small study, on a single issue with a controversial finding is more likely than a systematic review of the evidence to get widespread attention, as some of the headlines at the start of this book show. Single studies can be compelling. They can be well communicated (and this goes for poor quality as well as sound studies), and they often have a clear message. As the chapter on synthesis demonstrates, telling the systematic review story involves skill. Selling the story, or making sure key messages are heard is also important, although researchers may not always be the best people to do this. Researchers are, however, more likely than professional communicators to take account of some of the behavior change theories that are needed to move beyond dissemination into implementation. Marteau et al.'s observation on clinicians is equally true of those working in other areas:

> There is an asymmetry embedded in the notion of changing...behaviour. There are two parties, those who wish to change other people's behaviour and other people. But the latter are not impassively waiting to be changed; [those] whose behaviour is to be changed have their own ideas about whether and how such change might be effected. This means that behaviour change is not a one-sided business, a case of an enlightened intervention trying to change an old-fashioned [practitioner], but a process of negotiating whose model will prevail and whose behaviour will be changed. (Marteau et al., 2002)[3]

Effective dissemination involves considering who might want to use your work, producing good products and "getting inside the house" of those who might be in a position to use the findings. "Sexing up" a systematic review to make it interesting to those who need to hear about it is probably as unwise as it is unacceptable, and in many cases, it would tax even the most creative press officer. The messages from systematic reviews are often nuanced, and need careful interpretation. In many cases (as in most research), systematic reviews will result in small incremental additions to knowledge rather than major findings and a judgment needs to be made on whether the time and effort of wide dissemination are justified.

8.2   ORGANIZATIONAL MODELS OF GETTING RESEARCH INTO POLICY AND PRACTICE

A linear model in which findings are seamlessly disseminated to policy and practice users, and important findings acted on as night follows day has been largely discredited.[4, 5, 6] Lavis et al.[7] suggest that there are three key organ-izational models for dissemination:

1. Researchers responsible for transferring and facilitating the uptake of research knowledge (producer-push model).
2. Decision makers responsible for identifying and making use of research knowledge (user-pull model).
3. Researchers and decision makers jointly responsible for the uptake of research knowledge (exchange model).

Effective dissemination strategies will depend in part on the model your team embraces, and the extent to which you want to use your research for advocacy. A recent article in the *Journal of Epidemiology and Community Health* suggests that this is a legitimate activity for professionals, and reminds us that:

> Ever since John Snow removed the handle of the Broad Street Pump and faced the scepticism and wrath of water suppliers and residents, many public health initiatives have met with protracted, fraught, and often highly organised opposition. Road safety advocates have faced concerted opposition from the liquor and automobile industries, devotees of speed and critics of government revenue raising.[8]

Similar opposition is met by researchers in other disciplines, and beyond academia. Ibsen's "Enemy of the People" (and slightly more recently, Steven Spielberg's "Jaws") provide further examples of unpopular findings which people would rather not act on. A real-life example of this from a systematic review of driver education, is described in Box 8.1.

Box 8.1   Can dissemination of systematic reviews lead to changes in policy?

While helping to run a course on systematic reviewing, public health epidemiologist Ian Roberts received a communication from Bridget Chaudhury, the secretary of RoadPeace <http://www.roadpeace.org/>, a charity for road traffic victims.

There were plans, she said, for the UK government to introduce funding for schemes to teach young people to drive while they were at

(Continued)

Box 8.1 *(Cont'd)*

school. "What," she asked, "is the evidence that this does more good than harm?" With an intervention like this – something which is apparently a good idea, it can be hard for people to get their heads round the idea that it be harmful.

After discussion, the student group decided to carry out a systematic review, which was completed over a period of about four weeks. Different people were allocated different roles – including press officer and parliamentary liaison.

A careful search was carried out, and a systematic review produced which showed that driver education leads to early licensing. It found no evidence that driver education reduces road crash involvement, and it may lead to a modest but potentially important increase in the proportion of teenagers involved in traffic crashes (see <http://www.update-software.com/abstracts/ab003201.htm>).[9] In short, training drivers can increase the rate of road crashes, by encouraging young people to drive sooner than they would in the absence of such programmes.[10]

Carrying out a systematic review and having worthwhile findings are only half the battle. Getting them read and used is the other half. This is where press skills and contacts came in. In the face of other lobbies suggesting that education couldn't possibly do any harm, the researchers wrote to the Prime Minister, asking that the policy be stopped. They also wrote to the Chancellor, arguing that driver education is a waste of the scarce resources for road safety, to the Secretary of State for Education asking that the program be stopped, and to Her Majesty's Chief Inspector of Schools, asking that schools' participation in the Driving Standards Agency program be audited. Subsequently, Ian Roberts was able to raise concerns highlighted by the systematic review with the Parliamentary Under Secretary of State for the DETR with responsibility for road safety (see <http://www.cemcentre.org/eb2003>).

Despite all these efforts, it is unclear whether the review had any immediate impact: "We did get a lot of coverage but I think they went ahead with the policy despite the evidence." (Ian Roberts, pers. comm.)

(See Box 8.2 for the sequel . . .)

Roberts' view may be right. Change can be slow. For all sorts of reasons, decision makers may not want to take forward research messages, however well disseminated they may be. Box 8.2 gives one response to the review.

Box 8.2   Another view...

A senior user of systematic reviews in the USA cast doubt on the usefulness of the review described in Box 8.1, though he declared a competing interest: "As someone who used to supervise driver education programs for the state of Rhode Island... I would never think of canceling driver education requirements on the basis of a review such as [this]." He suggested some caution in expectations of the possible impact of systematic reviews of social policies. "While we need to be optimistic, we should not oversell the ability of systematic reviews... to shape (or in some people's views even determine) policy." (Dennis Cheek, pers. comm.)

He also advised: "[The review] is not capable of saying 'what should be done.' First, because all studies are by their very nature limited. For example, no studies followed the long-term effects (5–10 years out) of driver education on driver safety. A wide variety of contexts and driver education programs would have to be studied before a definitive conclusion could be reached. It is hard to imagine how to easily calculate how many are enough – it is not simply a matter of numbers within the studied populations but also rural, urban, suburban contexts; numbers of types of miles driven; the form of driver education and its content; the stringency of driver tests that are administered at the end of driver education programs (i.e., perhaps it is the fault of the particular type of driver screening test for licensure and not the education program per se or maybe it is the qualifications of the driver instructor that is critical) and many other issues. There may be issues besides safety that are affected (positively or negatively) by driver education programs, e.g., driver courtesy, better mileage per gallon/liter due to less of a tendency to press the gas pedal to the floor when accelerating, smoother traffic flows, general driver confidence in handling a vehicle."

"Second, if a single class of drivers has more accidents due to driver education you cannot generally, as a practical matter of public policy, deny driver education to that group of drivers. Third, even if you

(Continued)

Box 8.2 *(Cont'd)*

could, statistics are about populations and not individuals. There are some individuals within the class of 'suspect' drivers who in fact, could and would, benefit from driver education instruction. So you might also need to find out who, under what circumstances, would benefit at the level of the individual with some degree of confidence rather than just remaining at the population level."

Dr Cheek's caution serves as an important reminder of the part played by values in setting public policy.

Realistically, it will probably never be the case, even with the most straightforward intervention and the clearest evidence, that the government minister, the policy people, the practitioners and the users will say: "Hey, we'll have some of that, and we'll have it now." But systematic reviews provide a method that enables the steady accumulation of knowledge, and can increase the possibilities for that knowledge to be picked up and used. Timeliness is important, but even if the research evidence doesn't hit the mark the first time round, it is still there to be used in future. Good evidence has a long shelf-life.[11] Particularly for lobbying and special interest groups, stickability, and spotting opportunities where you can use a bit of evidence in your favor, can help bring about change.

The team at Research to Policy <http://www.researchtopolicy.ca> has taken a systematic approach to knowledge transfer, and maintain that this can be enhanced by answering five questions:

1. *What message do you want to transfer?* The message should be clear, compelling, and relate to a decision faced by decision-makers.
2. *To whom should the message be delivered?* The target audience should be specified and the message should be made specific to them and the context within which they work.
3. *By whom should the message be delivered?* The messenger should be credible, both to the target audience and to researchers.
4. *How should the message be delivered?* The mechanism used to transfer the message should be interactive where possible.
5. *With what effect?* Evaluation should be against explicit objectives that are appropriate to the target audience.

8.3   GETTING THE MESSAGE OUT AND GETTING IT USED

There is a clear need to get evidence into practice for the benefit of those who commission research, those who use services, and for the effective creation and running of services. There is little point in undertaking applied social research if the findings, once they have been critically appraised and synthesized, cannot be accessed by those whose lives they might affect. For research to be useful, it needs to be available for use. For that to happen, a prerequisite is that research findings are communicated effectively. But as the example above of teaching car drivers while they are young shows, this is only part of the story. The Research and Development (R&D) team of the UK childcare charity Barnardo's, investigated links between social care research and practice.[2] Their report lists some of the features of effective dissemination (Figure 8.1).

A different example of wide dissemination, but low take up, is given in Box 8.3, indicating the need for implementation as well as dissemination.

A more recent example from a systematic review of cot deaths shows that the data could have been used much earlier than they were, to support a change in the sleeping position of babies. When advice did change, following the UK's "back to sleep" campaign (started in 1991), which advised parents to place babies on their back or their side to sleep, there was a steep fall in deaths from SIDS (sudden infant death syndrome), although in the

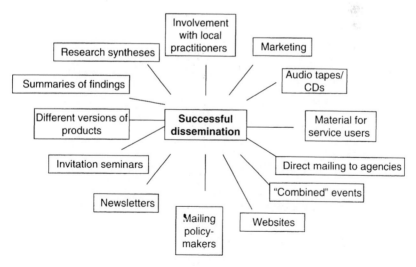

Figure 8.1   Effective dissemination: Who to involve, and how to do it
Source: Adapted from Barnardo's R&D (2000)[2]

Box 8.3   Dissemination is only half the battle

It is over a hundred and fifty years since Semmelweiss assembled research evidence to demonstrate the importance of a simple intervention, in this case handwashing, in preventing an important and unambiguous outcome – death.

It has been suggested that Semmelweiss was not a great publisher, nor was he a self-publicist. Reviewing a critical biography of Semmelweiss, Richard Horton, the editor of *The Lancet* writes: "For whatever reason, Semmelweiss was unable to match his discoveries with an appreciation of how best to persuade colleagues of their devastating responsibility for provoking an epidemic."[12]

It cannot be claimed today that Semmelweiss's findings are unknown. However, in July 2004, as the UK Health Protection Agency released figures on hospital infections, its chief executive, Dr Pat Troop announced: "Prevention of cross infection is of paramount importance, which will include good hand hygiene and healthcare professionals should ensure they always wash or decontaminate their hands thoroughly in-between treating patients." Which all goes to show that having the research knowledge is not enough, and even disseminating it does not mean that it is acted upon (<http://www.hpa.org.uk/hpa/news/articles/press_releases/2004/040714_mrsa.htm>).

UK, the death rate was already falling by then (Ruth Gilbert, pers. comm.). Campaigning and advocacy, as well as research, played a part in this decline.[13, 14, 15]

8.4   FEATURES OF EFFECTIVE DISSEMINATION

There have been a number of systematic reviews of the most effective approaches to dissemination and implementation in health care, including a report by Bero et al.[16] and the *Effective health care bulletin on getting evidence into practice* produced by the Centre for Reviews and Dissemination (CRD).[17] The CRD review suggests that in order for evidence to get into practice, there need to be routine mechanisms by which individual and organizational change can occur. Organizational, community and economic factors as well as individual behavior need to be considered when trying to influence practitioner behavior. A diagnostic analysis needs to precede any attempt to bring about change; multiple interventions are more likely to be effective than single interventions and successful strategies need to be adequately resourced by people with appropriate knowledge and skills. Any systematic approach to changing professional practice should include plans to monitor, evaluate, and reinforce any change.

The need for regular updating of reviews is demonstrated by a subsequent report on the effectiveness and efficiency of clinical guideline implementation strategies by Grimshaw et al.[18] Like Bero et al., the authors conclude that there is an imperfect evidence base to support decisions about which guideline dissemination and implementation strategies are likely to be efficient in different circumstances. In particular, they suggest that further research is needed to develop and validate a coherent theoretical framework to underpin professional and organizational change, and to estimate the efficiency of dissemination and implementation strategies in the presence of different barriers and effect modifiers. A small-scale survey on implementation with key informants highlighted a more practical issue. There tended to be no dedicated resources for dissemination and implementation strategies, so that within current resources, only the dissemination of educational materials and short educational meetings were considered feasible. In the light of this, it is fortunate that this review is rather more positive about the dissemination of educational materials to practitioners than was the earlier review, though they remain cautious, concluding that printed educational materials may lead to improvements in care. Key recommendations for policymakers include the need to decide which guidelines to prioritize on the basis of local needs; identification of the resources to support dissemination and implementation, consideration of the likely barriers and local circumstances, and the need to rigorously evaluate the effects of any interventions. Decision makers are urged to use their judgment on which interventions are likely to be effective in any given circumstances, but where possible, to include paper-based or computerized reminders, and to consider in some circumstances using a cheaper more feasible but less effective intervention (such as passive dissemination of guidelines), than a more expensive but potentially more effective intervention.

On the social care side, the Barnardo's report,[2] drawing in part on work in health care (including the Bero et al. review and the subsequent effectiveness bulletin), provided a summary of the factors that contribute to effective dissemination and implementation, much of which is consistent with the findings of Grimshaw et al.'s review. These are described in Figure 8.2, and

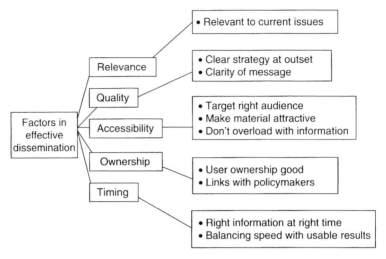

Figure 8.2   Linking research and practice
Source: Barnardo's R&D (2002)[2]

derive from a (traditional) literature review (see, for example, Crossland et al.; Everitt; Richardson et al.),[19, 20, 21] and from interviews with practitioners, policymakers, funders and researchers. Other work on effective dissemination in social care and other sectors[22, 23] comes to similar conclusions, with the latter making the important point that particular tensions are likely to arise from facilitating research informed practice and ensuring compliance with research findings. Subsequent studies have also emphasized the importance of identifying, and then addressing obstacles and barriers.

8.5   POINTERS TO THE EFFECTIVE DISSEMINATION OF SYSTEMATIC REVIEWS

Engage users early

Knowledge sharing is a two-way process, and if end-point users have been involved in setting the research questions, and have participated in advisory groups, some of the work of dissemination will already have been done and some of the potential problems of "Well it won't work round here because..." will have been ironed out at an early stage. As the enuresis example earlier in the book (chapter 2) demonstrates, in some cases users will have actually demanded the systematic review in the first place, and will be keen to use the findings.

Putting the "D" in "R&D"

Not every academic believes that it is within their remit to disseminate and implement. There is a strong argument that it is the business of universities and academic researchers to produce knowledge, not to meddle with the policy process; to inform policy rather than to support or undermine it. For the purposes of this book however, we are assuming that the reviewer, or whoever commissions your review, will want to see it used, and may want to play a part in that process.

In terms of products that work, there is a good deal to be learned from the organizations that make a major investment in R&D. The pharmaceutical companies for instance, do not send out their directors of research or their research technicians to "sell" their goods. It may well be that the knowledge sharing that should go alongside systematic reviewing needs its own dissemination and implementation structure.

In the UK, the Economic and Social Research Council (ESRC) has produced a guide for researchers wishing to disseminate their findings and a template to enable researchers to plan for this – see <http://www.esrc.ac.uk/commstoolkit/strategy/strategytemplate.doc>. The ESRC Communication Strategy offers their "top ten" tips for putting together a communication strategy (Box 8.4).

8.6 DISSEMINATING TO THE MEDIA

Journalist David Walker has interviewed a number of "Heroes of dissemination," and from these interviews identified lessons for researchers on using the media for dissemination, including the following:

- Researchers need to be aware of the different time scales and language codes with which media and research operate.
- In the pressured academic life, dissemination itself needs to be planned. It should be done consciously on a time budget, as a deliberate part of the research life.
- It is good for researchers to have a certain humility in their dealings with the media. They should not assume the possessor of academic knowledge necessarily knows more or better.

Box 8.4 ESRC's "Top ten" tips for putting together a communication strategy

1. Check external perceptions of your research among potential target audiences before you start.
2. Begin with a statement of your objectives in communicating the project, don't simply restate the objectives of the project itself.
3. Be clear on the principles underpinning your strategy. Some may be self-evident, like producing honest, succinct, credible, and cost-effective communications.
4. Develop some simple messages and model how these might work in different contexts – a press release, a report, a newspaper article, a website page.
5. Be clear about your target audiences and user groups and prioritize them according to importance and influence relative to your objectives.
6. Think about both the actual and preferred channels your target audiences might use and challenge yourself about whether you are planning to use the right ones for maximum impact.
7. Include a full list of all the relevant communication activities, developed into a working project plan with deadlines and responsibilities.
8. Keep it manageable and don't underestimate the time involved in communication.
9. Estimate the time and money involved.
10. Build in some simple evaluation measures at the start so that you'll know if and how you have succeeded in meeting your communication objectives.

(Adapted from the ESRC Communication Strategy Toolkit: <http://www. esrc.ac.uk/commstoolkit/strategy/topten.asp>)

- Doing dissemination is challenging and a source of intellectual stimulation, because simplifying an argument is a good test of its inner strength.
- Many social scientists would benefit from a reporter's training, from learning how to structure a "story."

- Talking to the public can provide unique feedback about the quality of research.
- The media agenda can change. Good intentions about dissemination do not matter if the media are indifferent to the subject matter.
- Communicating is a skilled business and it is worthwhile being trained.
- Dissemination requires faith – that there is an audience out there able to take part in debate (and who deserve the effort) and that society would be enriched by the sharing of social science results.
- To thine own self be true – when engaging with journalists and the media, stick to what you can say with confidence, and never say anything that would not pass muster with academic colleagues.

(Adapted from an ESRC publication, Heroes of Dissemination[24])

8.7 THE SPECIAL CASE OF SYSTEMATIC REVIEWS

Systematic reviews are distinctive, and as such, they have distinctive means through which they are disseminated, in addition to the means described above. There are, for example, journal guidelines relating to the publication of systematic reviews, which help to assure consistency of reporting. These are described in Appendix 2 (MOOSE guidelines) and Appendix 3 (the QUORUM guidelines).

Extensive advice on dissemination can also be found on the CRD website on the dissemination page <http://www.york.ac.uk/inst/crd/dissinfo1.htm> and in their handbook for systematic reviewers <http://www.york.ac.uk/inst/crd/report4.htm>.

Publishing or disseminating protocols

Publishing or otherwise disseminating protocols of reviews can contribute to the transparency of the review process. (An example is given in chapter 1, Box 1.7, which describes this process in relation to a systematic review of water fluoridation.) The Cochrane Collaboration includes a consumer group <http://www.cochrane.no/consumers/> and their "consumer panel" comments on:

- the language of the protocols and reviews;
- the rationale for the reviews;
- the interventions that should be included in the search and in future research;

- the outcomes that should be included in the search and in future research; and
- review topic priorities.

Sandy Oliver and Caroline Selai from the EPPI Centre at the University of London Institute of Education have produced a checklist for consumers (users/citizens/patients) to use when they are participating in this process: <http://www.cochrane.no/consumers/checklist%20for%20consumer%20 peer %20reviewers.pdf>.

The Campbell Collaboration similarly has goals of disseminating and promoting access to its reviews to meet the needs of policy and practice users worldwide, and includes a coordinating group focusing specifically on communication and dissemination issues <http://www.campbellcollaboration. org/Fracoorgroups.html>.

8.8 PRESENTATION AND TIMING

Certain steps can be taken to help get the review's message across to its intended audiences. For example:

- *Structure*: Consider producing both a longer version of the review, which is transparent and open to verification by others, and a shorter, more user-friendly version.
- *Identify key messages*: The *British Medical Journal* suggests that journal articles should include a brief description of "What do we already know?," and "What does this article add?" Answering these questions are key first steps to presenting key messages, and it is useful to keep them in mind when writing up a systematic review for publication, or for wider dissemination. It can sometimes be difficult to give a clear message on the basis of sound evidence. In this case, stand your ground. Do not be persuaded by stakeholders, journalists, or other interested parties to go beyond what the research tells you. (Look what happened in relation to Iraq's "weapons of mass destruction" (WMD).)
- *Identify recommendations for policy, practice and research*: For some researchers, moving from findings to recommendations is a step too far and goes beyond what they feel to be their legitimate remit. But for those working on systematic reviews with user groups who want to get findings into practice, turning findings into recommendations, and targeting the recommendations to specific groups is a logical step. This can involve, for example, targeting people with specific responsibilities,

such as commissioners of services, managers of services, and people who deliver services. Research funders are a key audience for systematic reviews, since reviews can help identify important gaps in knowledge.

- *Timing*: Timing is clearly important in the dissemination of reviews, as one respondent in the Barnardo's R&D work pointed out: "We did the review...at the time at which ministers were about to say something. Had they already said it, and the review results had come out, I doubt if they would have stood up and said, 'No, we've changed our minds.' And had we published two years ago, [the review] would...have been hidden in some publication database." (Systematic reviewer responding to Barnardo's R&D.)[2]

- *Prioritise the research messages*: We all have only so much time and energy. It is important to consider which messages have the strongest research evidence base: "You have to say, is this really important enough to...put the money in and...get people to change. If it isn't, then don't bother them, because people have got enough on their plates. And that's quite important in dissemination because you want to be able to say these are the key things and this is the expected benefit...Prioritising is important because the capacity for people to change what they're doing is very limited."[2]

- *Facts rarely speak for themselves*: Simply because something has been shown to work does not necessarily mean that it should be implemented. This step depends on factors including social values, priorities and resources.[25] All those involved in the production of systematic reviews can do is to ensure relevant people are aware of the findings and take them into account in decision making.

- *Consider carefully where to publish*: Journal publication in many cases, and particularly before online access, involves very small readerships, but those communities of "expert" readers are exceptionally well placed to criticize, peer review, and build on the work reported in your review. You may, however, wish to take into account the impact a journal has, and its accessibility. For academic reviewers in the UK and Australasia, exercises to assess academic production may well influence the choice of journal in which to publish. If you have worked from the start with potential users, their views will influence whether you produce your review in other formats (on the web, on tape, in large print, and so on). There are website guidelines for disability friendly formats. (See for example <http://www.ncddr.org/du/products/ufm/ufm.html>.)

- *Evaluate the impact of your review.* Does your review make a difference? Does anything change as a result? Does it change in the direction you might have anticipated, or are there any unexpected side effects? Long term tracking of a review's impacts can be difficult, particularly in the social policy world, where impacts may take a long time to appear and may be unexpected. (The driver education review referred to above was misdescribed by a participant at a UK conference as a review "showing that driving tests don't work," and thus held up as an example of the craziness of systematic reviews.)

Key learning points from this chapter

- Dissemination must be tied to implementation if findings are to be used.
- The "D" should be closely allied to the "R" in Research and Development. In other words, dissemination plans need to be made from an early stage, and built into, rather than bolted on to the review process.
- Users can be a powerful force for dissemination.
- Much of the literature implies a one-way process in dissemination; we need to know more about how researchers and others learn from frontline practitioners and users.

Finally:

- Think about dissemination from the start, not at the end of your work.
- Build in financial and time budgets for these activities.
- Get expert help from your university or organization's press officer and (if you are using your systematic review for advocacy), from user groups.
- As a researcher, you don't have to do it alone. Some aspects of dissemination and implementation are best carried forward by users or others.
- Remember the importance of timing, and accessibility to your target readerships.

REFERENCES

1. Blunkett, D. Influence or irrelevance: Can social science improve government?: Economic and Social Research Council, Swindon, online at: http://www.bera.ac.uk/ri/no71/ri71blunkett.html, 2000.
2. Barnardo's R&D. *What works? Making connections linking research and practice.* Barkingside, 2000.
3. Marteau, T., Sowden, A., and Armstrong, D. Implementing research findings into practice: Beyond the information deficit model. In A, Haines and A. Donald (eds.) *Getting research findings into practice.* London: BMJ Books, 2nd edn, 2002: 68–76.
4. Weiss, C. The interface between evaluation and public policy. *Evaluation: The International Journal of Theory, Research, and Practice* 1999, 5: 468–86.
5. Weiss, C. Research for policy's sake: The enlightenment function of social research. *Policy Analysis* 1977, 3: 531–47.
6. Lomas, J. Using linkage and exchange to move research into policy at a Canadian Foundation. *Health Affairs* 2000, 19: 236–40.
7. Lavis, J., Ross, S., McLeod, C., and Gildiner, A. Measuring the impact of health research. *Journal of Health Services & Research Policy* 2003, 8(3): 165–70.
8. Chapman, S. Advocacy for public health: A primer. *Journal of Epidemiology and Community Health* 2004, 58: 361–5.
9. Cochrane Injuries Group Driver Education Reviewers. Evidence based road safety: the Driving Standards Agency's schools programme. *Lancet* 2001, 358: 230–2.
10. Mohan, D. and Roberts, I. Global road safety and the contribution of big business: Road safety policies must be based on evidence. *British Medical Journal* 2001, 323: 648.
11. Whitehead, M., Petticrew, M., Graham, H., Macintyre, S., Bambra, C., and Egan, M. Evidence for public health policy: II: Assembling the evidence jigsaw. *Journal of Epidemiology & Community Health* 2004, 58: 817–21.
12. Horton, R. Review of *The Fool of Pest*, by Sherwin B Nuland. *The New York Review of Books* February 26 2004, 11(3): 10.
13. Dwyer, T. and Ponsonby, A. Sudden infant death syndrome: After the "back to sleep" campaign. *British Medical Journal* 1996, 313: 180–1.
14. Gilbert, R., Salanti, G., Harden, M., and See, S. Infant sleeping position and the sudden infant death syndrome: Systematic review of observational studies and historical review of recommendations from 1940 to 2002. *International Journal of Epidemiology* (in press).
15. Camps, F. and Carpenter, R. (eds.) *Sudden and unexpected deaths in infancy (Cot Deaths): Report of the proceedings of the Sir Samuel Bedson symposium, held at Addenbrooke's Hospital, Cambridge, on 17 and 18 April 1970:* J. Wright for the Foundation for the Study of Infant Deaths Ltd, 1972.
16. Bero, L., Grilli, R., Grimshaw, J., Harvey, E., Oxman, A., and Thomson, M. Getting research findings into practice: Closing the gap between research and

practice: An overview of systematic reviews of interventions to promote the implementation of research findings. *British Medical Journal* 1998, 465–9.

17. Centre for Reviews and Dissemination (CRD). *Effective Health Care Bulletin, Getting Evidence into Practice*, 5(1) February, online at: http://www.york.ac.uk/inst/crd/ehc51.pdf, 1999.

18. Grimshaw, J., Thomas, R., MacLennan, G., Fraser, C., Ramsay, C., Vale, L., et al. Effectiveness and efficiency of guideline dissemination and implementation strategies. *Health Technology Assessment* 2004, 8: 1–72.

19. Crossland, P., Deakin, S., Gelsthorpe, L., Jones, G., Quince, T., and Sutherland, H. Using social science: A pilot of non-academic exploitation of social science research in The University of Cambridge. Cambridge: University of Cambridge, 1998.

20. Everitt, A. *Applied research for better practice*. Basingstoke: Macmillan, 1992.

21. Richardson, A., Jackson, C., and Sykes, W. *Taking research seriously: Means of improving and assessing the use and dissemination of research*. London: HMSO, 1990.

22. Walter, I., Nutley, I., Percy-Smith, J., McNeish, D., and Frost, S.. Research Utilisation and the Social Care Workforce: A review commissioned by the Social Care Institute for Excellence (SCIE): Research Unit for Research Utilisation and Barnardo's Research and Development Team, 2004.

23. Walter, I., Nutley, S., and Davies, H. Research impact: A cross-sector review: Research Unit for Research Utilisation, University of St. Andrew's, Scotland, 2003, online at: http://www.st-andrews.ac.uk/~ruru/

24. Walker, D. *Heroes of dissemination*. Swindon: ESRC, 2001, online at: http://www.esrc.ac.uk/esrccontent/PublicationsList/4books/heroframeset.html

25. Rawlins, M. and Culyer, A. National Institute for Clinical Excellence and its value judgments. *British Medical Journal* 2004, 329: 224–7.

Chapter 9

Systematic reviews: Urban myths and fairy tales

Some non-scientists, and perhaps scientists, look with alarm at the progress of science, at the enormous accumulation of facts. They fear that we shall all be overwhelmed by the sheer size of the store of information. On the contrary, the ballast of factual information, so far from being just about to sink us, is growing daily less . . . In all sciences we are being progressively relieved of the burden of singular instances, the tyranny of the particular. We need no longer record the fall of every apple. (Pyke, 1996)[1]

This final part of the book challenges some common myths about what reviews can and cannot do . . . and ends with a fairy tale.

9.1   SYSTEMATIC REVIEWS AND URBAN MYTHS

The idea of a systematic review is a nonsense and the sooner those advocates of it are tried at the International Court of Human Rights in the Hague (or worse still sent for counselling) the better. (Rees, 2002)[2]

There are many misperceptions about what systematic reviews can and cannot do, and systematic reviews have had a bad press among some social scientists. These criticisms are often based on major misconceptions about the history, purpose, methods, and uses of systematic reviews. This section recaps some of the more common myths.

Systematic reviews are the same as ordinary reviews, only bigger

There is a common but erroneous belief that systematic reviews are just the same as traditional reviews, only bigger; in other words, they just involve searching more databases. Systematic reviews are not just big literature reviews. Their main aim is not simply to be "comprehensive" (many biased reviews are "comprehensive") but to answer a specific question, to reduce bias in the selection and inclusion of studies, to appraise the quality of the included studies, and to summarize them objectively, with transparency in the methods employed. As a result, they may actually be smaller, not bigger, partly because they apply more stringent inclusion criteria to the studies they review. They also differ in the measures they typically take to reduce bias, such as using several reviewers working independently to screen papers for inclusion and assess their quality. Even "small" systematic reviews are likely to involve several reviewers screening thousands of abstracts. As a result of these measures, systematic reviews commonly require more time, staff, and money than traditional reviews. Systematic reviews are not simply "bigger," they are qualitatively different.

Systematic reviews include only randomized controlled trials

There is a widespread belief that systematic reviews are only capable of summarizing the results of randomized controlled trials, and that they cannot be used to synthesize studies of other designs. Earlier chapters of the book have tried to lay this myth to rest. There is no logical reason why systematic reviews of study designs other than randomized controlled trials cannot be carried out. Systematic reviews of non-randomized studies are common and it is increasingly common to see qualitative studies included in systematic reviews. The choice of which study designs to include is a choice that is made by the reviewers, and will depend on the review question. It is not a restriction of the methodology.

Systematic reviews require the adoption of a biomedical model of health

This common myth holds that systematic reviews intrinsically adopt a biomedical model that is of relevance only to medicine and that should not be applied to other domains. Systematic reviews do not, however, have any preferred "biomedical model," which is why there are systematic reviews in such diverse topics as advertising, agriculture, archaeology, astronomy, biology, chemistry, criminology, ecology, education, entomology, law, manufacturing, parapsychology, psychology, public policy, and zoology.[3] In short, the systematic review is an efficient technique for hypothesis testing, for summarizing the results of existing studies, and for assessing consistency among previous studies. These tasks are not unique to medicine.

One key difference, however, between biomedically oriented systematic reviews and social science reviews lies in the importance of theory. Healthcare systematic reviews, for example, are often quite atheoretical. By comparison social science reviews will often require a sound understanding of the theories underpinning the studies being reviewed. In the case of a systematic review examining the effectiveness of an intervention, a knowledge of the underlying theory of change will help with refining the review question, and defining the inclusion and exclusion criteria. Decisions about subgroup analyses and explorations of heterogeneity and moderator effects will also be strongly influenced by theoretical considerations, as will the reviewer's interpretation of the review's findings. Theory is an important practical tool for systematic reviewers.

Systematic reviews necessarily involve statistical synthesis

This myth derives from a misunderstanding about the different methods used by systematic reviewers. Some reviews summarize the primary studies by narratively describing their methods and results. Other reviews take a statistical approach (meta-analysis) Many systematic reviews, however, do not use meta-analytic methods. Some of those that do, probably shouldn't; for example, it is common practice to pool studies without taking into account variations in study quality, which can bias the review's conclusions. It has been pointed out that one of the allures of meta-analysis is that it gives an answer, no matter whether studies are being combined meaningfully or not.[4]

Systematic reviews can be done without experienced information/library support

As should be clear from earlier chapters, a good systematic review requires skill in the design of search strategies, and benefits from professional advice. Systematic reviews can indeed be carried out without proper information or library support, but researchers are not typically experienced in information retrieval and their searches are likely to be less sensitive, less specific, and slower than those done by information professionals.[5, 6]

Systematic reviews can be done only by methodological experts or practitioners

Potential users of systematic reviews, such as consumers and policymakers, can be – and are – involved in the process. This can help to ensure that reviews are well-focused, ask relevant questions, and are disseminated effectively to appropriate audiences.[7] Users can influence the types of reviews that are carried out, and the questions that are answered; in this context Harden and Oliver refer to "systematically reviewing for ethics and empowerment" and this is certainly an important role for reviews.[8]

Systematic reviews are of no relevance to the real world

This book has presented systematic reviews that have been used to examine an array of contemporary and often contentious "real world" issues, from reviews of the effectiveness of policy and other interventions to systematic reviews of observational studies of social issues. Social researchers have been carrying out systematic reviews of policy and other social interventions since the early 1970s, if not before.[9]

Systematic reviews are a substitute for doing good quality individual studies

It would be comforting to think that systematic reviews were a sort of panacea, producing final definitive answers and precluding the need for further primary studies. Yet they do not always provide definitive answers and are not intended to be a substitute for primary research. Rather, they often identify the need for *additional* research as they are an efficient method of identifying where research is currently lacking.

As well as being the subject of myths, systematic reviews can also be helpful in dispelling them (see Box 9.1).

Box 9.1 Water, water everywhere (but do we really need to drink 8 glasses a day?)[22]

Sales of "lifestyle" bottled water are huge in many countries, bolstered by advertising and statements on bottle labels, on numerous websites, by alternative therapists and in the lay press that we need to drink at least eight glasses a day. But is this really true? Don't we get enough fluid from food, and other drinks?

Heinz Valtin, curious about such heath messages, wanted to find out. With the assistance of librarian Sheila A. Gorman he conducted extensive searches of electronic databases, websites, and used personal contacts, contacts with nutritionists specializing in fluid intake, and with authors of lay articles, to try to identify the scientific basis for this statement. The recommendation to drink 8×8 oz glasses a day (approximately 1.9 liters) appeared to be an offhand comment, un-supported by any scientific study, in a book co-written by renowned nutritionist Fredrick Stare in 1974: "For the average adult, some-where around 6 to 8 glasses per 24 hours, and this can be in the form of coffee, tea, milk, soft drinks, beer, etc. Fruits and vegetables are also good sources of water."[23]

However, according to Valtin, another possibility is that the rec-ommendation comes from a misreading of advice from the Food and Nutrition Board of the National Research Council who wrote in a 1945 report: "A suitable allowance of water for adults is 2.5 liters daily in most instances. An ordinary standard for diverse persons is 1 milliliter for each calorie of food. Most of this quantity is contained in prepared foods."[24]

Valtin felt that this last sentence may have been unheeded, or misinterpreted as a recommendation to *drink* 8 glasses a day. He conducted a search of the literature to identify any scientific studies that showed that we all need to drink eight 8 oz glasses of water a day, and found none. On the contrary, surveys of food and fluid intake on thousands of adults of both genders strongly suggested that such large amounts are not needed in healthy people.

He also found reports suggesting that the recommendation could be harmful " ... both in precipitating potentially dangerous hypona-tremia and exposure to pollutants, and also in making many people

(Continued)

> **Box 9.1** *(Cont'd)*
>
> feel guilty for not drinking enough. The [figure] does not include the water we derive from solid foods and metabolism."
>
> Many other urban myths and examples of quack science go un-challenged, but are suitable topics for a systematic review. Some of these are no more than "factoids" – assumptions or speculations repeated till they seem true.[25]

9.2 OPPORTUNITIES LOST (AND RE-GAINED)

In a little book I once wrote I said that a good thesis is like a pig. You don't throw anything away, and even after decades you can still re-use it. (Umberto Eco, 2004)[10]

Reflecting on the quotation that opened this chapter: there are clearly opportunities to relieve people of the necessity to record the fall of every apple, unless, of course, that is their choice. Many opportunities to carry out such reviews are however lost. Many Masters' and PhD dissertations are currently general, non-systematic trawls through a selection of the literature, and thereafter remain little read. (The typical PhD literature review has been referred to as "the shifting of bones from one graveyard to another."[11]) Many such theses could usefully incorporate a systematic review, thereby teaching the researcher an additional important scientific skill while making a useful scientific contribution. As well as showing where current research stands in relation to past work, the process of identifying and appraising previous studies also allows an insight into the major methodological and other shortcomings to be avoided; this is an invaluable training opportunity, as in science (as in so many other things), those who do not learn from the past are condemned to repeat it.

9.3 VARIATIONS IN THE QUALITY OF SYSTEMATIC REVIEWS

To end with a note of caution: the possibility that "traditional" literature reviews may be seriously biased is widely acknowledged. It must also be acknowledged that similar biases can apply to systematic reviews, and these have been extensively documented by systematic reviewers and meta-analysts themselves. The most common and probably the most serious flaw is the lack of any systematic critical appraisal of the included studies, but other flaws are common, including a restricted search for relevant studies, a lack of exploration of heterogeneity among the studies, lack of information on the inclusion and exclusion criteria, and inappropriate statistical combination of studies (Egger and Davey Smith remark that: "It is our impression that reviewers often find it hard to resist the temptation of combining studies when such meta-analysis is questionable or clearly inappropriate."[12]) A 1999 review of 480 healthcare systematic reviews (other than those in the Cochrane Library) found that only about a half of the reviews had carried out a detailed critical appraisal of the studies, yet this is a basic prerequisite for a robust systematic review. Many other studies have shown similar findings, and more importantly, have shown that the quality of systematic reviews is associated with their conclusions. For example, it has been shown that the lower the quality of a meta-analysis, the more likely it is that it will produce a statistically positive result.[13] (See Appendix 5 for a brief guide to appraising the quality of systematic reviews.)

9.4 FURTHER READING

There are now numerous guides to healthcare systematic reviews on the Web and elsewhere. Among the most useful and accessible are CRD's Report 4 <http://www.york.ac.uk/inst/crd/report4.htm>, which is a freely downloadable detailed guide to the stages in preparing and disseminating a systematic review. The Cochrane Handbook <http://www.cochrane.org/resources/handbook/index.htm> is another excellent and comprehensive guide to all stages and includes detailed description of all technical aspects of reviewing. This is not of value just to those carrying out reviews of healthcare interventions.[14]

Cooper and Hedges' authoritative handbook is another essential standby,[15] along with Lipsey and Wilson's practical guide to meta-analysis.[16] Egger et al.'s *Systematic reviews* is written primarily for a healthcare audience, but is of much wider relevance, and covers in more detail many of the methodological issues discussed in this book.[17] Morton Hunt's *How science takes stock* is a readable general overview of the development of systematic reviews and meta-analyses, and provides many illustrations of how they have been used to influence policy.[9] For a much shorter read, Reeves et al.'s paper "Twelve tips for undertaking a systematic review," referred to in chapter 2, gives some very sensible and practical advice to novice reviewers.[18]

9.5 CONCLUSION

> There is a need for producers of systematic reviews to better understand the
> evidence needs of policy customers and to produce reviews and other types of
> evidence that meet these needs. . . . This might be referred to as the "intel-
> ligent provider" role. (Davies, 2004)[19]

There are still many methodological challenges to be faced in the application of systematic reviews in the wider social world. There are difficulties
in locating and synthesizing appropriate contextual information and in
incorporating the results of qualitative research. There are ongoing challenges around implementation and dissemination. The results of reviews are
often provisional (and may be overturned by a single large, robust study) and
indicative, rather than definitive. They require regular updating to retain
their currency. All these challenges are being addressed, and the methods are
continually being adapted and revised by review groups around the world.
Systematic reviews, as has been emphasized throughout this book, are a
flexible tool. However in the drive to develop and extend the methodology
the needs of users should continue to be borne in mind.

Warren Walker, Senior Policy Analyst at RAND Europe (citing Schön)
outlines the problem this way: "In the varied topography of professional
practice there is a hard, high ground where theory, policy, and practice can be
based on research, and there is a swampy lowland where confusing messes,
often intractable to technical solutions, predominate."[20, 21] In reality, the

---

**Box 9.2   Rumpelstiltskin and the
systematic reviewer**

By Jacob and Wilhelm Grimm (mostly)

Once upon a time there was a poor miller. Well, not
exactly poor, maybe from Social Class III–M, so we're
talking skilled manual worker here. But anyway, like
all fairy tale manual workers, he had a beautiful
daughter. Now, it so happened that the miller got
into a conversation with the Chief Government
Policymaker, and seeking to make an impression, he
blurted out "I have a daughter who can spin straw
into gold." "Ah!" said the Chief Policymaker, "*This*
I gotta see. Bring her here."

"Well …" said the miller worriedly, backtracking quickly, "when I say she can spin straw into gold, I don't mean literally – it's a sort of metaphor. She is actually a systematic reviewer."

At this, the Chief Policymaker said to the miller, "Same thing, mate. I'm a big fan of systematic reviewing, and if your daughter is as skilful as you say, then bring her to my castle tomorrow. I will put her to the test."

The next day the girl was brought to the castle and taken into a room that was entirely filled to the ceiling with journal articles, of all things! It was that sort of castle. (More of a library, really.) Anyway, giving her a spinning wheel, the Chief Policymaker said with a dramatic gesture: "Get to work. Take this spinning wheel and spin all night, and if by morning you have not spun this straw into gold, then you will have to die."

With that, he locked her into the room, and she was there all alone. A few seconds later, he unlocked the door again, saying "Sorry, Spinning Wheel? Spinning Wheel? What was I thinking of? I mean 'laptop' of course. I'm getting too old for this fairy tale business …" Muttering to himself, he dragged the spinning wheel out of the room and thrust into her shaking hands a gleaming laptop. "Now get on with it. And I know I said 'spin all night,' but don't take that 'spinning' business too literally … or the 'dying' bit."

The poor miller's daughter sat there, but did not know what to do, because she had no idea how to spin straw into gold. She became more and more afraid, and finally began to cry. Then suddenly the door opened. A little man dressed all in green stepped inside, and said: "Good evening, Mistress Miller, why are you crying so?"

"Oh," answered the girl, "I am supposed to spin straw into gold, and I do not know how to do it."

The little man looked around, wrinkling his nose in distaste at the moldering heaps of articles from long-forgotten social policy journals, and finally said, "What will you give me if I spin it for you?"

"My necklace," said the girl. The little man took the necklace, sat down before the laptop, and his gnarled hands were a blur as he sorted the papers into piles: then, snapping them up quickly one by one, he extracted and entered the data, and within seconds, a shiny CD was filled with the first completed systematic review. Then he reached for another pile, and "whirr, whirr, whirr," a second shiny CD was filled too. So it went until morning, and then all the journal articles were dealt with, and all the CDs were filled with gold (metaphorically speaking, of course).

(Continued)

Box 9.2   *(Cont'd)*

At sunrise the Chief Policymaker came back, and when he saw the gold he was surprised and happy – but like all policymakers, his black heart was greedy for even more information. He took the miller's daughter to another room filled with journal articles. This room was even larger, and he ordered her to spin it all in one night, if she valued her life.

The girl did, of course, value her life (though in truth, like most people, she knew nothing of health economics) but still she did not know what to do, and so she simply sat and cried. Once again the door opened, and the little man appeared, saying, "What will you give me if I spin the straw into gold for you?" "The ring from my finger," answered the girl. "No way!" said the little man, "I think you'll find that the going rate for systematic reviews is about £80,000, but it depends on the size of the review. But stand back and give me some room, and I'll see what I can do."

The little man began once again to "whirr, whirr, whirr" with the spinning wheel – sorry "click, click, click" with the mouse. In the morning the Chief Policymaker arrived, and was happy beyond measure, but when he looked closer he saw that in fact the girl had not produced gold at all. Instead, it was still just straw, but piled differently.

"Dammit, girl!" he shouted. "I thought you said you'd turn the straw into gold? Not just sort it into neat piles!"

"Well", she said, slightly haughtily, "The process of systematic reviewing is not some sort of *alchemy*, you know. You can't *actually* turn straw into gold – particularly if you don't have much straw to start with. Your problem," she concluded, pointing rather rudely at the Chief Policymaker, "is that you really need more good quality straw."

"But there's loads of straw here! Roomfuls of the stuff!" cried the Chief Policymaker in exasperation. "I've been paying for the stuff for years! Now look: we have high hopes of systematic reviews. We need them to come up with quick, easy answers. Not thinly disguised recommendations that we collect 'more evidence.' Now get out, and take your short chum Rumpelstiltskin with you."

The miller's daughter shook her head.

"Listen, you've got the wrong sort of straw. You've got too much of the long, thin, gold-colored, pretty stuff, when what you really need is the short, thick, useful stuff. But at least you know that now. Systematic reviews might well be flavor of the month in your department, but really, there is no fairy tale ending. But …" and here she paused – "If you want to give Rumpelstiltskin and me some money, we'll do the primary research for you. After all, having done the systematic review, we now know exactly what sort of new studies are needed."
But the Chief Policymaker was not convinced. "Listen, pal," he snarled, pushing his face close to hers, "You systematic reviewers can't pull the wool over *my* eyes. Now, get out – I've got a meeting in 15 minutes with a sharp young guy from the Treasury called Jack. He's got a great new research proposal to evaluate the outcomes of swapping 5 beans for a cow. It can't fail."

preoccupations of the high ground are often less important to society, while the problems down in the swampy lowlands are those of greatest human concern. Systematic reviews, used thoughtfully, can succeed at both levels.

As promised we end with a fairy tale (see Box 9.2).

REFERENCES

1. Pyke, D. Foreword, in *The strange case of the spotted mice and other essays on science.* Oxford: Oxford Paperbacks, 1996.
2. Rees, J. Two cultures? *Journal of the American Academy of Dermatology* 2002 46: 313–16.
3. Petticrew, M. Systematic reviews from astronomy to zoology: Myths and misconceptions. *British Medical Journal* 2001, 322: 98–101.
4. Sutton, A., Abrams, K., Jones, K., Sheldon, T., and Song, F. Systematic reviews of trials and other studies. *Health Technology Assessment* 1998, 2, online at: http://www.hta.nhsweb.nhs.uk/ProjectData/3_publication_select.asp. Also available as: Sutton et al. *Methods for meta-analysis in medical research.* Chichester: Wiley & Sons, 2000.
5. Dickersin, K., Scherer, R., and Lefebvre, C. Identifying relevant studies for systematic reviews. *British Medical Journal* 1994, 309.

6. Glanville, J. Identification of research. In K. Khan, G. ter Riet, J. Glanville, A. Sowden, and J, Kleijnen (eds.) *Undertaking systematic reviews of research on effectiveness: CRD's guidance for carrying out or commissioning reviews.* CRD, University of York, online at: http://www.york.ac.uk/inst/crd/report4.htm, 2001.

7. Bero, L. and Jadad, A. How consumers and policymakers can use systematic reviews for decision making. *Annals of Internal Medicine* 1997, 127: 37–42.

8. Harden, A. and Oliver, S. Systematically reviewing for ethics and empowerment. In S. Oliver and G. Peersman (eds.) *Using research for effective health promotion.* Buckingham: Open University Press, 2001.

9. Hunt, M. *How science takes stock.* New York: Russell Sage Foundation, 1997.

10. Eco, U. It's not what you know... *The Guardian*, April 3, 2004.

11. Dobie, J. *A Texan in England.* Boston: Little, Brown, 1944.

12. Egger, M., Ebrahim, S., and Davey Smith, G. Where now for meta-analysis? *International Journal of Epidemiology* 2002, 31: 1–5.

13. Moher, D. and Olkin, I. Meta-analysis of randomized controlled trials. A concern for standards. *Journal of the American Medical Association* 1995, 24: 1962–4.

14. Alderson, P., Green, S., and Higgins, J. (eds.) Cochrane Reviewers' Handbook 4.2.2 [updated March 2004]. *The Cochrane Library*, Issue 1, 2004. Chichester, UK: John Wiley & Sons, Ltd.

15. Cooper, H. and L. Hedges (eds.) *The handbook of research synthesis.* New York: Russell Sage Foundation, 1994.

16. Lipsey, M. and Wilson, D. *Practical meta-analysis.* Thousand Oaks, CA: Sage, 2001.

17. Egger, M., Davey Smith, G. and Altman, D. *Systematic reviews in health care. Meta-analysis in context.* London: BMJ, 2001.

18. Reeves, R., Koppel, I., Barr, H., Freeth, D., and Hammick, M. Twelve tips for undertaking a systematic review. *Medical Teacher* 2002, 24: 358–63.

19. Davies, P. Is evidence-based government possible? Jerry Lee Lecture 2004, 4th Annual Campbell Colloquium, Washington DC.

20. Walker, W. Policy analysis: A systematic approach to supporting policymaking in the public sector. *Journal of Multi-Criteria Decision Analysis* 2000, 9: 11–27.

21. Schön, D. *The reflective practitioner: How professionals think in action.* New York: Basic Books, 1983.

22. Valtin, H. "Drink at least eight glasses of water a day." Really? Is there scientific evidence for "8 × 8"? *American Journal of Physiology. Regulatory, Integrative, and Comparative Physiology* 2002, 283: R993–R1004.

23. Stare, F. and McWilliams, M. *Nutrition for Good Health:* Fullerton, CA: Plycon, 1974.

24. Food and Nutrition Board, Recommended Dietary Allowances, revised 1945: Food and Nutrition Board, National Academy of Science. National Research Council, Reprint and Circular Series, No. 122, 1945 (Aug), 3–18.

25. Cummins, S. and Macintyre, S. "Food deserts": Evidence and assumption in health policy making. *British Medical Journal* 2002, 325: 436–8.

Glossary

(Entries appear in bold on their first use in the text.)

Allocation: Assignment of an individual to one or other arm of a study – for example, the intervention or control groups (arms) of a trial

ANCOVA: Analysis of covariance: Statistical method of assessing the effect of a variable on a dependent variable, while controlling for other variables (covariates)

ARIMA: Auto Regressive Integrative Moving Average (statistical method for analyzing time series data)

Attrition /attrition bias: Loss, or exclusion, of participants in a study. Those who are lost to follow-up are likely to differ systematically from those who are followed up until study completion – they may be more ill, for example. The bias this introduces in trials is referred to as attrition bias; it tends to result in over-estimates of the effectiveness of the intervention

Bayesian: Statistical approach to analysis of the effects of an intervention, based on Bayes' theorem, which takes into account prior beliefs about the distribution of likely effects (the "prior distribution"), and incorporates them with new data from the evaluation about the likely distribution of effect sizes ("the likelihood"), to form a new quantitative estimate ("the posterior distribution")[1]

Bayesian meta-analysis: Formal combination of qualitative information on prior beliefs with quantitative study data, using Bayesian methods[2]

Before and after study: Study in which data are collected before and after the implementation of an intervention of some sort (such as a project, or new service, or a policy). The comparison of these two sets of data may allow one to estimate the effects of the intervention – for example, a before and after study of the effects of television advertising on consumer behavior

Bias: Mis-estimation of an effect; bias may result in over-estimation or under-estimation

Blinding: "Blinding" occurs when participants in a trial do not know to which group (or which intervention) they have been allocated (single blinding). This reduces biases produced by placebo effects, or biases introduced by the researchers' or participants' expectancies about the effects of the intervention. The researcher may also be blinded (double blinding), along with those carrying out the statistical analysis of outcomes (triple blinding)

Campbell Collaboration: <http://www.campbellcollaboration.org/> International collaborative organization that produces syntheses of evidence in the fields of education, social welfare, crime and justice, and others. Named after eminent social scientist and methodologist, Donald T. Campbell

Case-control: Controlled, retrospective study design used to investigate risk factors, and sometimes to explore effects of interventions (particularly adverse effects). In a case-control study, people with some particular outcome or problem (for example, children with autism – *the cases*) are compared to those without (that is, otherwise healthy children – *the controls*)

Causality: The relationship between causes (such as interventions) and effects (outcomes)

CCT: Controlled clinical trial, which may or may not involve randomization

Cochrane Collaboration: <http://www.cochrane.org> International organization that carries out systematic reviews examining the effects of healthcare interventions. It also promotes the search for, and use of, evidence in the form of clinical trials and other studies of interventions. The Cochrane Collaboration was founded in 1993 and named for the British epidemiologist, Archie Cochrane

Community-level intervention: Intervention delivered to whole communities, as opposed to targeting specific individuals within that community

Complex intervention: Intervention comprising multiple component parts (or, one made up of multiple interventions delivered together)

Confidence interval (CI): A measure of uncertainty around an effect size or other parameter, wider confidence intervals indicating greater uncertainty. 95 percent CIs around an estimate are commonly calculated; this indicates the range within which the true effect is likely to lie (i.e., if we were to take repeated independent samples, and calculate the confidence intervals each time, they would contain the true estimate in 95 percent of cases)

Confounding/confounder: A situation in which an intervention effect is biased because of some difference between the comparison groups apart from the planned interventions, such as baseline characteristics, prognostic factors, or concomitant interventions. For a factor to be a confounder, it must differ between the comparison groups and predict the outcome of interest. (From the CONSORT statement, drawn up to improve the quality of reporting of RCTs: <http://www.consort-statement.org/>)

Controlled study: Usually refers to a study that employs a separate comparison group (usually one recruited at the same time as the intervention group)

Critical appraisal: Method of assessing the soundness and relevance of a research study

Data–dredging: Multiple statistical testing in the hope of finding (statistically) significant results

Decision analysis: Quantitative method of analyzing a decision that includes a range of heterogeneous information, for example information on an intervention's effectiveness, and the values of the stakeholders or users of the intervention. Used for comparing different options

Dose–response: Term used to refer to the relationship between the "amount" of some intervention that has been delivered (the "dose") and the outcome

Effect size: Statistical measure of the size of effect of an intervention, or of the relationship between two or more variables (a mean, or odds ratio, for example)

Effective(ness): The impact of an intervention in real life settings; assessing effectiveness implies considering both the positive *and* the negative effects

Efficacy: The impact of an intervention under ideal conditions (for example, in a hypothetical trial where everyone fully complies with the intervention)

Etiology: Study of the processes of development, or causation (for example the study of the causation of learning difficulties in children)

Exclusion criteria: Rules used (along with inclusion criteria) to determine which studies (for example, what study designs, and which interventions) should be excluded from a systematic review

Experiment(al): A scientific investigation carried out under carefully controlled circumstances, involving the deliberate manipulation of one or more independent variables while examining the effects on one or more dependent variables

External validity: The extent to which a study can be generalized to other populations, places, settings, and times[3]

Forest plot: Scatterplot of effect size estimates (with confidence intervals) from each study, ordered by country, year of publication, intervention, study design, or some other variable

Formative evaluation: Evaluation of the processes or components of an intervention while it is being developed, to help shape or change those components

Funnel plot: Scattergram of effect sizes against a measure of study precision (or study size)

Generalizability: See "External validity"

Gray literature: Information produced by government, academics, business, and industry in electronic and print formats that are not controlled by commercial publishing (see: <http://www.greynet.org/pages/1/>)

Hand searching: Process of reading though articles in key journals to determine if they are relevant for inclusion in a systematic review

Heterogeneity: Used to refer to differences between studies in a review, including differences between studies in terms of their outcomes and differences in populations, and study methods

Homogeneity: Similarity among study findings

Impact: Term sometimes used to refer to the effects of an intervention (e.g., "impacts," "impact assessment")

Inclusion criteria: Rules used to determine which studies (for example, what study designs, and which interventions) should be included in a systematic review

Intention to treat: An approach to the analysis of RCTs in which data on all those randomized are analyzed within the same arm of trial to which they were originally allocated

Intermediate outcome: An outcome of an intervention that is on the pathway to the intended, final outcome

Internal validity: The extent to which the design and conduct of a study eliminates the possibility of bias (from the CONSORT statement, as above)

Intervention: Term used to refer to an action intentionally undertaken to bring about some beneficial outcome – for example, a treatment, a program, or a policy

Kappa test: Statistical test for assessing degree of agreement between raters/judges – for example, agreement about the inclusion or exclusion of studies from a systematic review

Meta-analysis: Quantitative synthesis of study findings as a part of a systematic review

Meta-ethnography: An approach to evidence synthesis characterized by translation of the findings of one study into the context of another, by which means one can identify themes with the greatest explanatory power[4]

Meta-narrative mapping: New evidence synthesis technique involving the key conceptual, theoretical and other elements of a research paradigm, along with the development of the field, its main discoveries, along with identification and critical appraisal of the primary studies[5]

Moderator variable: Variable that affects the relationship between two other variables – for example by strengthening or weakening it (i.e., a moderator effect)

Non-experimental study: We use this term in the book to mean a study where no deliberate experimental manipulation has taken place – for example, where two interventions are compared, but there was no attempt by researchers to randomly allocate participants to one or other intervention

Observational study: There are multiple definitions, but this is often used to refer to a controlled or uncontrolled study of the effects of an intervention that did not involve randomization. This could include both prospective or retrospective studies. It is also used to refer to non-experimental studies of risk factors where no deliberate "intervention" has occurred

Odds ratio (OR): Measure of the association between two variables, often used to express the impact of an intervention; an odds ratio of significantly <1.0 indicates an effective intervention, compared to that which the control group received. If the OR is >1.0, then the control intervention may be more effective. An OR which is not significantly different from 1.0 signifies no effect

Outcome evaluation: A study which aims to assess the effects of an intervention; a randomized controlled trial is a form of outcome evaluation

Outcome(s): The effects of an intervention: for example, the outcomes of an educational intervention could include exam grades, and employability in later life

Population-level: Intervention delivered to a whole population (as opposed to specifically targeted individuals)

Post-hoc analysis: Statistical analysis conducted after the main study analyses have been completed, and which was not originally planned

Power: Likelihood that an analysis will be able to detect a statistically significant effect, if one really exists

Primary study: Term sometimes used to refer to the individual studies in a review (for example, before they are synthesized in a meta-analysis)

Process evaluation: An evaluation designed to investigate how an intervention and its components achieves its effects, and how it is implemented and received (as opposed to an analysis of its outcomes)

Prospective study: Study in which a group of individuals is assembled and their outcomes followed-up over time (an RCT is one example)

Protocol: A detailed plan of the procedures that a reviewer intends to adopt in order to identify, appraise, and synthesize the evidence, and disseminate the findings. Protocols may themselves be peer-reviewed (e.g., protocols prepared for Campbell and Cochrane systematic reviews)

Publication bias: Tendency for published and unpublished studies to differ systematically, such that the unpublished studies are more likely to report statistically non-significant findings

Quality: Term sometimes used to refer to the methodological soundness of a research study

RCT: Randomized controlled trial: experimental study in which participants are allocated randomly to receive an intervention of interest to the researcher, or to a comparison group (who may have received a different intervention, or none at all)

Realist synthesis: New methodology for systematic reviews, which has a strong focus on synthesizing evidence on theory and on the mechanisms by which interventions work, as opposed to solely synthesizing empirical evidence on outcomes[6]

Relative risk (Sometimes referred to as the Risk Ratio): Statistical measure of the influence an event has on some subsequent event – for example, the influence an intervention has on an outcome. (For a detailed explanation see: <http://www.cmaj.ca/cgi/content/full/171/4/353>)

Scoping review: A review sometimes carried out in advance of a full systematic review to scope the existing literature – that is to assess the types of studies carried out to date, and where they are located. This can help with refining the question for the full review, and with estimating the resources that will be needed

Search strategy: Procedure for identifying evidence for a systematic review. This includes specifying sources (such as databases), keywords, and search terms

Secular change/secular trend: Long-term change in an outcome (for example, the change in the average height of a human population over a period of decades)

Selection bias: Systematic error in creating intervention groups, such that they differ with respect to prognosis (from the CONSORT statement, as above)

Sensitivity analysis: Selective inclusion and exclusion of studies to explore their impact on the review's conclusions

Sensitivity (recall): In reviews, a measure of the ability of a search strategy to identify all relevant studies (see: <http://www.cebm.net/searching.asp>)

Standardized: When studies measure the same outcome in a variety of ways (for example using different measurement scales) they must be standardized to the same scale before they can be combined in a meta-analysis – for example by calculating the standardized mean difference for each study[7]

Stem-and-leaf diagram: Graph used to display the distribution of a set of data

Specificity (precision): The proportion of studies retrieved by a literature search that are relevant (see: <http://www.cebm.net/searching.asp>)

Systematic review: Overview of primary studies that use explicit and reproducible methods[8]

Triangulation: The employment of a variety of sources of data, and study methods and other information within a single study

Type I error: A false positive finding: Rejection of the null hypothesis (that is, that there is no statistically significant effect) when it is actually true (probability of Type I error $= \alpha$)

Type II error: A false negative finding: Accepting the null hypothesis when it is not true (probability of Type II error $= \beta$)

REFERENCES

1. Spiegelhalter, D., Myles, J., Jones, D., and Abrams, K. Methods in health services research: An introduction to Bayesian methods in health technology assessment. *British Medical Journal* 1999, 319: 508–12.
2. Roberts, K. A., Dixon-Woods, M., Fitzpatrick, R., Abrams, K. R., and Jones, D. R. Factors affecting uptake of childhood immunisation: A Bayesian synthesis of qualitative and quantitative evidence. *The Lancet* 2002, 360: 1596–9.
3. Cook, T. and Campbell, D. *Quasi-experimentation: Design and analysis issues for field settings.* Chicago: Rand McNally, 1979.
4. Dixon-Woods, M., Agarwal, S., Young, B., Jones, D., and Sutton, A. Integrative approaches to qualitative and quantitative evidence: Health Development Agency, London, online at: http://www.publichealth.nice.org.uk/page.aspx?o=508055, 2004.
5. Greenhalgh, T., Robert, G., Macfarlane, F., Bate, P., and Kyriakidou, O. Diffusion of innovations in service organizations: Systematic review and recommendations. *Milbank Quarterly* 2004, 82: 4, online at: http://www.milbank.org/quarterly/8204feat.html
6. Pawson, R. Evidence-based policy: The promise of "realist synthesis," *Evaluation* 2002, 8(3): 340–58.
7. Egger, M., Davey Smith, G., and Altman, D. *Systematic reviews in health care. Meta-analysis in context.* London: BMJ, 2001.
8. Greenhalgh, T. How to read a paper: Papers that summarise other papers (systematic reviews and meta-analyses). *British Medical Journal* 1997, 315: 672–5.

Appendix 1

The review process (and some questions to ask before starting a review)

Question 1. Is a systematic review actually needed?
What hypothesis are you testing? How do you know a review is needed? Are you sure there is not already a systematic review "out there?" Who will use the results of the review, and how?

↓

Question 2. Do you have the resources?
A systematic review can be costly in terms of time, money, and reviewer's energy. Do you have the resources? Do you know what it is likely to involve? Do you have the information support to help with the searching, and funds to cover obtaining copies of articles and books? Do you have another reviewer to help with screening and selecting the studies for review?

If the answer to the first two questions is "yes" then it is safe to proceed . . .

↓

Step 1. Define the question
Clearly specify the question that the review aims to answer. If it is a review of the effects of an intervention then specify the intervention, the population, the subpopulations, outcomes of interest, the time period within which you are interested, and the cultural or other context within which the intervention is delivered. Discuss the proposed review with stakeholders during this process.

↓

Step 2. Consider drawing together a steering or advisory group
It can be helpful to appoint a steering group, chosen to represent a range of interests; for example a review of a healthcare intervention may include a

practitioner who uses the intervention, a service manager who pays for it, a patient who has experience in its use, a researcher who has previously researched or perhaps evaluated the intervention, a statistician, an economist, and so on. They will also be able to advise on the review protocol.

↓

Step 3. Write a protocol and have it reviewed

It is essential to write a protocol stating the review question, the methods to be used, the study types and designs which the reviewer intends to locate, and by what means, and how these studies will be appraised and synthesized. It is good practice to have the protocol reviewed by people who are likely to know something about the topic area – for example, this could include topic experts as well as the intended users.

↓

Step 4. Carry out the literature search

Having decided the question, and discussed it with your advisory group, you will know what sort of studies you need to answer the review question. The next step is to find them, most probably searching electronic databases, bibliographies, book chapters and conference proceedings, and contacts with experts (including your advisory group).

↓

Step 5. Screen the references

The literature search retrieves hundreds, or thousands of references, often with abstracts. These need to be sifted to identify which ones are needed for further review.

↓

Step 6. Assess the remaining studies against the inclusion/exclusion criteria

After the clearly irrelevant studies are excluded (keeping a detailed note of the number of studies included and excluded at each stage) there are still likely to be many studies left – sometimes several hundred. Some can be confidently excluded after further examination of the abstract, but full copies of the rest of the papers may need to be obtained. These are examined to determine whether they meet the review's inclusion and exclusion criteria.

↓

Step 7. Data extraction

Systematic reviews adopt a formal, systematic approach to extracting relevant information from primary studies; this often involves developing a data extraction form, which the reviewer completes for every study in the review. This outlines the population, details of the intervention (if any), outcomes of interest, and relevant methodological and other information. This method is intended to ensure consistency and objectivity. Data extraction also involves drawing up a detailed table describing every study that is reviewed in detail (*not* every study that was located in the review – only those studies that meet all the inclusion criteria).

↓

Step 8. Critical appraisal

Every study in the review that meets the inclusion criteria needs to be assessed with respect to its methodological soundness. This process helps to identify any important biases. It also helps the reader interpret the data. The results of the critical appraisal are used when synthesizing the results of the primary studies.

↓

Step 9. Synthesis of the primary studies

The included studies need to be integrated, taking into account variations in population, intervention (if any), context and setting, study design, outcomes, and the degree to which they are affected by bias. This integration can be done statistically (meta-analysis), and/or narratively – by systematically describing, reporting, tabulating, and integrating the results of the studies. Graphical displays (such as Forest plots) of quantitative data are also helpful in achieving this synthesis.

↓

Step 10. Consider the effects of publication bias, and other internal and external biases

It is known that issues such as study size, study quality, source of funding, and publication bias can affect the results of primary studies. This can have a major impact on the conclusions of a systematic review of quantitative studies; at worst, a review may over-represent the true size of the effect in question. For quantitative studies, the effects of such a bias can be explored graphically (for example, using funnel plots) or narratively.

↓

Step 11. Writing up the report

For many reviews, the final output is a report or journal article. In some cases it first involves producing an electronic version of the review (for example, Campbell or Cochrane reviews are made available on the Web and/or on CD). The final version of the review needs to include details of the full search, and the "flow" of studies through the review process, including how many studies were excluded at each stage, and why. Providing this information (for example, in a flow chart) is a prerequisite for publication in some journals. Some health journals also require the authors to follow the *QUORUM* (*QU*ality *O*f *R*eporting *O*f *M*eta-analyses – see

Appendix 3) or MOOSE (see Appendix 2) guidelines for reporting systematic reviews.

↓

Step 12. Wider dissemination

At the start of the review, you will have defined clearly who you expect the audience for the review to be, and perhaps will have developed a plan in advance for disseminating your review's findings to them, and helping them to interpret and use them. Now you have to implement that plan. This may involve producing summaries or other versions of the review for decision-makers and non-research audiences, but may also involve working with users to implement the results, and helping potential users to understand the implications of the review's findings for policy, practice, and future research, where appropriate. Conferences, briefings of groups and individuals, seminars, public meetings, public inquiries, the media, the Web, and many other outlets may play a role. You should also consider assessing the impact your review has on relevant outcomes. This may involve measuring either social or health outcomes, or process outcomes (such as how the review was perceived, and used, and whether it in fact made any contribution to decision-making). The ability of a reviewer to do any of these wider dissemination tasks is, of course, highly dependent on time, resources, and the length of their research contract.

Appendix 2

MOOSE Guidelines

MOOSE: (Meta-analysis of observational studies in epidemiology): A checklist for authors, editors, and reviewers of meta-analyses of observational studies.[1]
(See chapter 2)

Reporting of the background should include:

- problem definition;
- hypothesis statement;
- description of study outcome(s);
- type of exposure or intervention used;
- type of study designs used; and
- study population.

Reporting of the search strategy should include:

- qualifications of searchers (e.g., librarians and investigators);
- search strategy, including time period included in the synthesis and keywords;
- effort to include all available studies, including contact with authors;
- databases and registries searched;
- search software used, name and version, including special features used (e.g., explosion);
- use of hand searching (e.g., reference lists of obtained articles);
- list of citations located and those excluded, including justification;
- method of addressing articles published in languages other than English;
- method of handling abstracts and unpublished studies; and
- description of any contact with authors.

Reporting of methods should include:

- description of relevance or appropriateness of studies assembled for assessing the hypothesis to be tested;
- rationale for the selection and coding of data (e.g., sound clinical principles or convenience);
- documentation of how data were classified and coded (e.g., multiple raters, blinding, and inter-rater reliability);
- assessment of confounding (e.g., comparability of cases and controls in studies where appropriate);
- assessment of study quality, including blinding of quality assessors; stratification or regression on possible predictors of study results;
- assessment of heterogeneity;
- description of statistical methods (e.g., complete description of fixed or random effects models, justification of whether the chosen models account for predictors of study results, dose-response models, or cumulative meta-analysis) in sufficient detail to be replicated; and
- provision of appropriate tables and graphics.

Reporting of results should include:

- graphical summary of individual study estimates and the overall estimate of effect;
- a table giving descriptive information for each study included;
- results of sensitivity testing (e.g., subgroup analysis); and
- indication of statistical uncertainty of findings.

Reporting of discussion should include:

- quantitative assessment of bias (e.g., publication bias);
- justification for exclusion (e.g., exclusion of non-English-language citations);
- assessment of quality of included studies; and
- the discussion should also include discussion of issues related to bias, including publication bias, confounding, and quality.

Reporting of conclusions should include:

- consideration of alternative explanations for observed results;
- generalizability of the conclusions (i.e., appropriate to the data presented);

- guidelines for future research; and
- disclosure of funding source.

REFERENCE

1. Stroup, D. F., Berlin, J. A., Morton, S. C., Olkin, I., Williamson, G. D., Rennie, D., et al. Meta-analysis of observational studies in epidemiology: A proposal for reporting. Meta-analysis of Observational Studies in Epidemiology (MOOSE) group. *Journal of the American Medical Association* 2000, 283: 2008–12.

Appendix 3

Example of a flow diagram from a systematic review

Many health-related journals have adopted the QUORUM guidelines, which cover the reporting and presentation of systematic reviews and meta-analysis, and among other things require that a detailed flowchart is produced which illustrates the inclusion and exclusion of studies from the review (example given below). In practice this means that if you submit your review to one of these journals you must follow these guidelines, which can be consulted at: <http://www.consort-statement.org/QUOROM.pdf>.[1]

EXAMPLE OF A QUORUM FLOWCHART[2]

Numbers in brackets in the flow chart refer to citations identified by electronic database searching + citations identified by other searches.

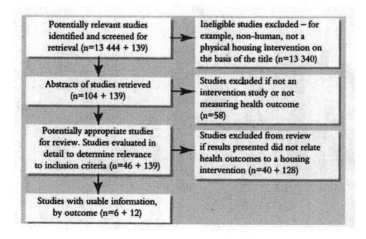

REFERENCES

1. Moher, D., Cook, D. J., Eastwood, S., Olkin, I., Rennie, D., and Stroup, D. F. Improving the quality of reports of meta-analyses of randomised controlled trials: The QUORUM statement. *Lancet* 1999, 354: 1896–900.
2. Thomson, H., Petticrew, M., and Morrison, D. Housing interventions and health – a systematic review. *British Medical Journal* 2001, 323: 187–90.

Appendix 4

Example data
extraction form

Example data extraction/critical appraisal form, used in this case to guide
data extraction of studies in a systematic review of the health and social
impacts of new road building.[1]

Data to be extracted	Notes to reviewer
Title of study	
Author	
Year of publication	
Study of new road?	If "no" – exclude.
Setting	Town/region and country of intervention
Time	Time when study took place (rather than date of publication)
Study objective clearly stated?	
Study objective as stated by authors	
Study methodology (or methodologies) used	
Inclusion of sufficient data to assess validity of conclusions?	Including statistical tables; in the case of qualitative studies, it can mean including direct quotes from respondents, rather than relying only on reported speech and interpretations.
Data source	(e.g. police accident statistics, survey of residents, etc.)
Size of achieved sample	Also include size of total population if stated

(Continued)

Data to be extracted (Cont'd)

Response rate	If not stated, calculate it if possible
Length of follow up	Specify number of years before and after the intervention
Type of road	(bypass/arterial/motorway, etc.)
Urban or rural location?	
Other relevant details of road (e.g. at grade/elevated? intersections?)	Only include details if they are shown to have some bearing on the results of the study.

Road accidents	
Reported effect on accident rate	Include details of significance testing, if reported
Effect on accident injury rate	
Effect on serious injury/fatality rate	
Specific information re injuries	Include other useful information given such as percentage of accidents involving pedestrians, or severity of injuries
Control for regression to mean?	
Control for general trends?	General trends are often assessed by looking at statistics for the entire region in which the new road is built
Use of control area or population?	Was an area similar to the intervention area (but with no new road) used as control/comparison?
List any confounders controlled for in the analysis statistically or by matching	

Pollution	
Health impact being measured	e.g., annoyance, asthma, stress, etc.
Type of pollution	e.g., noise, dirt, carbon monoxide, etc.
Method of measurement	e.g., self-reported questionnaire, interview, hospital records, etc.
Separate control group?	
Confounders controlled for	Confounders tend to fall into two groups – physical environment (e.g., other sources of pollution such as factories or household) and

	population characteristics (age, sex, class, occupation, smoking).
Health impact of pollutant	Include details of significance testing if any

Severance	
Method of measurement	e.g., questionnaires about social contacts, counts of road-crossing, etc.
Separate control group?	
Confounders controlled for	e.g., aspects of physical environment (e.g., proximity to crossing places, distance of residence from road, position of amenities), population characteristics (age and social class)
Effect on community severance	Severance studies tend to distinguish between perceptions and behavior in that people may perceive that a new road has increased or decreased severance, but this does not necessarily affect their behavior.
Effect on behavior	

Validity	
Overall impression of internal validity (low, medium, high)	Assessment based on the quality of the sampling and response and the treatment of confounding factors.
External validity	In some circumstances, the results of a study may be so dependent on the local context that it must be considered to have low external validity regardless of the quality of the study.
Conditions affecting external validity	e.g., urban/rural area, old population, etc.

Also see <http://www.epoc.uottawa.ca/checklist2002.doc> and CRD Report 4 <http://www.york.ac.uk/inst/crd/crdrep.htm>for other examples of data extraction forms.

REFERENCE

1. Egan, M., Petticrew, M., Hamilton, V., and Ogilvie, D. Health impacts of new roads: A systematic review. *American Journal of Public Health* 2003, 93(9): 1463–71

Appendix 5

Variations in the quality of systematic reviews

The words "systematic review" in the title of a journal article are no stamp of quality, and offer no firm guarantee that the review will be robust, or meaningful. Guidelines for reviewers should help improve review quality (such as the QUORUM guidelines, and the guidelines to which Campbell and Cochrane reviewers adhere). But this still leaves the rest of the iceberg, and it is important for readers and users to be aware that systematic reviews, like all research (and everything else) vary in reliability. Oxman and Guyatt have provided a validated checklist for assessing review quality.[1,2] As a short

---

Box A5.1 Some pointers to help assess the quality of a systematic review

1. Are the review's inclusion and exclusion criteria described *and* appropriate?
2. Is the literature search likely to have uncovered all relevant studies?
3. Did the reviewers assess the quality of the included studies?
4. Did the reviewers take study quality into account in summarizing their results?
5. If there was a statistical summary (meta-analysis), was it appropriate (that is were the studies similar enough to be statistically synthesized? (See Box 6.13.)
6. Was study heterogeneity assessed?
7. Were the reviewers' conclusions supported by the results of the studies reviewed?

guide, the seven points in Box A5.1 should be borne in mind when reading any systematic review or meta-analysis.

Systematic reviews are a form of retrospective, observational research and it is not surprising that many of the biases that attend any other piece of research also apply to systematic reviews. Retrospective studies in general are affected by the problem that the data may not have been originally intended to answer the questions that the researcher wants to address; the same applies to systematic reviews. Surveys can be affected by selection and response biases; as we have seen, the same may apply to systematic reviews. The same applies to issues of transferability. Moreover, like any retrospective study, time may have passed since the data were collected, and much may have changed in the interim: in the case of reviews of interventions, the context, the intervention, and even the population may have changed. What was effective once, may no longer be (though a review should be able to examine this issue – for example by means of cumulative meta-analysis). Systematic reviews, like other studies, need to be critically appraised.

REFERENCES

1. Oxman, A. D. and Guyatt, G. H. Validation of an index of the quality of review articles. *Journal of Clinical Epidemiology* 1991, 44: 1271–8.
2. Oxman, A. Checklists for review articles. *British Medical Journal* 1994, 309: 648–51.

Bibliography

Acheson, D. *Independent inquiry into inequalities in health*. London: Department of Health, 1998.

Alderson, P., Green, S., and Higgins, J. (eds.) Cochrane Reviewers' Handbook 4.2.2 [updated March 2004]. *The Cochrane Library*, Issue 1, 2004. Chichester, UK: John Wiley & Sons, Ltd.

Allen, I. and Olkin, I. Estimating time to conduct a meta-analysis from number of citations retrieved. *Journal of the American Medical Association* 1999, 282: 634–5.

Allen, M. and Burrell, N. Comparing the impact of homosexual and heterosexual parents on children: A meta-analysis of existing research. *Journal of Homosexuality* 1996, 32: 19–35.

Anderson, B. and Greenberg, E. Educational production functions for teacher-technology mixes: Problems and possibilities: Report: M-72-2. Washington, DC: National Aeronautics and Space Administration, March 1972.

Anderson, L., Shinn, C., Fullilove, M., Scrimshaw, S., Fielding, J., Normand, J., et al. The effectiveness of early childhood development programs. A systematic review. *American Journal of Preventive Medicine* 2003, 24(3 Suppl): 32–46.

Antman, E., Lau, J., Kupelnick, B., Mosteller, F., and Chalmers, T. A comparison of results of meta-analyses of randomized control trials and recommendations of clinical experts. *Journal of the American Medical Association* 1992, 268: 240–8.

Arai, L., Popay, J., Roberts, H., and Roen, K. *Preventing accidents in children – how can we improve our understanding of what really works? Exploring methodological and practical issues in the systematic review of factors affecting the implementation of child injury prevention initiatives*. London: Health Development Agency, 2003.

Arai, L., Roen, K., Roberts, H., and Popay, J. It might work in Oklahoma but will it work in Oakhampton? What does the effectiveness literature on domestic smoke detectors tell us about context and implementation? *Injury Prevention* 2005, 11: 148–51.

Arksey, H. and O'Malley, L. Scoping studies: Towards a methodological framework. *International Journal of Research Methodology, Theory and Practice* (in press).

Armstrong, C. and Wheatley, A. Writing abstracts for online databases: Results of an investigation of database producers' guidelines. *Program* 1998, 32: 359–71.

Atkinson, R. Does gentrification help or harm urban neighbourhoods? An assessment of the evidence-base in the context of the new urban agenda. Glasgow: ESRC Centre for Neighbourhood Research, Paper 5, 2002, online at: http://www.bristol.ac.uk/sps/cnrpaperspdf/cnr5pap.pdf [accessed February 24, 2005].

Badger, D., Nursten, P., Williams, P., and Woodward, M.. Should all literature reviews be systematic? *Evaluation and Research in Education* 2000, 14: 220–30.

Bambra, C., Whitehead, M., and Hamilton, V. Does "welfare to work" work? A systematic review of the effectiveness of the UK's "welfare to work" programmes for people with a disability or chronic illness. *Social Science & Medicine* 2005, 60(9): 1905–18.

Barbour, R. Checklists for improving rigour in qualitative research: A case of the tail wagging the dog? *British Medical Journal* 2001, 322: 1115–17.

Barnardo's R&D. *What works? Making connections linking research and practice.* Barking-side, 2000.

Bennett, D., Latham, N., Stretton, C., and Anderson, C. Capture-recapture is a potentially useful method for assessing publication bias. *Journal of Clinical Epidemiology* 2004, 57: 349–57.

Bero, L. and Jadad, A. How consumers and policymakers can use systematic reviews for decision making. *Annals of Internal Medicine* 1997, 127: 37–42.

Bero, L., Grilli, R., Grimshaw, J., Harvey, E., Oxman, A., and Thomson, M. Getting research findings into practice: Closing the gap between research and practice: An overview of systematic reviews of interventions to promote the implementation of research findings. *British Medical Journal* 1998, 465–9.

Beveridge, W. *The art of scientific investigation.* New York: Vintage Books, 1950.

Black, N. Why we need observational studies to evaluate the effectiveness of health care. *British Medical Journal* 1996, 312: 1215–18.

Blunkett, D. Influence or irrelevance: Can social science improve government? Swindon: Economic and Social Research Council, 2000, online at: http://www.bera.ac.uk/ri/no71/ri71blunkett.html [accessed February 2, 2005].

Boaz, A., Ashby, D., and Young, K. Systematic reviews: What have they got to offer evidence based policy and practice? ESRC UK Centre for Evidence Based Policy and Practice, Working Paper 2, 2002, online at: http://www.evidencenetwork.org/cgi-win/enet.exe/biblioview?538 [accessed February 2, 2005].

Bonta, J., Law, M., and Hanson, K. The prediction of criminal and violent recidivism among mentally disordered offenders: A meta-analysis. *Psychological Bulletin* 1998, 123: 123–42.

Booth, A. Cochrane or cock-eyed? How should we conduct systematic reviews of qualitative research? Qualitative Evidence-Based Practice Conference, Coventry University, May 14-16, 2001, online at: http://www.leeds.ac.uk/educol/documents/00001724.htm, 2001.

Booth, A., and Fry-Smith, A. Developing the research question. *Etext on Health Technology Assessment (HTA) Information Resources,* 2004, online at: http://www.nlm.nih.gov/nichsr/ehta/chapter2.html [accessed February 24, 2005].

Borenstein. M. and Borenstein H. *Comprehensive meta-analysis: A computer program for research synthesis*. New Jersey: Biostat <http://www.metaanalysis.com>, 1999.

Boulton, M. and Fitzpatrick, R. Quality in qualitative research. *Critical Public Health* 1994, 5: 19–26.

Boyce, M. Organizational story and storytelling: a critical review. *Journal of Organizational Change Management* 1996, 9: 5–26.

Boynton, J., Glanville, J., McDaid, D., and Lefebvre, C. Identifying systematic reviews in MEDLINE: Developing an objective approach to search strategy design. *Journal of Information Science* 1998, 24: 137–57.

Bradshaw, J. (ed.) *The well-being of children in the UK*. London: Save the Children, 2002.

Briss, P., Pappaioanou, M., Fielding, J., Wright-de Aguero, L., Truman, B., Hopkins, D., et al. Developing an evidence-based guide to community preventive services – methods. *American Journal of Preventive Medicine* 2000, 18(1S): 35–43.

Britten, N., Campbell, R., Pope, C., Donovan, J., Morgan, M., and Pill, R. Using meta ethnography to synthesise qualitative research: A worked example. *Journal of Health Services Research and Policy* 2002, 7: 209–15.

Britton, A., McKee, M., Black, N., McPherson, K., Sanderson, C., and Bain, C. Choosing between randomised and non-randomised studies: A systematic review. *Health Technology Assessment* 1998, 2, online at: http://www.hta.nhsweb.nhs.uk/htapubs.htm

Brookes, S., Whitley, E., Peters, T., Mulheran, P., Egger, M., and Davey Smith, G. Subgroup analyses in randomised controlled trials: Quantifying the risks of false positives and false negatives. *Health Technology Assessment* 2001, 5, online at: http://www.hta.nhsweb.nhs.uk/htapubs.htm

Browman, H. Negative results: Theme section. *Marine Ecology Progress Series* 1999, 191: 301–9.

Burdett, S., Stewart, L., and Tierney, J. Publication bias and meta-analyses. *International Journal of Technology Assessment in Health Care* 2003, 19: 129–34.

Bush, G. *State of the Union Address, 2003*, online at: http://www.whitehouse.gov/news/releases/2003/01/20030128-19.html [accessed February 2, 2005].

Bushman, B. and Wells, G. Narrative impressions of literature: The availability bias and the corrective properties of meta-analytic approaches. *Personality and Social Psychology Bulletin* 2001, 27: 1123–30, online at: http://www-personal.umich.edu/~bbushman/bw01.pdf

Button, K. and Kerr, J. The effectiveness of traffic restraint policies: A simple meta-regression analysis. *International Journal of Transport Economics* 1996, XXIII.

Callaham, M., Wears, R., and Weber, E. Journal prestige, publication bias, and other characteristics associated with citation of published studies in peer-reviewed journals. *Journal of the American Medical Association* 2002, 287: 2847–50.

Campbell, D. and Stanley, J. *Experimental and quasi-experimental designs for research*. Chicago: Rand McNally, 1966.

Campbell, K., Waters, E., O'Meara, S., and Summerbell, C. Interventions for preventing obesity in children. *The Cochrane Library*, Issue 2, 2004. Chichester, UK: John Wiley & Sons, 2004.

Campbell, M., Fitzpatrick, R., Haines, A., Kinmonth, A., Sandercock, P., Spiegel-halter, D., et al. Framework for design and evaluation of complex interventions to improve health. *British Medical Journal* 2000, 321: 694–6.

Campbell, R., Pound, P., Pope, C., Britten, N., Pill, R., Morgan, M., et al. Evaluating meta-ethnography: a synthesis of qualitative research on lay experiences of diabetes and diabetes care. *Social Science and Medicine* 2003, 56: 671–84.

Camps, F. and Carpenter, R. (eds.) *Sudden and unexpected deaths in infancy (Cot Deaths): Report of the proceedings of the Sir Samuel Bedson symposium, held at Addenbrooke's Hospital, Cambridge, on 17 and 18 April 1970*: J. Wright for the Foundation for the Study of Infant Deaths Ltd, 1972.

CDC Evaluation Working Group: Steps in Program Evaluation: Centers for Disease Control, Atlanta, US, online at: http://www.cdc.gov/steps/resources.htm, 2004.

Centre for Reviews and Dissemination (CRD). *Effective Health Care Bulletin, Getting Evidence into Practice*, 5(1) February, online at: http://www.york.ac.uk/inst/crd/ehc51.pdf, 1999.

Chalmers, I. Underreporting research is scientific misconduct. *Journal of the American Medical Association* 1990, 263: 1405–8.

Chalmers, I., Dickersin, K., and Chalmers, T. Getting to grips with Archie Cochrane's agenda. *British Medical Journal* 1992, 305: 786–8.

Chalmers, I., Enkin, M., and Keirse, M. Preparing and updating systematic reviews of randomized controlled trials of health care. *Millbank Quarterly* 1993, 71: 411–37.

Chalmers, I., Hedges, L., and Cooper, H. A brief history of research synthesis. *Evaluation and the Health Professions* 2002, 25: 12–37.

Chalmers, T. Meta-analytic stimulus for changes in clinical trials. *Statistical Methods in Medicine* 1993, 2: 161–72.

Chalmers, T., Smith, H., Blackburn, C., Silverman, B., Schroeder, B., Reitman, D., et al. A method for assessing the quality of a randomized controlled trial. *Controlled Clinical Trials* 1981, 2: 31–49.

Chang, J., Morton, S., Rubenstein, L., Mojica, W., Maglione, M., Suttorp, M., et al. Interventions for the prevention of falls in older adults: Systematic review and meta-analysis of randomised clinical trials. *British Medical Journal* 2004, 328: 653–4.

Chapman, S. Advocacy for public health: A primer. *Journal of Epidemiology and Community Health* 2004, 58: 361–5.

Chelimsky, E. On the social science contribution to governmental decision-making. *Science* 1991, 254: 226–30.

Chilcott, J., Brennan, A., Booth, A., Karnon, J., and Tappenden, P. The role of modelling in prioritising and planning clinical trials. *Health Technology Assessment* 2003, 7, online at: http://www.hta.nhsweb.nhs.uk/htapubs.htm

Chowka, P. Linus Pauling: The last interview. 1996, online at: http://members.aol.com/erealmedia/pauling.html [accessed February 2, 2005].

Clark, O. and Djulbegovic, B. Forest plots in Excel software (data sheet), online at: http://www.evidencias.com/forest01.xls, 2001.

Clarke, M. and Stewart, L. Obtaining data from randomised controlled trials: How much do we need for reliable and informative meta-analyses? *British Medical Journal* 1994, 309: 1007–10.

Cochrane Injuries Group Driver Education Reviewers. Evidence based road safety: the Driving Standards Agency's schools programme. *Lancet* 2001, 358: 230–2.

Committee on the Social and Economic Impact of Pathological Gambling [and] Committee on Law and Justice, Commission on Behavioral and Social Sciences and Education, National Research Council *Pathological gambling: A critical review*. Washington: National Academy Press, 1999.

CONSORT Guidelines, online at: http://www.consort-statement.org/

Cook, T. and Campbell, D. *Quasi-experimentation: Design and analysis issues for field settings*. Chicago: Rand McNally, 1979.

Cooper, H. and Hedges, L. (eds.) *The handbook of research synthesis*. New York: Russell Sage Foundation, 1994.

Cooper, H. and Rosenthal, R. Statistical versus traditional procedures for summarizing research findings. *Psychological Bulletin* 1980, 87: 442–9.

Cooper, H. and Valentine, J. What Works Clearinghouse Cumulative Research Evidence Assessment Device (Version 0.6). Washington, DC: US Department of Education, online at: http://www.w-w-c.org/, 2003.

Cooper, H. *Integrating research: A guide for literature reviews*. London: Sage, 1989.

Cooper, H. *The integrative research review: A systematic approach*. Newbury Park, CA: Sage, 1984.

Cooper, N., Sutton, A., and Abrams, K. Decision analytic economic modelling within a Bayesian framework: Application to prophylactic antibiotics use for caesarian section. *Statistical Methods in Medical Research* 2002, 11: 491–512, online at: http://www.hs.le.ac.uk/~keitha/SMMR%202002%20NJC.pdf

Coren, E. and Barlow, J. Individual and group based parenting for improving psychosocial outcomes for teenage parents and their children (Campbell Collaboration review), online at: http://www.campbellcollaboration.org/doc-pdf/teen par.pdf, 2004.

Cowley, D. Prostheses for primary total hip replacement: A critical appraisal of the literature. *International Journal of Technology Assessment in Health Care* 1995, 11: 770–8.

Crombie, I. *The pocket guide to critical appraisal*. London: BMJ Publishing Group, 1996.

Crossland, P., Deakin, S., Gelsthorpe, L., Jones, G., Quince, T., and Sutherland, H. Using social science: A pilot of non-academic exploitation of social science research in The University of Cambridge. Cambridge: University of Cambridge, 1998.

Cummins, S. and Macintyre, S. "Food deserts": Evidence and assumption in health policy making. *British Medical Journal* 2002, 325: 436–8.

Davey Smith, G., Egger, M., and Phillips, A. Beyond the grand mean? *British Medical Journal* 1997, 315: 1610–14.

Davies, P. Is evidence-based government possible? Jerry Lee Lecture 2004, 4th Annual Campbell Colloquium, Washington DC.

Davies, P. and Boruch, R. The Campbell Collaboration. *British Medical Journal* 2001, 323: 294–5.

Declaration of Helsinki, online at: http://www.wma.net/e/policy/b3.htm, 1964.

Deeks, J. Systematic reviews of evaluations of diagnostic and screening tests. In M. Egger, G. Davey Smith, and D. Altman (eds.) *Systematic reviews in health care. Meta-analysis in context.* London: BMJ, 2001.

Deeks, J., Dinnes, J., D'Amico, R., Sowden, A., Sakarovitch, C., Song, F., et al. Evaluating non-randomised intervention studies. *Health Technology Assessment* 2003, 7, online at: http://www.hta.nhsweb.nhs.uk/fullmono/mon727.pdf [accessed February 24. 2005].

Devillé, W., Buntinx, F., Bouter, L., Montori, V., de Vet, H., van der Windt, D., et al. Conducting systematic reviews of diagnostic studies: Didactic guidelines. *BMC Medical Research Methodology* 2002, 2, online at: www.biomedcentral.com/1471-2288/2/9 [accessed February 24, 2005].

Devine, E. and Cook, T. A meta-analytic analysis of effects of psychoeducational interventions on length of postsurgical hospital stay. *Nursing Research* 1983, 32: 267–74.

DiCenso, A., Guyatt, G., Willan, A., and Griffith, L. Interventions to reduce unintended pregnancies among adolescents: Systematic review of randomised controlled trials. *British Medical Journal* 2002, 324: 1426–34.

Dickersin, K. Reducing reporting biases. In I. Chalmers, I. Milne, and U. Tröhler, (eds.) *The James Lind Library* <www.jameslindlibrary.org>, 2004.

Dickersin, K., Olson, C., Rennie, D., Cook, D., Flanagin, A., Zhu, Q., et al. Association between time interval to publication and statistical significance. *Journal of the American Medical Association* 2002, 287(21): 2829–31.

Dickersin, K., Scherer, R., and Lefebvre, C. Identifying relevant studies for systematic reviews. *British Medical Journal* 1994, 309.

DiGuiseppi, C., Roberts, I., and Speirs, N. Smoke alarm installation and function in inner London council housing. *Archives of Disease in Childhood* 1999, 81: 400–3.

Dingwall, R., Murphy, E., Greatbatch, D., Watson, P., and Parker, S. Catching goldfish: Quality in qualitative research. *Journal of Health Services Research and Policy* 1998, 3: 167–72.

Dixon-Woods, M. and Fitzpatrick, R. Qualitative research in systematic reviews has established a place for itself. *British Medical Journal* 2001, 323: 765–6.

Dixon-Woods, M., Agarwal, S., Young, B., Jones, D., and Sutton, A. Integrative approaches to qualitative and quantitative evidence: Health Development Agency, London, online at: http://www.publichealth.nice.org.uk/page.aspx?o=508055, 2004.

Dixon-Woods, M., Shaw, R., Agarwal, S., and Smith, J. The problem of appraising qualitative research. *Quality & Safety in Healthcare* 2004, 13: 223–5.

Dobie, J. *A Texan in England.* Boston: Little, Brown, 1944.

Doll, R. and Hill, A. A study of the aetiology of carcinoma of the lung. *British Medical Journal* 1952, ii: 1271–86.

Doll, R., Peto, R., Boreham, J., and Sutherland, I. Mortality in relation to smoking: 50 years' observations on male British doctors. *British Medical Journal* 2004, 328: 1519–33.

Donaldson, C., Mugford, M., and Vale, L. (eds.) *Evidence-based health economics: From effectiveness to efficiency in systematic review.* London: BMJ Books, 2002.

Downs, S. and Black, N. The feasibility of creating a checklist for the assessment of the methodological quality of both randomised and non-randomised studies of healthcare interventions. *Journal of Epidemiology and Community Health* 1998, 52: 377–84.

DuBois, D., Holloway, B., Valentine, J., and Cooper, H. Effectiveness of mentoring programs for youth: A meta-analytic review. *American Journal of Community Psychology* 2002, 30: 157–97.

Duval, S. and Tweedie, R. Trim and fill: A simple funnel-plot-based method of testing and adjusting for publication bias in meta-analysis. *Biometrics* 2000, 56: 455–63.

Dwyer, T. and Ponsonby, A. Sudden infant death syndrome: After the "back to sleep" campaign. *British Medical Journal* 1996, 313: 180–1.

Eagly, A. and Wood, W. Using research synthesis to plan future research. In H. Cooper and L. Hedges (eds.) *The handbook of research synthesis.* New York: Russell Sage Foundation, 1994.

Easterbrook, P., Berlin, J., Gopalan, R., and Matthews, D. Publication bias in clinical research. *Lancet* 1991, 337: 867–72.

Eco, U. It's not what you know … *The Guardian*, April 3, 2004.

Effron, B. and Morris, C. Stein's paradox in statistics. *Scientific American* 1977, 236: 119–27.

Egan, M., Petticrew, M., Hamilton, V., and Ogilvie, D. Health impacts of new roads: A systematic review. *American Journal of Public Health* 2003, 93(9): 1463–71.

Egan, M., Petticrew, M., Ogilvie, D., and Hamilton, V. Privatisation, deregulation and state subsidies: A systematic review of health impacts of interventions affecting direct public investment in business. (in press), online at: http://www.msoc-mrc.gla.ac.uk/Evidence/Research/Review%2004/Review4_MAIN.html

Egger, M. Meta-analysis: Bias in location and selection of studies. *British Medical Journal* 1998, 316: 61–6.

Egger, M. and Davey Smith, G. Misleading meta-analysis. Lessons from "an effective, safe, simple" intervention that wasn't. *British Medical Journal* 1995, 310: 752–4.

Egger, M., Davey Smith, G. and Altman, D. *Systematic reviews in health care. Meta-analysis in context.* London: BMJ, 2001.

Egger, M., Davey Smith, G., Schneider, M., and Minder, C. Bias in meta-analysis detected by a simple graphical test. *British Medical Journal* 1997, 315: 629–34.

Egger, M., Ebrahim, S., and Davey Smith, G. Where now for meta-analysis? *International Journal of Epidemiology* 2002, 31: 1–5.

Egger, M., Jüni, P., Bartlett, C., Holenstein, F., and Sterne, J. How important are comprehensive literature searches and the assessment of trial quality in systematic reviews? *Health Technology Assessment* 2003, 7, online at: http://www.hta. nhsweb.nhs.uk/htapubs.htm

Egger, M., Schneider, M., and Davey Smith, G. Spurious precision? Meta-analysis of observational studies. *British Medical Journal* 1998, 316: 140–4.

Elbourne, D., Oakley, A., and Gough, D. EPPI Centre reviews will aim to disseminate systematic reviews in education. *British Medical Journal* 2001, 323: 1252.

Elvik, R. A meta-analysis of studies concerning the safety of daytime running lights on cars. *Accident, Analysis and Prevention* 1996, 28: 685–94.

Evans, D. Database searches for qualitative research. *Journal of the Medical Library Association* 2002, 90: 290–3.

Evans, S. Misleading meta-analysis: Statistician's comment. *Lancet* 1996, 312: 125.

Everitt, A. *Applied research for better practice.* Basingstoke: Macmillan, 1992.

Eysenck, H. An exercise in mega-silliness. *American Psychologist* 1978, 33: 517.

Eysenck, H. Systematic Reviews: Meta-analysis and its problems. *British Medical Journal* 1994, 309: 789–92, online at: http://bmj.bmjjournals.com/cgi/content/ full/309/6957/789

Eysenck, H. Meta-analysis squared. Does it make sense? *American Psychologist* 1995, 50: 110–11.

Farrington, D. Methodological quality standards for evaluation research. *Annals of the American Academy of Political and Social Science* 2003, 587: 49–68.

Farrington, D., Gottfredson, D., Sherman, L., and Welsh, B. The Maryland Scientific Methods Scale. In L. Sherman, D. Farrington, B. Welsh, and D. MacKenzie (eds.) *Evidence-based crime prevention.* London: Routledge, 2002.

Feinstein, A. Meta-analysis: Statistical alchemy for the 21st century. *Journal of Clinical Epidemiology* 1995, 48: 71–9.

Fitzpatrick, R. and Boulton, M. Qualitative methods for assessing health care. *Quality in Health Care* 1994, 3: 107–13.

Food and Nutrition Board, Recommended Dietary Allowances, revised 1945: Food and Nutrition Board, National Academy of Science. National Research Council, Reprint and Circular Series, No. 122, 1945 (Aug), 3–18.

Freeman, R. The idea of prevention: A critical review. In S. Scott, et al. (eds.) *Private Risks and Public Danger.* Ashgate: Avery, 1992.

Gaffan, E., Tsaousis, I., and Kemp-Wheeler, S. Researcher allegiance and meta-analysis: The case of cognitive therapy for depression. *Journal of Consulting and Clinical Psychology* 1995, 63: 966–80.

Gagnon, A., Tuck, J., and Barkun, L. A systematic review of questionnaires measuring the health of resettling refugee women. *Health Care for Women International* 2004, 25: 111–49.

Gennetian, L. and Knox, V. Staying single: The effects of welfare reform policies on marriage and cohabitation. New York and Oakland CA: MDRC Working Paper 13, 2002, online at: http://www.mdrc.org/publications/373/full.pdf [accessed February 24, 2005].

Gibson, L. and Strong, J. Expert review of an approach to functional capacity evaluation. *Work* 2002, 19: 231–42.

Gilbert, R., Salanti, G., Harden, M., and See, S. Infant sleeping position and the sudden infant death syndrome: Systematic review of observational studies and historical review of recommendations from 1940 to 2002. *International Journal of Epidemiology* (in press).

Gilland, T , Mayer, S., Durodie, B., Gibson, I., and Parr, D. *Science: Can we trust the experts?* London: Hodder & Stoughton, 2002.

Glanville, J. Identification of research. In K. Khan, G. ter Riet, J. Glanville, A. Sowden, and J. Kleijnen (eds.) *Undertaking systematic reviews of research on effectiveness: CRD's guidance for carrying out or commissioning reviews*: York: CRD, University of York, online at: http://www.york.ac.uk/inst/crd/report4.htm, 2001.

Glass, G. Meta-analysis at 25. College of Education, Arizona State University, 2000, online at: http://glass.ed.asu.edu/gene/papers/meta25.html

Glass, G. and Smith, M. *Meta-analysis of research on the relationship of class size and achievement.* San Francisco: Far West Laboratory for Educational Research and Development, 1978.

Glass, G., McGaw, B., and Smith, M. *Meta-analysis in social research.* Beverly Hills: Sage, 1981.

Glasziou, P., Vandenbroucke, J., and Chalmers, I. Assessing the quality of research. *British Medical Journal* 2004, 328: 39–41.

Gøetsche, P., Liberati, A., Torri, V., and Rosetti, L. Beware of surrogate outcome measures. *International Journal of Health Technology Assessment* 1996, 12: 238–46.

Gottfredson, D., Wilson, D., and Najaka, S. School-based crime prevention. In L. Sherman, D. Farrington, B. Welsh, and D. MacKenzie (eds.) *Evidence-based crime prevention.* London: Routledge, 2002.

Gough, D. and Elbourne, D. Systematic research synthesis to inform policy, practice, and democratic debate. *Social Policy and Society* 2002, 1: 225–36.

Green, J. Generalisability and validity in qualitative research. *British Medical Journal* 1999, 319: 418–21.

Greenhalgh, T. How to read a paper: Papers that report diagnostic or screening tests. *British Medical Journal* 1997, 315: 540–3.

Greenhalgh, T. How to read a paper: Papers that summarise other papers (systematic reviews and meta-analyses). *British Medical Journal* 1997, 315: 672–5.

Greenhalgh, T. Commentary: Meta-analysis is a blunt and potentially misleading instrument for analysing models of service delivery. *British Medical Journal* 1998, 317: 390–6.

Greenhalgh, T., Robert, G., Bate, P., Kyriakidou, O., MacFarlane, F., and Peacock. R. How to spread good ideas: A systematic review of the literature on diffusion, dissemination and sustainability of innovations in health service delivery and organisation. Report for the National Co-ordinating Centre for NHS Service Delivery and Organisation R & D (NCCSDO). 2004. Full report available online at: http://www.sdo.lshtm.ac.uk/pdf/changemanagement_greenhalgh_report.pdf [accessed February 24, 2005].

Greenhalgh, T., Robert, G., Macfarlane, F., Bate, P., and Kyriakidou, O. Diffusion of innovations in service organizations: Systematic review and recommendations. *Milbank Quarterly* 2004, 82: 4, online at: http://www.milbank.org/quarterly/8204feat.html

Greenhouse, J. and Iyengar, S. Sensitivity analysis and diagnostics. In H. Cooper and L. Hedges (eds.). *The handbook of research synthesis.* New York: Russell Sage Foundation, 1994.

Grimshaw, J. *How to find information: Social sciences.* London: British Library, 2000.

Grimshaw, J., Freemantle, N., Wallace, S., Russell, I., Hurwitz, B., Watt, I., et al. Developing and implementing clinical practice guidelines. *Quality in Health Care* 1995, 4: 55–64.

Grimshaw, J., Thomas, R., MacLennan, G., Fraser, C., Ramsay, C., Vale, L., et al. Effectiveness and efficiency of guideline dissemination and implementation strategies. *Health Technology Assessment* 2004, 8: 1–72.

Gruen, R., Bailie, R., McDonald, E., Weeramanthri, T., and Knight, S. The potential of systematic reviews to identify diversity and inequity in health care interventions. XI Cochrane Colloquium: Evidence, health care and culture, Barcelona, 2003.

Guyatt, G., Haynes, R., Jaeschke, R., Cook, D., Green, L., Naylor, C., et al. Users' Guides to the Medical Literature: XXV. Evidence-based medicine: Principles for applying the Users' Guides to patient care. Evidence-Based Medicine Working Group. *Journal of the American Medical Association* 2000, 284: 1290–6.

Guyatt, G., Sackett, D., Sinclair, J., Hayward, R., Cook, D., and Cook, R. Users' guides to the medical literature. IX. A method for grading health care recommendations. *Journal of the American Medical Association* 1995, 274: 1800–4.

Hahn, R., Bilukha, O., Crosby, A., Fullilove, M., Liberman, A., Moscicki, E., et al. First reports evaluating the effectiveness of strategies for preventing violence: Firearms laws. Findings from the Task Force on Community Preventive Services. *Morbidity and Mortality Weekly Report* 2003, 52: 11–20.

Hall, J., Tickle-Degnen, L., Rosenthal, R., and Mosteller, F. Hypotheses and problems in research synthesis. In H. Cooper and L. Hedges (eds.) *The handbook of research synthesis.* New York: Russell Sage Foundation, 1994.

Hall, W., Ross, J., Lynskey, M., Law, M., and Degenhardt, L. How many dependent heroin users are there in Australia? *Medical Journal of Australia* 2000, 173: 528–31.

Hanson, R. and Bussière, M. Predictors of sexual offender recidivism: A meta-analysis: Public Works and Government Services Canada, online at: http://home.wanadoo.nl/ipce/library_two/han/hanson_96_txt.htm, 1996.

Harden, A. and Oliver, S. Systematically reviewing for ethics and empowerment. In S. Oliver and G. Peersman (eds.) *Using research for effective health promotion.* Buckingham: Open University Press, 2001.

Harmon, C., Oosterbeek, H., and Walker, I. The returns to education: A review of evidence, issues and deficiencies in the Literature. London: Center for the Economics of Education (CEE) Discussion Papers no. 5, London School of Economics, 2000.

Harris, D. The socialization of the delinquent. *Child Development* 1948, 19: 143–54.

Hartley, R., Keen, R., Large, J., and Tedd, L. *Online searching: Principles and practice.* London: Bowker-Saur, 1990.

Hasselblad, V. and Hedges, L. Meta-analysis of screening and diagnostic tests. *Psychological Bulletin* 1995, 117: 167–78.

Hawe, P., Shiell, A., and Riley, T. Complex interventions: how "out of control" can a randomised controlled trial be? *British Medical Journal* 2004, 328: 1561–3.

Hawker, S., Payne, S., Kerr, C., Hardey, M., and Powell, J. Appraising the evidence: Reviewing disparate data systematically. *Qualitative Health Research* 2002, 12: 1284–99.

Heckman, J., Hohmann, N., and Smith, J. Substitution and dropout bias in social experiments: A study of an influential social experiment. *Quarterly Journal of Economics* 2000, 115: 651–94.

Hedges, L. Comment on: Selection models and the File Drawer problem (Iyengar and Greenhouse, 1988). *Statistical Science* 1988, 3: 118–20.

Hedges, L. and Olkin, I. *Statistical methods for meta-analysis.* New York: Academic Press, 1985.

Hedges, L. V., Laine, R. D., and Greenwald, R. Does money matter? A meta-analysis of studies of the effects of differential school inputs on student outcomes. *Educational Researcher* 1994, 23: 5–14.

Hemingway, H. and Marmot, M. Evidence based cardiology: Psychosocial factors in the aetiology and prognosis of coronary heart disease: Systematic review of prospective cohort studies. *British Medical Journal* 1999, 318: 1460–7.

Hetherington, J., Dickersin, K., Chalmers, I., and Meinert, C. Retrospective and prospective identification of unpublished controlled trials: Lessons from a survey of obstetricians and pediatricians. *Pediatrics* 1989, 84: 374–80.

Higgins, J. Assessing statistical heterogeneity: Chi-squared or I-squared? *Newsletter of the Cochrane Wounds Group* 2004, 3–4.

Higgins, J. and Thompson, S. The risk of false-positive findings from meta-regression. 4th Symposium on Systematic Reviews: Pushing the Boundaries; 2002; Oxford, online at: http://www.ihs.ox.ac.uk/csm/pushingtheboundaries/symp2002.html

Higgins, J., Thompson, S., Deeks, J., and Altman, D. Measuring inconsistency in meta-analyses. *British Medical Journal* 2003, 327: 557–60.

Hogarth, R. *Judgement and choice. The psychology of decision-making.* Chichester: John Wiley & Sons, 1987.

Hopewell, S., Clarke, M., Lefebvre, C., and Scherer, R. Handsearching versus electronic searching to identify reports of randomized trials (Cochrane Methodology Review). In *The Cochrane Library*, Issue 2, 2004. Chichester, UK: John Wiley & Sons, Ltd.

Horton, R. Review of *The Fool of Pest*, by Sherwin B Nuland. *The New York Review of Books* February 26 2004, 11(3): 10.

Hsieh, C. C. and Pugh, M. D. Poverty, income inequality, and violent crime: A meta-analysis of recent aggregate data studies. *Criminal Justice Review* 1993, 18: 182.

Hunt, M. *How science takes stock*. New York: Russell Sage Foundation, 1997.

Hurwitz, B., Greenhalgh, T., and Skultans, V. (eds.) *Narrative Research in Health and Illness*. BMJ Books, 2004.

Huwiler-Müntener, K., Jüni, P., Junker, C., and Egger, M. Quality of reporting of randomized trials as a measure of methodologic quality. *Journal of the American Medical Association* 2002, 287: 2801–4.

ISIS-2 (Second International Study of Infarct Survival) Collaborative Group: Randomised trial of intravenous streptokinase, oral aspirin, both or neither among 17,187 cases of suspected acute myocardial infarction. *Lancet* 1988 ii: 349–60.

Jadad, A. *Randomised controlled trials: A users guide*. London: BMJ Books, 1998.

Jadad, A., Moore, A., Carrol, D., Gavaghan, D., and McQuay, H. Assessing the quality of reports of randomised clinical trials: Is blinding necessary? *Controlled Clinical Trials* 1996, 17: 1–12.

Jones, D. Meta-analysis of observational studies: A review. *Journal of the Royal Society of Medicine* 1992, 85: 165–6.

Jowell, R. Introducing the survey. In R. Jowell and C. Airey (eds.) *British Social Attitudes: The 1984 report*. Aldershot: Gower, 1984.

Jüni, P., Witschi, A., Bloch, R., and Egger, M. The hazards of scoring the quality of clinical trials for meta-analysis. *Journal of the American Medical Association* 1999, 282: 1054–60.

Kahneman, D., Slovic, P., and Tversky, A. (eds.) *Judgement under uncertainty: Heuristics and biases*. Cambridge: Cambridge University Press, 1982.

Khan, S., Bhuiya, A., and Uddin, A. Application of the capture-recapture method for estimating number of mobile male sex workers in a port city of Bangladesh. *Journal of Health, Population and Nutrition* 2004, 22: 19–26.

Klebanoff, S., Singer, J., and Wilensky, H. Psychological consequences of brain lesions and ablations. *Psychological Bulletin* 1954, 51: 1–41.

Knipschild, P. Some examples of systematic reviews. *British Medical Journal* 1994, 309: 719–21.

Knipschild, P. Some examples of systematic reviews. In I. Chalmers and D. Altman (eds.), *Systematic reviews*. London: BMJ Publishing Group, 1995.

Krishnan, E., Murtagh, K., Bruce, B., Cline, D., Singh, G., and Fries, J. Attrition bias in rheumatoid arthritis databanks: A case study of 6,346 patients in 11 databanks and 65,649 administrations of the Health Assessment Questionnaire. *Journal of Rheumatology* 2004, 31: 1320–6.

Kristjansson, B., Robinson, V., Tugwell, P., Petticrew, M., Greenhalgh, T., Macdonald, B., et al. School feeding programs for improving outcomes of low-income children and for reducing socioeconomic inequalities in health (submitted).

Kuvlesky, W. Disability and family stress: Conceptual specification and research possibilities. Report: TAES-216-15-69; USDA-CSRS-RP-NC-90, paper presented at the Association of Southern Agricultural Workers Meeting, Atlanta, Georgia, February 1973, Washington, DC: Cooperative State Research Service (DOA).

Laska, E. The use of capture-recapture methods in public health. *Bulletin of the World Health Organization* 2002, 80: 845.

Lau, J., Antman, E., Jimenez-Silva, J., Kupelnick, B., Mosteller, F., and Chalmers, T. Cumulative meta-analysis of therapeutic trials for myocardial infarction. *New England Journal of Medicine* 1992, 327: 248–54.

Lau, J., Ioannidis, J., and Schmid, C. Quantitative synthesis in systematic reviews. In C. Mulrow and D Cook (eds.) *Systematic reviews: Synthesis of best evidence for health care decisions.* Philadelphia: ACP, 1998.

Lavin, R. and Sanders, J. *Synthesis of knowledge and practice in educational management and leadership.* Volumes 1 and 2. Project No. ED 73-241: Dayton, OH: Charles F. Kettering Foundation, 1973.

Lavis, J., Ross, S., McLeod, C., and Gildiner, A. Measuring the impact of health research. *Journal of Health Services & Research Policy* 2003, 8(3): 165–70.

Lazarus, R. S., Deese, J., and Osler, S. The effects of psychological stress upon performance. *Psychological Bulletin* 1952, 49(4): 293–317.

Lefebvre, C. and Clarke, M. Identifying randomised trials. In M. Egger, G. Davey Smith, and D. Altman (eds.) *Systematic reviews in health care: Meta-analysis in context.* London: BMJ, 2001.

Legge, J. T. *The Analects of Confucius*: Project Gutenberg, 1930.

Lewis, S. and Clarke, M. Forest plots: Trying to see the wood and the trees. *British Medical Journal* 2001, 322: 1479–80.

Liebesny, F. Lost information: Unpublished conference papers. *Proceedings of the International Conference on Scientific Information* 1959, 1: 475–9.

Light, R. and Smith, P. Accumulating evidence: Procedures for resolving contradictions among different research studies. *Harvard Educational Review* 1971, 41: 429–71.

Light, R., Singer, J., and Willett, J. The visual presentation and interpretation of meta-analyses. In H. Cooper and L. Hedges (eds.) *The handbook of research synthesis.* New York: Russell Sage Foundation, 1994.

Lipsey, M. and Wilson, D. Reply to comments. *American Psychologist* 1995, 50: 113–15.

Lipsey, M. and Wilson, D. *Practical meta-analysis*: Thousand Oaks, CA: Sage, 2001.

Liu, B., Ivers, R., Norton, R., Blows, S., and Lo, S. Helmets for preventing injury in motorcycle riders (Cochrane Review). *The Cochrane Library*, Issue 2, 2004. Chichester, UK: John Wiley & Sons, Ltd., 2004.

Lomas, J. Using linkage and exchange to move research into policy at a Canadian Foundation. *Health Affairs* 2000, 19: 236–40.

Lucas, P. et al. A systematic review of lay perspectives on infant size and growth, (for project description please see http://www.city.ac.uk/chrpu/projects/infant-growth.html.).

Lumley, J., Oliver, S., and Waters, E. Interventions for promoting smoking cessation during pregnancy (Cochrane Review). *The Cochrane Library*, Issue 2, 2004. Chichester, UK: John Wiley & Sons.

MacAuley, D., McCrum, E., and Brown, C. Randomised controlled trial of the READER method of critical appraisal in general practice. *British Medical Journal* 1998, 316: 1134–7.

MacCoun, R. Biases in the interpretation and use of research results. *Annual Review of Psychology* 1998, 49: 259–87.

Macdonald, G. Evidence-based social care: Wheels off the runway? *Public Money Management* 1999, 19: 25–32.

Macdonald, G. and Roberts, H. *What works in the early years*. London: Barnardo's, 1995, Report summary is online at: http://www.barnardos.org.uk/resources/researchpublications/documents/WW-E-YRS.PDF [accessed February 2, 2005].

Macintyre, S. Evidence based policy making. *British Medical Journal* 2003, 326: 5–6.

Mackenbach, J. Tackling inequalities in health: The need for building a systematic evidence base. *Journal of Epidemiology and Community Health* 2003, 57: 162.

Magnus, P. and Jaakkola, J. Secular trend in the occurrence of asthma among children and young adults: Critical appraisal of repeated cross sectional surveys. *British Medical Journal* 1997, 314: 1795.

Mallett, S. and Clarke, M. The typical Cochrane review: How many trials? How many participants? *International Journal of Technology Assessment in Health Care* 2002, 18: 820–31.

Manheimer, E. and Anderson, D. Survey of public information about ongoing clinical trials funded by industry: Evaluation of completeness and accessibility. *British Medical Journal* 2002, 325: 528–31.

Marteau, T., Sowden, A., and Armstrong, D. Implementing research findings into practice: Beyond the information deficit model. In A. Haines and A. Donald (eds.) *Getting research findings into practice*. London: BMJ Books, 2nd edn, 2002: 68–76.

Matthews, F. E., Chatfield, M., Freeman, C., McCracken, C., Brayne, C., and MRC CFAS. Attrition and bias in the MRC cognitive function and ageing study: An epidemiological investigation. *BMC Public Health* 2004, 4: 12.

Mays, N. and Pope, C. Assessing quality in qualitative research. *British Medical Journal* 2000, 320: 50–2.

McCormick, F. and Renfrew, M. E. *MIRIAD, The Midwifery Research Database, A sourcebook of information about research in midwifery*, 2nd edn. Hale: Books for Midwives Press, 1996.

McDermott, E. and Graham, H. Resilient young mothering: Social inequalities, late modernity and the "problem" of "teenage" motherhood. *Journal of Youth Studies* 2005, 8(1): 59–79.

McDonagh, M., Whiting, P., Wilson, P., Sutton, A., Chestnutt, I., Cooper, J., et al. Systematic review of water fluoridation. *British Medical Journal* 2000, 321: 855–9.

McDonald, S., Lefebvre, C., Antes, G., Galandi, D., Gøetsche, P., Hammarquist, C., et al. The contribution of handsearching European general health care journals to the Cochrane Controlled Trials Register. *Evaluation & the Health Professions* 2002, 25: 65–75.

McGrath, J., Davies, G., and Soares, K. Writing to authors of systematic reviews elicited further data in 17% of cases. *British Medical Journal* 1998, 316: 631.

McManus, R., Wilson, S., Delaney, B., Fitzmaurice, D., Hyde, C., Tobias, R., et al. Review of the usefulness of contacting other experts when conducting a literature search for systematic reviews. *British Medical Journal* 1998, 317: 1562–3.

Meltzer, H. Review of reviews in industrial psychology, 1950–1969. *Personnel Psychology* 1972, 25: 201–22.

Mibai, S. An experimental study of apparent movement. *Psychological Monographs* 1931, 42: 91.

Miller, N. and Pollock, V. Meta-analytic synthesis for theory development. In H. Cooper and L. Hedges (eds.), *The handbook of research synthesis.* New York: Russell Sage Foundation, 1994.

Milton, B. and Whitehead, M. Social consequences of poor health in childhood. *Child* (in press).

Mirza, I. and Jenkins, R. Risk factors, prevalence, and treatment of anxiety and depressive disorders in Pakistan: Systematic review. *British Medical Journal* 2004, 328: 794.

Mohan, D. and Roberts, I. Global road safety and the contribution of big business: Road safety policies must be based on evidence. *British Medical Journal* 2001, 323: 648.

Moher, D. and Olkin, I. Meta-analysis of randomized controlled trials. A concern for standards. *Journal of the American Medical Association* 1995, 24: 1962–4.

Moher, D., Cook, D. J., Eastwood, S., Olkin, I., Rennie, D., and Stroup, D. F. Improving the quality of reports of meta-analyses of randomised controlled trials: The QUORUM statement. *Lancet* 1999, 354: 1896–900.

Moher, M., Schulz, K. F, and Altman, D. The CONSORT statement: Revised recommendations for improving the quality of reports of parallel-group random-ized trials. *Journal of the American Medical Association* 2001, 285: 1987–91.

Morrison, D., Petticrew, M., and Thomson, H. Effectiveness of transport interventions in improving health: Evidence from systematic reviews. *Journal of Epidemiology and Community Health* 2003, 57: 327–33.

Muhlhauser, I. Systematic reviews do not allow appraisal of complex interventions. XI Cochrane Colloquium: Evidence, health care and culture, 2003, Barcelona.

Muir Gray, J. A. *Evidence-based healthcare.* London: Churchill Livingstone, 1997.

Mulrow, C. D. Systematic reviews: Rationale for systematic reviews. *British Medical Journal* 1994, 309: 597–9.

Myers, R. The synthesis of dynamic and historical data on marine populations and communities. *Oceanography* 2000, 13: 56–9.

Myers, R., MacKenzie, B., Bowen, K., and Barrowman, N. What is the carrying capacity for fish in the ocean? A meta-analysis of population dynamics of North Atlantic Cod. *Canadian Journal of Fisheries and Aquatic Sciences* 2001, 58.

Mytton, J., DiGuiseppi, C., Gough, D., Taylor, R., and Logan, S. School based violence prevention programs: Systematic review of secondary prevention trials. *Archives of Paediatrics and Adolescent Medicine* 2002, 156: 748–9.

National Statistics. *Britain update: November 2000.* London: National Statistics, 2000.

Nelson, G., Westhues, A., and MacLeod, J. A meta-analysis of longitudinal research on preschool prevention programs for children. *Prevention & Treatment* 2003, Article 31, online at: http://journals.apa.org/prevention/volume6/pre0060031a.html

Nelson, H., Nygren, P., McInerney, Y., and Klein, J. Screening women and elderly adults for family and intimate partner violence: A review of the evidence for the US Preventive Services Task Force. *Annals of Internal Medicine* 2004, 140: 387–96.

NHS Centre for Reviews and Dissemination. Undertaking systematic reviews of research on effectiveness: CRD's guidance for those carrying out or commissioning reviews. CRD Report Number 4 (2nd edn): University of York, 2001, online at: http://www1.york.ac.uk/inst/crd/report4.htm

Nichols, H. The psychology of time. *American Journal of Psychology* 1891, 3: 453–529.

Noblit, G. and Hare, R. *Meta-ethnography: Synthesizing qualitative studies.* London: Sage, 1988.

Nutley, S., Davies, H., and Walter, I. Conceptual synthesis 1: Learning from the Diffusion of Innovations. University of St. Andrews, Research Unit for Research Utilisation, 2002, online at: http://www.st-andrews.ac.uk/~ruru/Learning%20from%20the%20Diffusion%20of%20Innovations.pdf [accessed February 24, 2005].

Nutley, S., Davies, H., and Walter, I. What is a conceptual synthesis? University of St. Andrews, Research Unit for Research Utilisation Briefing Note 1, 2002, online at: http://www.st-andrews.ac.uk/~ruru/Conceptual%20synthesis.pdf [accessed February 24, 2005].

Oakley, A. *Experiments in knowing: Gender and method in the social sciences.* Cambridge: Polity Press, 2000.

Oakley, A. Social science and evidence-based everything: The case of education. *Educational Review* 2002, 54: 277–86.

Oakley, A. and Fullerton, D. *A systematic review of smoking prevention programmes for young people.* London: EPPI Centre, Institute of Education, 1995.

Ogilvie, D. and Petticrew, M. Smoking policies and health inequalities. *Tobacco Control* 2004, 13: 129–31.

Ogilvie, D., Egan, M., Hamilton, V., and Petticrew, M. Promoting walking and cycling as an alternative to using cars: What works? A systematic review. *British Medical Journal* 2004, 329: 763.

Oliver, S., Peersman, G., Harden, A., and Oakley, A. Discrepancies in findings from effectiveness reviews: The case of health promotion for older people in accident and injury prevention. *Health Education Journal* 1999, 58: 66–77.

Olson, C., Rennie, D., Cook, D., Dickersin, K., Flanagin, A., Hogan, J., et al. Publication bias in editorial decision making. *Journal of the American Medical Association* 2002, 287(21): 2825–8.

Oxman, A. Checklists for review articles. *British Medical Journal* 1994, 309: 648–51.

Oxman, A. and Guyatt, G. The science of reviewing research. *Annals of the New York Academy of Sciences* 1993, 703: 125–33.

Oxman, A. D. and Guyatt, G. H. Validation of an index of the quality of review articles. *Journal of Clinical Epidemiology* 1991, 44: 1271–8.

Parry, O., Bancroft, A., Gnich, W., and Amos, A. Nobody home? Issues of respondent recruitment in areas of deprivation. *Critical Public Health* 2001, 11: 305–17.

Patton, M. Q. *Utilization-focused evaluation* (3rd edn.). Newbury Park, CA: Sage Publications, 1996.

Pawlicki, R. Behavior-therapy research with children: A critical review. *Canadian Journal of Behavioural Science* 1970, 2: 163–73.

Pawson, R. Evidence and policy and naming and shaming: ESRC UK Centre for Evidence Based Policy and Practice: Working paper no. 5, 2001, online at: http://www.evidencenetwork.org/home.asp

Pawson, R. Evidence-based policy: The promise of "realist synthesis," *Evaluation* 2002, 8(3): 340–58.

Pawson, R. Does Megan's Law work? A theory-driven systematic review: ESRC UK Centre for Evidence Based Policy and Practice, Working Paper, 2002, online at: http://www.evidencenetwork.org/Documents/wp8.pdf [accessed February 24, 2005].

Pawson, R., Boaz, A., Grayson, L., Long, A., and Barnes, C. Types and quality of knowledge in social care: Social Care Institute for Excellence. Online at: http://www.evidencenetwork.org/project1.asp, 2003.

Pawson, R., Greenhalgh, T., Harvey, G., and Walshe, K. Realist synthesis: An introduction: ESRC Research Methods Programme, University of Manchester. RMP Methods Paper 2/2004, online at: http://www.ccsr.ac.uk/methods/publications/documents/RMPmethods2.pdf, 2004.

Pearson, A., Wiechula, A., and Long, L. QARI: A systematic approach to the appraisal, extraction and synthesis of the findings of qualitative research. XI Cochrane Colloquium: Evidence, health care and culture, 2003, Barcelona.

Pearson, K. Report on certain enteric fever inoculation statistics. *British Medical Journal* 1904, 3: 1243–6.

Petrosino, A. The hunt for experimental reports: Document search and efforts for a "What works?" meta-analysis. *Journal of Crime and Justice* 1995, 18: 63–80.

Petrosino, A. What works revisited again: A meta-analysis of randomized experiments in delinquency prevention, rehabilitation, and deterrence. Doctoral dissertation. Rutgers University (New Jersey, USA): University Microfilms Inc., 1997.

Petrosino, A., Turpin-Petrosino, C., and Buehler, J. Scared Straight and other juvenile awareness programs for preventing juvenile delinquency: A systematic review of the randomized experimental evidence. *Annals of the American Academy of Political and Social Science* 2003, 589.

Petrosino, A., Turpin-Petrosino, C., and Buehler, J. "Scared Straight" and other juvenile awareness programs for preventing juvenile delinquency. *The Cochrane Library*, Issue 2, 2004. Oxford: Update Software, 2004.

Petticrew, M. Systematic reviews from astronomy to zoology: Myths and misconceptions. *British Medical Journal* 2001, 322: 98–101.

Petticrew, M. Why certain systematic reviews reach uncertain conclusions. *British Medical Journal* 2003, 326: 756–8.

Petticrew, M. and Roberts, H. Evidence, hierarchies and typologies: Horses for Courses. *Journal of Epidemiology and Community Health* 2003, 57: 527–9.

Petticrew, M., Fraser, J., and Regan, M. Adverse life events and breast cancer: A meta-analysis. *British Journal of Health Psychology* 1999, 4: 1–17.

Petticrew, M., Song, F., Wilson, P., and Wright, K. The DARE database of abstracts of systematic reviews: A summary and analysis. *International Journal of Technology Assessment in Health Care* 2000, 15: 671–8.

Petticrew, M., Whitehead, M., Bambra, C., Egan, M., Graham, H., Macintyre, S., et al. *Systematic reviews in public health: The work of the ESRC Centre for Evidence Based Public Health Policy. An evidence-based approach to public health and tackling health inequalities.* Milton Keynes: Open University Press (in press).

Popay, J. and Roen, K. Synthesis of evidence from research using diverse study designs: A preliminary review of methodological work: Social Care Institute of Excellence, 2003.

Popay, J., Rogers, A., and Williams, G. Rationale and standards for the systematic review of qualitative literature in health services research. *Qualitative Health Research* 1998, 8: 341–51.

Powell, S. and Tod, J. A systematic review of how theories explain learning behaviour in school contexts. Research Evidence in Education Library. London: EPPI-Centre, Social Science Research Unit, Institute of Education, online at: http://eppi.ioe.ac.uk/EPPIWeb/home.aspx?&page=/reel/reviews.htm, 2004.

Power, C. and Hertzman, C. Social and biological pathways linking early life and adult disease. *British Medical Bulletin* 1997, 53: 210–21.

Prescott, R., Counsell, C., Gillespie, W., Grant, A., Russell, I., Kiauka, S., et al. Factors influencing the quality, number and progress of randomised controlled trials. *Health Technology Assessment* 1999, 3, online at: http://www.hta.nhsweb.nhs.uk/htapubs.htm

Puffer, S., Torgerson, D., and Watson, J. Evidence for risk of bias in cluster randomised trials: Review of recent trials published in three general medical journals. *British Medical Journal* 2003, 327: 785–9.

Pulkingham, J. and Ternowetsky, G. A state of the art review of income security reform in Canada. Ottawa, Canada: International Development Research Centre, 1998.

Pyke, D. Foreword, in *The strange case of the spotted mice and other essays on science.* Oxford: Oxford Paperbacks, 1996.

Rachman, S. and Wilson, G. *The effects of psychological therapy.* New York: Pergamon Press, 1980.

Ravetz, J. *Scientific knowledge and its social problems.* Middlesex: Penguin University Books, 1973.

Rawlins, M. and Culyer, A. National Institute for Clinical Excellence and its value judgments. *British Medical Journal* 2004, 329: 224–7.

Rees, J. Two cultures? *Journal of the American Academy of Dermatology* 2002 46: 313–16.

Rees, R., Harden, A., Shepherd, J., Brunton, G., Oliver, S., and Oakley, A. Young people and physical activity: A systematic review of research on barriers and facilitators. London: EPPI Centre, Institute of Education, University of London, online at: http://eppi.ioe.ac.uk/EPPIWeb/home.aspx, 2001.

Rees, R., Potter, S., and Penn, H. Searching for studies of the outcomes of education: A bibliometric study. XI Cochrane Colloquium: Evidence, health care, and culture, Barcelona, 2003.

Reeves, R., Koppel, I., Barr, H., Freeth, D., and Hammick, M. Twelve tips for undertaking a systematic review. *Medical Teacher* 2002, 24: 358–63.

Reisch, J., Tyson, J., and Mize, S. Aid to the evaluation of therapeutic studies. *Pediatrics* 1989, 84: 815–27.

Richardson, A., Jackson, C., and Sykes, W. *Taking research seriously: Means of improving and assessing the use and dissemination of research.* London: HMSO, 1990.

Riemsma, R., Pattenden, J., Bridle, C., Sowden, A., Mather, L., Watt, I., et al. A systematic review of the effectiveness of interventions based on a stages-of-change approach to promote individual behaviour change. *Health Technology Assessment* 2002, 6, online at: http://www.hta.nhsweb.nhs.uk/fullmono/mon624.pdf [accessed February 2, 2005].

Rigby, K. *A meta-evaluation of methods and approaches to reducing bullying in pre-schools and in early primary school in Australia.* Canberra: Commonwealth Attorney-General's Department. 2002. (See: http://www.education.unisa.edu.au/bullying/countering.htm [accessed February 2, 2005] for details of how to obtain this report.)

Ritchie, D. "Breathing Space" – reflecting upon the realities of community partner-ships and workers' beliefs about promoting health. *Health Education Journal* 2001, 60: 73–92.

Roberts, H., Curtis, C., Liabo, K., Rowland, D., DiGuiseppi, C., and Roberts, I. Putting public health evidence into practice: Increasing the prevalence of working smoke alarms in disadvantaged inner city housing. *Journal of Epidemiology and Community Health* 2004, 58: 280–5.

Roberts, H., Liabo, K., Lucas, P., DuBois, D., and Sheldon, T. Mentoring to reduce antisocial behaviour in childhood. *British Medical Journal* 2004, 328: 512-14, online at: http://bmj.bmjjournals.com/cgi/content/full/328/7438/512 [accessed February 2, 2005].

Roberts, H., Smith, S., and Bryce, C. Prevention is better . . . *Sociology of Health and Illness* 1993, 15: 447-63.

Roberts, K. A., Dixon-Woods, M., Fitzpatrick, R., Abrams, K. R., and Jones, D. R. Factors affecting uptake of childhood immunisation: A Bayesian synthesis of qualitative and quantitative evidence. *The Lancet* 2002, 360: 1596–9.

Rose, S., Bisson, J., and Wessely, S. Psychological debriefing for preventing post traumatic stress disorder (PTSD) (Cochrane Review). *The Cochrane Library,* Issue 2, 2004. Chichester, UK: John Wiley & Sons.

Rosenthal, R. The "File Drawer Problem" and tolerance for null results. *Psychological Bulletin* 1979, 86: 638–41.

Rosenthal, R. *Meta-analytic procedures for social research.* Newbury Park: Sage, 1991.

Rosenthal, R. Parametric measures of effect size. In H. Cooper and L. Hedges (eds.) *The handbook of research synthesis.* New York: Russell Sage Foundation, 1994.

Rossi, P. The iron law of evaluation and other metallic rules. *Research in Social Problems and Public Policy* 1987, 4: 3–20.

Rowland, D., DiGiuseppi, C., Roberts, I., Curtis, K., Roberts, H., Ginelli, L., et al. Increasing the prevalence of working smoke alarms in disadvantaged inner city housing: A randomised controlled trial. *British Medical Journal* 2002, 325: 998–1001.

Rumsfeld, D. Department of Defense news briefing, Feb. 12, 2002, online at: http://slate.msn.com/id/2081042/ [accessed February 2, 2005].

Rychetnik, L., Frommer, M., Hawe, P., and Shiell, A. Criteria for evaluating evidence on public health interventions. *Journal of Epidemiology and Community Health* 2002, 56: 119–27.

Sackett, D. Bias in analytic research. *Journal of Chronic Diseases* 1979, 32: 51–63.

Scherer, R., von Elm, E., and Langenberg, P. Full publication of results initially presented in abstracts (Cochrane Methodology Review). *The Cochrane Library*, Issue 2, 2005. Chichester, UK: John Wiley & Sons, Ltd.

Schön, D. *The reflective practitioner: How professionals think in action.* New York: Basic Books, 1983.

Schulz, K., Chalmers, I., Hayes, R., and Altman, D. Empirical evidence of bias. Dimensions of methodological quality associated with estimates of treatment effects in controlled trials. *Journal of the American Medical Association* 1995, 273: 408–12.

Scully, D. and Bart, P. A funny thing happened on the way to the orifice. *American Journal of Sociology* 1973, 78: 1045–50.

Searching for the best evidence in clinical journals. Oxford: Centre for Evidence-Based Medicine, online at: http://www.cebm.net/

Secker-Walker, R., Gnich, W., Platt, S., and Lancaster, T. Community interventions for reducing smoking among adults (Cochrane Review). *The Cochrane Library*, Issue 2, 2004. Chichester, UK: John Wiley & Sons.

Shadish, W. Author judgements about works they cite: Three studies from psychological journals. *Social Studies of Science* 1995, 25: 477–98.

Shadish, W. Meta-analysis and the exploration of causal mediating processes: A primer of examples, methods, and issues. *Psychological Methods* 1996, 1: 47–65.

Shadish, W. and Haddock, C. Combining estimates of effect size. In H. Cooper and L. Hedges (eds.) *The handbook of research synthesis.* New York: Russell Sage Foundation, 1994.

Shadish, W. and Ragsdale, K. Random versus nonrandom assignment in controlled experiments: Do you get the same answer? *Journal of Consulting and Clinical Psychology* 1996, 64: 1290–1305.

Shadish, W., Cook, T., and Campbell, D. *Experimental and quasi-experimental designs for generalized causal inference.* Boston: Houghton-Mifflin, 2002.

Shadish, W. R. Policy research: Lessons from the implementation of deinstitutionalization. *American Psychologist* 1984, 39: 725–38.

Shadish, W. R., Cook, T. D., and Leviton, L. C. *Foundations of program evaluation: Theories of practice.* Newbury Park, CA: Sage Publications, 1991.

Sharpe, D. Of apples and oranges, file drawers and garbage: Why validity issues in meta-analysis will not go away. *Clinical Psychology Review* 1997, 17: 881–901.

Sharpe, S., Thompson, S., and Altman, D. The relation between treatment benefit and underlying risk in meta-analysis. *British Medical Journal* 1996, 313: 735–8.

Shaw, R., Booth, A., Sutton, A., Miller, T., Smith, J., Young, B., et al. Finding qualitative research: An evaluation of search strategies. *BMC Medical Research Methodology* 2004, 4, online (free) at: http://www.biomedcentral.com/1471 2288/4/5

Sheikh, A., Gopalakrishnan Netuveli, G., Kai, J., and Singh Panesar, S. Comparison of reporting of ethnicity in US and European randomised controlled trials. *British Medical Journal* 2004, 329: 87–8.

Sheldon, B. and Chilvers, R. *Evidence-based social care: A study of prospects and problems.* Lyme Regis, Dorset: Russell House Publishing, 2000.

Sheldon, B. and Macdonald, G. Mind the gap: Research and practice in social care. Centre for Evidence Based Social Services, 1999, online at: http://www.ex.ac.uk/cebss/files/MindtheGap.pdf [accessed February 2, 2005].

Sheldon, T. *An evidence-based resource in the social sciences,* Report of a scoping study for the Economic and Social Research Council (ESRC), 1998.

Shepherd, J., Harden, A., Rees, R., Brunton, G., Garcia, J., Oliver, S., et al. Young people and healthy eating: A systematic review of research on barriers and facilitators. London: Evidence for Policy and Practice Information and Co-ordinating Centre, Institute of Education, University of London, online at: http://eppi.ioe.ac.uk/EPPIWeb/home.aspx, 2001.

Siddiqui, O., Flay, B. R., and Hu, F. B. Factors affecting attrition in a longitudinal smoking prevention study. *Preventive Medicine* 1996, 25: 554–60.

Silagy, C., Middleton, P., and Hopewell, S. Publishing protocols of systematic reviews: Comparing what was done to what was planned. *Journal of the American Medical Association* 2002, 287: 2831–4.

Silverman, W. *Retrolental fibroplasia: A modern parable.* New York: Grune and Stratton, 1980.

Silverman, W. and Chalmers, I. Casting and drawing lots: A time honoured way of dealing with uncertainty and ensuring fairness. *British Medical Journal* 2001, 323: 1467–8.

Simons, K. and Watson, D. Day services for people with learning disabilities in the 1990s. Exeter: Centre for Evidence-Based Social Services, University of Exeter, 1999, online at: http://www.cebss.org/files/LDReview.pdf [accessed February 24, 2005].

Slavin, R. Best-evidence synthesis: An alternative to meta-analytic and traditional reviews. *Educational Researcher* 1986, 15: 5–11.

Slavin, R. Best evidence synthesis: An intelligent alternative to meta-analysis. *Journal of Clinical Epidemiology* 1995, 48: 9–18.

Slavin, R. and Cheung, A. *Effective reading programs for English language learners: A best evidence synthesis.* Baltimore: CRESPAR/Johns Hopkins University, www.csos.jhu.edu., 2003.

Sleight. P. Debate: Subgroup analyses in clinical trials: Fun to look at – but don't believe them! *Current Controlled Trials in Cardiovascular Medicine* 2000, 1: 25–7.

Smith, M. and Glass G. Meta-analysis of psychotherapy outcome studies. *American Psychologist* 1977, 32: 752–60.

Smith, R. Doctors information: Excessive, crummy, and bent. *British Medical Journal* 1997, 315: 13, online at: http://bmj.bmjjournals.com/cgi/content/full/315/7109/0

Smith, R. and Roberts, I. An amnesty for unpublished trials. *British Medical Journal* 1997, 315: 622.

Solesbury, W. Evidence based policy: Whence it came and where it's going. ESRC UK Centre for Evidence Based Policy and Practice: Working Paper 1, 2001, online at: http://www.evidencenetwork.org/Documents/wp1.pdf [accessed February 2, 2005].

Sønbø Kristiansen, I. and Gosden, T. Evaluating economic interventions: A role for non-randomised designs? In C. Donaldson, M. Mugford, and L. Vale (eds.) *Evidence-based health economics: From effectiveness to efficiency in systematic review.* London: BMJ Books, 2002.

Song, F., Abrams, K., and Jones, D. Methods for exploring heterogeneity in meta-analysis. *Evaluation and the Health Professions* 2001, 24: 126–51.

Song, F., Altman, D., Glenny, A., and Deeks, J. Validity of indirect comparison for estimating efficacy of competing interventions: Empirical evidence from published meta-analyses. *British Medical Journal* 2003, 326: 472.

Song, F., Eastwood, A., Gilbody, S., Duley, L., and Sutton, A. Publication and related biases. *Health Technology Assessment* 2000, 4, online at: http://www.hta.nhs-web.nhs.uk/htapubs.htm

Sowden, A. and Arblaster, L. Mass media interventions for preventing smoking in young people (Cochrane Review). *The Cochrane Library.* Chichester, UK: John Wiley & Sons, 2004, issue 2.

Spencer, L., Ritchie, J., Lewis, J., and Dillon, L. *Quality in qualitative evaluation: A framework for assessing research evidence.* London: Government Chief Social Researcher's Office, 2003.

Spiegelhalter, D., Myles, J., Jones, D., and Abrams, K. Methods in health services research: An introduction to Bayesian methods in health technology assessment. *British Medical Journal* 1999, 319: 508–12.

Spohn, W. Can mathematics be saved? *Notices of the American Mathematical Society* 1969, 16: 890–4.

Spoor, P., Airey, M., Bennett, C., Greensill, J., and Williams, R. Use of the capture-recapture technique to evaluate the completeness of systematic literature searches. *British Medical Journal* 1996, 313: 342–3.

Stare, F. and McWilliams, M. *Nutrition for Good Health*: Fullerton, CA: Plycon, 1974.

Stead, L. and Lancaster, T. Interventions for preventing tobacco sales to minors (Cochrane Review). *The Cochrane Library.* Chichester, UK: John Wiley & Sons, 2004, issue 2.

Sterling, T. Publication decisions and their possible effects on inferences drawn from tests of significance – or vice versa. *American Statistical Association Journal* 1959, 54: 30–4.

Sterne, J., Egger, M., and Davey Smith, G. Investigating and dealing with publication and other biases. In M. Egger, G. Davey Smith, and D. Altman (eds.) *Systematic reviews in health care*. London: BMJ Publishing Group, 2001.

Sterne, J., Egger, M., and Davey Smith, G. Systematic reviews in health care: Investigating and dealing with publication and other biases in meta-analysis. *British Medical Journal* 2001, 323: 101–5.

Stevenson, F. A., Cox, K., Britten, N., and Dundar, Y. A systematic review of the research on communication between patients and health care professionals about medicines: The consequences for concordance. *Health Expectations* 2004, 7(3): 235–45.

Stroup, D., Thacker, S., Olson, C., Glass, R., and Hutwagner, L. Characteristics of meta-analyses related to acceptance for publication in a medical journal. *Journal of Clinical Epidemiology* 2001, 54: 655–60.

Stroup, D. F., Berlin, J. A., Morton, S. C., Olkin, I., Williamson, G. D., Rennie, D., et al. Meta-analysis of observational studies in epidemiology: A proposal for reporting. Meta-analysis of Observational Studies in Epidemiology (MOOSE) group. *Journal of the American Medical Association* 2000, 283: 2008–12.

Suarez-Almazor, M., Belseck, E., Homik, J., Dorgan, M., and Ramos-Remus, C. Identifying clinical trials in the medical literature with electronic databases: MED-LINE alone is not enough. *Controlled Clinical Trials* 2000, 21: 476–87.

Suri, H. A critique of contemporary methods of research synthesis. Paper presented at the Annual Meeting of the Australian Association of Research in Education (AARE), Melbourne, November 29–December 2, 1999, online at: http://www.aare.edu.au/99pap/sur99673.htm

Sutton, A., Abrams, K., Jones, K., Sheldon, T., and Song, F. Systematic reviews of trials and other studies. *Health Technology Assessment* 1998, 2, online at: http://www.hta.nhsweb.nhs.uk/ProjectData/3_publication_select.asp. Also available as: Sutton et al. *Methods for meta-analysis in medical research*. Chichester: Wiley & Sons, 2000.

Sutton, A., Duval, S., Tweedie, R., Abrams, K., and Jones, D. Empirical assessment of effect of publication bias on meta-analyses. *British Medical Journal* 2000, 320: 1574–7.

Taylor, B., Dempster, M., and Donnelly, M. Hidden gems: Systematically searching electronic databases for research publications for social work and social care. *British Journal of Social Work* 2003, 33: 423–39.

Thomas, H. Quality assessment tool for quantitative studies. Effective Public Health Practice Project. Toronto: McMaster University, 2003, online at: http://www.hamilton.ca/phcs/ephpp/Research/Tools/QualityTool2003.pdf

Thomas, J., Harden, A., Oakley, A., Sutcliffe, K., Rees, R., Brunton, G., et al. Integrating qualitative research with trials in systematic reviews. *British Medical Journal* 2004, 328: 1010–12.

Thompson, S. Systematic review: Why sources of heterogeneity in meta-analysis should be investigated. *British Medical Journal* 1994, 309: 1351–5.

Thomson, H., Petticrew, M., and Morrison, D. Housing interventions and health – a systematic review. *British Medical Journal* 2001, 323: 187–90.

Thomson, H., Hoskins, R., Petticrew, M., Ogilvie, D., Craig, N., Quinn, T., et al. Evaluating the health effects of social interventions. *British Medical Journal* 2004, 328: 282–5.

Titchener, E. A plea for summaries and indexes. *American Journal of Psychology* 1903, 14: 84–7.

Tonks, A. A clinical trials register for Europe. *British Medical Journal* 2002, 325: 1314-15.

Toroyan, T., Roberts, I., Oakley, A., Laing, G., Mugford, M., and Frost, C. Effectiveness of out-of-home day care for disadvantaged families: Randomised controlled trial. *British Medical Journal* 2003, 327: 906.

Tramer, M., Reynolds, D., Moore, R., and McQuay, H. Impact of covert duplication on meta-analysis: A case study. *British Medical Journal* 1997, 315: 635–40.

Tsikata, S., Robinson, V., Petticrew, M., Kristjansson, B., Moher, D., McGowan, J., et al. Do Cochrane systematic reviews contain useful information about health equity? XI Cochrane Colloquium: Evidence, health care, and culture, Barcelona, 2003.

Tugwell, P. and Kristjansson, B. Moving from description to action: Challenges in researching socio-economic inequalities in health. *Canadian Medical Association Journal* 2004, 95: 85–7.

Turner, H., Boruch, R., Petrosino, A., Lavenberg, J., De Moya, D., and Rothstein, H. Populating an international web-based randomized trials register in the social, behavioral, criminological, and education sciences. *Annals of the American Academy of Political and Social Science* 2003, 589: 203–23.

Ukoumunne, O., Gulliford, M., Chinn, S., Sterne, J., and Burney, P. Methods for evaluating area-wide and organisation-based interventions in health and health care: A systematic review. *Health Technology Assessment* 1999, 3, online at: http://www.hta.nhsweb.nhs.uk/htapubs.htm

US General Accounting Office. Cross-design synthesis: A new strategy for medical effectiveness research (GAO/PEMD-92-18), 1992.

Uttl, K. Vegetative centres in the diencephalon. *Review of Neuroogical Psychiatry (Praha)* 1935, 32: 104–14.

Valtin, H. "Drink at least eight glasses of water a day." Really? Is there scientific evidence for "8 x 8"? *American Journal of Physiology. Regulatory, Integrative, and Comparative Physiology* 2002, 283: R993–R1004.

Vickers, A., Goyal, N., Harland, R., and Rees, R. Do certain countries produce only positive results? A systematic review of controlled trials. *Controlled Clinical Trials* 1998, 19: 159–66.

Vitaliano, P., Zhang, J., and Scanlan, J. Is caregiving hazardous to one's physical health? A meta-analysis. *Psychological Bulletin* 2003, 129, online at: http://www.apa.org/releases/caregiving_article.pdf [accessed February 24, 2005].

Wadsworth, M. *The imprint of time: Childhood, history and adult life*. Oxford: Oxford University Press, 1991.

Walker, D. *Heroes of dissemination*. Swindon: ESRC, 2001, online at: http://www. esrc.ac.uk/esrccontent/PublicationsList/4books/heroframeset.html

Walker, W. Policy analysis: A systematic approach to supporting policymaking in the public sector. *Journal of Multi-Criteria Decision Analysis* 2000, 9: 11–27.

Wallace, A., Croucher, K., Quilgars, D., and Baldwin, S. Meeting the challenge: Developing systematic reviewing in social policy. *Policy and Politics* 2004, 32: 455–70.

Walter, I., Nutley, S., and Davies, H. Research impact: A cross-sector review: Research Unit for Research Utilisation, University of St. Andrew's, Scotland, 2003, online at: http://www.st-andrews.ac.uk/~ruru/

Walter, I., Nutley, I., Percy-Smith, J., McNeish, D., and Frost, S.. Research Utilisation and the Social Care Workforce: A review commissioned by the Social Care Institute for Excellence (SCIE): Research Unit for Research Utilisation and Barnardo's Research and Development Team, 2004.

Wanless, D. *Securing good health for the whole population: Final report*. London: HM Treasury, 2004.

Ware, W. and Dupagne, M. Effects of US television programs on foreign audiences: A meta-analysis. *Journalism Quarterly* 1994, 71: 947–59.

Weingarten, M., Paul, M., and Leibovici, L. Assessing ethics of trials in systematic reviews. *British Medical Journal* 2004, 328: 1013–14.

Weisburd, D., Sherman, L., Petrosino, A. *Registry of randomized experiments in criminal sanctions, 1950–1983*. Los Altos, CA: Sociometics Corporation, Data Holdings of the National Institute of Justice, 1990.

Weiss, C. Research for policy's sake: The enlightenment function of social research. *Policy Analysis* 1977, 3: 531–47.

Weiss, C. The interface between evaluation and public policy. *Evaluation: The International Journal of Theory, Research, and Practice* 1999, 5: 468–86.

Wells, G., Shea, B., O'Connell, D., Peterson, J., Welch, V., Tugwell, P. et al. *The Newcastle-Ottawa Scale (NOS) for assessing the quality of nonrandomised studies in meta-analyses*. Ottawa: Clinical Epidemiology Unit, University of Ottawa, 1999.

Wentz, R., Roberts, I., Bunn, F., Edwards, P., Kwan, I., and Lefebvre, C. Identifying controlled evaluation studies of road safety interventions: Searching for needles in a haystack. *Journal of Safety Research* 2001, 32(3): 267–76.

Whitehead, M., Petticrew, M., Graham, H., Macintyre, S., Bambra, C., and Egan, M. Evidence for public health policy: II: Assembling the evidence jigsaw. *Journal of Epidemiology & Community Health* 2004, 58: 817–21.

Williams, G., O'Callaghan, M., Najman, J., Bor, W., Andersen, M., and Richards, D. Maternal cigarette smoking and child psychiatric morbidity: A longitudinal study. *Pediatrics* 1998, 102(1): e11.

Wilson, P. Muddy waters: The use and abuse of findings from the "York Review" on fluoridation, ESRC Reseach Methods Festival, July 2, 2004.

Wilson, S. and Lipsey, M. Effects of school-based social information processing interventions on aggressive behavior, *Campbell Collaboration Systematic Review*, 2004, online at: http://www.campbellcollaboration.org/doc-pdf/agbhprt.pdf, [accessed February 24, 2005].

Windle, C. The shift to research synthesis. *Administration and Policy in Mental Health* 1994, 21: 263–7.

Winsor, A. The relative variability of boys and girls. *Journal of Educational Psychology* 1927, 18: 327–36.

Woolf, S. Taking critical appraisal to extremes: The need for balance in the evaluation of evidence. *Journal of Family Practice* 2000, 49(12), December: 1081–5.

Wortman, P. Judging research quality. In H. Cooper and L. Hedges (eds.) *The handbook of research synthesis*. New York: Russell Sage Foundation, 1994.

Yardley, L. Dilemmas in qualitative health research. *Psychology and Health* 2000, 15: 215–28.

Younge, G. President sets aside £1.5bn to boost marriage. *The Guardian*, January 15, 2004, online at: http://www.guardian.co.uk/international/story/0,1123417,00.html [accessed February 2, 2005].

Zaza, S., Wright-de Aguero, L., Briss, P., Truman, B., Hopkins, D., Hennessy, H., et al. Data collection instrument and procedure for systematic reviews in the "Guide to Community Preventive Services." *American Journal of Preventive Medicine* 2000, 18: 44–74.

Ziman, J. Is science losing its objectivity? *Nature* 382 (1996): 751–4.

Zoritch, B., Roberts, I., and Oakley, A. Day care for pre-school children (Cochrane Review). *The Cochrane Library*, Chichester, UK: John Wiley & Sons, Ltd.

Index

L'Abbé plot 228–9, 230 (fig)
abstracts: bibliographic databases 103–4;
    dissertations 90 (box), 97–8;
    keywords 84 (box), 101, 117;
    non-English language papers 156;
    writing 84 (box)
accountability 13–14
Acompline 92 (box)
advisory groups 104–5, 248, 284–5
African Studies Companion 117 (box)
Ageinfo 106 (box)
Agency for Health Care Research and
    Quality 96
AIDSInfo 106 (box)
AIDSLINE 106 (box)
Allen, I. 49–50
AMED 106 (box)
American Institutes for Research 95–6
American Journal of Psychology 16
Anderson, L. 147
anti-smoking intervention: *see* smoking
    cessation
anti-social behavior 4 (box), 42
Antman, E. 35
apples and oranges problem 203–4
appraisal questions 152 (box)
appropriateness 127, 149
Arai, L. 148 (box)
Armstrong, C. 84 (box)
article length 240 (box)
aspirin trial 221
assessment/implementation 144, 145 (box)
ASSIA 36, 106 (box)

astrological study 221
attrition bias 126
Australian Digital Theses 98
Australian Domestic and Family Violence
    Clearinghouse 112 (box)

Babelfish 156
Bacon, Francis 85, 86 (box)
Badger, D. 103, 118, 120
Barlow, J. 182 (box)
Barnardo's 253, 255, 256 (fig), 261
Bayesian approach 191, 208–9
before-and-after studies 59, 134, 188
behavior change theories 248
behavior therapy 17 (tab)
behavioral interventions 132
Bennett, D. 239
Berkeley, George 20
Berkeley Systematic Reviews Group 201
Bero, L. 254, 255
best evidence synthesis 181–3, 185–7
Beveridge, W. 237 (box)
bias 3–6; attrition 126; citations 6, 234
    (box); country 234 (box); data
    extraction 155; database 234 (box);
    detection 139–40 (box); drop-
    outs 129; funding 234 (box); hierarchy
    of evidence 58; individual studies 125,
    157; internal/external 286;
    language 234 (box); literature
    reviews 3–6; location 234–5 (box);
    methodology 130–1;
    publication 230–6; quality

assessment   154; quantitative studies   126; randomized controlled trials   133, 134 (box), 167; recall   137–8; systematic   166–7; uncontrolled studies   65
bias-reduction   193–4, 206–7, 266
bibliographic databases   80, 84 (box), 102–4
bilingual instruction methods   182–3
biomedical model   266–7
BIOSIS   106 (box)
Black, N.   132, 135 (tab)
blinding   132–3, 140 (box); lack of   126
Blue books   96
Blunkett, D.   24n25
Booth, A.   89–90
Boulton, M.   153
Breathing Space study   64 (box)
British Education Index   106 (box)
British Humanities Index   117 (box)
British Library   97; Index of conference proceedings   90–1 (box), 98
British Medical Journal   59, 75 (box), 102–3, 260
British Social Attitudes Survey   141
Brookes, S.   223 (box)
Bubl   94
bullying   8–9 (box)
Bush, George W.   4 (box)
Bushman, B.   202
Bussière, M.   198
Button, K.   224 (box)

C2-SPECTR   115 (box), 119 (box)
Campbell, D.   131
Campbell Collaboration   xiii, 20, 37 (box); coordinating group   260; equity-focused reviews   219; methodology   208; website   181
Campbell Implementation Process Methods Group   89
Canada: Effective Public Health Practice   36; theses   97–8
Canadian Health Services Research Foundation   116 (box)
Canadian Institutes of Health Research   116 (box)
Cancerlit   98, 106 (box)
capture-recapture technique   238–9

cardiovascular health   177–8 (box)
CareData   106 (box)
Carroll, Lewis: *The Hunting of the Snark*   238; *The Walrus and the Carpenter*   186 (box)
cars: *see* road building; transport choice
case control study   67, 134, 137–8, 137 (box)
CCTR   114 (box), 119 (box)
Centers for Disease Control and Prevention   96
CENTRAL   86
Centre for Economic Evaluation   95
Centre for Economic Policy Research   95
Centre for Evidence-Based Public Health Policy   95
Centre for Evidence in Health, Ethnicity and Diversity   95
Centre for Evidence-Informed Policy and Practice in Education   38 (box)
Centre for Neighbourhood Research   95
Centre for Reviews and Dissemination   13 (box), 20; *Effective Health Care*   254–5, 271; Enuresis Society   30 (box); guide   154; handbook   135, 136 (box); Information Services   85; Register   94; search strategies   81; website   36, 259
Chalmers, Iain   16, 193
Chalmers, Thomas   131, 223 (box)
Chapman's method   239
Charity Organization Society   12
Chaudhury, Bridget   249–50 (box)
Cheek, Dennis   251 (box), 252
CHEPA   112 (box)
Cheung, Alan   182
Chilcott, J.   100
ChildData   107 (box)
children: behavior therapy   17 (tab); cognitive development   219, 229–30; healthy eating   155, 192 (box); obesity   171 (box); parents' sexual orientation   45; poverty   66; sudden infant death syndrome   253–4
Chilvers, R.   235 (box)
CINAHL database   87, 88–9 (box), 107 (box)
citations   6, 98–9, 234 (box)

Clark, O. 226
Clarke, M. 225, 233 (box)
clinical psychology vi
clinical trials 86
Clinicaltrials.gov 114 (box)
ClinPSYC 107 (box)
cluster randomized controlled trials 133,
 134 (box)
Cochrane, Archie 16
Cochrane Central Register of Controlled
 Trials 86
Cochrane Child Health Field
 30 (box)
Cochrane Collaboration xiii, 20, 36;
 consumer group 259–60;
 handbook 75 (box), 204 (box), 271;
 information search 85;
 methodology 89; qualitative
 studies 72 (box); systematic
 reviews 187
Cochrane Database of Systematic
 Reviews 37 (box), 93
Cochrane Effective Practice and
 Organization of Care 66, 138
Cochrane Health Promotions and Public
 Health Field 216
Cochrane Library 179
Cochrane Tobacco Addiction Group 66,
 138
cognitive development 219, 229–30
cohort studies 66–8, 134
communication: ESRC 258 (box); social
 policy 247–8
community intervention 64 (box), 146,
 179–81 (box)
Community WISE 107 (box)
Comprehensive Meta-Analysis 202, 226
conceptual review 39 (tab)
conference proceedings 98
confidence intervals 182 (box), 200
Confucius 2 (box)
congestion charging 224 (box)
consumer group 259–60
consumers' checklist 260
contamination 129
context 147–8
control groups 14
controlled trials 85, 86

Cook, T. 131, 144
Cooper, H. 134, 193, 196, 197 (box), 198,
 203, 205 (box), 208, 271
COPAC 90 (box)
CORDIS 93
Coren, E. 182 (box)
coronary heart disease 73
costings 49
cot deaths 253–4
Cowley, D. 135 (tab)
CRD: see Centre for Reviews and
 Dissemination
CRESPAR 182
CRiB 114 (box)
crime reduction 118, 119–20 (box), 135
Criminal Justice Abstracts 112 (box)
criminology 111–12 (box)
CRISP 96
critical appraisal 38, 125–6,
 157, 286, 297; case control studies 137
 (box); checklists 128–9, 131–2;
 lacking 271; methodology 131;
 multiple 190; observational
 studies 136 (box); randomized
 controlled trials 126, 154;
 surveys 142–3 (box); teenage
 mothers 150–1 (box); usability 134;
 see also study quality
critical review 41 (tab)
Crombie, I. 141, 142–3 (box)
cross-design synthesis 166, 185
cross-sectional surveys 138, 141
Current Contents 99
Current Index to Journals in
 Education 111 (box)
cut-off point 100, 103
cycling 74–5 (box),
 168–9 (box)

Daily Graphic 87 (box)
DARE database 37 (box), 114
data analysis 171–2
data collection 139–40 (box)
data-dredging 223 (box)
data extraction 154, 155, 285–6, 293–5
databases: abstracts 103–4;
 accessibility 103–4; bias 234 (box);
 cross-design synthesis 185;

indexing   105; search strategies   101–2;
  see also bibliographic databases; electronic
  databases
Davey Smith, G.   271
day care   62–3 (box)
decision analyses   209
decision-makers: effectiveness   255;
  evidence-based practice   45; question
  framing   28–9
Deeks, J.   65–6, 134, 135 (tab)
democratization of knowledge   7
Department for Education and Skills,
  UK   8 (box), 38 (box)
Department of Education, US   36, 97
Department of Health, UK   13 (box)
Department of Health and Human Services,
  US   107 (box)
detection bias   139–40 (box)
DETR   250 (box)
Devine, E.   144
diagnosis   46 (tab)
differential effects   155
Dingwall, R.   209
DIPEx   117 (box)
disability/family stress   16, 18 (tab)
disadvantaged families   62–3 (box)
disappointing findings   235 (box)
dissemination   viii; effectiveness   253 (fig),
  254–5; heroes of   257–9;
  implementation   248, 255, 262;
  limitations   254 (box); media   257–9;
  models for   249; widening   287
Dissertation Abstracts   90 (box), 97
Dixon-Woods, M.   71
Djulbegovic, B.   226
dose-response   178 (box)
double-blinding   132–3
Downs, S.   132, 135 (tab)
driver education   249–50 (box), 251–2
  (box), 262
Driving Standards Agency   250 (box)
drop-outs   129, 133
DuBois, D.   144, 145 (box)
duplication   234 (box)

early childhood development
  programs   147
Early Years, Hackney   62–3 (box)

ECMT TRANSDOC   91 (box)
Economic and Social Research Council,
  UK   92, 258 (box); *Heroes of
  Dissemination*   257–9
economic factors   12, 47 (tab), 112–13
  (box), 208 (box)
Edison, Thomas   85, 87 (box)
education: anti-smoking   5 (box);
  bilingual   182–3; driving
  249–50 (box), 251–2 (box),
  262; as investment   208 (box);
  pre-school   221 (fig), 229,
  231 (fig); television/computer use   17
  (tab)
educational research   110–11 (box)
educational status   129, 155
EEVL   94
effect size: comparing   197–9, 202; Forest
  plot   199–200, 225–6; missing   236;
  pooling of difference   195–6; smoking
  review   179
Effective Health Care Bulletin   92
Effective Public Health Practice,
  Canada   36
effectiveness: decision makers   58, 255;
  dissemination   253 (fig), 254–5;
  heterogeneity   215–16;
  interventions   1–2, 21, 35, 43–4,
  189–90, 231–2; process
  information   138, 141;
  psychotherapy   193; question
  framing   45, 46 (tab), 48; randomized
  controlled trials   61–3; search terms   82
  (box); study design   143–4
effects: adverse   146; differential   155;
  fixed   196; intention   12;
  random   196; subgroup   157, 218; *see
  also* effect size
Egan, M.   141 (box)
Egger, M.   67–8, 100, 207 (box), 232, 234
  (box), 235, 236, 271
electronic databases: criminology   111–12
  (box); economics   112–13 (box);
  educational research   110–11 (box);
  justice   111–12 (box); search
  strategies   79, 80–1; social work and
  welfare   106–10
ELSC   107 (box)

EMBASE   107 (box)
employment rates   147–8
English language journals   105, 234 (box)
English language teaching   182–3
Enuresis Society   30 (box), 256–7
EPOC group   133, 140 (box), 154
EPPI Centre   20, 111 (box), 141, 147, 151 (box), 191; consumers' checklist   260; synthesis of evidence   192 (box); *see also* Social Science Research Unit
equity-focused reviews   219
Equity Gauge, World Bank   218
ERIC   107 (box), 119 (box)
error types   128
ethical implications   127, 149
ethnicity   129, 219
ethnography   viii, 87
etiology   xiii, 66–7, 134, 136 (box), 167
ETOH   107 (box)
evaluation studies   89; *see also* process evaluation
Evans, D.   86–7
evidence: absence   188; adequacy   131; best available   181, 185–7; complex   188–90; hierarchies   57–8, 59–61, 129–30, 135; implementation   148 (box); reporting   235; synthesis   23, 125, 192 (box)
evidence-based practice   vi, 11–12, 13–14, 45
Evidence Network   95
excluded studies   120–1
exclusion, subgroups   218
experimental studies   16, 59, 167–8
expert reviews   6–7, 10, 41(tab)
experts   104–5, 268
exposure to media   178 (box)
external validity   127, 148–9
Eysenck, Hans   203

Fabian Socialists   12
Fail-safe N   236
Federal Research in Progress   115 (box)
Feinstein, A.   203
Filkin, Lord   4 (box)
fire deaths   69–70 (box)
fiscal interventions   138

fish population   207 (box)
fit for purpose criterion   127, 131
Fitzpatrick, R.   71, 153
fixed effects model   196
flow diagram example   291
flowchart   102
fluoridation of water   13 (box)
Food and Drug Administration, US   96
Food and Nutrition Board, NRC   269 (box)
Forest plots   164, 181, 195, 199–201, 201 (fig), 217, 225–6
funding   22 (box), 92, 93–5, 100, 234 (box)
funnel plots   200, 227–8, 229 (fig)

gender factors: healthy eating   155; persistence   193
General Accounting Office, US   96, 185
generalizability: healthcare studies   43–4; hierarchies of evidence   130; individual studies   2–3; narrative synthesis   165; qualitative studies   153, 240 (box); randomized controlled trials   166, 185; study populations   148–9
GEOBASE   116 (box)
Geographical abstracts   116 (box)
Glass, G.   19, 192–3, 194, 203
Goetsche, Peter   73
Google   100
Gore, Al   79
Gorman, Sheila   269 (box)
Graham, Liz   151 (box)
graphical presentations   209, 225–6
gray literature   50, 80, 85, 90–2 (box), 121, 235
Green, J.   153
Greenhalgh, T.   34, 204 (box)
Grimm, Jacob and Wilhelm   272–5 (box)
Grimshaw, J.   113 (box), 255
group-forming process   51–2 (box)
Guyatt, G.   184 (box), 296

Haldane, J. B. S.   187–8
Hall, J.   204 (box)
Hamilton, Val   84 (box)
hand searching   30 (box), 80, 89, 102, 116–18

Handbook of research synthesis (Cooper and
   Hedges)   196–7
handwashing   254 (box)
Hanson, R.   198
Harden, A.   268
Harmon, C.   208 (box)
Hawaii Medical Library   87, 88–9 (box)
Hawker, S.   89
headlines   1–2, 3
health   67, 220 (box)
health care   19–20, 43–4, 188–9, 199 (box),
   271
health education reviews   5 (box)
health journals   286–7
health promotion   155
Health Resources and Services
   Administration   96
Health Technology Assessment Agency,
   UK   49, 65, 197 (box)
healthy eating   155, 192 (box)
Heckman, J.   129
Hedges, L.   196, 197 (box), 198,
   232, 271
HEED   112 (box)
HELMIS   108 (box)
Helsinki Declaration   105
HERO   115 (box)
heterogeneity   209; Chi-square test   200;
   effectiveness   215–16;
   homogeneity   196–7; narrative
   review   217; process indicators   145–6;
   sensitivity analysis   170; social   216;
   statistical   203, 215–16, 217, 241;
   study   215–16, 241
Hetherington, J.   105
heuristics   130
hierarchies of evidence   57–8, 59–61,
   129–30, 135
Higgins, J.   217, 225
Higher Education Abstracts   110 (box)
Hill, Octavia   12
HMIC   108 (box)
Hom, Wade   1–2
Home Office (UK)   93
home ownership study   34 (fig)
homogeneity   196–7
Horton, Richard   254 (box)
Housing Abstracts   92 (box)

Housing Information Digest   92 (box)
How science takes stock (Hunt)   271
HSRProj   114 (box)
HSTAT   108 (box)
Hunt, Morton   271
Huwiler-Müntener, K.   127
hygiene   254 (box)
hypothesis-testing   35, 267

Ibsen, Henrik   249
IDOX   91 (box)
implementation: assessment   144, 145
   (box); dissemination   248, 255, 262;
   evidence   148 (box);
   interventions   143–4, 189; sensitivity
   analysis   218
inclusion/exclusion criteria: Best
   Evidence   183; cohort studies   67–8;
   etiological studies   66–7;
   outcomes   71–3; quasi-
   experiments   63–5; randomized
   controlled trials   61–3; reviews   74–6;
   search hits   187; search strategies   80–1;
   sifting   118–21; systematic reviews   188,
   266, 271, 285; translation   156 (box)
index of best practice   144–5
Index of Conference Proceedings   90–1
   (box), 98
Index to Scientific and Technical
   Proceedings   91 (box)
Index to Social Sciences and Humanities
   Proceedings   91 (box)
indexes   84 (box), 87 (box), 89,
   105, 117
indirect comparison   199 (box)
individual studies   vi–vii, 268; bias   125,
   157; generalizability   2–3;
   publicity   248; statistics   193–4;
   systematic reviews   15
industrial psychology   16, 18 (tab)
inequalities   218–19
infant growth study   156 (box), 209
information overload   7–8, 22;
   bullying   8–9 (box); historical
   example   7 (box)
information policy   79
information science   79–80, 85–92, 95–7,
   267–8

Institute for Fiscal Studies, UK
113 (box)
Institute of Education Sciences,
US 97
Institute of Health Economics 113 (box)
Integrating research (Cooper) 203, 205 (box)
intention to treat 133
internal validity 58, 61, 127, 130, 154,
166, 172
International Bibliography of the Social
Sciences 108 (box)
International Development Abstracts 116
(box)
International Standard Randomized
Controlled Trial Number 113–14
interrupted time series 134, 138, 139–40
(box)
interventions: categorized 135;
comparisons 198–9 (box);
complex 43, 190; differential
effects 155; effectiveness 1–2, 21, 35,
43–4, 189–90, 231–2; experimental
studies 167–8; fiscal 138;
headlines 1–2, 3;
implementation 143–4, 189;
outcomes 46 (tab)
INVOLVE 30 (box)
Iron Law of Evaluation 126, 132
ISRCTN Register 114 (box)
iterative processes 89
ITRD 91 (box)

Jadad, A. 127, 132–3
Jadad Scale 132–3 (box)
Joanna Briggs Institute 191
Joseph Rowntree Foundation 93
*Journal of Epidemiology and Community
Health* 249
*Journal of Negative Results: Ecology and
Evolutionary Biology* 238 (box)
*Journal of Negative Results in
BioMedicine* 237 (box)
*Journal of Negative Results in Speech and Audio
Sciences* 237 (box)
journals: editors 148 (box), 231; English
language 105; guidelines 259; hand
searching 102, 116–18; health
care 286–7; information overload 7;

negative findings 237–8 (box); peer-
reviewed 232; printed/electronic
forms 118; referees 207–8; systematic
reviews 233 (box)
Jowell, Roger 141
Jüni, P. 129
justice 111–12 (box)

Kahneman, D. 130
Kappa test 121
Kerr, J. 224 (box)
key informants 89–90
key recommendations 255
keywords 84 (box), 101, 117
Knipschild, Paul 6
knowledge sharing 7, 257
knowledge transfer 252, 256–7
Kristjansson, B. 133, 219
Kuvlesky, William 16

Labordoc 113 (box)
Lao-Tze 2 (box)
Lavin, R. 16, 19
Lavis, J. 249
Legendre, A.-M. 193
Leisure, Recreation and Tourism
Abstracts 117 (box)
Lewis, S. 225
LexisNexis 108 (box)
Liebesny, Felix 230–1, 232
Light, R. 183, 225–6
LILACS 108 (box)
Lipsey, M. 203, 271
literature reviews xiii, 2, 285; bias 3–6;
methodological quality 184 (box); non-
systematic 10, 270; PhD 270;
surveys 15; up-to-dateness 99; *see also*
systematic reviews
Liu, B. 225, 228
LMS Bibliographic Database 112 (box)
location bias 234–5 (box)
logic 100
logic model 146, 147
London School of Economics 113 (box)
London University, Institute of
Education 260
longitudinal study 129, 138
Lucas, Patricia 156 (box)

Lumley, J. 145
lumping 48 (box)

MacCoun, R. 206, 207 (box)
McDermott, Liz 151 (box)
McGrath, J. 105
McManus, R. 105
Marine Ecology Journal 238 (box)
marriage/co-habitation 36
Marteau, T. 248
Maryland Scientific Methods Scale
  (SMS) 135
MDRC 36, 96
media factors 66, 178 (box), 257–9; *see also*
  headlines
mediating variables 178 (box), 179
medical interventions 188–9; *see also*
  health care
Medical Research Council, UK 35
Medline 38, 108 (box); citations 99;
  dates of articles 102; Ovid HealthSTAR
  Database 91 (box); search
  strategies 81, 83, 84 (box), 85
Meltzer, H. 16
Menlo Park 87 (box)
Mental Health Act, UK 103
mentoring 4 (box), 144–5
meta-analysis 19, 202–5, 267; apples
  and oranges 4 (box);
  bias-reduction 193–4, 206–7;
  economics 208 (box);
  inappropriate 205 (box); marine 207
  (box); methodology 194–5;
  observational studies 68, 206, 207 (box);
  patterns in data 199–200; quantitative
  studies 172, 192–9; sausage machine
  metaphor 205–8; sexual orientation of
  parents 45; software packages 201–3;
  statistical heterogeneity 217; systematic
  reviews 19 (box), 164
meta-narrative mapping 34
meta-register 113, 115 (box)
meta-regression 207–8, 224–5,
  224 (box)
meta-search engines 100
methodology 129, 208; bias 130–1;
  critical appraisal 131; meta-
  analysis 194–5; quality 171 (box),

181 (box), 184 (box); research tools
  47 (tab)
MIDIRS 93
MIRIAD 93
moderator variables 157, 170, 202, 218–23
MOOSE guidelines 259, 287, 288–90
mortgage safety nets 33
motherhood, teenagers 150–1 (box)
motorcycle helmets 225, 226 (fig), 228,
  229 (fig)
Mulrow, C. 35
Multicultural Education Abstracts 111
  (box)
Myers, R. 207 (box)

naming and shaming 149
narrative review 19 (box), 39 (tab);
  conclusions 194; heterogeneity 217;
  meta-analysis 202; titles 202–3;
  weighting of studies 165
narrative synthesis 166 (box); cross-study
  synthesis 178–81; organization of
  studies 171–7; within study
  analysis 177–8
National Bureau of Economic Research,
  US 113 (box)
National Cancer Institute 98
National Centre for Social Research 94
National Centre for Survey Research,
  UK 151–2
National Childcare Information Center
  Online Library 109 (box)
National Clearinghouse for Bilingual
  Education 111 (box)
National Clearinghouse on Child Abuse and
  Neglect Information 108 (box)
National Electronic Library for Health 93
National Health Service, UK 93; CRD
  Guide 141; CRD Report 137 (box);
  EED 112–13 (box); Research and
  Development Programme 113
National Institute for Health and Clinical
  Excellence *see* NICE
National Institutes of Health 96
National Research Council 269 (box)
National Research Register 93, 94
NCJRS Abstracts Database 111 (box)
NCJRS Virtual Library 111 (box)

negative findings 231, 232, 236, 237–8 (box)

Nelson, G. 219, 229

"Netting the Evidence" website 21

New Towns Record 92 (box)

New Zealand Ministry of Education 183

Newcastle-Ottawa tool 135 (tab)

Newton, Sir Isaac 4, 21

NHMRC 114 (box)

NICE 36

Nichols, Herbert 16

NMAP 94

NOD 114 (box)

non-English language papers 50, 156, 235

non-experimental studies 81, 82 (box), 101

non-indexed studies 235

non-qualitative data 191

non-randomized comparison studies 65–6

non-randomized controlled trials 266

non-reporting 126–7

non-responders 125–6

Nutrition Abstracts and Review Series A 109 (box)

Oakley, Ann 5 (box), 187

obesity 33, 171 (box)

objectivity 23

observational studies 46 (tab), 133–5; critical appraisal 136 (box); meta-analysis 68, 206, 207 (box); phenomena/outcomes 45

odds ratios 154, 200

Office of Assistant Secretary of Health 96

Office of Health Economics 113 (box)

Office of Policy 96–7

Office of the Deputy Prime Minister, UK 93–4

Ogilvie, David 74–5 (box), 169 (box)

Oliver, Sandy 260, 268

Olkin, I. 49–50, 197 (box), 198

OMNI 94

OSH-ROM 109 (box)

outcomes: blinding 140 (box); inclusion/exclusion criteria 71–3; intermediate 73; interventions 46 (tab); multiple 197 (box); study organization 172; unknown 125–6; variability 216

Ovid HealthSTAR Database 91 (box)

Oxman, A. 184 (box), 296

paradigm-shifting 20–1

parenthood 14, 45, 150–1 (box), 182 (box)

Pauling, Linus 6

Pawlicki, R. 16

Pawson, R. 149, 191

PDQ 115 (box)

pearl growing 98–9

Pearson, Sir Karl vi

performance/stress 17 (tab)

persistence 193

Petersen's method 239–40

Petrosino, Anthony 118, 200–1

pharmaceutical industry 257

PhD literature review 270

phenomena/outcomes 45

PICO model 38, 42

PICOC model 43–4, 44 (fig), 52

Planex 91 (box)

Policy Hub 94

policymakers 11–12, 33–4, 255

POPLINE 109 (box)

population-level interventions 132

post-traumatic stress disorder example 188

poverty 14, 66, 67

practice/research 256 (fig)

pre-school education programs 221 (fig), 229, 231 (fig)

pregnancy 145–6, 150–1 (box)

prevalence 47 (tab)

preventing cross-infection 254 (box)

Preventive Services Task Force, US 128

primary research 31, 92–8, 216, 286

process evaluation 89, 178 (box)

process information 138, 141

PROGRESS dimensions 219

prospective registration 114

prospective studies 63, 134

protection 46 (tab)

protocol 30 (box), 44–5, 52, 285

Psychlit 36

psychotherapy 193

PsycINFO 109 (box)

public health 249

publication: choice of journal   261–2;
    multiple   234 (box); systematic
    reviews   233 (box), 259
publication bias   230–5, 286;
    non-randomized controlled trials   233
    (fig); qualitative studies   239–40, 240
    (box); randomized controlled
    trials   233 (fig)
PubMed   89, 108 (box)
Puffer, S.   133

qualitative analysis software   89
qualitative data   57, 58, 117 (box)
qualitative studies   xiv, 72 (box); appraisal
    questions   152 (box); checklists   153;
    experimental studies   59;
    generalizability   153, 240 (box);
    identifying   85–90; indexes   89; mixed
    methods   190–2; publication
    bias   239–40, 240 (box); quality
    assessment   149–53; quantitative studies
    vii, 177; smoke alarm trials   69–70 (box);
    social interventions   85–6;
    synthesis   208–9; systematic
    reviews   68–70, 72 (box); uncountable
    data   191
quality assessment: bias   154;
    characteristics   127–8;
    frameworks   131; qualitative
    studies   149–53; quantitative
    studies   135 (tab); road
    building   141 (box)
quantitative studies   59, 191;
    bias   126; graphical presentations   209;
    meta-analysis   172, 192–9;
    methodological quality   171 (box);
    qualitative studies   vii, 177;
    quality assessment   135 (tab);
    study quality   165–70; tabulating
    included studies   165; tools for
    systematic reviews   135 (tab);
    weighting   132
quasi-experimental studies   63–6, 177–8
    (box)
question framing   52; appraisal   152 (box);
    effectiveness   45, 46 (tab), 48;
    meaningfulness   32 (box); policy
    issues   32–4; suitability of study

design   60 (tab); users'
    involvement   29–30 (box)
QUORUM guidelines   259, 291, 296

race   219
Ragsdale, K.   167
random effects model   196
randomization   126
randomized controlled trials (RCTs)   57;
    bias   133, 167; clustered   133, 134
    (box); critical appraisal   126, 154;
    database analysis   185;
    effectiveness   61–3; evidence   33;
    generalizability   166, 185;
    hierarchy   60; Jadad Scale   132–3 (box);
    smoke alarm trials   69–70 (box); social
    interventions   63; suitability   58;
    validity   130, 132–3
rapid review   40 (tab)
Ravetz, J.   7
realist synthesis   191
realistic review   40 (tab)
recall bias   137–8
record-keeping   102
REEL   111 (box), 114
Rees, R.   151 (box)
Reeves, R.   271
Reeves, S.   50, 51–2 (box)
referees, journals   207–8
reference management   104
references, screening   285
Regard database   93, 115 (box)
registers of trials   105–116
Registry of Randomized Experiments in
    Criminal Sanctions   119 (box)
Reisch, J.   135 (tab)
relevance   22 (box), 79, 127, 268
reliability: see bias; error types
reoffending study: see Scared Straight
REPEC   113 (box)
replication   149
report, writing up   286–7
reporting evidence   235
research   viii, xiii, 3; gaps   186;
    information overload   7; practice   256
    (fig); registers   114–15 (box);
    synthesis   193, 208–9
Research and Development (R&D),
    Barnardo's   253

Research Council, UK   113
Research Evidence in Education
   Library   37–8 (box), 141
Research Findings Register   93
Research into Higher Education
   Abstracts 1980   110 (box)
Research to Policy   252
Research Unit for Research Utilisation   95
retrospective studies   188
review, traditional   41 (tab), 184, 193
review process   3–6, 284–7
RevMan   201, 226
risks   46 (tab), 197
road building   141 (box), 293–5
road safety interventions   84, 249
road traffic injuries   42
RoadPeace   249–50 (box)
Roberts, Ian   249–50 (box), 251
robustness   215
Rosenthal, R.   193, 198, 208, 236
Rossi, P.   126
Rumpelstiltskin and the systematic
   review   272–5 (box)
Rumsfeld, Donald   2 (box)
Rychetnik, L.   147–8, 149

Sackett, D.   126
Sainsbury, J.   206 (fig)
salience, titles of papers   202–3
Sanders, J.   16, 19
SAS   201
saturation   100–1
sausage makers   206 (fig)
Scared Straight   119–20 (box); Forest
   plot   201 (fig); L'Abbé plot   229;
   sensitivity   200–1; systematic
   reviews   118
scattergram   231 (fig)
SCHARR   22 (box), 58, 85
Scherer, R.   232, 233 (fig)
Schön, D.   272
school feeding program   133, 220 (box)
Schulz, K.   154
Schwarzer, Ralf   202
science-practitioner model   vi
scoping review   32, 36, 40 (tab), 48–9
screening   46 (tab), 120, 149, 285
search filters   88–9 (box)

search hits   187
search strategies: databases   101–2;
   electronic databases   79, 80–2, 90;
   information science   85; Medline   81,
   83, 84 (box), 85; stopping rules   100–1
search terms   82 (box), 89
Secker-Walker, R.   146
secular changes   139 (box)
Selai, Caroline   260
selection bias   133, 134 (box)
Semmelweiss, I. P.   254 (box)
sensitivity   81–4, 83 (box)
sensitivity analysis   170, 200–1, 218
SERLINE   118
sex education example   42
sexual offender recidivism   198
sexual orientation of parents   45
Shadish, W.   6, 21, 63, 167, 201
Sharpe, S.   229
Shaw, R.   87, 89
Sheffield University: see SCHARR
Sheldon, B.   235 (box)
Shepherd, J.   155
SIGLE   91 (box), 92
Silagy, C.   44–5
single studies: see individual studies
Slavin, Robert   181–2
Sleight, P.   221–2
Smith, M.   19, 192–3
Smith, P.   183
Smith, Richard   75 (box)
smoke alarm trials   69–70 (box)
smoking cessation: community
   intervention   64 (box), 146, 179–81
   (box); effect sizes   179; longitudinal
   study   129; pregnancy   145–6; Stanford
   Three-city study   177–8 (box);
   suicide   67–8; youth education
   5 (box)
Snow, John   249
social interventions: comparisons   199
   (box); complex   216; headlines   1–2;
   meaning/processes   47 (tab); qualitative
   studies   85–6; randomized controlled
   trials   63
Social Policy and Practice   94
Social Policy and Social Care   95
social policy reviews   33, 247–8

Social Science Research Unit 192 (box)
Social Sciences Citation Index 109 (box)
Social Services Abstracts 110 (box)
Social Work Abstracts 110 (box)
social work and welfare databases 105–10
socioeconomic inequalities 219–20 (box)
Sociofile 109 (box)
Sociological abstracts 109 (box)
Sociology of Education Abstracts 111 (box)
Song, F. 199 (box), 234 (box)
SOSIG 94
Special Educational Needs Abstracts 111 (box)
special interest groups 252
specificity 81–4, 83 (box)
Spencer, L. 151–3, 152 (box)
Spielberg, Steven 249
splitting 48 (box)
Spoor, P. 239
SPORTDiscus 110 (box)
SPSS 201
stakeholders 29–30 (box), 31, 90, 284
Standardized Mean Difference 194, 195–6
Stanford Three-city project 177–8 (box)
Stare, Frederick 269 (box)
STATA 201
state of the art review 41(tab)
statistical methods 193–4
Stein, C. 222
Stein's paradox 222
stem-and-leaf diagram 181
Sterling, T. 231
Sterne, J. 225, 238
Stewart, L. 233 (box)
stopping rules 100–1
streptomycin 102–3
stress/performance 17 (tab)
Stroup, D. 232
Studies on Women and Gender Abstracts 117 (box)
study design 60 (tab), 143–4, 216
study populations 148–9, 216, 239
study quality 125, 127–8, 165–70, 209, 266
subgroup analysis 218–23
subgroup effects 157, 218

subquestions 38
Substance Abuse and Mental Health Services 96
sudden infant death syndrome 253–4
suicide 67–8
SUMARI package 191
Suri, H. 183
surrogate outcome measures 73
surveys vii, 15, 59, 138, 141, 142–3 (box)
sustainability 146
Sutton, A. 196, 197 (box), 201–2, 237
systematic reviews: alternatives 38, 39 (tab); collaborations 19–20; history of 16–19; misperceptions 265–70; need for 15, 21–2, 29 (box), 284; presentation and timing 260–2; quality 270–1, 296–7, 296 (box); Rumpelstiltskin 272–5 (box); seven stages 27 (box); twelve tips 51–2 (box); uses 9–10; value 10–11, 15

tabulation 165
Taylor, B. 105–6 (box)
teenagers 150–1 (box), 182 (box)
television/computer use, education 17 (tab)
theoretical models 149, 267
theses 97–8
Thomas, H. 135 (tab)
Thomson, S. 215, 225
Thorne's Better Medical Writing 57–8
time factors 49–50, 100
time, psychology of 17 (tab), 73
timeliness 251 (box), 252, 261
titles of papers 101, 120, 202–3
tobacco consumption 138; see also smoking cessation
tokenism 31
Toroyan, T. 63 (box)
Tramer, M. 234 (box)
TRANSDOC 91 (box)
transferability 149
translation 156, 156 (box)
TRANSPORT 91 (box)
transport choice example 167, 168–9 (box), 173–6 (tab)
transport research 224 (box)
treatment integrity 144–8
trials 129, 237

trials registers   105–16, 114–15 (box), 237
triangulation   89, 166, 187–8
trim and fill method   236–8
TRIS   91 (box)
Troop, Pat   254 (box)
Tversky, A.   130
Type A behavior pattern   73

UKCCCR   115 (box)
uncontrolled studies   65–6
United Kingdom: Charity Organization
    Society   13; Department for Education
    and Skills   8 (box), 38 (box); Department
    of Health   12–13 (box); DETR   250
    (box); Economic and Social Research
    Council   92, 258 (box), 258–9; Health
    Technology Assessment
    Agency   49, 65, 197 (box); Home
    Office   93; Institute for Fiscal
    Studies   113 (box); Medical Research
    Council   35; Mental Health
    Act   103; National Centre for Survey
    Research, UK   151–2; National Health
    Service   93, 112–13 (box), 137 (box),
    141; Office of the Deputy Prime
    Minister   93–4; Research
    Council   94, 113
United States of America: Department of
    Education   36, 97; Department of Health
    and Human Services   107 (box); Federal
    Research in Progress   115 (box); Food
    and Drug Administration   96; General
    Accounting Office   96, 185; information
    science websites   95–7; National Bureau
    of Economic Research   113 (box);
    Preventive Services Task Force   128;
    What Works Clearinghouse   36
unpublished papers   231, 235
up-to-dateness   99
Urbadisc   92 (box)
Urbaline   92 (box)
Urban Institute   97
urban myths   265–70
Urban Studies Abstracts   92 (box)
usability   134
users' involvement   29–30 (box), 31, 256–7

validity: external   127, 148–9;
    internal   58, 61, 127, 130, 154, 166, 172;
    randomized controlled trials   130, 132–3;
    threats to   131
Valtin, Heinz   269–70 (box)
variability   216
Vickers, A.   234 (box)
vitamin C   6
vote counting reviews   126, 183–5

Walker, David   257–9
Walker, Warren   272
walking   74–5 (box), 168–9 (box)
Wallace, A.   33, 34 (fig)
Walrus and Carpenter (Carroll)   186 (box)
water, bottled   269 (box)
water, daily requirements   269–70 (box)
water fluoridation   12–13 (box)
weapons of mass destruction   260
Web of Science   99
Webb, Beatrice   12
Weber's Law   16
websites   7–8, 99–100
weighting of studies   128, 131–2, 165,
    195–6
welfare to work programs   147, 148, 189
Wells, G.   135 (tab), 202
Wentz, R.   84
What Works Clearinghouse, US   36, 97
What works for children   95
Wheatley, A.   84 (box)
Wilson, D.   203, 271
Woolf, Steven   128–9
World Bank   113 (box); Equity
    Gauge   218
Wortman, P.   131, 155
writing up stage   286–7

York University: see Centre for Reviews and
    Dissemination
youth mentoring   144–5

Zaza, S.   135 (tab)
ZETOC   99
Ziman, John   22
Zoritch, B.   63 (box)